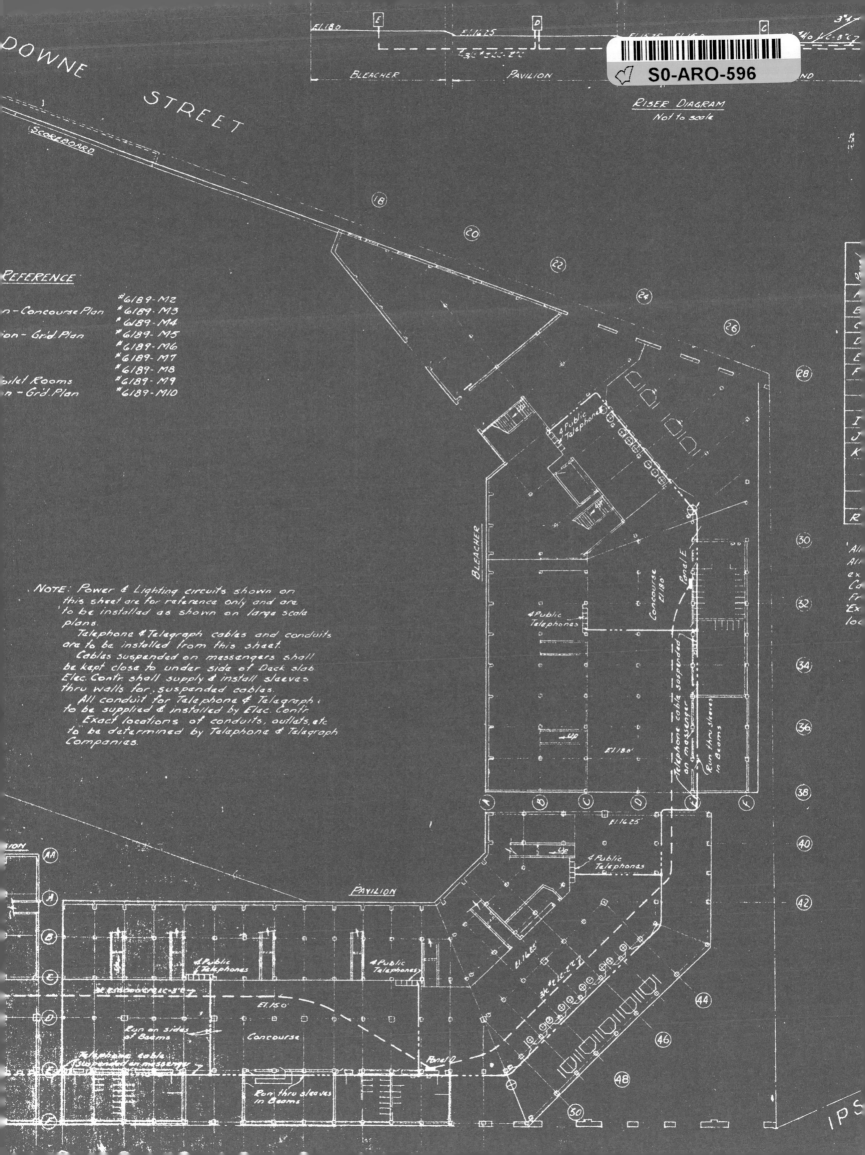

DOWNE STREET

SCOREBOARD

BLEACHER   PAVILION

RISER DIAGRAM
Not to scale

REFERENCE

n - Concourse Plan   #6189-M2
                        #6189-M3
ion - Grid. Plan   #6189-M4
                        #6189-M5
                        #6189-M6
                        #6189-M7
oilet Rooms   #6189-M8
                        #6189-M9
on - Grid. Plan   #6189-M10

NOTE: Power & Lighting circuits shown on
this sheet are for reference only and are
to be installed as shown on large scale
plans.
   Telephone & Telegraph cables and conduits
are to be installed from this sheet.
   Cables suspended on messengers shall
be kept close to under side of Deck slab.
Elec. Contr. shall supply & install sleeves
thru walls for suspended cables.
   All conduit for Telephone & Telegraph
to be supplied & installed by Elec. Contr.
   Exact locations of conduits, outlets, etc
to be determined by Telephone & Telegraph
Companies.

4 Public Telephones

BLEACHER

4 Public Telephones

Concourse El.180

Panel E

Telephone cable suspended on messenger

Run thru sleeves in Beams

El.180'

PAVILION

4 Public Telephones

4 Public Telephones

4 Public Telephones

Run on sides of Beams   Concourse

Telephone cable suspended on messenger

El.150'

Panel D

Run thru sleeves in Beams

IPS

Field of Our Fathers

An Illustrated History of Fenway Park

RICHARD A. JOHNSON

TRIUMPH
BOOKS

To my home team of Mary, Lizzy, and Bobby

To the memory of:

James Lou Gorman (Red Sox general manager)

Cynthia Atlas Goff (education director, The Sports Museum, Boston)

Andy Jurinko (artist)

Minna Flynn Johnson (fellow, American Antiquarian Society; director, Edward Street Day Care Center, Worcester, Massachusetts)

All of whom loved Fenway Park, baseball, Boston, and all the things that make life worth living including love, literature, art, and laughter. They were great citizens, accomplished professionals, and cherished friends. Rest in peace.

Triumph Books and colophon are registered trademarks of Random House, Inc.

Library of Congress Cataloging-in-Publication Data
Johnson, Richard A., 1955-
  Field of our fathers : an illustrated history of Fenway Park / Richard A. Johnson.
    p. cm.
  ISBN 978-1-60078-423-1 (alk. paper)
  1. Fenway Park (Boston, Mass.)—History. 2. Fenway Park (Boston, Mass.)—History—Pictorial works. 3. Boston Red Sox (Baseball team)—History—Pictorial works. I. Title.
  GV416.B674J65 2011
  796.357'640974461—dc23
                    2011027978

This book is available in quantity at special discounts for your group or organization. For further information, contact:

Triumph Books
542 South Dearborn Street
Suite 750
Chicago, Illinois 60605
(312) 939-3330
Fax (312) 663-3557
www.triumphbooks.com

Printed in China.
ISBN: 978-1-60078-423-1
Design by Eileen Wagner Design

Contents

Fenway Park, Boston, Mass.

Acknowledgments

The primary challenge, as with all books, was to create a work original in content that aspires to enlighten, educate, and entertain the reader.

In this endeavor I was helped to a huge extent by my old friend Kathryn Maynes who cheerfully performed yeoman service in selecting and transcribing many of the firsthand accounts included in this volume.

I am also most grateful to the staff of the microtext room of the Copley Square branch of the Boston Public Library. Their number include: curator Henry F. Scannell, Diane Parks, Cecile Gardner, Melir Esguerre, Dawn Barnes, and Theresa Rourke. In recent years this department has fallen victim to some inexplicable management strategies despite being the library's research center. Likewise, the library's print department, once the domain of the astute and indispensable Aaron Schmidt, was of tremendous help with images. The Boston Public Library deserves the support of every author and reader.

I am also grateful for the support of my colleagues at The Sports Museum whose number includes Rusty Sullivan, Brian Codagnone, and Michelle Gormley. A hearty thanks to Glenn Stout, my great friend and esteemed colleague, who encouraged me even as he wrote the definitive tale of Fenway's first season. In my opinion, Glenn is the best writer currently covering the sports history "waterfront" in America. I am also grateful to old friends Luke Salisbury, Steve Buckley, Leigh Montville, Bob Ryan, and Janet Marie Smith for the wonderful pieces they contributed to the text.

I am especially grateful to Ed "Moose" Savage for his sharing the amazing scrapbooks of the Pere Marquette Football team with me. They include incredible photographs and compelling documentary evidence of one of Fenway's and Boston's greatest sports tales of the roaring twenties.

The library of *The Boston Herald* was also incredibly supportive, and for that I extend a big high five to chief librarian Martha Reagan.

Thanks also to Mike Andersen, ballpark maven and Dorchester guy Bob Bluthardt, Ted Spencer, Wes Dow, Rich Paisley, the late Dennis Brearley, Robert Flynn Johnson, Bill Nowlin, Dan Desrochers, Saul Wisnia, Albie Walton, Todd Gipstein, Bob Walsh, and Richard Thaler.

And finally, the Red Sox Fenway centennial team of Dave Friedman, Sarah McKenna, Nick Roper, Dan Rea, as well as old friends Dick Bresciani, Debbie Matson, Paul Hanlon, and Dan Lyons helped in more ways than I can possibly describe here.

The Red Sox could not have been more supportive.

Most especially I am grateful to my home team of Mary, Lizzy, and Bobby for their love and undying support through the many long grumpy days it took to complete this work.

Introduction

Only in Boston, where one can disembark at a subway stop—State, whose signature structure was built in 1713—could one make plans to meet friends for a game at either Harvard Stadium (c.1903), Matthews/Boston Arena (1910), or Fenway Park (c.1912). Ah, tradition.

Before I began work on this ambitious project I was well aware that most of the literary and historical treatments of Fenway Park played shamelessly off John Updike's unforgettable peeping-egg description of the ballyard included in his 50-year-old *New Yorker* paean to Ted Williams. Either that or they were pretty picture books with breathless quotes from needy celebrities seeking fan-cred while opining about Calvinism, curses, and the green of the grass.

Who doesn't love Fenway Park? It endures as a place of narrow seats, little parking, good times, and abundant history. However, the true story of Fenway is more compelling than pithy quotations of famous folk who couldn't pick Joe Lahoud or Billy Mike Smithson out of a mug book if their lives depended on it. The real and mostly hidden history of this tiny ballyard is that of a place that was home to an impressive variety of events and performers.

It became clear after pouring through hundreds of news clippings and scrapbooks that this project presented many of the same challenges that confronted Glenn Stout and myself when we undertook researching and writing *Red Sox Century* a dozen years ago. The primary challenge simply being: to create a definitive history of Fenway Park where there'd been none before. It is my sincere hope that this book comes close to meeting that expectation.

After reading of the thousands of athletes that competed on its turf—many of whom did so as high school, collegiate, and amateur athletes—I felt compelled, driven actually, to honor their legacies by telling as many of their stories as I could find. For the true measure of New England's and now Red Sox Nation's relationship to and obsession with all things Fenway lies not exclusively with the fans but also with the multitude of New Englanders that literally carried the park's dirt in their fingernails.

I also made a conscious decision to compile, rather than simply interpret, the history that lay before me. As a result I've collected what I thought were the best pieces about the hidden history of Fenway Park as well as pieces that chronicle events more familiar to Red Sox fans.

During the period from 1912–62 it was far more likely that Bostonians actually knew someone who'd competed there than merely experienced the place as a paying customer. For two generations, the place was nothing less than a People's Park where high school and college baseball and football was as much a part of the schedule as the mostly hopeless Red Sox.

Among the more improbable events that took place at Fenway were the two National High School Football title games showcasing mighty Everett High in 1912 and 1914; the baseball/lacrosse doubleheader that featured the Red Sox and Boston Lacrosse Club on June 15, 1915; the football game between South Boston's Pere Marquette AC and the NFL's New York Giants on November 19, 1927; boxer Kid Chocolate's tune up for the world lightweight title in 1932; Satchel Paige facing the team from the Fore River shipyard in 1943; the Harlem Globetrotter's 1954 exhibition; 2010's NHL and NCAA hockey games; and the many high school and collegiate football and baseball games played in the shadow of the Green Monster through the generations.

For the past century, Fenway Park has served the fans of the world's greatest sports town as the venerable and versatile venue of a variety of sporting, entertainment, social, and political activities. It is the one address in town that connects Barry Goldwater to Eugene McCarthy, Kid Chocolate to Pinky Higgins, Keith Richards to Neil Diamond, Cliff Battles to Gino Cappelletti, Joe Wood to Pedro Martinez, and Meadowlark Lemon with Zdeno Chara.

Built over a period of seven months in 1911 and 1912, Fenway Park has been home to two major league baseball teams, five pro football teams, many college football teams, and a vast array of local high school and amateur teams. For much of its first half century the park was as apt to host a local high school football game as it was an NFL War Bond game or an MLB All-Star Game.

As with any of the books I've written or edited, my first motivation was to create a book that I'd both buy for myself and friends. Apart from that, my sincere hope is that I've done my homework and captured much, if not the entire story of this precious ballpark in as colorful and engaging a manner as possible. Such is the debt I owe to the generations of athletes, public figures, and spectators who've made Fenway Park their very own for the past century.

The Braves take on the Philadelphia Athletics at Fenway Park in the third game of the 1914 World Series. Note the construction of the structure later known as the Jeano Building in the foreground and the majestic Christian Science Church in the adjacent Back Bay. *(Photograph by Leslie Jones, courtesy of the Boston Public Library)*

CHAPTER ONE

Fenway Park 1911-1920

"Architecture has its political Use; Publick Buildings being the Ornament of a Country;
it establishes a Nation, draws People and Commerce; makes the People love their native Country,
which Passion is the Original of all great Actions in a Common-wealth....
Architecture aims at Eternity."

—SIR CHRISTOPHER WREN

Field of Our Fathers

The roots of Fenway Park's bluegrass are sunk deep into soil that was once owned by a family that boasted a signer of the Articles of Confederation and a member of the Continental Congress as well as the author of the acclaimed *Two Years Before the Mast*. The park was built on land acquired by General Charles H. Taylor from the Danas, one of the Bay Colony's founding families along with the likes of the Cabots, Lowells, and Delanos.

The most prominent member of the famous clan was Francis Dana, a Boston attorney and diplomatic partner of John Adams during the American Revolution. Not only was Dana an early member of the Sons of Liberty and Continental Congress, but he also traveled to Valley Forge where he helped reorganize the Continental Army. He later served John Adams as secretary to the American diplomatic delegation in France and England.

In 1793 he helped build the West Boston Bridge on the site of what is now the Longfellow Bridge and did much to support his alma mater, Harvard.

The other famous Dana is Richard Henry Dana Jr., author of the classic memoir *Two Years Before the Mast*, who also was a noted lawyer and politician who devoted much of his career to helping the downtrodden. Dana was a leading abolitionist who helped found the anti-slavery Free Soil Party in 1848 and famously represented the fugitive slave Anthony Burns in Boston in 1854. He later served as the U.S. attorney

for Massachusetts and was one of the lead prosecutors in the trial of Confederate president Jefferson Davis.

His family owned property that stretched from the tidal flats of the Charles River to the Muddy River and adjoining Fens. This extensive parcel was known at various times as the "Dana Lands," and it was on eight acres of this centrally located but soggy land that the Red Sox would sink roots that remain to this day as the site of America's most beloved ballpark.

James E. McLaughlin/ Fenway's Architect

Like many in Boston's early 20th century ascendant Irish-American upper middle class, 37-year-old architect James F. McLaughlin was an immigrant having arrived in Roxbury from Nova Scotia at the age of 12 in 1885. Though the details of his education are unclear, it is likely he was trained at MIT as it offered the nation's first formal architectural course of study.

By 1911 McLaughlin had already established himself as one of Boston's better known architects, having designed many civic buildings such as schools, municipal offices, churches, and rectories. His buildings were basic, elegant, and in the best New England tradition didn't call attention to themselves while blending in with their surroundings. It also didn't hurt that McLaughlin was plugged into Boston's Catholic power elite.

It was for all of these reasons that the Taylor family selected McLaughlin in 1911 to build their ballpark, soon to be named Fenway Park, both in recognition of its location and as a promotional boost to the Taylor's Fenway Realty Company.

McLaughlin's design was based on the following conditions:

- The grandstand, which stretched from sections 14 to 27, had to be built of fireproof concrete and steel.
- The concrete footprint of the grandstand was to be strong enough to support a full upper deck. (As historian Glenn Stout has observed, this feature is the main reason the ballpark has survived to this day. The Taylors simply ran out of time to add the upper deck in time for the park's opening in April 1912.)
- The configuration of the playing field had to match that of the old home at the Huntington Avenue Grounds with right field serving as the "sun" field. Unlike much of the Back Bay, the acreage upon which Fenway Park was built was not filled land, although its proximity to the Muddy and Charles Rivers contributes to its notoriously bad drainage.

Completed in roughly eight months, the new park was built by contractor Charles Logue, civil engineer L. Kopczynski of the Concrete and Expanded Metal Construction Company, New England Structural Steel, and Osborn Engineering Company of Cleveland.

Among the distinguishing features of the park were:

- McLaughlin's brick facade for the Jersey St. (now Yawkey Way) main entrance. The park nameplate has since become a virtual trademark, and the arches and doorways of the team offices, a near perfect fit with those of the surrounding period buildings.
- The original left-field wall, festooned with a montage of advertisements, and fronted by a 6' high rise of earth called "Duffy's Cliff" in honor of left-fielder George "Duffy" Lewis. The wall also included baseball's first electric scoreboard, all the better for the significant constituency of gamblers that congregated in the right-field stands and bet on balls and strikes.
- A deep center field, marked by a flagpole some 550 feet from home plate.
- A parking lot adjacent to the right field stands.
- The first screen ever placed behind home plate to protect fans from foul balls.
- Fifteen thousand reserved seats and another 13,000 unreserved seats and bleacher seats that nearly doubles the capacity of their old home of the Huntington Avenue Grounds.

While much of the original park has been remodeled or replaced, the essential character of McLaughlin's creation survives as the sweep of the grandstand still allows one to see the treetops on Van Ness street, and the sun that challenged right fielder Harry Hooper remains a nightmare for J.D. Drew.

The Fenway neighborhood was just being developed when the Taylor family built their new ballpark in 1911-12. *(Collection of the author)*

Boston, The Fenway and Somerset Hotel.

APRIL 17, 1911

Boston Beauty Will Be Enhanced by a New Ballpark

THE BOSTON AMERICAN LEAGUE CLUB TO BE PERMANENTLY DOMICILED ON ITS OWN GROUND IN THE BAY DISTRICT WITHIN A YEAR OR TWO

Special to "Sporting Life"

It is understood that the purchase recently by Gen. Charles. H. Taylor, of a large tract of land in Back Bay, means that the Boston American League Club, of which his son, John I. Taylor, is president, will have a new park within a year or two. From time to time it has been reported that the Red Sox would have new grounds at Forest Hills, with concrete and steel grand stand and bleachers, but it is evident that the Taylors concluded a location nearer the center of the city would be more profitable. The property purchased by Gen. Taylor is what has been known, as the Dana Lands, located on Lansdowne and Ipswich streets. It comprises 365,308 square feet, or about eight acres, having a frontage of 900 feet on Lansdowne street and 500 on Ipswich street. It was sold at auction about two months ago to an insurance company for $120,000, and its assessed valuation is $219,200. Plans are now being considered for a new subway through the Bay Back section which will bring the proposed new ballpark within a few minutes' ride of the State House. (*A.H. Mitchell*)

MARCH 25, 1912

The New Park at Boston

Fenway Park the new home of the Boston Red Sox, is rapidly nearing completion and will be ready for a game between the Red Sox and the Harvard nine on April 9. The big grand stand, built of concrete and steel, will have 95 private boxes, each seating four persons, in the front row. The Boston Club has fixed a special price of $250 for a box calling for 77 championship games at home, and many prominent citizens have sent in reservations. In the second row there are 45 boxes, each providing room for six persons each. Behind the boxes are 10 rows of reserved seats, with 50 seats in a row. With an upper tier the stand will seat more than 12,000 spectators, half as many as the big structure at the Polo Grounds. The open stands will provide seating accommodations for at least 20,000 more. As there is room in the outfield for standees, it is estimated that nearly 40,000 persons can see the Red Sox play a championship game. The Boston plant will cost nearly $300,000. (*A.H. Mitchell for* Sporting Life)

APRIL 9, 1912

Red Sox Beat Fair Harvard, 2-0, in Fenway Opener

By Paul H. Shannon

The wind blew in fitful gusts across the new Red Sox field yesterday afternoon, and whirling flurries of snow did their best to drive two husky squads of athletes under cover, but in spite of the frostiest of receptions from the local weather dispenser, Boston's great Red Sox team made their unofficial debut and christened their splendid new home with a defeat for fair Harvard to the tune of 2 to 0.

PLAY ON SOGGY FIELD

Upon a wet and soggy field, and under conditions far more favorable for football, the speedy squad that Jake Stahl expects will follow him to ultimate victory this season gave the fans a demonstration of their worth, and local fandom is well satisfied with the team that the giant first sacker commands. And while opportunities for cheering were few and far between, save when one of the Harvard pitchers managed to sneak a strike across the rubber, the composition of the Red Sox team for 1912 seems one that may well justify the confidence of owners and leader.

A big delegation was on hand from Harvard, and the Red Sox rooters swelled the attendance to about 3,000. The field looked gray and soggy, as the workmen had not yet succeeded in offsetting the labors of the weather man. The grand stand is still far from completion, but there was every indication that things would be in readiness when Stahl's men come back to open the regular season.

HOW RUNS WERE SCORED

For the first four innings the Crimson went out in order. In the first session for Boston, although Yerkes singled and Speaker was safe on Wigglesworth's muff, there was no score resulting.

Passes to Krug and Thomas, with a wild throw to second by Felton, and Hageman's single sent Boston's first run across.

In the third two of the Sox were passed, only to have chances for a score killed by a pretty double play by Potter, Clarke and Wingate.

In the fifth Boston's other score came across. Gardner opened up with a clean single, and Lewis fanned the Back Bay breezes. Krug drew a pass and then Hageman drove in a run for the second time with a clean single.

Harvard's one change to register came in the sixth, through passes to Wigglesworth and Coon, the latter batting for Felton. A passed ball was thrown in after Wingate had forced Coon. Then came the attempt at a double steal, which failed when Wigglesworth was caught at the plate.

Rain Causes Fenway Opening Delays

By Paul H. Shannon

Hardly half an hour after President McAleer, manager Jake Stahl and Manager Harry Wolverton had agreed that there was no prospect of the two teams meeting yesterday afternoon, the sun broke out and the unwelcome rainfall ceased, but there was no use in lamentation then. The fates had decided against the Boston American management, and for the second day in succession the formal opening of the magnificent new park had to be postponed.

BLOW TO BOX OFFICE

The failure to play on Thursday with yesterday's double postponement puts an awful crimp in the club's box office receipts. These postponed games will, of course, be played off later on, but the money that would have poured into the treasury on Thursday and Friday will never return. Thursday was a State holiday up in New Hampshire and hundreds of excursionists had arranged with the railroads for transportation to Boston in time to be present at the opening of the Fenway park. Yesterday it is only reasonable to presume that the attendance at both morning and afternoon contests would have approximated 35,000.

Not without severe mental struggle did the two clubs finally resign themselves to the inevitable. In spite of the incessant rain and the frightful condition of the ground, President McAleer hoped against hope and remained at the park from 10 o'clock until 1 p.m., in the hope that J. Pluvius would relent. Notwithstanding the wretched condition of the outfield, the diamond itself would have been in passable condition, as canvas had sheltered the playing space and a few barrels of sawdust spread in the vicinity of the home plate would have made play possible by 3 o'clock.

This afternoon, however, it really looks as though the long deferred clash would come off. The weather man has sent out word that the two days' storm has drifted away from vicinity of the Hub and there is every reason to believe that the weather conditions this afternoon will be favorable. It should be much warmer, the grounds ought to be pretty well dried out, and it goes without saying that the seating accommodations at Fenway Park should be taxed to the limit.

Buck O'Brien was selected to work yesterday afternoon, and it will be up to either him or Charlie Hall to pitch this afternoon. Hall may be the final selection, as the Californian pitched a masterly game against the Highlanders in the last game in New York, and Manager Stahl believes that the Sea Lion can trim them again today. Then, too, either Wood or O'Brien will be scheduled to work against Washington, who open here next Monday, and Stahl is especially anxious to down the Senators in the game in which Walter Johnson works.

With the right kind of weather, therefore, the bleacherites will get busy and whoop her up this afternoon. The Sox are in fine trim, the Highlanders are in better shape after their enforced layoff, and Wolverton will do his utmost to win this remaining game from the locals. The home rooters are all expected to be on hand and it will be up to them to stand by Stahl in royal style and cheer the Sox in their efforts to remain at the head of the American league race.

Speaker's Scorcher Wins Opener

By Paul H. Shannon

Over the winding roads and across the narrow bridge that leads to Fenway Park, the baseball-hungry fans of Boston threaded their impatient way yesterday noon to get a long awaited glimpse of the stalwart crew that big Jake Stahl leads to action.

Into the mammoth stand, out upon the sun-kissed bleachers and swarming over the field, forming a human fringe to the expansive playing space where the Red Sox were to make their initial bow of the 1912 season, the fans of Boston forced their way, until when the umpire gave the word for play to begin more than 24,000 loyal Red Sox supporters were waiting to pass judgment upon park and team.

FANS LIKE THE PARK

The mammoth plant, with its commodious fittings, met with distinct approval, and as for the team, well – the cheer that arose when the great Tris Speaker scorched that single to left in the 11th, sending Steve Yerkes home with the winning run, was a fitting tribute to the estimation in which Boston holds its Red Sox.

Three hours before, a curious, impatient crowd had gathered within the big inclosure, hoping for a Red Sox victory and a fourth straight win from New York. It was well along toward twilight when that same crowd, no longer a mildly enthusiastic body but a yelling, cheering mob, hurried back to the four corners of Greater Boston to spread the news of an uphill fight, a thrilling finish and a great 11th inning defeat of Wolverton's Highlanders.

It was an old time Red Sox victory. Handicapped at the very start by a temporary weakness in the pitcher's box, and forced to come from behind all the way until Jack Stahl's timely two-bagger had tied up the contest in the eighth, the Boston team has seldom before given such an exhibition of bulldog tenacity and fight. If ever a team

The South End Grounds resembled a magnificent Queen Anne–style mansion and was the home of the great Boston Nationals teams that featured such stars as King Kelly, Kid Nichols, John Clarkson, and "Sliding Billy" Hamilton among many others. It burned to the ground in May 1894 after an errant lit cigar tossed by a fan ignited a trash heap. *(Courtesy of the Boston Public Library)*

The Huntington Avenue Grounds was built directly across the tracks of the Providence and Boston railroad from the park of the rival Braves, the South End Grounds. It served as the home of the Boston Americans from 1901–11. The sod from the old park was transplanted to Fenway Park in 1912. *(Courtesy of the Boston Public Library)*

deserved to win the Red Sox did yesterday, and this in spite of errors and loose play that would have put a high school team to blush.

It was well for Jake Stahl's team that it has a pitcher of Charlie Hall's calibre for just such emergencies. It is a fortunate thing, as well, that the Red Sox squad can boast of so many lusty hitters, and that Yerkes and Tris Speaker came through as they did in this nerve-racking, 11-inning fight. For, while the Boston team was threatened with disaster by a seeming collapse in the first few innings of the game, it was nerve and fight of this great trio that finally enabled the Sox to come up on even terms with their opponents and ultimately win out.

YERKES' HEAVY HITTING

On a soft and slippery field, whose condition might well have excused the commission of even more frequent blunders, the work of these three men shone like beacons. Yerkes, in spite of three errors, for which the soft spots around the second bag were almost wholly to blame, made up for his misdeeds by grand work at the bat. In seven times up he hammered out three singles, a brace of doubles, scored three of the seven runs and helped to drive in two more himself. Speaker drove in Boston's first and last tally, made three hits and was robbed of two more by catches that were little short of miraculous. Hall also had his day.

Buck O'Brien, picked by the majority to find the Highlanders easy money, had to pay the penalty of an eight-day layoff and was found signally wanting. From the very start it was easily to be seen that the Brockton lad possessed little of his usual effectiveness, and

when his wildness robbed him of the least pretence to an ability to locate the plate, his quick departure was foreshadowed. Nevertheless, in the hope that Buck might settle down, Manager Stahl kept him on the rubber until the Highlanders had taken his measure for four innings and piled up five big runs.

RED SOX NARROW THE GAP

A likely-looking rally in Boston's fourth and the acquisition of three runs that brought the home team up to within a solitary score of the invaders, had forced Relief Pitcher Hall into the fray, and right nobly did the Californian acquit himself. From the moment that the "Sea Lion" took his position upon the rubber the game assumed a different aspect, and hope which had been glimmering but feebly broke into a quick flame.

In the seven innings that Hall worked but three hits were made off him, and the one run that the Highlanders got was the result of a base on balls and an ill advised throw to second base. At the bat, however, Hall atoned for this one tally that he gave the New Yorkers, scoring one run, and driving out a lusty two-bagger that should have ended the game in the ninth inning. His pitching was a duplication of the fine work that he had performed against New York on the latter's own grounds, and the Californian finished as strongly as he had begun.

The Highlanders, desperately anxious to win this one game in Boston and put an end to their monotonous string of defeats, used up no less than three pitchers, but all to no avail. Against the heavy cannonading of the Red Sox hitters they fell one by one, Vaughan,

the redoubtable left hander, being the pitcher who has to stomach the blame for defeat, Caldwell was yanked at the first sign of weakening, Quinn was removed when an incipient rally threatened in the ninth, and finally the bats of Yerkes and Speaker put Vaughan to the bad in the 11th inning.

FOURTEEN RED SOX HITS

While the Highlanders were scratching out eight scattered singles, the Red Sox were running up a tally of 14 safe drives with a total of 19 bases, and had it not been for the ground rule, which limits hits into the crowd to two bases each, the contest would have been ended without the necessity of playing two extra sessions. Five long two-baggers did the Red Sox make, drives by Hall, Stahl and Speaker counting for two sacks when they might just as easily have gone for three sackers or home runs.

The fielding of neither team was of very high class, but, as explained before, the condition of the diamond was largely accountable. Yerkes had three boots, while Wagner, Stahl, O'Brien and Hall are credited with one each. The New York errors were much fewer, but they were very costly, one of Dolan's bad errors and a passed ball by Charlie Street in the 11th allowing the Sox to score the run that robbed the fast gathering darkness of a chance to call the game with the teams on even terms.

Contrary to expectation, there were none of the usual opening-day functions, the two days' postponement calling off the parade and flag-raising, and making that far-famed Letter Carriers' band conspicuous by its absence. The only pretension to the opening day frill was the hurling of the ball by Mayor Fitzgerald, but Boston's modest chief executive pulled off this feat so quietly that few excepting those within closest proximity knew that this important duty had been transacted.

FIRST INNING BAD FOR BOSTON

The first inning as usual was a bad one for Boston. Zinn, the first man up, hit when Buck O'Brien covered the sack on a grounder to Stahl rather lamely. Chase sacrificed, Hartzell singled to left, but Wolter knew the strength of Lewis' arm and but one run came in. Daniels hit to O'Brien, Buck made a good stop and caught Wolter 15 feet from the plate, but he threw low to Nunamaker and Daniels was safe, while Wolter scored. Dolan was hit by the pitcher after Nunamaker had caught Hartzell off second base. Gardner singled and Daniels counted. Street ended the agony by fanning.

In the last half two-baggers by Yerkes and Speaker gave Boston one run.

The third inning was another bad session for O'Brien. Hartzell got his base on Yerkes' fumble and Dolan singled after Daniels fanned. Then came a wild pitch, a pass to Street and a single by Caldwell. This accounted for two runs.

In the fourth O'Brien hit one man and passed two more, but a lucky wild pitch that struck Gardner's bat resulted in an easy roller to Stahl and a fortunate escape from runs. This ended O'Brien.

SOX GET AFTER CALDWELL

The Sox started after Caldwell in the last half. Gardner began by hitting safely and Lewis drew a pass. Dolan's error filled the bases with none down. Nunamaker fanned. Henriksen was sent in to hit for O'Brien and drew

a base on balls, forcing Gardner in. Quinn replaced Caldwell at this point. Hooper forced Henriksen and Lewis counted. Yerkes dropped a single in left and Wagner came across. Speaker ended the inning with a grounder to Chase.

A pass to Hall, Hooper's sacrifice and Yerkes' fourth safe hit sent in the tieing run in the sixth. The seventh passed without a score, but both teams got a man across in the eighth. A pass to Wolter, a steal and a bad throw to second let Kauff, who had replaced Wolter, go to third with one down and Chase's single scored him. In Boston's half, two-baggers by Yerkes and Stahl tied the game up again.

The ninth and 10th were critical moments for both sides, sensational catches by Lewis and Daniels cutting off likely scores. Vaughan replaced Quinn in the ninth, after Hall had doubled with one out, and this left the Californian languishing upon the sacks.

In the 11th, when it became apparent that this inning would end matters in case of no decision, Yerkes got a life on Dolan's fumble and continued on to second when the New Yorker made a bad throw. A short passed ball let him move on to third, and a wild yell arose when Speaker drove a scorcher between Dolan and Hartzell and sent the winning run across.

APRIL 26, 1912

Bradley First to Clear the Wall

Worcester native and Red Sox reserve first baseman Hugh Bradley confounded many in the press box who thought Fenway Park's new left (right) Author/attorney Richard Henry Dana Jr. along with grandfather Frances (a signer of the Articles of Confederation) were two of the more famous members of the family from whom the Taylors purchased the 8-acre tract known as the "Dana Lands" for their new ballpark. *(Collection of the author)*

(below) Much of the beauty of Fenway Park lies in the fact that the ever-changing Boston sky is as much a backdrop for the action as the horizontal sweep of the grandstand. *(Courtesy of the Boston Public Library)*

RICHARD HENRY DANA.

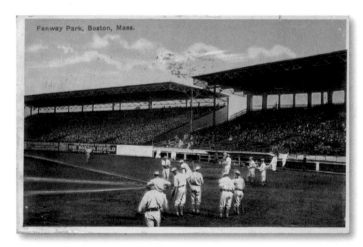

The architecture of Fenway Park remains the perfect counterpart to the brick and brownstone buildings of the Fens and Back Bay. Its brick façade is as much a part of Boston's historic DNA as the USS *Constitution* and the old and new State Houses. *(Courtesy of the Boston Public Library)*

field wall insurmountable when he socked the first of the now 10,000+ home runs at Fenway Park just six days after the park's first game.

Paul Shannon described the blow in *The Boston Post*: "It looked to be all over but the shouting at the eventful moment when Bradley pulled off a feat that may never be duplicated. It was in the seventh inning that there were two men out and two men on base with the Athletics leading by a score of 6-4 and seemingly little chance that they would be headed when Bradley lifted the ball over the left-field fence for a home run, which won the game for the Red Sox." It was the second and final home run of Bradley's three year stint with Boston.

A cartoon in the *Post* showed Bradley's blast hitting City Hall in Philadelphia to the surprise of an admiring Quaker.

JUNE 2, 1912

SEATTLE, WASH.,
Mr. F. C. Lane,
Editor, The Baseball Magazine,
65 Fifth Avenue, New York City.

Dear Sir:

I am a traveling man, and on my numerous visits in the East I have the extreme pleasure of seeing major league ball in all the cities of that class, a treat denied the average fan on the Coast. On my last trip I had occasion to stop in Boston for a while and, among other things, visited that new temple of modern baseball, Fenway Park. I was considerably annoyed to find on each of my several trips to the park that gambling was as open there as at any race-course in the country. With the constantly

growing attendance of ladies at the games, this is a great pity, even at a distance from the grandstand and "under cover." But to have gambling in the open, in the fifty-cent bleachers, within easy earshot of the grandstand and the lady patrons, is a disgrace to Boston and the American League.

At the old Huntington Avenue grounds there were always to be seen a large body of men who took rather poor seats away down near the left field foul-line when there were plenty back of third base to be had. These men habitually stayed after the game was over, supposedly to discuss plays and look over the scenery that had escaped their glances during the heat of the conflict. And before the game these same men were to be found on Washington Street, near Clarke's Hotel, with suspicious-looking books in their hands. But now! they, the habitual attendants, the professional gamblers, go about among the crowd shouting their odds in the boldest, most audacious manner, to the disgust of everyone but the "short-enders" and themselves, and near the end of the game openly settle their bets right in the stand.

There never was any attempt to stop this vicious practice in Boston on the American League grounds, and since the passing of the late George Dovey, the same is true at the South End Grounds. And what is true of Boston is true of many other cities, particularly Forbes Field, Pittsburgh. With the decline of horse-racing, made rotten by the gamblers and their methods, the latter have turned to baseball, and are reaping large dividends. Must this practice go on? Must our great national game be sacrificed to the needs of these snakes in the grass?

What is the matter with the club that permits these gamblers to do as they please? What is the matter with the league behind the teams? Surely the whole league knows of the practice in Boston, as what visiting team could remain ignorant after one series? What is the matter with the press, that mighty wielder of public opinion, that it does not protest vigorously, both editorially and through its news and sporting columns? To be sure, the Boston Traveler did make a short but praiseworthy attempt last summer when I was in Boston, but the general press has been pretty silent. These and kindred questions those who have the best interest of the game at heart would like to have answered. I have read Ban Johnson's article in your June number, and it strikes me that while he is claiming so much success for the American League on "clean baseball" it would not be out of place to have him bring a little pressure to bear on the management of the Boston team toward the stamping out of this gambling evil. I cite Boston particularly because any schoolboy there could point out a score of the gamblers in the fifty-cent stand on mighty short notice, but what is true of Boston is pretty true all over the circuit.

Some people question the success of the American League because of their promises of "quarter ball" eleven years ago. I do not, even though I do think the quarter seats in places like Fenway Park are a joke; baseball to-day and baseball in 1901 are two different subjects; that is another subject entirely. But the gambling question, and it is just as true, mark my words, in the National League as in the American, is one that we have constantly before us with the threatening ruin of the "greatest game on earth." Do I implore in vain, Mr. Lane? Can The Baseball Magazine remain silent in such a case? I am an individual; I can do nothing; but hope you can do a lot, editorially and in special articles illustrating the evils of the present system to wake up the press, the leagues, and the public whose good money is after all what makes the baseball "mare" go. Bring this matter to the attention of Messrs. Johnson and Lynch; to Mr. Dreyfus; to Mr. McAleer; to Mr. Ward, and to all the other magnates, and in so doing know that you have the backing of every clean-minded lover of baseball in the country.

Very truly yours,
Harold Bowne.

AUGUST 3, 1912

CHRISTIAN SCIENCE MONITOR 4 SOMERVILLE INDEPENDENTS 1

AUGUST 8, 1912

CHRISTIAN SCIENCE MONITOR 2 BOSTON TRANSCRIPT 1

AUGUST 10, 1912

WINTHROP KNIGHTS OF COLUMBUS 3 LYNN ELKS 1 (7 INNINGS)

AUGUST 10

BOSTON LODGE OF ELKS FIELD DAY FEATURING U.S. OLYMPIAN JIM THORPE

OCTOBER 16, 1912

Desperate Finish Wins Series for Red Sox in Tenth, 3 to 2

MATHEWSON WEAKENS AFTER SNODGRASS DROPS ENGLE'S EASY FLY – SPEAKER'S SINGLE AND GARDNER'S SACRIFICE FLY GIVE BOSTON TWO RUNS AND THE FINAL GAME – ERRORS LOST FOR NEW YORK

HENRIKSEN, BATTLING FOR BEDIENT, SAVES GAME FOR BOSTON IN SEVENTH WITH SLASHING TWO-BAGGER, TIEING THE SCORE

HOOPER'S WONDERFUL CATCH ROBS DOYLE OF HOME RUN – WOOD PITCHES LAST THREE INNINGS

HOW THE RED SOX WON GAME IN TENTH INNING

This is the story of how the Red Sox won the game and the championship of the world in the 10th inning of the deciding game of the most sensational series for the big title ever waged. The Giants had managed to take a one-run lead in their half of the inning, so that the Red Sox faced the loss of the game, the title and the big end of the players share of the receipts unless they scored at least one run. They made two.

In the emergency Engle was called to be in place of Wood. He sent a fly to left centre which Snodgrass muffed, Engle taking second on the error. Hooper sent another fly to Snodgrass, but this time the New York centre fielder made no mistake and Hooper was

out. Mathewson walked Yerkes. Speaker, coming up amidst an ovation from the now frenzied spectators, swung hard at the first ball pitched, but a groan went up when it was seen that he had raised a puny foul near the coacher's box at first. Merkle and Meyers, both started for it, became mixed up and let the ball drop between them. Then Speaker singled to right, scoring Engle with the run that again tied up the game. Yerkes took third and Speaker second on Devore's throw to catch Engle at the plate. Lewis was purposely passed, the Giants planning on a double play with the bases filled. But Gardner sent a long fly to right. Devore caught it and threw to the plate, but not in time to catch Yerkes, who came across with the winning run.

Supreme Court Justices Get Bulletins of Contest

WASHINGTON, Oct. 16. – Unprecedented procedure was permitted today in the Supreme Court of the United States, when the justices, sitting on the bench hearing the government's argument in the "bath tub trust" case, received bulletins, inning by inning, of the world's championship baseball game at Boston. The progress of the playing was clearly watched by the members of the highest court in the land, especially by Associate Justice Day, who had requested the baseball bulletins during the luncheon recess from 2 to 2:30 p.m. The little slips giving the progress

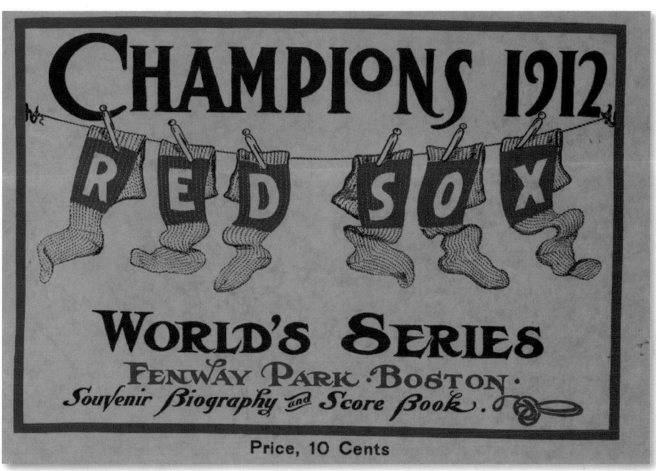

Gambling was so prevalent at Fenway Park that tickets, such as this from 1942, informed fans that gambling was forbidden. Though the penne ante touts have vanished from the right-field bleachers fans can still take their chances with a Red Sox theme scratch ticket from the state lottery. *(Collection of the author)*

Jim Thorpe (left) is shown racing Thomas McLoughlin of the Boston Lyceum in a race held prior to his field day appearance at Fenway Park. Thorpe would go on to win the decathlon at the 1912 Summer Olympics in Stockholm. *(Courtesy of the Library of Congress)*

The Royal Rooters are rousted by Boston police after their seats had been mistakenly re-sold to the seventh game of the 1912 World Series. Many of this loyal band protested their treatment and didn't attend this next afternoon's championship-clinching finale. *(Courtesy of the Boston Public Library)*

of the play went to him not only during the luncheon recess but when the court resumed its sitting. They were passed along the bench from justice to justice.

Smallest Crowd of Series Sees Victory

Either the weather, the disaffection of the rooters or the poor showing of the Red Sox in the first five games this week had a woeful effect upon the attendance. Only 17,034 paid admissions were registered. The greatest game of all in the greatest world series of all was witnessed by far the smallest crowd.

World Champions at Faneuil Hall Today

Faneuil Hall will be thrown open today at 1 o'clock for a public demonstration by the baseball fans of Boston to the Boston Red Sox, the world's champions.

Mayor Fitzgerald was the first to get to the Red Sox dressing rooms after the game yesterday to congratulate them on their splendid victory and at once set machinery working for the demonstration today.

He engaged a band over the telephone, and with President McAleer and Vice-President Taylor made arrangements for the Red Sox players to assemble at Fenway Park today at noon and parade down town in automobiles to Faneuil Hall, headed by the band.

Speeches will be made by the Mayor and other city and State officials, as well as prominent fans, and congratulating the champions on the work accomplished.

Rooters Angry

That the Boston rooters, as well as the "royal rooters" were much incensed at the Red Sox management was manifested yesterday afternoon, when but a few more than 17,000 fans turned out to witness the deciding game of the world series.

It was less than half of the tremendous throng that witnessed the Sox lose on Tuesday, and it is alleged that yesterday's poor attendance was nothing more than a demonstration of the fans who wished to show their dissatisfaction with the manner in which the Boston club management treated the royal rooters.

Early yesterday morning John I. Taylor, vice president of the Red Sox, went to the Mayor's office and attempted to settle the wrangle. The Mayor turned Mr. Taylor over to Mr. Mooney, who looked after the rooters' tickets. The latter stated the rooters had secured their tickets before noon, despite Treasurer McRoy's statement to the contrary, and that Mr. McRoy had some motive in not reserving the seats.

Red Sox President Apologizes to Mayor

MCALEER SAYS MISTAKE MADE IN NOT HOLDING USUAL ROOTERS' SEATS UNTIL GAME TIME

The failure to hold the seats for the royal rooters on the occasion of the seventh series game was due to a mistake, according to President McAleer.

The incident certainly caused a turmoil which is still waxing merrily, and it will be recalled that Mayor Fitzgerald came on strong on behalf of the rooters.

FROSTY ATTENDANCE

Whether it was the treatment accorded the rooters by the Sox club on Tuesday, or other causes, the fact remains that the attendance on Wednesday was a frosty one for a world's series game, and a final one at that.

In a letter to the fans issued last night, President McAleer expresses regret over the affair as follows:

HIS APOLOGY
"On behalf of the Boston American league ball club I desire to make an apology to the Mayor of Boston and the Boston rooters for the failure to secure the seats at the seventh game of the world series.

"We regret very much that this unfortunate affair should have occurred to mar what was in every

The 1912 Red Sox won 105 games prior to beating the New York Giants in an epic eight-game World Series. They are shown here at the new home. Note the lack of fixed seats in the box seat area where free-standing chairs were utilized. *(Courtesy of Bob Wood)*

The first significant non-baseball event at Fenway Park was the 1912 National High School Football Championship Game between Oak Park (Illinois) High School and Everett (Massachusetts) High School. *(Collection of the author)*

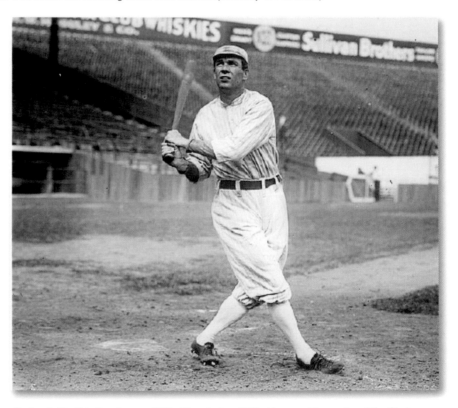

Center fielder Tris Speaker was Willie Mays before Willie Mays, and he captured the Chalmers Award in 1912 as American League MVP. *(Courtesy of the Library of Congress)*

respect the most sensational series of games ever played, and we appreciate the splendid support and encouragement given the Red Sox in their efforts to bring to Boston the baseball championship of the world.

"A mistake was made in not holding the usual seats until game time, but I can assure Mayor Fitzgerald and all the Royal Rooters it was unintentional.

James R. M'aleer,
President American League Club

NOVEMBER 28, 1912

BOSTON LATIN 7, BOSTON ENGLISH 6

NOVEMBER 30, 1912

Oak Park High School (Ill) defeats Everett High School (Ma) in National High School Football Championship Game 32-14

In the first significant non-baseball event at Fenway Park Oak Park High School (Ill) led by future Hall of Fame coach Robert Zuppke defeated Everett High School by a score of 32-14 in the National High School Football Championship before a crowd of over ten thousand. The fans filled the bleachers and were described in the following excerpt from the game account in *The Evening Record.*

"The Oak Park squad came onto the field amid a momentary hush and then the Everett cohorts gave a lusty yell for the westerners that seemed to put added life into the practice, and they charged up and down the gridiron with speed, their husky backs keeping well together in interference.

The Everett players watched their antagonists with a great deal of attention, each man giving his opponent for the afternoon a sizing up.

When the Everett boys went out for their practice the entire crowd rose and gave a cheer that would have done credit to the Harvard cheering section."

Just prior to the game fans spilled from the bleachers onto the field and had to be restrained by mounted police summoned by Boston Mayor John "Honeyfitz" Fitzgerald.

Despite the heroics of Everett captain Charlie Brickley coach Cleo O'Donnell's Everett team couldn't match the razzle dazzle style employed by Oak Park. At times the champions made as many as six laterals before charging forward in an attack that dazzled fans and sportswriters alike.

Oak Park's victory represented their third title in the first three years of the competition and also was Zuppke's last game at Oak Park prior to taking over the football program at the University of Illinois. At Illinois Zuppke coached the great Red Grange and led his squad to four national titles.

JANUARY 15, 1913

Red Sox announce the removal of auxillary seating at ballpark left over from '12 World Series but also announce they'll have more (8,000) 25-cent seats than any team in the majors.

APRIL 19, 1913

NEW YORK GIANTS 7
BOSTON BRAVES 2
NEW YORK GIANTS 10
BOSTON BRAVES 3

MAY 6, 1913

Commerce Defeats Coast Ball Team

The High School of Commerce baseball team had a very easy time yesterday afternoon at Fenway Park, for the Columbia Park Boys' Club of San Francisco was defeated by the score of 24 to 0 in six innings of very sensational but ragged baseball. The visitors, who are making a short stay in the Hub while on their trip around the world, essayed to take on the local high school team and also tested its strength in a few track events.

The visitors never had a look-in, while the local boys pasted the ball all over the lot.

MAY 30, 1913

BROOKLYN DODGERS 2,
BOSTON BRAVES 1

**BOSTON BRAVES 7,
BROOKLYN DODGERS 6**

**OCTOBER 11, 1913 OBRION,
RUSSELL & CO 9, OLD
COLONY TRUST COMPANY 5**

**NOVEMBER 18, 1913
MECHANIC ARTS 6, BOSTON
LATIN 3**

**NOVEMBER 19, 1913   HIGH
SCHOOL OF COMMERCE 3,
BOSTON ENGLISH 3**

**NOVEMBER 27, 1913
BOSTON ENGLISH 21,
BOSTON LATIN 0**

**APRIL 11, 1914 TUFTS 6,
DARTMOUTH 4**

**JUNE 1 , 1914
BOSTON 7, UNIVERSITY OF
TORONTO 2 (LACROSSE)**

JUNE 7, 1914

50,000 CHILDREN SHRIEK WELCOME TO ELEPHANTS

Fenway Park Packed With Cheering Small Humanity – Greatest Crowd in Inclosure in America's History – All Seats Taken Early and Overflow Takes to Field – Thousands Unable to Gain Entrance to Park – Governor Presents Mollie, Waddy and Tony to City and Mayor Accepts – Stirring Scenes on the Children's Gala Day – No Accident – Elephants in New Home at Franklin Park

Largest Crowd Ever Seen by Governor

By Governor David I. Walsh

"The feature of the day at Fenway Park, which impressed me most was the mighty enjoyment of the kiddies. It was an inspiring sight to look on that sea of child faces and to witness their expression of pleasure when the three elephants purchased by them were led on the field.

"It was the largest crowd that I ever saw assembled in one place in my life. It was truly a remarkable occasion and it gave me great satisfaction to be able to participate in it, actng for the children of New England presenting Mollie, Waddy and Tony to the city of Boston. I wish to especially compliment the police on the order and kind manner in which they handled the great crowd of children."

By Paul Waite, the "Elephant Editor, Boston Post"

Harvard and Yale football gatherings and world series baseball crowds of the past stand almost insignificant beside the mighty child host of far more than 50,000 that stormed Fenway Park yesterday morning to bid welcome to the city of Boston their own elephants, Mollie, Waddy and Tony. Hundreds who could not gain admission welcomed the spectacle from roofs of nearby buildings.

Never before in the history of the United States has there been such a remarkable gathering of tiny humanity.

The spectacle for its vastness and enthusiasm was wonderful to behold and surely the children of Greater Boston will never forget the day.

Neither will the thousands upon thousands more who witnessed the parade of the elephants following the event at the baseball park.

Not a single child was hurt in that vast throng. Sixty were taken to the police station as lost, to be sure, but *Post* automobiles quickly effected family reunions to the last child.

At last Mollie, Waddy and Tony are in their new life home at Franklin Park, having arrived there yesterday after the exercises.

It so happened that with the exception of one article in the *Boston Traveler* and a brief mention in the *Transcript*, the public received all of its advance information as to Elephant Day from the *Post*. That the crowd attained the size it did indicated the vast army of *Post* readers.

Last night, however, the *Boston Evening Globe* printed a good account of the affair, with illustrations. The *Evening Transcript* had an appreciative story of the event. *The Record, Christian Science Monitor* and *Traveler* also reported the exercises. The early edition of today's *Sunday American* also contained an account of the celebration.

The rush came with such impetus that it was with only the greatest difficulty that the boxes allotted to Governor Walsh and Mayor Curley were held. Even then they had to be emptied at least a dozen times and seats found somewhere for the persistent occupants.

Fenway Park, with its immense seating capacity of 33,000 adults, was filled by 9:45. Thousands of chairs held two children.

Crowd Most Good-Natured

The *Post* regretted its inability to save the boxes for the various people, State and city dignitaries, assigned, but under the circumstances it would have been folly to have attempted it.

Everybody allotted to seats who failed to get them were magnificently good-natured, for all knew little folks who were having the time of their lives were occupying them.

Most Remarkable of Campaigns

The great day was the culmination of the most remarkable child campaign on record – a campaign during which 75,000 boys and girls of New England contributed their savings of pennies, nickels and dimes to the extent of $6,700 for the sentimental purpose of purchasing three famous elephants for the city of Boston zoo.

The crowd, like a human tidal wave, fairly engulfed Fenway Park. It was an undreamed of throng.

In order to accommodate a tremendous gathering, the *Post* sought the largest amphitheatre available, and Fenway Park was generously donated for the occasion by President J.J. Lannin of the Boston American league baseball team.

However, it proved to be small when the thousands of childish elephant enthusiasts made assault upon it.

Nearly 70,000 Boston-area schoolchildren donated pennies and nickels to purchase three former circus elephants, Molly, Waddy, and Tony, for the Franklin Park Zoo for a total of $6,700. They were welcomed to Boston on June 6, 1914, at Fenway Park before a crowd of more than 50,000. *(Collection of the author)*

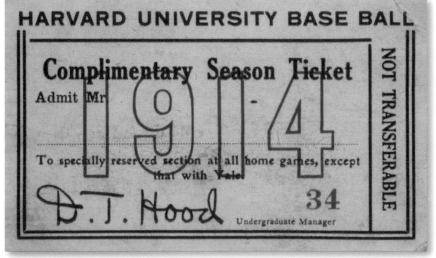

Season pass for Harvard baseball. In 1914 the Harvard baseball team returned to Fenway Park to play their rivals from Yale. *(Collection of the author)*

Babe Ruth arrived in Boston on July 11, 1914, and met his future wife and won his first major league game that same day. Ruth was a member of three world championship teams in 5-1/2 seasons in Boston and only 4-of-15 seasons with the Yankees. *(Courtesy of the Library of Congress)*

There were 50,000 people in Fenway Park during the gala exercises yesterday morning.

The *Post* makes this conservative estimate as follows: Forty thousand people seated somehow in the stands, and 10,000 on the field.

Some of the police experts who have handled crowds for years stated that 60,000 were in Fenway Park and that from 10,000 to 20,000 were outside. Little folks were in the majority, two to one. They shrieked with delight over every funny antic of the clowns and the bewildering array of dancers and novelty attractions that was ever going on in the center of the diamond.

And at the height of it all came in Mollie, Waddy and Tony, the beloved, amid a din of childish delight that probably before has never been equaled.

They howled and they shrieked. The band, situated in the centre of the grounds, blared forth. Every child was on his feet and the stands

and field were a sea of handkerchiefs waving frantically back and forth.

The great day started this way:

It was about 7:00 yesterday morning, just at a time when the sun burst forth from behind some questionable white, puffy clouds, that one lone boy of five was found sitting all by himself on the Fenway Park steps.

He was Charles Friedburg of Lamont street, Roxbury, and he had walked in from the other side of Dudley street – "to see Tony." He was the first of that great concourse to come.

The entrances of Jersey street already began to show signs of something going on. Perhaps 200 had gathered. Then a wonderful thing happened all at once.

Juvenile Boston at that moment took Fenway Park by storm. They climbed over the backs of the seats. They rushed down the aisles, all heading for front seats. On came the flow behind them, on, on, on – never ending.

In the meantime the crowd had become so great in the street, as the car-lines began to empty their human freight, it became necessary to throw open the gates which had been assigned for the performers in order to lessen the congestion. In came the deluge from this quarter. How the little Indians yelled.

GRANDSTAND IS PACKED, RECORD CROWD FOR PARK

Already the grandstand with its 18,000 seats was filled. Allotted seats had been confiscated and the steady inpouring stream of people made it impossible even to attempt to remove the boys and girls from the seats.

After all, it was their day, and what is the difference? A hurry call was sent to open the bleacher entrances on Ipswich street and on Lansdowne street.

There was no sign of an end to the inrush to the grandstand. Already the bleachers were becoming black with children and their escorts.

Then it seemed but minutes before they were solidly packed. Still came the not-to-be-daunted tide.

Orders came to close the gates. This was done and for a moment the police were able to move about 2000 out of the grandstand who had no seats. They were placed on the field, over on the great bank back of third base.

Not to disappoint the enormous crowd outside, it was decided to admit as many to the field as possible. Open went certain gates. Again came the rush. The field became black with people. Shut went the gates again.

Tremendous excitement was created when Mr. and Mrs. William Orford, the people who have owned

Mollie, Waddy and Tony for so many years, came on the field headed for the Governor's box. Presently Mr. Orford disappeared. The band was getting a breath while the officers and mounted men were getting the crowd farther back in the field.

Then over at one side of the field some gates opened. A strange form loomed into sight, shadowed by two monstrous forms. There were the elephants.

The band crashed into a march. The whole field went wild. It was the mightiest kind of a welcome. The din continued as the big fellows, Tony in the lead, with Mollie next and Waddy last, marched around the green. As they came to a stop in the centre, the demonstration reached its height, for already the Governor, Mayor Curley, Mrs. Orford and Park Commissioners Gibson and Dillon, with the Post reception committee, Robert L. Norton, Edward J. Dunn, Edward Maguire and Malcolm E. Nichols, were walking to the centre of the green.

HAIL TO THE CHIEF

The band quickly switched from the march into "Hail to the Chief."

Fenway Park never saw such a scene, not even at the world series.

After some minutes quiet was restored and Governor Walsh was introduced. On behalf of the children he presented the elephants to the city of Boston, through Mayor Curley, making an address of about five minutes.

Mayor Curley responded feelingly, and both executives were loud in their praise of the *Post* and the children.

Another tremendous ovation followed a moment later—probably the greatest ovation ever accorded a

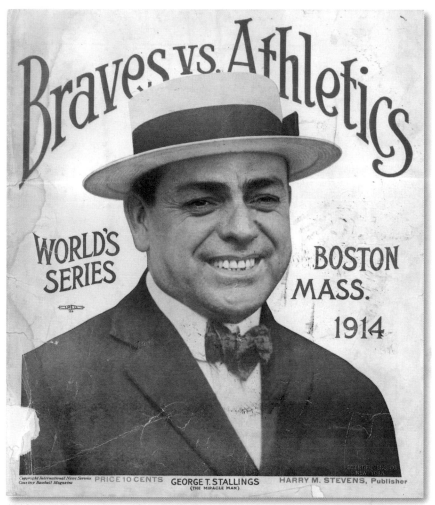

1914 World Series scorecard featuring Boston manager George Tweedy Stallings. Stallings, the son of a Confederate war hero admonished his team with the slogan, "You can win, you must win, you will win." Their world championship was selected by the Associated Press as the greatest sports upset of the first half of the 20th century. They also played their final World Series games against the Athletics at Fenway Park. *(Collection of the author)*

Emblem of the Philadelpia Athletics, who played the Boston Braves at Fenway Park in the 1914 World Series. *(Collection of the author)*

woman in this country, when Mrs. William Orford was introduced. In order came Mr. Orford. It was a magnificent tribute to these two people, who have sacrificed thousands of dollars so as the elephants would be assured the best kind of a home for the rest of their lives. At the height of the demonstration the little French clown, Pauline Mason, presented Mrs. Orford, on behalf of the *Post*, a huge bouquet of American Beauty roses.

The performance of Mollie, Waddy and Tony that followed, with both Mr. and Mrs. Orford participating, will never be forgotten by those who witnessed it. Tremendous excitement was created when Mrs. Orford was swung aloft by Waddy's trunk.

And there was that silly little rascal Tony. How the children laughed at him and his funny antics. Yes, he put the baby to bed.

A moment later and the gates swung open. With the band leading the way and Mollie, Waddy and Tony close behind, the parade was begun. Thus ended a child-demonstration that will go down in history – a day when the children and Mollie and Waddy and Tony came into their own.

JUNE 12, 1914

ENGLISH HIGH SCHOOL 16, HIGH SCHOOL OF COMMERCE 3

JUNE 15, 1914

B.C. High Defeats Rindge Tech 2 to 1

Boston College High emerged the victor in the contest with Rindge yesterday at Fenway Park. The James street boys won 2 to 1, in a most interesting and exciting contest.

Bob Gill pitched superb ball all through the game, striking out 11. His opponent, Cedarstrand, put up a fine article of ball also, and mowed down nine of his opponents via the strikeout route.

Over a thousand boys from Boston College High were in the stands with a couple of bands, and their cheering lent much color to the otherwise exciting contest.

JUNE 15, 1914 HOLY CROSS 8, BOSTON COLLEGE 0

JUNE 17, 1914 HARVARD 7, YALE 3

JUNE 20, 1914 YALE 13, HARVARD 8

JUNE 20, 1914

Speaker Hooted

Something must be wrong in Boston when the fans hoot Tris Speaker who is receiving $16,500 this year. During a recent double-header with the Athletics at Fenway Park the crowd got after Speaker in merciless fashion. Every time he came to bat and failed to make a hit he was hooted. Speaker, who had not been hitting with his usual skill lost his head completely and as he walked out to center field each time he made gestures and faces at the crowd. The fans in the open stands kept up their groans and catcalls all through the series until Speaker was glad to leave on the Western trip.

(A.H. Mitchell for Sporting Life)

JULY 11, 1914

RUTH SHAPES UP WELL

By T.H. Murnane

The Red Sox introduced Mr. Ruth, one of the Baltimore recruits yesterday to the crowd at Fenway Park and with the assistance of Leonard, the Fresno fruit grower, the young man led the home club over the wire by a score of 4 to 3. There was a fine crowd and they enjoyed the short, snappy contest immensely, as only one hour and 33 minutes were taken up in playing the game.

All eyes were turned on Ruth, the giant left-hander, who proved a natural ball player and went through his act like a veteran of many years. He has a natural delivery, fine control and a curve ball that bothers the batsmen, but has room for improvement and will, undoubtedly become a fine pitcher under the care of Manager Carrigan.

He held the Naps to five hits in six innings, with one strikeout, but was hit hard in the seventh, when the visitors tied the score by scoring two earned runs on singles by Kirke and Chapman, a sacrifice and a single by O'Neill. That was the curtain for the oriole importation, and he looked weak only in comparison with Dutch Leonard, who pitched the last two innings, putting six men out in order, four of them on strikes.

Leonard is really pitching the best ball of any man in the American League, and is the one man whom manager Bill can depend on to hold a game once won.

Boston scored one in the first on a single by Scott and a triple by Gardner. The two runs in the fourth came on a pass, singles by Gardner and Carrigan and a wild throw by O'Neill.

The Naps scored one in the fourth on a muff by Speaker, a sacrifice and a single by Jackson. The two runs in the seventh tied the score, and with Mitchell pitching high class ball there was trouble ahead for the home team. Lewis, batting for Ruth, hit a grounder that Kirke made a fine one-hand stop of and then threw wild, so that Lewis went to second and then to third on Scott's out. Speaker responded with a fine drive to center, scoring Lewis with the winning run.

There was some fine fielding by Turner, Graney, Scott, Yerkes, Janvrin and Speaker. The same teams will meet Monday (No Sunday baseball at Fenway Park) and by that time the Red Sox players should all line up for a week of good, hard play when called up.

AUGUST 1, 1914 BOSTON BRAVES 4, ST LOUIS CARDINALS 3 (10 INNINGS)

AUGUST 4, 1914

AMITY IN BOSTON

PRESIDENT LANNIN OFFERS THE USE OF FENWAY PARK TO THE BOSTON NATIONAL CLUB FOR BALANCE OF SEASON

That the best of good feelings exists between the owners of the Boston Red Sox and the Boston Braves, both regarded as pennant contenders because of recent spurts, is shown in the following telegrams which passed today between Joseph J. Lannin and James E. Gaffney. Mr. Lannin has generously offered the use of Fenway Park to the Braves

Fans make their way down Brookline Avenue toward Fenway Park during the 1914 World Series. Note the sartorial elegance of most fans who wore hats, suits, and ties to the games. *(Photograph by Leslie Jones, courtesy of the Boston Public Library)*

Braves fans including Boston Mayor and JFK granddad John "Honey Fitz" Fitzgerald (fourth from left), Braves catcher Hank Gowdy (fifth from left) and owner James Gaffney (seventh from left). *(Courtesy of the Boston Public Library)*

The first "bus" to Fenway Park cost a nickel back in 1915. The entrance to Park Street Church can be seen in the upper left-hand corner. *(Courtesy of the Boston Public Library)*

Lacrosse was an infrequent activity at Fenway Park but was encouraged by Red Sox owner Joe Lannin, who also served as president of the Boston Lacrosse Club. *(Courtesy of the Boston Public Library)*

for the remainder of the season and that offer has been accepted in part.

Mr. Gaffney announced this morning that the following telegrams had been received and sent:"

St. Louis, August 3
James B. Gaffney,
President Boston National
League Club, Boston, Mass.:

If it would be of any advantage to play at Fenway Park for the balance of the season you are welcome to use it free of all charges. Congratulations to you and Mr. Stallings on the fine showing of your club.

Joseph J. Lannin,
Boston Red Sox.

Boston, Mass., August 4.
Joseph J. Lannin, Boston Red Sox, St. Louis, Mo.:

Please accept my thanks for your most generous offer. It is the thought of a true sportsman and is appreciated not only by myself but also the public of New England. The Braves look like contenders so we may take advantage of your offer on Saturdays and holidays.

Permit me to congratulate you on the fine progress the Red Sox have made under your ownership. Boston needs two pennants. Let us go after them.
James E. Gaffney
Boston Braves
(Sporting Life)

AUGUST 8, 1914

BOSTON BRAVES 4, CINCINNATI REDS 3 (10 INNINGS)

AUGUST 17, 1914

Roosevelt at Fenway Park Today

EXPECTED TO SOUND KEYNOTE OF BULL MOOSE CAMPAIGN

(Author's Note: Roosevelt's speech was rained out a Fenway Park and given instead at the Boston Arena. The Arena, now known as Matthews Arena, opened in 1910, and endures as the oldest indoor ice arena in the world.)

AUGUST 17

BEVERLY PROGRESSIVES 5, IRISH ATHLETIC ASSOCIATION CLUB 0 (5 INNINGS)

LABOR DAY 1914

Boston's Biggest Baseball Crowd

BRAVES AND GIANTS PLAY HOST OF 75,000 AT FENWAY PARK

BOSTON LANDS FIRST GAME BY SENSATIONAL FINISH, SECOND IS ALL NEW YORK'S

From Boston Post *correspondent*

Two crowds, totaling 75,000 people, the largest gatherings that ever witnessed two baseball games in a single day in this city, saw the Braves and Giants break even at Fenway Park yesterday. The Braves captured the morning game 5 to 4 and the afternoon session was an easy victory for the Giants who won 10 to 1. The

teams are still in a tie for the leadership of the national League.

The afternoon game was enlivened by what at one time threatened to be a riot, worse than anything recorded at a baseball game in recent years. It came as the result of unsportsmanlike actions on the part of Fred Snodgrass, the Giants center fielder, who invited the crowd to hiss and boo him and following his actions at the time he was met with a shower of pop bottles from the crowd.

POLICE INTERFERE

It was the timely interence of the police and some cool headed members of the New York team that averted what might have been the most serious affair that baseball has yet knowm. As it was, the incident was considered the most unfortunate thing that has ever happened in Boston's baseball history.

The affair started in the sixth inning after the Giants had scored four runs. Snodgrass was at bat and was hit by one of Tyler's inshoots. The Giants center fielder was so elated at getting his way to first that he danced his way to first and on his way danced towards the pitcher's box. Once he was perched on the initial bag he kept yelling at Tyler to throw the ball, pointing his finger in the direction of the bag, and his actions became so prominent that Tyler tossed the ball in the air five different times and each time let it drop to the ground. This of course was intended as an imitation of Snodgrass famous $30,000 muff in the world series between Boston and New York in 1912.

The great crowd started to yell their disapproval of the antics of Snodgrass before Tyler added to the excitement by reminding him of his still-famous muff, and when the New Yorker was tagged out by Schmidt upon his trying to steal home, after reaching third on Doyle's single to centre the crowd yelled as few crowds have done in Boston

CROWD THROWS BOTTLES

When Snodgrass started for his position in center field the crowd hissed and booed and they were invited to show their disapproval of his actions in louder tones by the player himself. When the tumult had reached its greatest Snodgrass thumbed his nose at the crowd. That should have resulted in his banishment from the game at that time, but the umpires did not act and the crowd greeted him with scores of empty tonic bottles. They kept the fusillade up until the mounted police galloped in. Snodgrass held up one of the bottles in the air and started to pick another up when one just grazed his head and then several members of the Giants rushed to center field.

Capt. Larry Doyle, with Fletcher, Grant and Murray, began picking the bottles up and tossing them out of the playing field, when one of the fans on Duffy's Cliff made a remark which so angered Doyle that he started after him but he was grabbed by a policeman and Fletcher also grabbed him. Just then, Mayor Curley, who had been watching the game from the grandstand, jumped onto the field and protested to umpire Emsile that Snodgrass was inciting a riot and should be ordered from the game, but no action was taken. The game was started again after this incident had held it up for fully 10 minutes.

It was one of the incidents that can do baseball no good and it will

be surprising if some punishment commensurate with the actions of Snodgrass is meted out to him when the facts come known to President Tener. There was no question in the minds of the 40,000 people who attended the afternoon game but what Snodgrass was responsible for the entire proceeding. He invited it and is a fortunate man tonight that he got away as easily as he did.

CROWD AFTER SNODGRASS

McGraw sent Beecher into play in place of Snodgrass in the last half of the ninth and averted another demonstration that might have been more serious than the first as when the game was over fully 1,000 angry fans gathered in front of the New York dugout and yelled for Snodgrass to come out. The mounted police had to be called again to disperse them.

This excitement gave those who attended the afternoon game more thrills by far than the game itself, but all who journeyed to Fenway Park yesterday were entertained in one way or another. The morning game produced some of the best baseball seen this year.

Yesterday's crowd made history in more ways than one. It was the largest crowd that ever witnessed a National League game in Boston. It was the greatest throng by far that attended a holiday game in Boston and it was also believed a record for the country. The afternoon has been exceeded in numbers but once before, that being when the *Post* elephants were presented to the city. It was also the first time a Boston mayor protested the actions of a player on the field.

It was stated yesterday that the crowd was larger by far than that which attended the last world series during any two games.

TERRIBLE CRUSH

From early in the morning cars brought men, women and boys to the side of Fenway Park and hours before the ticket offices were opened lines stretched far into Lansdowne Street. It was estimated that 20,000 people were lined outside the gates by 8:30 AM. When the gates were finally opened there was a terrible crush and the efforts of the police for a time were futile. The mounted force arrived and it was with great difficulty they kept the men in line.

While a good portion of the grandstand had been sold long before yesterday there was the same demonstration in front of the park and it became necessary to close the gates to all but ticket-holders fully 45 minutes before the game was started. At this time there was such a great crowd waiting for tickets admitting them to the bleachers and on the field that hundreds started home convinced that no more could be jammed inside the park.

It was estimated that fully 35,000 persons watched the morning game, and this, in itself created a new record for National League attendance in Boston. It stood but a short time, however, as the afternoon session entertained a full 5,000 more than the morning.

GATHER ALL DAY

An idea of the great throng may be gleaned through the fact that as early as 7:30 yesterday morning the crowd started to assemble outside the park. At 8:30, the elevated road had added 50 cars to its full quota for holiday games at this same park and these cars were kept running back and forth from that time until the game was nearly ended as long before the first game closed another crowd was gathering for the afternoon set-to.

It was to be expected that ticket speculators would be busy for these two games and a small harvest was reaped by them.

September 8 Boston Braves 8, New York Giants 3

September 9 Philadelphia Phillies 10, Boston Braves 3

September 9 Boston Braves 7, Philadelphia Phillies 0

September 10 Boston Braves 3, Philadelphia Phillies 0

September 10 Boston Braves 7, Philadelphia Phillies 2

September 11 Boston Braves 6, Philadelphia Phillies 5

September 12 Brooklyn Robins 4, Boston Braves 3

September 14 Boston Braves 4, Brooklyn Robins 3

September 15 Boston Braves 7, Brooklyn Robins 5

September 16 Boston Braves 6, St. Louis Cardinals 3

September 17 Boston Braves 5, St. Louis Cardinals 1

September 18 Boston Braves 1, St. Louis Cardinals 1 (Tie)

September 19 Boston Braves 9, Pittsburgh Pirates 3

September 21 Boston Braves 6, Pittsburgh Pirates 5

September 22 Boston Braves 8, Pittsburgh Pirates 2

September 23 Boston Braves 3, Cincinnati Reds 2

September 23 Cincinnati Reds 3, Boston Braves 0

September 24 Boston Braves 5, Cincinnati Reds 0

September 24 Boston Braves 2, Cincinnati Reds 2 (Tie)

September 25 Boston Braves 2, Cincinnati Reds 0

September 25 Boston Braves 4, Cincinnati Reds 3

September 26 Boston Braves 6, Chicago Cubs 2

September 26 Boston Braves 12, Chicago Cubs 2

September 28 Boston Braves 7, Chicago Cubs 6

September 29 Boston Braves 3, Chicago Cubs 2

OCTOBER 12, 1914

BRAVES WIN DRAMATIC 12 INNING 5-4 VICTORY OVER PHILADELPHIA TO TAKE A 3 TO NOTHING LEAD IN THE WORLD SERIES

OCTOBER 13, 1914

Braves Conclude Miracle Season with Sweep of Athletics to Claim World Title

Despite drawing a crowd that was slightly smaller than the Labor Day throng from a month earlier the Braves scraped their way to a 3-1 victory over the heavily favored Philadelphia Athletics as team captain Johnny Evers scored the game's first run and drove in the other two to complete their unprecedented Worlds Series sweep.

In the wake of the Braves mighty achievement there was a demonstration of genuine enthusiasm that has never before been approached, much less has it ever been equaled, upon the ball field. It started the moment that Charley Deal retired "Stuffy" McInnis for the third hand out in the ninth inning, and for more than an hour the greater portion of the big Fenway Park crowd –all but as large as that of Monday's Columbus Day gathering-thronged about the Boston dug-out, cheering for everybody and everything in sight and doing it with an enthusiasm that could not leave the slightest doubt whether it was genuine or not. (Walter Hapgood, Boston Herald, October 14, 1914)

SEPTEMBER 9, 1914

Harvard Law Student Tosses Fenway's First No-Hitter

George "Iron" Davis made the most of his first starting appearance for the Boston Braves when he pitched a no-hitter to lead the Braves to a split of the double-header with the Phillies. Not only did Davis get three hits in four plate appearances, but he got himself out of a monumental jam in the fifth inning when he notched a strikeout and double play after walking the first three batters. (Author's note: This would be the career highlight for the spitball artist who later practiced law in Buffalo and was also recognized as one of the nation's top amateur astronomers.)

OCTOBER 30, 1914

HIGH SCHOOL OF COMMERCE 7, BOSTON LATIN 0

OCTOBER 31, 1914

Boston College 28 Norwich 6

In a game that was originally slated to be played in Montpelier, Vermont, Norwich University played Boston College on Halloween in what was to be the first of the Eagles' many home games at Fenway Park.

The correspondent's report from *The Boston Post* described the action as follows:

"The best football team that has represented Norwich University this season went down to defeat yesterday afternoon at the hands of the Boston College football team to the tune of 28 to 6. The game was played at Fenway Park, and was one of the finest exhibitions of the new style of open play that has been seen in Boston this year. The Norwich team was greatly strengthened by the half back of Bishop who has been kept out of the lineup until to-day because of his condition."

Sources Boston Post, November 1, 1914

Boston Evening Record , October 31, 1914

November 4, 1914 Boston English 10, Mechanic Arts 0

November 6 , 1914 High School of Commerce 34, Dorchester High 12

November 12, 1914 High School of Commerce 17, Mechanic Arts 0

November 13, 1914 Volkmann School 13, Noble & Greenough 7

November 18, 1914 Boston Latin 7, Mechanic Arts 7

November 19, 1914 Boston English 19, High School of Commerce 0

NOVEMBER 22, 1914

Dartmouth 40 Syracuse 0

A soggy Fenway Park was filled with crowd of over twenty thousand who cheered on a Darttmouth football squad coached by the legendary Frank "The Iron Major" Cavanagh. The men from Hanover started slowly leading by a score of 7-0 after the first quarter but a 25 yard interception by Murdock of Dartmouth led to quick second quarter touchdown and pushed their lead to 14-0 by halftime. The remainder of the game was marked by what eyewitnesses called "flukes," a euphemism for fumbles and Dartmouth racked up an additional 26 points.

Sources: Lowell Sun, page 5, November 23, 1914

Syracuse Herald, November 22, 1914

NOVEMBER 26, 1914

Boston Latin 3, Boston English 3

Boston College 14 Catholic University 0

In a rare Thanksgiving college game the Eagles of Boston College raced out to a two touchdown first half

lead that was never threatened by the visitors from Washington DC.

Typical of the era every player for both teams was listed as playing the full sixty minutes on both offense and defense.

Source: The Washington Post, page 8, November 27, 1914

NOVEMBER 28, 1914

Everett High School 80 Oak Park, Ill High School 0

Fenway Park played host to its second national high school championship game in three years as Oak Park High School returned to the site of ther triumph in 1912. Taking a measure of revenge against Oak Park High the Everett High School juggernaut of coach Cleo O'Donnell pounded Oak Park by a score of 80 to 0 to conclude a season in which Everett outscored their opponents by an aggregate score of 600 to 0.

Everett football historian Arn Boardman wrote of the game:

"Six thousand saw the complete triumph of eastern schoolboy football. The day could not have been better adapted for a championship game, though overnight frost and a mid-day sun made the field soft in spots, a failure which prevented both teams from playing with the brilliance they might have displayed on a firm gridiron.

"Everett was so perfect a machine, the parts were so cannily fitted together to make the irresistible whole that it seems a bootless task to indicate the stellar individual performers for the winners."

In 1960 "Sport" magazine named the 1914 Everett squad the greatest high school football team in history.

Source: "112 Years of Crimson Tide Football, Everett High School 1893-2004" by Arnold Boardman

**DECEMBER 9, 1914
SOMERVILLE HIGH 7,
DEPAUL (IL) ACADEMY 0**

JANUARY 19, 1915

Red Sox Lower Ticket Prices

The Red Sox announced they'd LOWER their ticket prices following winning the 1915 World Series. Perhaps this was in reaction to the fact that the Braves, who just a season earlier had also won the series, was about to open their 43,000 seat Braves Field in Allston just up Commonwealth Avenue from Fenway. According to Red Sox historian Bill Nowlin in his indispensable *Day By Day With The Boston Red Sox* the team cut the price of box seats (the first five rows at Fenway) from $1.50 to $1.00 and the balance of the grandstand from $1.00 to 75 cents. Most of the outfield seats were priced at 50 and 25 cents and team President Lannin expressed his feelings that a dollar was plenty to pay to see a regular. (Author's Note: Over the years Red Sox ticket prices sustained their value, even with the advent of free agency and rising salaries. In fact the $6 bleacher seat in 1989 and the handful of $10 upper row bleacher seats in 2010 are an even bigger bargain than the 25-cent ticket of 1916.)

April 10 Boston College High School 19, Cambridge Latin 2

April 12 Boston Braves 7, Harvard College 3

April 13 Boston Braves 6, Brown University 0

April 14 Philadelphia Phillies 3, Boston Braves 0

April 15 Philadelphia Phillies 7, Boston Braves 1

April 17 Boston Braves 5, Brooklyn Robins 1

April 19 Boston Braves 7, Brooklyn Robins 2

April 19 Boston Braves 6, Brooklyn Robins 4

April 20 Boston Braves 4, Brooklyn Robins 3

April 21 Brooklyn Robins 8, Boston Braves 4

May 6 New York Giants 3, Boston Braves 1

May 7 Boston Braves 11, New York Giants 7

MAY 7, 1915

N. & G. Nine Wins in Closing Rally

Noble & Greenough defeated the Volkmann School baseball team yesterday afternoon at Fenway Park by the score of 1 to 0. Pratt opened the nine with a safe hit and Kenney was safe on Howe's error. Abbott was out bunting the third strike. Minot hit to Wiswait forcing Kenney at second, and in attempting to complete a double play, Wiswail threw wild to first base, allowing Pratt to score the only and winning run.

May 8, 1915 Boston Braves 4, New York Giants 3

May 10, 1915 Boston Braves 14, New York Giants 9

May 11, 1915 St. Louis Cardinals 5, Boston Braves 1

May 13, 1915 Boston Braves 6, St. Louis Cardinals 2

May 14, 1915 St. Louis Cardinals 5, Boston Braves 4

May 15, 1915 Pittsburgh Pirates 10, Boston Braves 6

May 18, 1915 Boston Braves 3, Pittsburgh Pirates 2

May 19, 1915 Pittsburgh Pirates 7, Boston Braves 0

May 20 , 1915 Boston Braves 4, Cincinnati Reds 2

May 21, 1915 Chicago Cubs 3, Boston Braves 2

May 22, 1915 Chicago Cubs 5, Boston Braves 4

May 23, 1915 Spanish-American War Memorial Mass

May 24, 1915 Chicago Cubs 9, Boston Braves 1

May 25, 1915 Boston Braves 3, Cincinnati Reds 1

May 27, 1915 Cincinnati Reds 6, Boston Braves 0

May 28, 1915 Boston Braves 5, Philadelphia Phillies 2

May 28, 1915 Boston Braves 5, Philadelphia Phillies 4

May 29, 1915 Boston Braves 9, Philadelphia Phillies 4

May 31, 1915 Boston Braves 2, Philadelphia Phillies 1

May 31, 1915 Philadelphia Phillies 5, Boston Braves 2

June 1, 1915 Boston Braves 7, New York Giants 0

June 2, 1915 Boston Braves 5, New York Giants 5 (Tie)

June 3, 1915 New York Giants 10, Boston Braves 3

An early postcard view of Fenway's grandstand. Note the tiny press box and the major league's first home plate protective screen. *(Courtesy of the Boston Public Library)*

Section of Grand Stand, Fenway Park, Boston, Mass.

JUNE 5, 1915

Fenway Park Hosts Red Sox and Boston Lacrosse Club Doubleheader

Red Sox owner Joseph Lannin achieved his American dream when the former bellhop emigrated to America from Quebec and made his fortune. Apart from leading the Red Sox Lannin maintained strong ties to his childhood sport of lacrosse and on Saturday June 5th hosted an unprecedented baseball/lacrosse doubleheader at Fenway Park.

In the opening game the Red Sox beat the first place White Sox 4-2 before 10,000 fans who saw George Foster pitch a superb 4 hit complete game.

Roughly half the crowd remained for the lacrosse game between the Boston Lacrosse Club and the New York Lacrosse A.A.

The game started just 15 minutes after the Red Sox game and was played on a field laid out in roughly the same layout as the 2010 Winter Classic rink between the two dugouts on the crest between the infield and outfield. The Boston team prevailed by a score of 9 to 2 in a game marked by aggressive play and superb passing.

Sources: The Boston Sunday Globe, pages 18,19, June 6, 1915

Boston Globe, page 7, June 5, 1915

June 22, 1915 Boston Braves 3, Brooklyn Robins 2

June 23, 1915 Boston Braves 3, Brooklyn Robins 2

June 24, 1915 Boston Braves 6, Brooklyn Robins 0

July 9, 1915 Boston Braves 4, St. Louis Cardinals 3

July 10, 1915 St. Louis Cardinals 7, Boston Braves 1

July 10, 1915 Boston Braves 3, St. Louis Cardinals 1

July 12 St. Louis Cardinals 2, Boston Braves 1

July 12 St. Louis Cardinals 4, Boston Braves 3

July 13 Pittsburgh Pirates 3, Boston Braves 1

July 13 Boston Braves 7, Pittsburgh Pirates 6

July 15 Boston Braves 3, Pittsburgh Pirates 2

July 16 Boston Braves 6, Pittsburgh Pirates 5

July 17 Boston Braves 3, Cincinnati Reds 2

July 17 Boston Braves 3, Cincinnati Reds 2

July 19 Boston Braves 4, Cincinnati Reds 1

July 20 Boston Braves 6, Cincinnati Reds 2

July 21 Cincinnati Reds 2, Boston Braves 1

July 22 Boston Braves 4, Chicago Cubs 3

July 23 Boston Braves 2, Chicago Cubs 1

July 24 Boston Braves 1, Chicago Cubs 0

July 26 Boston Braves 1, Chicago Cubs 0

Not only did lanky right-hander Ernie Shore arrive in Boston via the same trade that sent Babe Ruth to the Red Sox, but on June 23, 1917, Shore replaced Ruth after one batter and an ugly scene in which Ruth punched umpire Brick Owen. Shore proceeded to pick off the base runner allowed by the Babe and retire the next 26 batters for a historic perfect game. *(Courtesy of the Boston Public Library)*

SEPTEMBER 16, 1915

Tigers Win Brawl Game, 6-1 as Fans Incite Cobb

In the heat of a torrid pennant race the Tigers and Red Sox faced off at Fenway Park where the crowd began hooting at Ty Cobb from the first inning onward. After the Tigers jumped to a 5-0 lead Boston relief pitcher Carl Mays threw two pitches at Cobb's head before hitting him on the wrist. After Cobb came around to score and returned to his spot in the outfield fans began showering him with wads of paper. A police escort soon escorted Cobb from the field.

SEPTEMBER 18, 1915

The Red Sox Pennant Battle

The Red Sox have been having a high old time during the past few days. They took four out of five from the White Sox, effectively putting a damper on whatever hopes Comiskey's men might have had for winning the pennant. The visitors had been enjoying quite a winning streak up to the time they hit Boston, a few days ago. They were within striking distance of the goal provided they could clean up the series with the Red Sox. But they failed dismally. Superb pitching by the Boston pitchers sent them away with only one victory to their credit. Then came the Tigers. Jenniugs'

crew gave Boston a bad beating on Thursday, before more than 20,000. But on Friday, Carrigan's men came back strong and with Leonard in the box, beat the Tigers badly, 7 to 2, before an even larger crowd. Leonard let the visitors down with one hit up to the ninth. Then, with one on,

COBB DROVE THE BALL into the right-field seats for a home run and Veach followed with a single, making three hits off Dutch. The recent games in Boston have been marked by fierce rooting by the populace. It is something new to this old base ball town. The Red Sox have run up against organized bands of rooters in other cities, but Boston crowds have always been very polite and seemed as anxious to applaud good plays by the visitors as much as if made by the home players. But some of the newspapermen called attention to the fact that crowds in other cities sometimes went to extremes to rattle the Boston Club, and they called on the local fans to pay the visiting teams back in some of their own medicine. So the rooters went out to Fenway Park in force and with tin horns, cow-bells, and other instruments calculated to rattle the opponents, they set up a terrific din in the Chicago series. The noise was something awful, and no doubt had a lot to do with subduing the White Sox. At any rate, they were effectually tamed. The noise....

FINALLY BECAME OBNOXIOUS to many of the regular patrons and one or two writers called for a halt of it. Just now it seems to be a fight between newspapers, some of the writers calling for more noise and others demanding the "roughnecks" cease their din. Today, it was announced that the Royal Rooters will take a hand in the proceedings and march to the park, 300 strong, with a band and instruments for making noise. The song "Tessie" is expected to play an important part. Clark Griffith recently remarked: "You can't play ball in Boston with that infernal 'Tessie' ringing in your ears. I was 'Tessieized' out of a pennant in 1905. That song certainly nets the goats of the visiting teams." The Royal Rooters, heretofore, have never mixed up in the winning of league pennants. They have always reserved their energies for the World's Series, in which Boston clubs have participated. But now they are horning into the regular season, and, with their band, propose to root another pennant into Boston. There were...

SCENES OF NEAR DISORDER in the Thursday game. The crowd got after Cobb (it was the first game of the Detroit series) and Cobb got back at the crowd. In one part of the game, with Carl Mays pitching for Boston, Cobb declared that the pitcher was trying to "bean" him, and threw his bat at the boxman. Fortunately, it went wide and did no damage. The crowd surrounded Ty as soon as the game closed, but the police rushed to his assistance and escorted him off the grounds. All this is simply paying the Tigers back in their own coin. When the Red Sox visit Detroit, the Tigers and the Detroit fans leave no stone unturned in order to put it over our boys. They wrangle, they incite the public, they play "roughhouse" and stop at nothing to win. Yet hitherto the Detroit Club has always received nothing but the best of treatment whenever it came to Boston.

THE RECENT UPRISING of the fans here may mean that hereafter visiting teams will be treated the way the Red Sox are treated when they are in the West. Crowds continue very large at Fenway Park, and Mr. Lannin has undoubtedly made good early losses. Including today's game, the Red Sox have 18 more games to play, 11 in Boston and two in Washington and five in New York. If the Tigers take the two remaining games here they cannot leave town leading the American League. So by every way of figuring, the Red Sox have distinctly the best chance to land the flag. A victory over the Tigers today and Monday would spell the death-knell to Jennings' hopes. The Red Sox are all in good shape, no cripples or sore arms, except Joe Wood's. If Joe had continued in good shape the race would be all over by this time,
(A.H. Mitchell for Sporting Life)

November 1, 1915 Boston Latin 9, High School of Commerce 7

November 3, 1915 Boston English 20, Mechanic Arts 7

November 5, 1915 Boston College High 19, St. John's Prep 0

NOVEMBER 6, 1915

Dartmouth 7 Pennsylvania 3

On the day after the British had taken Baghdad in the spreading conflict that was the First World War, *The Boston Globe* front page headline reported "Dartmouth Snatches Game Out of The Fire." A crowd of 12,000 was sent home cheering by a last minute Dartmouth touchdown pass from Holbrook to Emery. Following the game hundreds of Dartmouth students raced onto the field where they did a snake dance around the field led by the college band. Not only did they sing "Fight for Dartmouth," a song written expressly for this game but they also marched from the ballpark to The Colonial Theater where they took in an evening performance of "Watch Your Step."
Source, The Boston Sunday Globe, November 7, 1915

November 11, 1915 High School of Commerce 10, Mechanic Arts 3

November 17, 1915 Boston Latin 21, Mechanic Arts 3

November 18, 1915 Boston English 10, High School of Commerce 6

November 25, 1915 Boston College 35, Norwich 0

Military mass honoring the war dead of World War I is held on the field at Fenway Park. *(Photograph by Leslie Jones, courtesy of the Boston Public Library)*

Red Sox owner Harry Frazee (second from right) views a game at Fenway Park with family and friends. *(Courtesy of the Boston Public Library)*

November 25, 1915 Boston Latin 14, Boston English 13

November 27, 1915 Everett High 6, Waltham High 0

February 25, 1916 Women's Prices and Separate Turnstiles Adopted Sox President Lannin issues an announcement regarding special women's prices set at 50 cents instead of 75 cents. Separate turnstiles will be installed for women, too.

May 26, 1916 Noble and Greenough 16, Volkmann 2

JUNE 21, 1916

Foster Pitches Fenway's 1st No-Hit Game, 2-0 Over New York

Boston's barrel chested "Little Giant" five foot seven George "Rube" Foster only allowed 3 Yankee batters to reach first base as he tossed the fifth no-hit, no-run game in Red Sox history and the first no hitter at Fenway Park as Boston beat New York by a score of 2-0. Manager Bill Carrigan caught the game despite playing with a broken finger. The Oklahoma farmer's masterpiece was the second no hitter recorded in Boston within a week as it matched Tom Hughes no-hit victory over the Pirates by the same score at Braves Field just six days earlier.

AUGUST 30, 1916

Leonard Fires No-Hitter Over Browns, 4-0

Red Sox southpaw Dutch Leonard dominated the fourth place Browns and helped Boston hold onto first as catcher/manager Bill Carrigan caught his second no-hitter of the season. Only two bases on balls prevented Leonard from perfection in a game marked by two superb catches by right fielder Harry Hooper, the first a show stopper in the first inning off a drive by George Sisler.

September 2, 1916 Pere Marquette Council, Knights of Columbus/ South Boston 3, Salvador Council of New York 2

September 4, 1916 Galway Men's Association Field Day

SEPTEMBER 10, 1916

Thousands Cheer Odd Fellows on Their Three Mile March to Fenway Park

On a week-end during which the Red Sox battled the Washington Senators at Griffith Park in their quest for back to back pennants, Fenway Park answered to a higher calling.

Under sunny skies and balmy conditions thousands of Bostonians cheered the 15,000 Odd Fellows that represented the 200 lodges of Massachusetts as they marched down Boylston and Tremont streets before heading down Commonwealth Avenue towards Fenway Park to hold their annual Church Day of the Triple Link League of the I.O.O.F.

Among the highlights of their ballpark ceremony was a flag parade featuring 75 flag bearers who marched and countermarched across the Fenway diamond before standing at attention as the crowd thundered forth "The Star Spangled Banner."

In the principal address delivered from a platform located directly over the pitcher's mound Past Grand Master Joseph Belcher remarked, "In the olden days, our forefathers in their deep religious feeling, worshipped only in a building of God, deeming it somewhat irreligious to worship in the open air. But who among us cannot feel the inspiration of worshipping our lord and master under the blue canopy of heaven? Surely there can be no one in this present day and generation, who, because of inherited prejudice can fail to catch the splendor of this hour."

After several more speakers the ceremony closed with the crowd singing "America" to the accompaniment of ten bands. (*Boston Post*)

September 21, 1916 Boston Police 10, Newton Police 6

October 20, 1916 High School of Commerce 21, Lowell High 19

October 27, 1916 Boston College High 52, South Boston High 0

October 30, 1916 High School of Commerce 13, Brockton High 0

November 1, 1916 Boston English 25, Mechanic Arts 0

November 15, 1916 Boston Latin 3, Mechanic Arts 0

November 16, 1916 Boston English 27, Brockton High 0

November 17, 1916 High School of Commerce 27, Dorchester High 0

November 18, 1916 Rindge Tech 17, Boston College High 0

November 23, 1916 Boston English 20, High School of Commerce 7

November 25, 1916 Syracuse 20, Tufts 13

November 30, 1916 Boston English 13, Boston Latin 0

DECEMBER 2, 1916

Boston College 17 Holy Cross 14

On a Saturday that Bostonians celebrated Thanksgiving the fans of Boston College were justified in feeling Christmas may have come early.

Of their historic victory *Boston Globe* sportswriter Lawrence J. Sweeney wrote of Boston College, "For 17 long years Boston College had awaited the day when her football team should triumph over its time-honored rival from Worcester and yesterday at Fenway Park, as the shadows of eventide crept over the gridiron her fondest hopes were realized.

"Great was the joy in the Boston stands when Jimmy Fitzpatrick, the clever right halfback of the brickleyized team stood upon his rival's 34 yard line and lofted a beautiful drop kick over the bar."

A crowd of 8,000 that included Mayor James M. Curley and Cardinal O'Connell attended the historic game.
Source: The Boston Sunday Globe, page 1, 16, December 3, 1916

December 9, 1916 Somerville High 7, DePaul Academy (IL) 0

March 19, 1917 Shepard Norwell Women's Military Company First Public Drill

March 27, 1917 Spanish-American War Memorial Mass

May 25, 1917 Volkmann School 5, Noble and Greenough 4

June 20, 1917, Mechanic Arts High 8, High School of Commerce 3

JUNE 23, 1917

Pitcher Ernie Shore Achieves Perfection Following Ruth Ejection, Sox Win, 4-0

Babe Ruth had faced just one batter before he lost his temper following the base on balls awarded Senators leadoff man Ray Morgan. After screaming at home plate umpire Brick Owens, Ruth was warned he'd be thrown out of the game if he kept protesting which prompted the Red Sox pitcher to retort, "If you chase me, I'll punch your face." His immediate ejection provoked Ruth to make good on his promise and teammates grabbed Ruth only after he'd landed a solid punch to Owen's ear

Player/manager Jack Barry quickly gestured to towering right-hander Ernie Shore to warm up in preparation to take Ruth's place.

After Morgan was thrown out trying to steal second Shore was perfect retiring the next twenty six batters in a row. In fact only six balls were hit as far as the Boston outfield. Shortstop Everett Scott and second baseman Jack Barry made several great plays to preserve Shore's gem including a sensational first inning snare of a Texas leaguer by Barry and a sixth inning scoop of a ball hit off Shore's glove by Scott.

July 21, 1917 Harry Hooper Day at Fenway Park.

August 3, 1917 St John's AC/ Cambridge 6, Boston Tigers 5

August 4, 1917 Pitcher Carl Mays digs for fishing worms under the stands at Fenway and loses his wallet.

August 11, 1917 Police arrest 5 gamblers in Fenway Park bleachers.

August 13, 1917 Boston Printers 8, New York Printers 2

OCTOBER 3, 1917

Senators Win Benefit Game vs Red Sox Featuring Babe Ruth and Walter Johnson

PROCEEDS BENEFIT 101ST REGIMENT FUND

Not only did Walter Johnson shut out Babe Ruth and the Red Sox by a 6-0 score he also cleared the bases with a double before 2,070 at Fenway Park. The game was highlighted by a ceremonial first pitch tossed by Lieutenant Governor and future President Calvin Coolidge and a speech by Mayor Curley. Curley also presented members of the 101st regiment with baseball equipment donated by Senators owner Clark Griffith.

October 12, 1917 Boston College 20, Tufts 0

Fenway interior looking from center field bleachers to the wooden bleachers that once sat alongside the left field wall.

October 26, 1917 High School of Commerce 26, Brockton High 7

OCTOBER 31, 1917

Boston English Blanks Mechanics and Arts High 34-0

Boston English led by Captain Bill Bridges, who scored 22 of their 34 points, defeated Mechanics and Arts High at Fenway Park in City of Boston High School League action.

The Boston Globe reported, English scored all its touchdowns on straight line plays. The first one was made possible in the opening period when McDonald made a 25 yard run the five yard line and tallied on the following play. One more touchdown came for English High before the period ended. In the second period English High continued its scoring,

making another touchdown. Two more came in the third while there was little doing in the fourth period.

November 8, 1917 Boston English 21, Boston College High 6

NOVEMBER 10, 1917

Boston College Blasts Holy Cross 34-6 Before 5,000

November 13, 1917 High School of Commerce, 37, Arlington High 0

November 16, 1917 Boston Latin 34, Mechanic Arts 0

November 29, 1917 Boston English 13, Boston Latin 6

MAY 26, 1918

Red Sox Postpone Red Cross War Fund Benefit to Monday May 27th to Hold Military Mass at Fenway Park

Over 30,000 attended a solemn war memorial mass at Fenway Park on a day the team had originally slated for a game versus the defending world champion Chicago White Sox in which owner Harry Frazee was going to donate the entire proceeds of the game. The game would wait for a day while Bostonians, including large delegations from local businesses such as Jordan Marsh, Filenes, R.H. White, Lee Higgonson Company, Heitzer-Cabot Company and American Express marched to the park in with, in the words of an eyewitness, "the vigor and spirit of soldiers."

The head of the Boston Archdiocese, Cardinal O'Connell presided over the mass which was also attended by Governor McCall, Mayor Peters, and many other politicians and public officials.

A large group of recently drafted men joined with coast guard sailors, radio and aviation cadets, and parish society members as the crowd sang "Keep The Home Fires Burning," "Onward Christian Soldiers," and "Over There."

In his sermon O'Connell called for the gathering to "remember that the voice of Congress and the President is for us the voice of God, and though we do not understand the motive underlying their several enactments let us not forget that their horizon is all the more expansive by reason of their exalted position." (*Boston Post*)

AUGUST 31, 1918

Red Sox Possess Full Title To The Championship Of American League

BABE RUTH'S VICTORY GIVES PENNANT TO RED SOX

Colossus, Who Had Done so Much During the Season, Wins Deciding Game, A's Win Second Contest

Hanging the Ribbon Aloft

BY FRANK GAFFNEY, BOSTON POST

The Boston Red Sox by winning the first game of yesterday's double-header with the Philadelphia Athletics 6 to 1, copped the American League pennant and will meet the Chicago Cubs, the winners of the National League pennant in the world series this week. Babe Ruth twirled the Barrowites to victory. The home club lost the second game 1 to 0.

SEPTEMBER 9, 1918

The "Star Spangled Banner" is played for the first time prior to a major league game at Fenway prior to game four of the World Series against the Cubs. (In 1912 the Red Sox were also the first team to market series souvenirs.)

SEPTEMBER 11, 1918

RED SOX ARE AGAIN WORLD'S CHAMPIONS

MAYS HOLDS CUBS IN CHECK WHILE TYLER FAILS TO BLOCK SOX–WHITEMAN'S WONDERFUL WORK MAINLY RESPONSIBLE FOR 2 TO 1 VICTORY

By Paul H. Shannon Boston Post

Again are the Boston Red Sox champions of the world.

At exactly five minutes past three o'clock yesterday afternoon, even before the wires began to tell the country that Barrow's men had delivered the punch that was to win the deciding contest in this great struggle for the supreme title, a carrier pigeon, released from the press stand by exultant soldiers started on its long flight to Camp Devens with the news of the fatal third inning and the downfall of the Chicago Cubs.

For six innings after this the contest endured, but this one eventful frame gave the veteran Whiteman a chance to pen the closing chapter in the championship battle of 1918.

KEEPS CLEAN SLATE

Once more a Boston team had arisen in its might and preserved a reputation never smirched in the postseason contests for the big stakes. For the fifth time in seven years Boston's championship prestige had been maintained by a team well worthy of upholding its reputation.

Just one unfortunate play by the National Leaguers blasted the Cubs' faint hopes of winning and gave George Whitemen, easily the star of the entire series, the opportunity of writing his record indelibly in the annals of a bitterly waged struggle. Just one sad muff by a player who had been one of the real bulwarks of the Chicago defense sent that team from Fenway Park defeated after one of the gamest fights that a losing outfit has ever made.

Many will blame Flack for Chicago's downfall, and by the strict rules of scoring he must bear the stigma for the Cubs defeat, yet the 18,000 fans who witnessed the closing game will be inclined to extend praise rather than blame.

WHITEMAN THE STAR

In nearly every run that the Red Sox scored in the six games Whiteman, the little Texas veteran, has figured mightily, and yesterday was again the bat that sent both of the Boston runs across.

Two bases-on-balls in the third inning—one to Mays, the other to Shean—had put two men on the sacks, and they were on third and second respectively when Whitey came to bat with two men out. A consultation followed and for a moment it looked as though the Chicago team would pass him and take a chance on the even more dangerous McInnis. Finally the Cub board of strategy decided to make the batter hit.

With one ball and one strike the count Whitey got hold of a ball that was just on the outside and drove it with the speed of a bullet into right field. Flack, who was playing well out tore in to catch the liner. He reached it by a desperate sprint but the ball had been driven with such

force that it tore his hands apart and dropped to the ground while Shean followed Mays across the plate. The crestfallen Flack made a futile throw home, but there was no play. The second run had been registered and as it turned out, the championship had been decided right then and there.

It was said afterward that Flack, in the belief that but one man was out at the time, tried to throw the ball before he caught it in the hope of stopping a man from going home. This was denied by Manager Mitchell, who said after the game that it was an out and out muff, that Flack knew two men had been retired and the only excuse was that the ball was driven with far greater force than the fielder anticipated. At any rate, Chicago's hopes of wresting the championship from the Boston team died at the same time.

So thus it was the good fortune of the Red Sox left fielder to close his big league career in a blaze of glory, such as he had never dared to hope for since he first entered the majors eleven long years ago. To Whiteman it has been given to star both on the offense and defense as few world series heroes ever have. He can always look back with pride upon the splendid part he took in bringing the 1918 world championship home to Boston.

MAKES GREAT CATCH

Whiteman's active participation in the struggle did not end with that telling drive in the eighth. In that same frame Barber, leading off as a pinch hitter for the Cubs, made a gallant effort to start what might have proven a dangerous rally but for the enterprise and game-ness of the Texan.

Hitting the ball squarely on the trade mark and lining it into short left field his chances for starting this round with a two bagger were good until Whiteman made his marvelous as well as sensational play. Tearing in at breakneck speed Whiteman made a shoestring catch, grabbing the ball just before it reached the ground and turning a complete somersault after making the catch. The achievement completely stopped the opposition and gave the stands a chance to cheer and shriek for three full minutes.

In accomplishing this feat, however Whiteman was hit on his head and badly wrenched the muscles of his neck. Compelled to leave the game a minute later after courageously trying to resume play, he was given a tremendous tribute as he passed into the dugout. After the game, Manager Mitchell in warmly commending this man's work during all six games, said that the catch was one of the most spectacular he has ever witnessed in post-season battle.

By the score of 2 to 1 the Red Sox vanquished the Cubs in a twirling duel that was anticipated when the nominations had Mays opposing Tyler on the rubber. Just as expected Mays proved a baffling proposition for the Cubs, the one run scored off him coming in the only round where the submarine was not completely the master of the situation. As for Lefty Tyler, grandly as he worked, he as well as his manager must realize today that he suffered the fate of the pitcher sent too often to the well.

Fully as effective as Mays and every whit as efficient as in either of his other appearances against the Red Sox Tyler paid the penalty for his lack of control as well as for the fatal though excusable error by his

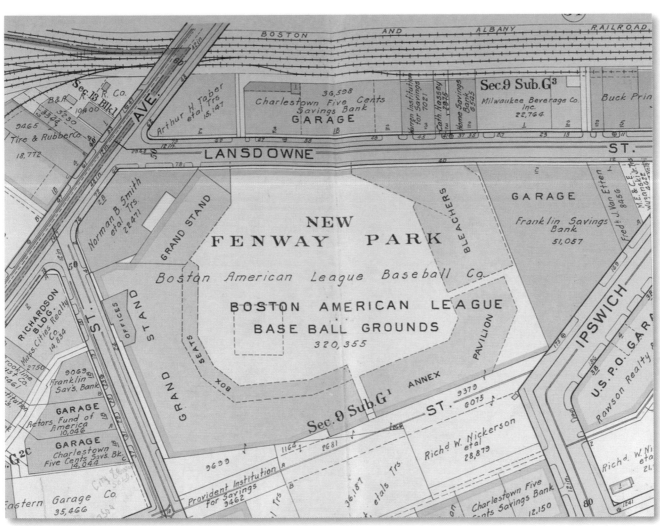

Insurance map of Fenway Park c.1915, showing the adjacent properties and their owners. The park was built on property that once touched the shoreline of the Charles River prior to the massive landfills of the 19th century. *(Courtesy of the Boston Public Library)*

unlucky right fielder. All through the rash of bases on balls have been the cause of serious trouble for the Cub southpaws and the history of the earlier games in the sextet were repeated yesterday.

PASSES PROVE FATAL

In his opening essay against the Red Sox a pass in the fourth inning was the cause of Jim Vaughn's defeat. On Saturday last the run that beat this same twirler was started by a batter being hit. Both the men that scored on Ruth's terrific three bagger last Monday were sent to first on passes by Tyler and yesterday again these fatal passes caused or

rather led up to the clever southpaw's undoing.

All along it has been conceded that the Red Sox lacked the punch against left-handers and that these same twirlers of the southpaw variety would be very apt to beat them if they possessed control. But lack of control at critical times shattered the hope of Mitchell and failed to confirm Mitchell's judgment in vesting his whole reliance on two left-handers while great right-handers like Hendrix and Douglas were compelled to sit upon the bench.

Tyler was in splendid form yesterday but for the third and fourth innings. In each of these frames he issued two bases on balls and had

not Flack muffed Whiteman's drive he might have pitched himself out of the hole as he did in the fourth. Of the six hits made off Tyler only one was a clean cut one and this was a single by Strunk was safe because it bounded between Hollocher and Pick who both came within an ace of stopping the ball.

Mays, on the other hand, was possessed of far better control than Tyler. He pitched one of his finest games and was given superb support as, indeed, have all the Boston twirlers in a series which was marked by but one Red Sox error in six games.

The work of Whiteman, Scott, Thomas and Hooper went a long way yesterday. In adding to Carl's efficiency while the sharp way in which both he and Schang watched the bases kept the opposition from taking any undue risks.

AND STUFFY MCINNIS

Right here it might be added that McInnis, whose first base play has been the finest ever provided for any world series struggle, added a great deal to the Red Sox defense by co-operating so splendidly with the battery. In the second inning, for instance, he kept Pick who was on first constantly guessing until Mays picked the runner off the bag by an unexpected and lightning throw. Later on the same sort of play, executed by Schang and McInnis held the Cubs in check in the only round where there was any real danger of Mays being punished.

The victory of the Boston team, undoubtedly expected by the majority of the Cubs, was no signal for any great demonstration. The Boston players were in a very subdued mood through long consideration of the scanty purse which will reward their achievement. This money they will split at Fenway Park at noon today. The Cubs left the field without any fuss and took occasion before dressing to visit the Red Sox clubhouse and congratulate the new champions.

Strike Rumor To Blame for Small Attendance

Strike talk in the air and on fans tongues kept down the attendance at the last game of the world series yesterday at Fenway Park. It was unfortunate in a way that fans throughout New England could not have been certain that the sixth game would be played. Many were afraid that the players would not appear for the game and so stayed away. Telephones to the papers were continually tinkling yesterday morning and early in the afternoon, asking if the game would be played. Both President Weeghman of the Cubs and President Frazee of the Red Sox assured their players that they would do everything in their power to persuade the national commission and National League and the American League to agree to a redivision of the players share in the spoils, an arrangement which would give the participants in the series a worthwhile amount. The Sox meet at noon today to say the last fond farewells and divide their spoils.

November 5, 1918 High School of Commerce 33, Revere High School 0

November 7, 1918 Dorchester High 7, Boston English 6

November 8, 1918 Boston College High School 7, Boston Latin 7

November 14, 1918 Boston Latin 0, Dorchester High 0

November 15, 1918 Boston College High School 21, Boston English 0

November 16, 1918 High School of Commerce practice

November 28, 1918 Boston Latin 28, Boston English 0

December 7, 1918 High School of Commerce 3, Medford High 0

May 25, 1919 Spanish-American War Memorial Service

60,000 Storm Fenway Park to Cheer the Irish President

JAM SO GREAT THAT THOUSANDS FAIL TO GET IN – ENTHUSIASM IS TREMENDOUS – CHEERS AND TEARS MINGLE IN DRAMATIC SCENES AS PRESIDENT DE VALERA TELLS OF HOPES OF IRELAND – APPEALS TO AMERICA AS THE SAVIOR OF THE SMALL NATIONS – SENATOR DAVID I. WALSH PAYS ELOQUENT TRIBUTE TO DE VALERA AS GREAT CHIEFTAIN OF IRELAND

ALL NEW ENGLAND IS REPRESENTED IN GREAT THRONG WHO SEEK JUSTICE FOR ERIN

PRESIDENT DE VALERA MAKES REMARKABLE IMPRESSION AND WINS HEARTS OF AUDIENCE

DEMAND RECOGNITION OF IRISH REPUBLIC

The following resolutions were unanimously adopted at yesterday's meeting at Fenway Park:

Resolved: That we return thanks to the United States Senate for the American delegates at Paris to bring the case of Ireland, through its representatives to the peace conference, that her case may be heard.

Resolved: That we declare ourselves unreservedly in favor of the independence of Ireland and

Irish leader Eamon De Valera packed Fenway Park to overflowing while giving a historic address on Irish freedom in 1919. *(Photograph by Leslie Jones, courtesy of the Boston Public Library)*

demand that our government recognize the Irish republic.

Resolved: That we register our opposition to any proposal of League of Nations which does not protect all American rights and ideals and which binds us to guarantee the territorial integrity of the British and Japanese empires.

Sixty-thousand freedom-loving men, women and children packed into Fenway Park yesterday afternoon, thundered encouragement to Edward De Valera, President of the Irish Republic, assured him by their cheers that the hopes of his race are their hopes, and in resolutions unanimously adopted demanded of the government of the United States that the new Erin government be recognized immediately.

An ideal day brought men and women from all parts of New England to the park to welcome the Irish leader. An hour before the scheduled starting time, 3 o'clock, entrances were blocked and cordons of police thrown round them prevented thousands more from entering. Between rows of seats and in the aisles the crowds jammed in, overflowing to the field, massing tightly about the platform on which De Valera and his escort of honor had their places.

Cheering was so vociferous, enthusiasm reached such a high pitch that at times the safety of those in stands and on the speakers' platform was in jeopardy. Scores of women fainted because of the crush to get a close view of the distinguished visitor.

Mounted police officers and several hundred others on duty restrained with great effort the thousands, turbulent with job and veritably wild with enthusiasm, who fought for places in the forefront of the great assembly.

AMERICANS HOPE OF THE WORLD

De Valera voiced a message in which he declared that "American is the hope of the world," and prophesied that "If America fails the good people of small nations seeking to wrest themselves from tyranny and oppression, then, Democracy dies or else goes mad."

"There is no compromise between right and wrong," he shouted. "There is no compromise between justice and expediency. There will be no peace, there must be no

Fenway Park was nothing less than the hub of the baseball universe while hosting five world championship clubs in its first seven seasons from 1912-18. (Courtesy of the Library of Congress)

worldly relations, trade or otherwise, between this country and Great Britain until Ireland first of all is free."

GREAT THRONG IN DANGER

"Again the crushing, pushing and surging movement broke loose in the great crowds about the platform as the cheers became almost ear-splitting. Men climbed to precarious positions on the frail framework that held the screening in front of the boxes in the central stands, and speakers urged them down.

Then, for once, the serious tone of the whole assembly was burst for the moment when one man persisted in holding his vantage point high up on the screening, when all others had climbed down. Police and soldiers urged him down, but he persisted in retaining the place he had reached with much difficulty.

The crowds hooted and jeered him, but he refused to be moved. The humor of the situation struck thousands at once and laughter broke forth. What jeers had failed to do, laughter accomplished. The man smiled in defeat and made an undignified descent."

LIKENS DE VALERA TO LINCOLN

Senator Walsh declared that the Irish leader reminded him of another great man. In form, face, intellect and the cause he advocates, De Valera reminds him, he said, of Abraham Lincoln, the Great Emancipator. "As that great man took the shackles off the black man, the 'Lincoln of Ireland' will take the shackles of tyranny and oppression from Ireland."

"Born of lowly parents, in humble circumstances, how like Lincoln he is," the Senator remarked. "Now he is here with us,

pleading for equality – pleading for what we have gained in America, what our boys fought for, shall not be denied to the race from which he comes."

Twenty races of people in the old world are to be free, for which he thanked God. America, he said, has helped in bringing freedom to them, but now are insisting and demanding that the boy of Irish parentage who fought in the last war will not in the future have to say, "I brought liberty and freedom to all the white races of the world except my own."

Make this cause a holy one, a sacred one, he urged. Make it your first thought day and night. Think how best we may assure the Irish people of freedom. He hoped the question never would become one of party politics, that it may never become the property of one group of men in America, for in his opinion it is too sacred, it belongs to all America, to America that welcomed our ancestors when they came "barefooted and naked with outstretched hands."

DE VALERA RISES TO SPEAK

De Valera rose to speak. He said a word in Gaelic, and the storm broke in fury – a storm of applause that eclipsed all others that had gone before. Ex-Congressman O'Connell led three cheers and they were given "thrice three times." Three more for the Irish republic were given with a will, and when Senator Walsh called for "three United States cheers for the President of the Irish republic," the roars of the response could be heard surely a mile away.

It was some time before the visitor, smiling and bowing, could make himself heard. He never completed an Irish sentence, and his first Yankee words audible were: "Gaels and friends of the Gael," in addressing the greatest multitude ever gathered within his hearing since he became a great leader of a great people.

Visibly he was impressed by the demonstration. He stood erect, a trifle nervous, smiling continually, joyous in the extreme. After voicing the greetings of the patriots overseas, he launched into his address, which frequently was punctuated by cheers. He looked like the Lincoln that people here have likened him to.

When he declared that people of Ireland have told him during the war that the sympathy of the people of America had been lost, the crowds yelled back: "Lies! Lies!" He never doubted the help of Americans, he insisted, for he knew that people of the true land of liberty, the land in which he "had the honor to be born," according to his own word, were not going to desert

a people fighting against a tyranny far greater than that of Germany.

As he told the people of Clare a few months ago, when he emerged from Lincoln jail, he told his audience yesterday, that though branded by England as a criminal and traitor, he was willing to be judged by the Irish people, and if they call him a traitor, he said, he will hang his head in shame.

SEPTEMBER 7, 1919

Odd Fellows Hold Open Services at Fenway Park Amidst Much Pomp and Color

Led by the Waltham Watch Company Marching Band, over a thousand members of the Odd Fellows, be-decked in top hats, straw boaters and colorful trademark aprons made their way from Charles Street through the Back Bay to Fenway Park to celebrate both a mass and ceremony that focused on America's solidarity with England during the First World War.

Speaking before a crowd of 15,000 at Fenway Park the Rev. Brother Allan A. Rideout remarked, "America must never forget the part played by England in the great war. We are in the position of the son who has grown bigger than his mother. Our ties with the mother country, England, should become closer than ever after our joint struggle against the common enemy."

After praising the allied victory in the First World War Rideout

added a scathing indictment of Bolshevism: "There are men in this country, followers of the atrocious Russian Trotsky who would throw the 'Star-Spangled Banner' into the dust and elevate in its place the red flag of revolution and riot. This is an enemy even more menacing than the one we have just conquered. We are facing a new world, and there is no room in it for the exponents of revolution and bloodshed, of riot and disorder. Real Americans must unite against this movement, must stamp it out the instant it starts to raise its head."

The rest of the ceremony was marked by the communal singing of hymns concluding with the traditional parting anthem, "America,"

August 23, 1919 Boston Navy Yard 6, New York Navy Yard 4

SEPTEMBER 11, 1919

Attempt to Rob Box Office at Fenway Park is Foiled

A plan to rob the box office at Fenway Park was frustrated by Capt. Goode of Station 16 who received a tip that the robbery was contemplated. He sent 100 police officers and two companies of States Guardsmen to the park.

They formed a line from the park to Kenmore Station along which the spectators were allowed to pass. The crooks who were to rob the box office were said to be in the crowd.

Military mass honoring the war dead of World War I is held on the field at Fenway Park. *(Photograph by Leslie Jones, courtesy of the Boston Public Library)*

(Author's Note: The rank and file of the Boston Police Dept went out on strike on September 9, 1919. Derided by the press as "agents of Lenin," "deserters," and Bolsheviks," the police were criticized severely by Massachusetts Governor Calvin Coolidge who remarked,

"There is no right to strike against the public safety, anywhere, anytime." He then replaced the striking members with un-employed First World War Veterans who were forced to wear civilian clothing as the members of the United Garment Workers refused to sew their new uniforms. It would take until 1965 for there to be a Boston Patrolman's Association. Coolidge rode the wave of public support he gained from the strike to the vice presidential nomination on the successful 1920 Republican ticket with Warren G. Harding.)

September 26, 1919 High School of Commerce 39, Revere High 0

OCTOBER 10, 1919

English Shuts Out Dorchester High

SCORE OF 20 TO 0 IN A LEAGUE GAME AT FENWAY PARK

In just one of the score of high school football games held at Fenway Park Boston English blanked Dorchester High by a score of 20-0 despite completing the only pass they attempted all afternoon. Only a fine display of punting by Dorchester captain Roger Mackay kept the score from being much

more lopsided. Like many high schools of the era it featured four 10 minute quarters.

Source: The Boston Globe page 7, October 11, 1919

October 12, 1919 Boston College High 9, Boston Latin 3
October 30, 1919 Dorchester High 47, Mechanic Arts 0
November 3, 1919 Boston Latin 7, High School of Commerce 0
November 7, 1919 Boston College High 24, Dorchester High 7

NOVEMBER 8, 1919

RUTGERS 13 BOSTON COLLEGE 7

November 11, 1919 Boston College High 10, Boston English 0
November 12, 1919 High School of Commerce 32, Brockton High 0
November 14, 1919 Boston Latin 7, Dorchester High 0

NOVEMBER 15, 1919

BOSTON COLLEGE BESTS HOLY CROSS 9-7

November 18, 1919 Boston English 14, High School of Commerce 0
November 27, 1919 10-mile New England Championship Run by the St. Alphonsus Association and the Dorchester Club starting and ending at Fenway Park.
November 27, 1919 St. Alphonsus 0, Pere Marquette Council, K of C 0
November 27, 1919 Boston Latin 0, Boston English 0
December 1, 1919 Boston College High 54, Mechanic Arts 0

The annual military mass at Fenway, c.1920. This photo provides one of the best early views of the left-field wall showing the crazy quilt of advertising as well as the slope of Duffy's Cliff fronting the wall. *(Courtesy of the Boston Public Library)*

CHAPTER TWO
The People's Park

"I guess God made Boston on a wet Sunday."

—RAYMOND CHANDLER

Fenway became a true "People's Park" during the twenties. As the Red Sox fortunes and attendance dwindled, management, led by Brooklyn native Bob Quinn, hosted a wide variety of events ranging from a band concert by the immortal John Philip Sousa, "Bloomer Girl" baseball, schoolboy and collegiate football, international soccer, integrated boxing cards, and an unforgettable football game that matched the mighty New York Giants against South Boston's Pere Marquette Knights of Columbus squad.

In the era just before sports radio broadcasts, events such as the 1920 baseball game between Harvard and Yale drew more than 15,000 to Fenway and nearly any game featuring the recently departed Babe Ruth automatically became the toughest ticket in town.

This was also a decade that part of the park burned down and was left alone as the cash-strapped Quinn didn't rebuild and instead used the insurance money to cover the Red Sox payroll.

Such was an era when people's identification with the park was formed both by the paying customers as well as the many school and collegiate competitors with Fenway's dirt under their fingernails.

The 1920 Harvard Baseball team faced rival Yale before a crowd of more than 20,000 at Fenway. *(Collection of the author)*

APRIL 18, 1920

Babe Ruth and Mays Play Sox

FORMER BOSTON STARS HERE WITH THE YANKEES ON HOLIDAY

Barrow's Hurling Staff is Strong

RUSSELL, PENNOCK, JONES, HOYT AND BUSH IN FINE SHAPE

"Babe" Ruth, home-run record holder and the highest-price piece of baseball brickabrac in captivity, makes his 1920 bow to Boston baseball fans tomorrow.

He will bow twice during the day, once in the morning and once in the afternoon, for the club which parted with 135,000 cold smackers to gain Babe's services is due for morning and afternoon battles against the Red Sox at Fenway Park.

"Babe" is glad to get to the Hub once more.

They hain't been doin' right by our Babe, over in New York, according to recent reports – possibly because Babe hain't been doin' the expected for his new club. Babe muffed a fly in his opening game which permitted the lowly Athletics to win the contest, and in the second clash between those two clubs the home run king whiffed the Gotham breeze on three successive occasions, once with the bases choked with runners, and in recognition of these achievements "Babe" was formally presented with a brown derby.

BABE EAGER TO GET GOING

"Babe" became a bit galled at this ceremony and once back on the old Hub ball yard he expects to perform such stunts that the bestowers of the brown skypiece will offer to eat it when Babe returns to Gotham.

Along with Babe will come Carl Mays, the centre of the stormiest baseball storm ever cracked, and those desiring to make a study of mob expression need go no further than Fenway Park to gain a rattling fine demonstration. Babe, a prime favorite with the big majority of most ball followers, is down for a rare ovation of cheers and handslapping, while Carl, who is in very Dutch with local fans, will probably be accorded a unanimous hiss varnished fore and aft with some beautiful books.

APRIL 20, 1920

Ruth Goes Hitless in Four At-Bats vs Red Sox

BIG-HEARTED 'BABE' REFUSES TO KNOCK ANY HOMERS AGAINST OLD CLUB

MAY 30, 1920
WAR MEMORIAL SERVICE

JUNE 27, 1920

Harvard Wins Third Game from Yale, 6-3

20,000 PEOPLE SEE CRIMSON TRIUMPH IN DECIDING DIAMOND STRUGGLE – "LEFTY" COXE KNOCKED OUT IN SIXTH – SUB'S HIT CINCHES GAME

By Wilton Vaugh

Harvard battered "Lefty" Coxe, the husky Yale pitcher, out of the box in the sixth inning of yesterday's game at Fenway Park, and won the third and decisive batter of the annual diamond series by a 6 to 3 score.

It capped the Harvard 1919-1920 athletic book with a glorious climax, for the Crimson had already triumphed over the Blue in three major sports, football, hockey and crew, leaving the Yalensians with nothing but the track laurels.

GRABS OPPORTUNITY

The capping was done by "Fish" Janin, a substitute outfielder. He was playing in the left garden instead of "Babe" Frothingham, who was "beaned" in the opening game of the series last Tuesday at New Haven and put in the repair shop for the rest of the season.

Perhaps it was a fortunate "beaning" for Harvard; perhaps not. But, at any rate, the gamey youngster came up to bat in the sixth session of the all-important struggle of the year for Harvard and Yale. The score was 3 to 1 in Yale's favor, and the Blue battlers were confident that the series was theirs. Perkins was waiting on third base and Jones was straining at the keystone leash. With one man down Janin was presented with the golden opportunity. And he grabbed it by the forelock.

He picked out a good ball served up by pitcher Coxe, who was passive through his first real dangerous situation, and smashed it far out into left field way up on "Duffy's Cliff" – or has it been changed to "Menosky's Cliff"? – for two bases. The wallop scored Perkins and Jones, sending Harvard into the lead and emblazoning the name of the struggling recruit on the pages of the Crimson sports album. It was a corker.

Senators great Walter Johnson pitched his only career no-hitter on July 1, 1920, at Fenway Park before a crowd that included future Speaker of the House Thomas P. "Tip" O'Neil. *(Courtesy of the Library of Congress)*

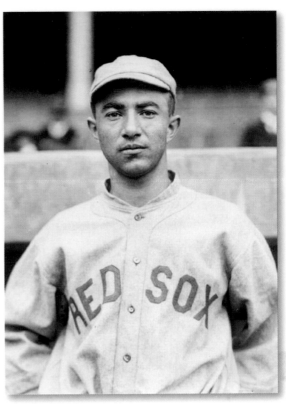

Shortstop Everett "Deacon" Scott was one of the last holdovers from the Red Sox championship years having started at shortstop for three Red Sox world champion teams before departing to the Yankees in 1922. *(Collection of the author)*

John Philip Sousa led his Navy Band in concert at Fenway Park during a national tour that featured appearances at many major league ballparks. *(Collection of the author)*

Massachusetts governor and future president Calvin Coolidge (third from left) assists in a flag-raising ceremony on Opening Day 1920. *(Photograph by Leslie Jones, Courtesy of the Boston Public Library)*

Dartmouth played many noteworthy football games at Fenway in the park's first four decades. *(Collection of the author)*

Boston native and future Hall of Fame outfielder Tommy McCarthy was feted at Fenway Park with an All-Star Game to raise money for his family following his death in 1922. *(Courtesy of the Library of Congress)*

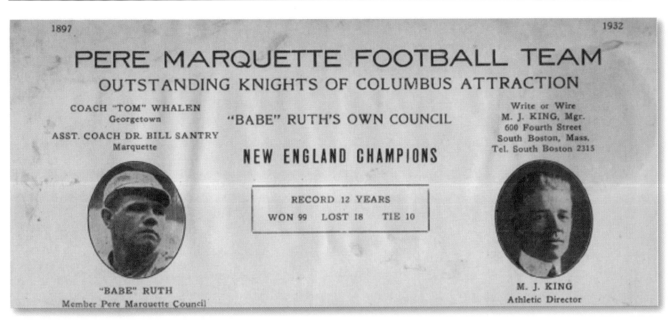

1897

1932

PERE MARQUETTE FOOTBALL TEAM

OUTSTANDING KNIGHTS OF COLUMBUS ATTRACTION

COACH "TOM" WHALEN
Georgetown

ASST. COACH DR. BILL SANTRY
Marquette

"BABE" RUTH'S OWN COUNCIL

NEW ENGLAND CHAMPIONS

Write or Wire
M. J. KING, Mgr.
600 Fourth Street
South Boston, Mass.
Tel. South Boston 2315

| RECORD 12 YEARS |
| WON 99   LOST 18   TIE 10 |

"BABE" RUTH
Member Pere Marquette Council

M. J. KING
Athletic Director

The Pere Marquette Football team of South Boston featured Babe Ruth as a director long after the Bambino had departed for New York. Ruth remained an avid fan of a team skilled enough to play the mighty New York Giants at Fenway in November 1927. *(Courtesy of Ed "Moose" Savage)*

KEPT 15,000 ON TOES

Fight such as is seen only in a Harvard-Yale athletic battle kept the 15,000 fans who packed the grandstand and the right-field bleachers keyed up. Fair feminine friends of the collegians were there in flocks to add a little color to the contest and cheer the boys on to victory. With "Heinie" Faxon, the football player, and "Johnny" Sessions, the Crimson gridiron manager, leading the cheers down in front with "Mike" Dinnehan, the original Harvard rooter, the Crimson fans made the most noise. But the visitors were not without support, for a large number of Eli graduates were on hand, and then the gang of baseball lovers were there to applaud every good play by either team.

It was a contest well worth seeing, for both coaches flashed the best players they had. "Babe" Felton, who had won the first of the three games, was picked to oppose Franklin Coxe, the big southpaw, who had proved a nemesis to the Harvard batters in the second

game. A win for Yale meant the series and the championship of the "Big Three." But the Crimson win sent Harvard, Yale and Princeton into a triple tie for the title, because Princeton had won the series with the Cantabridgians, and Yale had taken the Tigers into camp in two games out of three.

LAST CHANCE FOR HARVARD

Harvard took its last turn at bat in the eighth. Janin was thrown out at first by Holmes, but Hallock smashed a sound single down the first base line. He went to second on the play because Diamond, who fielded the ball, threw hurriedly and wildly to Pitcher Selleck, who ran to cover the bag. Hallock went to third while Aldrich was throwing Lincoln out at first, but he died there because Blair fouled to Peters.

Coach Jack Slattery rewarded Tom Gammack for his hustling all season by sending him to catch the last inning. After Diamond had flied out to Hallock and Parsons had lifted to Janin, Peters rapped to

Conlon, who threw to Jones for the last put-out. But the Harvard first baseman did not want to stop playing so soon, and he dropped the throw, giving Peters a life. Felton preferred to end the game in a flash of glory as well as a hurry, so he struck out Selleck, the opposing pitcher, and catcher Tom Gammack romped off to the clubhouse with the winning ball in his hip pocket as well as another varsity "H" in his athletic record.

JULY 1, 1920

W. Johnson Pitches a No-Hit, No-Run

HARPER ALSO TWIRLS TIGHT GAME, BUT RED SOX ON LOSING END OF CLOSE SCORE, 1-0

By Paul H. Shannon, Boston Post

Clark Griffiths' former great left hander faced Walter Johnson, still the Senator's big pitching ace, in the third game of the present series at Fenway Park yesterday and the meeting spelled disaster for the locals. For Johnson, twirling one of the most wonderful games of his career, not only shut out the Sox to the tune of 1-0, but he likewise achieved a no-hit game, the best during his many years of splendid service in the American League.

BOX MASTERS' DUEL

It was a great pitching duel between two of the most effective flingers in the American League, for Harper is always unhittable when he has control, and Johnson knows no peer when working at his best. Yesterday, Harper looked better than he has at any time in a Red Sox uniform at Fenway Park, while Walter Johnson was the real premier pitcher of old.

In addition to his terrific speed, the big Washington pitcher had superb control and he toyed with the Sox in feline fashion. Time after time, the batter had him for two or three straight balls before the big pitcher settled down to business. Then the sphere would cut the heart of the plate like a rifle shot, or the batter, bringing his club around too late, would swing vainly, with the ball already settling in the catcher's mitt.

The best hitters in the Barrow batting order were forced to pay tribute to the speed king. Schang struck out twice, while Hooper, McInnis and McNally were included in the long list of strikeout victims, and it was not extraordinary support that was in any measure responsible for his triumph as his unequalled effectiveness made all but two of the chances given the Washington fielders of the easiest kind.

Harper was splendidly effective, and while he was found for an occasional hit, was master of the situation till the fatal seventh. Here a combination of three single base hits, the last and destructive one the merest scratch, was what proved his Waterloo.

JUDGE SAVES THE DAY

In the eighth and ninth the Senators worked like fiends to win the honor for their popular pitcher, and Judge's great stop off Hooper in the ninth just made this possible.

The fans prepared for another long drawn out game when they saw Harry Hooper start, but the big southpaw showed gratifying control in the first round, fanning Judge after the latter had him in the hole, and then forcing Milan to give McNally an easy chance. He hit Sam Rice, who promptly stole only to see Roth called out on strikes. Johnson was in the hole against the three batsmen who opposed him, but none of the two reached first base.

AUGUST 8, 1920

Sousa's Band Heard By 4,000 Persons

Lieut. Commander John Philip Sousa and his famous band gave their opening concert of the season in this city at Fenway Park yesterday afternoon. The band drew an audience of nearly 4,000 persons.

The program was along the lines of a regular Sousa concert with a few added attractions, among which were some of the leader's most recent compositions. In each instance, the audience loudly applauded the numbers, especially the xylophone solo

by George J. Carey, the vocal solos given by Miss Marjorie Moody, and the cornet solo so well presented by John Dolan.

Sousa himself was the center of much attention and received much applause as the band played his composition, "The Stars and Stripes Forever." The cheering lasted nearly five minutes, after which the leader stood at attention and saluted the audience in true naval fashion.

OCTOBER 9, 1920

Open Air Boxing Show at Fenway Park Every Bout a Main Event

The first boxing event held at Fenway Park was a wild affair held on a beautiful Saturday afternoon that left the 5,000 in attendance stunned by the ferocity of the main bout and its unexpected aftermath.

After black heavyweight contender Battling McCreary won a clear 10-round decision over fellow African American John Lester Johnson, he went over to his opponent's corner to shake hands and was met by what the *Boston Globe* described as a "stiff wallop to the mouth."

This prompted another fight that saw McCreary not only knock Johnson out of the ring but also strike Johnson on the head with a stool McCreary had grabbed from his corner. Fan reaction was immediate and saw at least one tonic bottle tossed at McCreary as he scampered to his dressing room. To make matters worse the entire box office receipts were attached by one

In one of the earliest football action photos taken at Fenway Park the Pere Marquette squad, led by running back Billy O'Leary, faces off against the Providence Steam Rollers on October 11, 1924. Providence won 7-0.

More remarkable game action from the Pere Marquette–Steam Roller contest of October 11, 1924. *(Courtesy of Ed "Moose" Savage)*

Joseph Clancy, who claimed he was owed the money as secretary of the host Hanover Athletic Club.

In other bouts Eddie Shevlin of Roxbury won a 10-round decision over Paul Doyle of New York, "Pal" Reed of Framingham stopped Johnny Alecks of Philadelphia in the 8th round, and Young Sacco of East Boston scored a surprise win over Harry "Kid" Brown of Philadelphia in 10 rounds.

OCTOBER 12, 1920

Crowd of 7,000 Sees Dorchester and Latin Win at Fenway Park

Football Double-Header starting the Boston High Series-English is Beaten 7-6 and Mechanic Arts Shut Out, 18-0

High school football shared the same page of *The Boston Globe* that featured listings for burlesque shows at the legendary Old Howard Theater in Scolly Square as well as an announcement for the screening of the latest Norma Talmedge film, *The Branded Woman* at Gordon's Old South Theater.

After Latin and Mechanics Arts High opened with an 18-0 Latin victory, Dorchester High and English played a thriller in

Biggest Baseball Attraction of Today

THE ORIGINAL

American
CHAS. A. ABBOTT, Mgr.
Bloomer Girls

ORGANIZED
1906

AMERICAN BLOOMER GIRLS

A BALL TEAM
THAT IS A BALL TEAM

Outlives All Competition

A Word to the Public
This is a First Class, Respectable Organization in every particular, where you can bring mothers, wives, sisters and sweethearts. Truthfully advertised and honestly conducted. Indorsed by press and public.

There is a Reason

Only Female Club Recognized By League and Reputable Managers

The best players that money will hire.

IDLE PARKS DO NOT MAKE DOLLARS

The American Bloomer Girls were one of the many attractions that graced Fenway's eclectic itinerary during the Roaring Twenties. *(Collection of the author)*

the nightcap. The game was decided by the slimmest of margins as English missed the point after its lone touchdown which was scored in dramatic fashion following a blocked kick on the Dorchester 29 that rolled to the 2-yard line where it was grabbed by English's left tackle Mclean. In the fourth quarter Dorchester recovered an English fumble on their 28 yard line and quickly advanced upfield where right halfback George Kinally rushed for a touchdown and made the winning point after kick.

Both these games also featured four 10 minute quarters.

NOVEMBER 20, 1920

Boston College 13 Marietta College 3

Author's Note: In a game that received scant press coverage save for the fact that Cincinnati Reds outfielder Alfred Earle "Greasy" Neale was serving as coach of

tiny Marietta College roughly a year after he'd faced the infamous Chicago "Black Sox" in the 1919 World Series. This marked the beginning of a Hall of Fame coaching career that saw the former baseball star lead underdog Washington and Jefferson to the 1922 Rose Bowl as well as serving as head coach of the University of Virginia, University of West Virginia and the Philadelphia Eagles.

At Fenway Park his undermanned Marietta squad was no match for a powerhouse Boston College squad enjoying its best season to date under head coach Frank "Iron Major" Cavanagh. Despite leading 3-0 Marietta gave up touchdowns in the third and fourth quarters to lose to undefeated Boston College.

JULY 16, 1921

**BOSTON ALL-
INTERSCHOLASTIC
2, NEW YORK ALL-
INTERSCHOLASTIC 1**

AUGUST 9, 1921

Deacon Touches 'Em All

After nine years and 750-plus consecutive games Red Sox captain, shortstop Everett "Deacon" Scott hit the first home run of his career at Fenway Park against the Detroit Tigers. The rangy 160 lb. Scott sent a low blow to the gap where Ty Cobb and Harry Heilman failed to grab it after several bounces against the fence.

(Author's note: Scott is perhaps the most underrated Red Sox player in Fenway Park history as the skinny Indiana native was shortstop for

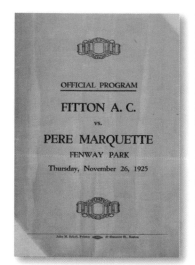  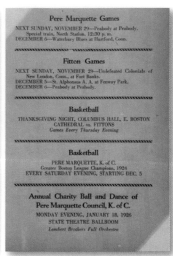

A rare Pere Marquette program for their game against the Fitton A.C. on November 26, 1925. Despite their semi-pro status and their many donations to church-related charities, many of their Peres were nearly as well compensated as members of the Red Sox during the same period. *(Courtesy of Ed "Moose" Savage)*

three world championship teams in 1915, 1916, and 1918. He later was shortstop of the Yankees first world championship team in 1923 and retired in 1926 as baseball's ironman having played in 1,307 consecutive games. This streak was subsequently broken by both Lou Gehrig and Cal Ripken, Jr.)

OCTOBER 12, 1921

Fenway Park Hosts High School Pigskin Double-header Mediocre Results as Boston English and Latin Triumph

On a Columbus Day in which Bostonians could have gone to see the Ziegfeld Follies at The Colonial Theater or D.W. Griffith's latest film *Way Down East* at The Globe Theater 4,000 football fans made their way to Fenway Park to watch a high school double-header the *Boston Globe* described as "mediocre." Boston English defeated Dorchester High by a score of 27-0 and Boston Latin beat Mechanics Arts High by a score of 6-0 on a day where the uncertainty of the weather attracted a crowd much smaller than anticipated.

NOVEMBER 12, 1921

HIGH SCHOOL OF COMMERCE 27, BROOKLYN COMMERCIAL HIGH SCHOOL 5

NOVEMBER 18, 1921

Dartmouth Freshman Defeat Dean Academy 21-0

PENALTIES MAR VICTORY, BOTH OFFENDING GREEN YOUNGSTERS' OVERHEAD PLAY EFFECTIVE

In a game that press accounts described as both disappointing and penalty marred, Dartmouth '25 showcased their talent against a strong Dean Academy squad before a crowd at Fenway Park that featured many alumni and former players. At the time Dartmouth was building a national collegiate powerhouse and within four seasons would secure lasting fame while capturing the 1925 national collegiate football championship. Their rare trips to Fenway Park served as a great recruiting vehicle as well as a rallying point for Boston alumni.

May 28, 1922 War Memorial Service

May 28, 1922 Irish Republican Army Meeting and Speech by Countess Markiewicz

Red Sox ace Howard Ehmke and Yankee pitcher Bob Shawkey pose in this 1924 photograph. Ehmke was a Fenway favorite, winning 20 of Boston's 61 victories in their last-place season of 1923. *(Courtesy of The Library of Congress)*

Havana native, and Red Sox infielder Ramon "Mike" Hererra greets Babe Ruth at Fenway Park in 1926. In part-time duty, Herrara batted .275 in 84 games as a reserve infielder in 1925 and '26. *(Collection of the author)*

JUNE 13, 1922

English High Provides Upset by Defeating Commerce at Fenway Park

SMITH HOLDS COMMERCE TO FOUR HITS; ENGLISH PUTS OVER 2-1 VICTORY

BLUE AND BLUE SECOND BASEMAN, PITCHING FIRST GAME OF SEASON, PROVES PUZZLE – COMMERCE BLANKED UNTIL 9TH INNING

By Tom McCabe

Bossism is rampant in the city schools. Without a chance to sit on the local diamond throne, English high rules the roost. Taking a sizzling 2 to 1 contest from Commerce yesterday at Fenway Park, the blue and blue athletes assumed more than passing interest in the baseball situation. Considering, too, that English high meets Mechanic Arts, the league leader, Friday, its methods ought to be investigated.

STEINY WHACKS ONE

It seems hardly fair to use a second baseman as a pitcher. Arthur Smith played the keystone sack for English High all year and yesterday he did the pitching. Did it so well all Commerce got was four scattered hits, and until the ninth had one beautiful time getting a runner around the bases. "Smith" may have a common tinge to it, but there was nothing common in the stock in trade yesterday. As a sign of the times, 10 Commercial travelers took three healthies.

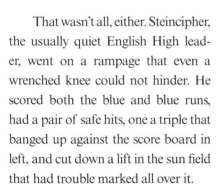

Boston Mayor James Michael Curley tosses out the first ball on Opening Day in 1924. *(Photograph by Leslie Jones, Courtesy of the Boston Public Library)*

A military mass is celebrated at Fenway Park in 1920.

That wasn't all, either. Steincipher, the usually quiet English High leader, went on a rampage that even a wrenched knee could not hinder. He scored both the blue and blue runs, had a pair of safe hits, one a triple that banged up against the score board in left, and cut down a lift in the sun field that had trouble marked all over it.

Then Healey and McVey were not a bit fair, either. Each had a pair of safe drives and they turned in a double killing that closed the contest tighter than a drum head. The double killing by way of a strikeout and sharp throw to first with a tying run on second base still has the boys talking. It cleared up a rather cloudy situation.

CROTTY SOMNOLENT

Another English run was chalked up in the eighth, Steincipher's hot shot to third being too fast for Crotty, for a starter. He stole second as McVey fanned and continued to third when

Santosuorro's throw went into centre-field. That toss hurt considerably for Healey's double to left broke up the ball game.

A pass to Caulkins, Mawn's single and Crotty's drive to right brought some balm to Commerce. With runners on first and second, one run in and just one batter out, Crotty went to sleep in the pinch and as Coughlin fanned was caught flat-footed off first base for the final out in the battle. Healey's throw was a gem to get Crotty but it was not a whit better than McVey's stab to get the runner.

JULY 14, 1922

Echo Park

The *Chicago Tribune* reports a paid attendance of only 68 patrons at Fenway Park for a game versus the White Sox

AUGUST 14, 1922

Benefit Game Played for Family of Tommy McCarthy

ALTROCK LEADS STARS AGAINST RED SOX

Thousands of Boston baseball fans paid tribute to the memory of Tommy McCarthy at Fenway Park and incidentally had a lot of fun and saw some pretty good baseball. More than $5,000 was realized for the family of the great outfielder of the old days, Boston as usual proving most generous and unforgetful.

The day was personally conducted by Nick Altrock, the well-known comedian. He managed the

Pere Marquette game action from a 1920s contest at Fenway. *(Courtesy of Ed "Moose" Savage)*

New England's Greatest Football Attraction 11-1-192?

The Pere Marquette Council, K. of C., Football Team will play the New York Giants, one of the greatest teams in this country, on Saturday, November 19th, at Fenway Park, Boston.

The New York squad will include Garvey of Notre Dame, Howard of Princeton, Biggs of Baylor, Stahlman of Chicago, Captain Owen of Phillips, Cal Hubbard of Geneva, Corgan of Arkansas, Murtagh of Georgetown, Harms of Vermont, Jappe of Syracuse, Zero White of Oklahoma, Wycoff of Georgia Tech., Hagerty of Georgetown, Imlay of California, Haines of Penn. State, McBride of Syracuse, Milstead of Yale, Guyon of Carlisle and Wilson of Texas.

The Pere Marquette team, with five straight victories, is also well represented with former college stars, among them being Captain Calman, O'Brien, Ohrenberger, Kobolinsky and Paten of Boston College, Wise, Wallis, Norton, Connors and Kittridge of Holy Cross, Tyler of Tufts, Murphy of B. U., Wentworth and O'Connor of New Hampshire State, Hurley of St. Bonaventure, Morrison of Canisius and O'Leary of Old Point Comfort, Va. As the Harvard and Yale game is the only contest in Boston, it is expected that one of the largest crowds that ever witnessed an Independent game at Fenway Park will be on hand. Reserved seats at $1.10 are on sale at the Horace Partridge Co., W. H. Brine Co., Wright & Ditson and J. W. Brine Co., leading sporting goods houses in Boston.

The game is scheduled to start at 2 P. M.

P. S. Will you please read to your members and post this notice on your bulletin.

A flyer promoting the Pere Marquette vs New York Giants game at Fenway Park.
(Courtesy of Ed "Moose" Savage)

Program for the St. Alphonsus A.A. vs Pere Marquette game on October 10, 1925. A good portion of the proceeds of these games went to fund church-related social services such as the Columbus child care center in South Boston.
(Courtesy of Ed "Moose" Savage)

The World Champion 1927 New York Giants. *(Courtesy of Ed "Moose" Savage)*

team of All-American stars that beat the Red Sox, 3 to 2, in ten innings.

He provided a continuous vaudeville show all by himself from shortly after noon until the sun was dropping out of sight back of the Newton Hills. To top it all off, he pitched the last four innings of the ball game, which was the one serious thing he did all day.

Nick used to be quite a south paw in the old days, and he brought a lot of his old stuff back to the peak. He didn't have much of a fast one, but he had the curve and slow ball, and he got the decisions on the close ones, as he called 'em himself.

Nicholas went through four innings and never was scored on, though he had a couple of narrow squeaks. For example, two triples were combed off his curve in the seventh, but the old-timer removed the curse by picking Minosky the first tripler off third base. He hadn't forgotten how to do that little stunt, anyhow.

ALL THE CLUBS IN THE AMERICAN LEAGUE REPRESENTED

The comedian manager had all the uniforms in the league on his bench.

Hoffman of the Yankees caught a while, and Elmer Smith played right field. Jim Bagby, of Cleveland, did a bit of pitching, with Leslie Nunamaker, teammate, back of the bat.

Doc Johnson, of the Athletics, first based after Lizzie Murphy had performed for one inning. Pep Young, of the Mack team, was on second. Tilly the left field job. Bruggy caught a while, and Hasty pitched three innings. Connie Mack couldn't get over himself, but he sure sent along plenty of his athletes.

Donnie Bush, of the Senators, was at short, wrapped up in a Sox road rig. McClellan, of the White Sox, covered third. Flagstead, of the Tigers, took the last half of the left field patrol, and Chick Shorten, of the Browns, was out in centre. So the league was represented 100 per cent, which was mighty fine, as Tommy did most of his playing in, and helped to make famous, the National League.

SNAPPY EXHIBITION SPUN OFF IN A FASHION TO COPY

The game was a pretty snappy exhibition, spun off in a fashion that might be copied to advantage at

the Fenway every day. The stars picked up a run in the second off Allan Russell, on Smith's triple against the right field bleachers and Walker's suicide fly.

The Sox went out ahead in the fifth, two hits and a pair of errors giving them a couple of counters. A hit by Flagstead, Pratt's error, and McClellan's infield out tangled it up in the sixth, and it stayed that way 'til the tenth, when Doc Johnston tripled, after Pep Young had pushed a hit to center off Alec Ferguson.

But the baseball was only a small part of the afternoon. There was a vaudeville show before the game, and a band concert before, during and after that. Teams from Keith's and the Howard helped in the vaudeville, as well as a flock of flappers from *Love and Kisses*.

MADE A GREAT HIT WITH NICK AND EVERYBODY ELSE

These flaps made a great hit with Manager Nick, who danced with them and acted with them and played ball with them for an hour or so while the athletes were warming up.

The Pere Marquette squad lost to the Giants before a crowd estimated to be anywhere from 8,000 to 10,000 fans *(Courtesy of Ed "Moose" Savage)*

The Columbus Day Nursery was one of the principle beneficiaries of the Pere Marquette Football team's fundraising as the squad kicked in 500 depression era dollars years before groups like Dorothy Day's Catholic Worker movement supported similar church related efforts. *(Courtesy of Ed "Moose" Savage)*

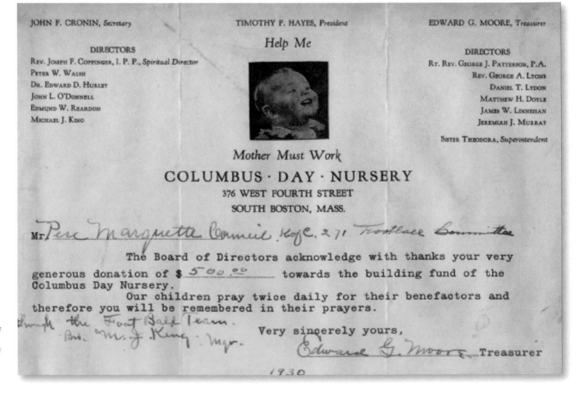

Babe Ruth signs autographs for Boston fans in 1929. He was Fenway's top drawing card until his Yankee career ended in 1934. *(Courtesy of The Boston Public Library)*

The girls went through the stand, too, and sold more score cards than a hundred ushers could have. They brought plenty of pep into the ball yard and spread it around very pleasantly. The girls were Elsie Lombard, Lucille Moore, Maude Lydiate, Lillian Thomas, Claire Martin, Bobby Breslaw, Bernice Goesline and Mildred Quinn.

Jimmy Coughlin's 101st band furnished the music and furnished plenty. They accompanied his former Honor, John F. Fitzgerald, as that remarkable individual warbled "Sweet Adeline." Fitzy's voice improves with the years, and his solo drew a tremendous hand.

All the way through, it was a very enjoyable afternoon, with the gang forgetting the horrible season we've been having, and cheered lustily as one good play followed another. The athletes didn't stall or bluff, but went through at top speed.

The pitchers put something on the ball, as the scarcity of hits shows, for all the boys were up there taking their cut at it. Nick figured in the assault, too, getting a nifty base blow when he went to the saucer for Hasty just before taking over the hurling job.

We saw hundreds of the close personal friends of Tommy's there—the boys who played with him, or cheered for him in his glorious hey day, and it softened the pang the flag fluttering at half-mast brought to them to realize that every one of the 4,000 present was there as a personal tribute to one of the most popular athletes who ever starred in the big show.
(The Boston Post)

OCTOBER 12, 1922

Double Header at Fenway Park: B.C. High and Boston English Battle 0-0; Dorchester Beats Mechanics Arts 18-0 After a Scoreless Fight in First Half

The games were played in the morning as a prelude to the big Columbus Day afternoon game less than a mile away from Braves Field where upwards of 25,000 fans flocked to see Boston College and Fordham. In what was now another Boston Columbus Day tradition Fenway Park played host to a high school football doubleheader featuring Boston English who drew with Boston College High School, and Dorchester High who scored three second half touchdowns to down their crosstown rivals at Mechanics Arts High by a score of 18-0.

NOVEMBER 25, 1922

Brown Upset By Dartmouth Green Delivers One Big Punch to Win 7-0. Fumble on 29 Yard Line is Bruins Death Knell

On a freezing day on which one could choose to see both the four Marx Brothers on stage at the Shubert Majestic Theater and college football at Fenway Park, some 20,000 hearty souls battled the elements and saw Wollaston native Dartmouth fullback Larry Leavitt recover a Brown fumble and then smash his way to score the game's lone touchdown in a 7-0 upset triumph for the Green. In an advertisement next to the game summary readers were informed of such holiday bargains as Men's Great Overcoats at the Filenes Automatic Bargain Annex for $16.75 and talking machines for only $16.50 in the home furnishing department at Ivor Johnson Sporting Goods Company on Washington and Tremont Streets.

DECEMBER 9, 1922

U.S.S. *Delaware* Eleven Defeats U.S.S. *Relief* for Atlantic Fleet Championship

On a Saturday afternoon where they could have escaped to the warmth of the Tremont Temple to watch child sensation Jackie Coogan in *Oliver Twist* both Mayor Curley and Governor Cox bundled up against the cold and joined 5,000 fellow Bostonians to watch the U.S.S. *Delaware* score a 27-21 victory over the U.S.S. *Relief* for the Atlantic Fleet football championship. The game was a free-admission event.

May 27, 1923 War Memorial Service

September 6, 1923 North Cambridge 4, St. Andrews 4 (Tie)

September 7, 1923 North Cambridge 5, St. Andrews 5 (Tie)

September 10, 1923 St. Andrews 5, North Cambridge 1

September 12, 1923 Fitchburg 7, North Cambridge 2

OCTOBER 12, 1923

Columbus Day Schoolboy Football Doubleheader

Boston College High 20 Boston English 0

Brockton High 33 Boston Latin

October 19 , 1923 Boston Latin 7, Boston College High 0

Glasgow Rangers attracted 10,000 fans to Fenway in 1928. *(Collection of the author)*

Red Sox President Bob Quinn displays scant amusement while posed between baseball clowns Nick Altrock (left) and Al Schacht (right) at Fenway Park in this undated photograph. *(Courtesy of the Boston Public Library)*

Ira Flagstead was one of the few stars of the Red Sox during the twenties and was given a day of honor at Fenway on July 21, 1928. *(Collection of the author)*

Boxer Al Mello defended his New England welterweight title against Billy Murphy on June 26, 1928 *(Courtesy of Bob Walsh)*

Fenway Park sits at the mid left-hand side of this 1925 aerial photograph of Boston's Back Bay. *(Courtesy of the Boston Public Library)*

NOVEMBER 10, 1923

Dartmouth Scores Over Brown 16-14 at Fenway Park

Bizarre plays and startling changes of fortune were the features of the game here today in which Dartmouth triumphed over Brown by 16 to 14. Dartmouth by reason of two punts blocked by "Swede" Oberlander went into the final period leading 16 to 0 and with half of the period gone Brown had yet failed to score. Then, in the last six minutes of play, the Brown bears astonished the stands and sent their supporters into ecstasies by scoring two touchdowns-one on a recovered kick and a 50-yard run by Reynolds; the other on a 38-yard forward pass, Eisenberg to Dixon and a 27-yard run by Dixon."

November 29, 1923 Pere Marquette 14, Fitton A.C. 9

May 25, 1924 War Memorial Service

June 2, 1924 Boston College 20, Georgetown 6

June 4, 1924 Harvard 5, Princeton 3 (10 innings)

June 7, 1924 Boy Scouts of Boston Council Rally

June 11, 1924 Holy Cross 12, Boston College 0

September 14, 1924 Boston Post Office 9, Hartford Post Office 0

October 11, 1924 Providence Steam Rollers 7, Pere Marquette 0

October 13, 1924 Boston College High 7, Boston English 0

October 13, 1924 Dorchester High 18, Mechanic Arts 0

November 27, 1924 Fitton A. C. 20, Pere Marquette 0

December 6, 1924 Neponset Warriors 7, Fitton A. C. 7

May 16, 1925 Holy Cross 5, Boston College 1

May 24, 1925 War Memorial Service

June 22, 1925 Bloomer Girl All-Stars 5, "Billie" Delaney's Peanut Hustlers 4

August 11, 1925 Unknowns (Chelsea, MA) 5, Eagle Juniors 4 ("Boys Day" Game)

August 25, 1925 Old Colony Trust 10, R. H. White 6

August 28, 1925 R. H. White 10, Old Colony Trust 1

September 8, 1925 Everett Tigers 1, Roxbury Braves 0 (Massachusetts Intercity League Championship)

September 27, 1925 Boston Post Office 10, Waterbury (CT) Post Office 3 (National Post Office Championship)

October 12, 1925 Boston English 6, Boston Trade School 0

October 12, 1925 Dorchester High 0, Mechanic Arts 0

October 17, 1925 Boston Woodsies 0, Fall River Marksmen 0 (Soccer)

October 31, 1925 Boston vs. Providence (Soccer)

NOVEMBER 14, 1925

Boston University 14 Providence College 0

This was a game marked by the fact that Providence College had rejected the request by Boston University to play the game not by timed periods but by a little used regimen that would have had each team use a 40-play period system that Boston University had used in the previous game against Brown in Providence.

Providence head coach Archie Golembeski remarked, "While the system may produce approximately the same results as the customary timing methods so far as the elapsed

time of periods and the number of plays per period are concerned, I believe it tends to devitalize the game by eliminating an element of suspense which is essential to football."

NOVEMBER 21, 1925

ST ALPHONSUS 7 PERE MARQUETTE 6

NOVEMBER 26, 1925

THANKSGIVING CLASH BETWEEN FITTONS (7) AND PERE MARQUETTE (9)

December 12, 1925 Hartford Blues 10, St. Alphonsus 0

APRIL 9, 1926

FIRST BRAVES/RED SOX CITY SERIES GAME PLAYED AT FENWAY PARK

Red Sox 6, Braves 1 (Winner, Howard Ehmke)

APRIL 13, 1926

Yankees Beat Sox 12-11 on Opening Day Game Broadcast on WNAC Radio

Opening Day 1926 at Fenway features the first ever Red Sox radio broadcast featuring Gus Rooney of WNAC. Rooney would last but a season on the WNAC microphone before being replaced by the legendary Fred Hoey. At first, only the home games of both the Braves and Red Sox were broadcast over the radio.

MAY 8, 1926

Sox Park Has Bleacher Fire

THIRD BASE SEATS AT FENWAY DESTROYED – GRAND STAND ALSO DAMAGED – BLAZE CAUSED BY BURNING CIGAR OR CIGARETTE – BREAKS OUT SHORTLY AFTER CONCLUSION OF GAME

HIGH WIND SHOOTS FLAMES ALL THROUGH STRUCTURE – MANY VOLUNTEER WORKERS

LOSS IS $25,000 – BRAVES FIELD OFFERED SOX MANAGEMENT FOR MONDAY'S GAME

A fire believed to have started from a cigar or cigarette stub early last evening swept through the third base bleachers at Fenway Park and completely ruined the stand. The fire also damaged the grandstand and destroyed a couple of large billboards

TRIPS ON WIRE, NOSE SPLIT

A strong breeze carried blazing embers over the roof of the grandstand and set fire in the dump on Jersey street. This dump fire at one time covered three acres of ground and extended along both sides of Jersey street from the ballpark to Boylston street

Three alarms were sounded because the third base bleachers at Fenway Park are wedged in close to a large garage and the entire vicinity of Landsdowne street and Brookline avenue is congested, being occupied by big garages, filling stations and tire concerns.

Lieutenant John Goode, aide to Chief Sennott of the fire

Pere Marquette Fenway Park Ticket. *(Courtesy of Ed "Moose" Savage)*

department, tripped over a wire while on duty at the fire and sustained a split nose. He refused to quit until after he had driven the chief back to his headquarters.

The fire was first noticed by Joseph Lunney, a night watchman at the park. He rushed to the Red Sox office and sent an emergency call for the fire department. Immediately on the arrival of the first apparatus, a box alarm was sent in and when Chief Sennott arrived he ordered a second and then a third alarm.

VOLUNTEERS PREVENT BIG LOSS

Lee Fohl, manager of the Red Sox, was in the office when Lunney rushed in to phone. He grabbed a hand fire extinguisher, as did Lunney and some of the other ball park employees. Their attempts were futile, for the strong wind was carrying the flame with remarkable rapidity the entire length of the stand.

A corps of drivers from the S.S. Pierce Company, under the leadership of Jeff Davis, rushed into the park before the apparatus arrived, and attached the hose used for watering the grass and played it on the third base side of the grandstand, extinguishing the burning embers that were being blown into

the grandstand. The action of these men prevented a great loss of property in the grandstand. Arthur Sousa, one of the drivers, was cut by a steel girder, and his wound treated by Mary Lynch, Red Sox bookkeeper.

EMBERS BLOWN ON GRANDSTAND

The fire was noticed by Lunney at 7:06. Within fifteen minutes, the entire third base bleachers were ablaze, and showers of blazing embers were being blown into the grandstand and onto the roof. Many of the embers were carried over the roof to the big dump where old automobiles and parts, dry grass, empty packing cases, barrels, etc., furnished fuel for a spectacular blaze.

FIGHT FIRES ON GRANDSTAND ROOF

Hose lines were directed toward the burning stands from Jersey street, Landsdowne street and Brookline avenue. Other engines pumped water from hydrants on Boylston street, Jersey street and Kilmarnock street on the three acres of blazing dump. A big billboard facing Boylston street at Jersey was partially destroyed by fire, and another billboard just inside the 75-cent entrance

to Fenway Park was destroyed. Firemen pulled down the back of the burning stand and the top of the fence along Landsdowne street opposite the Knickerbocker garage. Manager Patrick McMann of the Knickerbocker sent a force of his men with fire extinguishers to quench the fire running along the Landsdowne street fence top.

At several places holes were cut through the high fence by firemen in order to get hose lines into the park in a position to play on the burning stands. The firemen worked an hour after the third base bleacher fire was extinguished in fighting fires on the roof of the grandstand. Holes were dug into the roof and when the fire started running along the edge of the grandstand roof, it was necessary to chop out part of the woodwork which also resulted in uprooting the telegraph and telephone wires running to the grandstand press box.

DAMAGE OVER $25,000

During yesterday's game it was necessary to extinguish two small fires in the third base bleachers with pails of water.

The damage is estimated at between $25,000 and $30,000 and is partially covered by insurance. Owner "Bob" Quinn stated that he hopes the game with Cleveland can be played at Fenway Park with the burned section roped off. He was gratified, however, to receive a visit from Secretary Eddie Ridley of the Braves while the fire was in progress. Riley came hurrying to Fenway Park to inform Owner Quinn that he might have the use of Braves Field for Monday's game if Fenway Park cannot be used.

The third base bleachers had a seating capacity of about 2,200.

The last two rows of chairs in the grandstand on the base side was the only part of the interior of this stand injured by fire. The roof was badly burned, however.

Bleachers Burn in Fenway Park

GRANDSTAND DAMAGED AND GENERAL FIRES STARTED OUTSIDE GROUNDS

WOMAN EMPLOYEE THE HEROINE OF HOUR

Fire wiped out the third base bleachers of Fenway Park yesterday, damaged the western end of the grandstand and menaced several buildings, when flying embers started three serious brush blazes. Damage of $25,000 was caused to the park property. Three alarms were sent in.

Lt. John Goode, aide to Chief Dan Sennott, received cuts about the face when he fell from a steel girder on the first base side of the grandstand. He had mounted to ascertain the seriousness of the blaze between the ceiling and upper surface of the grandstand canopy.

EMPLOYEES ALERT

Arthur Sousa, an employee of the park, suffered cuts to his right hand when he tripped over a seat in the grand [stand at] the beginning of the fire. His injuries were dressed in the ball park offices by Miss Mary Lynch, a bookkeeper.

The vigilance of Miss Lynch and several employes about to leave the grounds for the day probably saved the administration offices and the remainder of the grandstand and first base bleachers from being swept away by the fire.

Miss Lynch said she was on her way home and had reached Kenmore station when she saw the smoke. Fearing that it might be at the park, she returned. When she noted the serious aspect, she entered the offices and sent in calls to the fire department and officials at the park. After her first call, she divided her time between the switchboard and the first aid kit. She remained at her post until the fire was extinguished.

The blaze was first discovered by John Stack, an employee of the park. His shouts attracted the attention of Louis Fishera, a driver of the Checker Taxi Company. Fishera raced his cab to box 234 and returned to give what aid he could.

ADDITIONAL ALARMS

A second alarm was sent in ten minutes later at 6:55. By that time the bleachers fronting on what is known as "Duffy's Cliff," was a mass of fire. It swept the dry seats like tinder, setting fire to the billboards and part of the fence on the Landsdowne street side. The flames then doubled back and leaped a narrow gap to the grandstand, touching off the roof ceiling and tarred top.

Meanwhile Stack, aided by his son, Joe; Jeff Davis, Art Sousa, W. Caswell and "Winnie" Green, all employes, broke out the park's hose lines and directed them at the flames. On the arrival of the fire department, they formed bucket brigades to fight the roof fire.

Clouds of embers, blown by a stiff northeast wind, swept over the roof and caught in the wooden gangway leading to the press boxes.

The gangway quickly caught fire. The flames spread to the back of the press boxes on the roof. Bucket brigades fought these incipient blazes until hose lines could be laid.

The windfall of blazing embers landed on the parking space on the Boylston street side of the field and spread to a brush tract along Boylston street between Ipswich and Jersey streets. The cut and dried brush flamed like cotton. Within five minutes the flames had bridged Jersey street and Boylston street.

FIRES IN THE BRUSH

The brush fires for a time seemed more serious than the original blaze. Their proximity jeopardized the Lalime and Partridge building at Boylston and Ipswich streets, housing the W.C. Sills Company and the American–La France Fire Engine Company.

In the vacant space between Jersey and Kilmarnock streets, the flames swept toward a gasoline station of the Standard Oil Company It was checked through the efforts of firemen and volunteers when it had come within 10 yards of the vents of a huge storage tank. Here men, women and children fought the ground fire with buckets, earth, pieces of tin and any other available weapon.

Another menace loomed when the brush on the opposite side of Boylston street caught fire. Fanned by the wind, the flames raced through the dry grass and brush toward the rear of a group of apartments fronting on Peterborough street.

A third alarm at 7:15 called additional apparatus. Men were thrown at the brush fires. Slowly they gained headway against the

Brothers Alex and Milt Gaston pose at Fenway Park in 1929. Alex was a catcher who played parts of two seasons with the Red Sox, batting .233, while his brother Milt was a pitcher who lost 19 and 20 games in consecutive seasons in 1929 and '30. *(Collection of the author)*

Following his departure to New York, Babe Ruth was baseball's biggest drawing card. He is shown here balancing on his rear foot while cocking his bat at Fenway Park in the late twenties. *(Donation by Joseph Copley, Courtesy of The Sports Museum)*

flames, checking all three before damage to buildings had been done.

Damage to a block of stores and offices at the northwest corner of the park was averted by a heavy fire wall. The destroyed bleachers were built against this wall. The roof was burned at one edge. The building housed, in the basement and on the second floor, the Cadillac Automobile Company of Boston.

Other occupants were Speedometer Service, Inc., of Boston, 64 Brookline avenue; General Welding & Equipment Company, 66 Brookline avenue; Butts & Ordway, 66 Brookline avenue; John V. Wilson Company, 74-76 Brookline avenue.

Nearly 200 seats in the grandstand adjoining the burned bleachers were consumed. For a while the offices were menaced. All telephone and telegraph wiring to the press boxes was destroyed, but the instruments escaped.

TRAFFIC IS HALTED

All traffic in the entire area was halted. Streetcars on Boylston street, the Ipswich street – Chestnut hill line, were held up more than half an hour. Squads of police from division 16, under the direction of Sgts. Shea and Waugh, handled traffic and kept the hundreds of spectators out of danger.

Thousands of feet of hose were brought into play, some lines of 1,200 to 1,500 feet being needed in the battles with the brush fires. Gallons of chemicals were also used on the main blaze and the brush fires.

Scarcely had the fire been extinguished when Secretary Eddie Riley of the Boston Braves communicated with Manager Bob Quinn of the Red Sox and offered the Americans the use of the Wigwam until the destroyed bleachers can be rebuilt. Quinn, expressing the appreciation of the Red Sox, declined the kindly offer, explaining the transfer would probably not be necessary.

Source: The Boston Post, May 9, 1926

(Author's note: The Red Sox declined to rebuild this section of the ballpark as attendance had dropped so low as to not be worth the expense or trouble)

May 23, 1926 War Memorial Mass

June 13, 1926 Holyoke 3, Boston Post Office 2, Boston Post Office 15, Springfield 2

JUNE 17, 1926

Holy Cross Bows to Boston College, 2-1, before 12,000 at Fenway Park

July 23, 1926 Lynn Flyers 6, White Eagles 2

August 25, 1926 Houghton & Dutton 3, R H. White 3

September 29, 1926 Jamaica Plain 7, Mechanic Arts 0 (Football)

September 29, 1926 Brighton High 0, South Boston High 0 (Football)

September 30, 1926 BU Terriers "B" Football Team Beats Varsity Squad in Scrimmage at Fenway (Football)

APRIL 8, 1927

CITY SERIES, RED SOX 13, BRAVES 2 (WINNER, SLIM HARRISS)

APRIL 9, 1927

CITY SERIES, BRAVES 6, RED SOX 5 (WINNER, GEORGE MOGRIDGE)

Despite the fact that this game was played at Fenway Park, the Red Sox batted first and the Braves last.

May 29, 1927 War Memorial Service

October 1, 1927 Duke 25, Boston College 9 (Football)

October 12, 1927 Dorchester High 19, Mechanic Arts 12 (Football)

October 12, 1927 Boston English 21, Boston Trade 0 (Football)

October 14, 1927 East Boston 12, High School of Commerce 0 (Football)

October 14, 1927 Brighton High 0, Hyde Park High 0 (Football)

October 25, 1927 Dorchester High 20, Boston Trade 18 (Football)

October 25, 1927 Hyde Park High 13, Charlestown High 12 (Football)

November 9, 1927 Boston Latin 19, Charlestown High 0 (Football)

November 10, 1927 Brighton High 0, East Boston High 0 (Football)

November 15, 1927 Hyde Park High 0, Dorchester High 0 (Football)

November 17, 1927 Boston English 26, High School of Commerce 0 (Football)

Ed Morris pitched superbly for some of the worst Red Sox teams in history while winning 19 and 14 games respectively for the 1928 and '29 American League last place finishers. The 31-year-old died tragically as the result of a stab wound suffered during a going-away party held in his honor in Century Florida prior to spring training in 1932. *(Collection of the author)*

NOVEMBER 18, 1927

New York Giants Clash with Pere Marquettes

PROFESSIONAL FOOTBALL INVADES BOSTON AGAIN SATURDAY.

The New York Giants, one of the greatest coin-getting gridiron machines of the universe, clash with the unconquered Pere Marquettes of South Boston at Fenway Park while the Yale bulldog is growling in the stadium against Harvard.

The contest may ultimately result in a pro league franchise being awarded the South Boston team.

Dr. Harry A. March, one of the leading powers of pro circles, will come to the Hub for the purpose of gaining first hand information of the possibilities of the game here.

The Boston Bulldogs tried the venture a couple of years ago and Bob McKirdy, local promoter, who backed the team was nearly sent to the cleaners.

The Giants command the pro football universe; in fact, the team leads the pro league and is regarded as the last word in gridiron machinery. Jack Hagerty, Dorchester kid, former Georgetown star, is one of the outstanding players of the Giants, while Pinky Haines, former Penn State star, is another leading light of the team.

Tom Whelen, Caseys coach, who has a most successful season at South Boston, is developing a new attack to uncover against the New Yorkers.

NOVEMBER 19, 1927

Giants Walk All Over Peres, 34-7

GOTHAM TEAM GIVES WONDERFUL GRID EXHIBITION—OUTSHINE SOUTHIE BOYS IN EVERY DEPARTMENT

The New York Giants, and Giants they were, beat the Pere Marquettes eleven, 34 to 7, before 10,000 fans at the Fenway Park gridiron yesterday afternoon. The Gotham team, first in its pro league, was indeed a sturdy lot and the visitors had their football down to a nicety, with all the tricks that are uncovered with a batch of seasoned players, most of them with All-America ratings.

OUTCLASS LOCALS

The Giants out-kicked, out-rushed, out-passed and out-played the Caseys and gave as clever an exhibition of the great fall sport as could be desired. If it has been said that the "pros" take it easy, this could not be said yesterday. They meant to show up the South Boston team and they scrapped their hardest to rub it in.

Each replacement looked bigger than the player going out and the whole lot of them sensed the position of the ball at all times and were on all the plays and on all the passes, and the Caseys generally discouraged.

Early in the game the Giants showed which way the wind was to blow for the afternoon, so far as victory was concerned. They got the ball on a short kick on the Casey 30-yard line. In one play McBride crashed the line and kept right on going for a touchdown. In the same period, after McBride ran in a kick for 20 yards, he tossed two passes to Corgan for 15 and 25 yards each for another touchdown.

FINE AIR ATTACK

More flashy forwards came in the second period and one from McBride to Hagerty, former Dorchester boy who went to Georgetown, landed on the 10-yard line. Pere Marquette put up a rugged fight with a goal-line defense but the Giants power could not be denied and on fourth down Haines crashed the line for a score.

Pere Marquette was forced to resort to trick plays and passes, but one was intercepted by Garvey on the Casey 40-yard line. Haines and Gagnon carried to the 11-yard line on slanting plays and Imlay swung an end for the score.

The Pere Marquette score came in the third period when the Giants kicked outside their 45-yard line. A forward, Kitteridge to Morrison, was good for 15 yards. Another to Wentworth went for a score but Kitteridge was not back five yards when he threw and the play was called back. It was tried again and went successfully for a touchdown.

GET IN GEAR AGAIN

In the final period the Giants opened up again. Passes from Hagerty to Kendrick, a new star end, worked twice in succession and were good for a touchdown.

After this score the Giants were not content and tried hard to keep it going. They were clever under punts and just when their punt catcher was about to be tackled he would side pass to one of his own men. Three times it took fine tackling by the Caseys to keep the runner from gaining a clear field.

Billy Wise, the regular quarter for the Pere Marquette team, could not get into uniform as his upstate high school team was playing. His cleverness was sadly missed.

The Casey players came out of the clash in fairly good shape and are fit to go up to Peabody this afternoon to meet the University of Peabody team in the fourth annual battle.

CHAMPIONS OF THE COMMUNITY

Nearly a decade before Dorothy Day and Peter Maurin founded the Catholic Worker Movement in New York City the South Boston Pere Marquette Council, known as "Babe Ruth's Own Council" even after the former Red Sox star had shipped to New York, supported progressive community charities such as the Columbus

Tony Rovinski of Holy Cross passes to Montelli in action against Boston College in 1929. *(Photograph by Leslie Jones, Courtesy of The Boston Public Library)*

Day Nursery. The Nursery, whose slogan was "Mother Must Work" is now known as the Laboure Center and celebrated its 100th anniversary in 2007. Now run by the Boston Archdiocese and renamed for St. Catherine Laboure, a Daughter of Charity in 1947, who was canonized that same year, the center was run and supported by the Knights of Columbus until the takeover. During that time the South Boston Knight's sports club, the Pere Marquettes fielded formidable semi-pro teams in basketball, hockey, baseball and football and donated funds generated by these programs to both the daycare center and other church-sponsored charities. Their example was emulated two decades later with the founding of The Jimmy Fund in support of the Dana Farber Cancer Institute. This legendary charity was initiated by Lou Perini and Billy Sullivan of the Boston Braves and later adopted by the Red Sox and championed by Tom Yawkey and Ted Williams.

November 22, 1927 Mechanic Arts 9, Boston Trade 7
November 24, 1927 Boston English 20, Boston Latin 13
November 24, 1927 Dorchester High 31, High School of Commerce 0
November 24, 1927 Pere Marquette 6, Fitton A.C. 0
May 20, 1928 War Memorial Service
June 9, 1928 Holy Cross 9, Boston College 6

JUNE 18, 1928

Glasgow Rangers Tie Boston Eleven at Fenway Park

Though outplayed throughout the Glasgow Rangers, Scottish soccer champions, were able to hold the Boston eleven (Wonder Workers of the American Soccer League) league champions to a 2-2 tie here at Fenway Park before 10,000 spectators. The Boston team displayed marvelous cooperation which enabled Johnny Ballantyne, inside left, to score twice."

JUNE 26, 1928

Mello Retains His Welter Title in Fast, Close Bout With Skillful Billy Murphy

The majority of the 12,000 fans that came to Fenway Park on the night of June 27th had taken the train from Lowell where they'd purchased their fight tickets at Bill Keenan's Diamond Diner. The main bout was the big attraction and featured two Lowell boxers, New England welterweight champion Al Mello, the darling of the Portugese community and "Irish" Billy Murphy.

The correspondent from the *Lowell Sun* wrote of the thrilling 10-round decision, "It was a great fight and it will be fought over again a thousand times verbally by those who were there. Mello won. It was a close win, but a win and the decision was just. It was one of those battles that calls for a repeat, the sooner the better for there still remains ample room for discussing who is the better man. Last night, Mello came through on top. Murphy seems to have the stuff to reverse the decision. He never looked better in a Boston ring, and it may be his turn next time. Both fighters are a credit to Lowell, no matter

how you look at it and both could wear the welterweight crown with equal grace."

Other winners in the card were featherweight Hy Diamond of Boston's West End, Roxbury's Jackie Donahue, Connie Holmes of the South End, Dorchester's Charlie Donovan, and Ray Cross of Milford.

July 21, 1928 Ira Flagstead Day

August 9, 1928 Worcester (MA) American Legion 5, Manchester (NH) American Legion 5 (Tie)

August 12, 1928 New York Printers 8, St. Louis Printers 2

August 12, 1928 Detroit 9, Indianapolis 2

August 31, 1928 Al Mello Knocks Out Charlie Donovan in Six Rounds (Boxing)

September 6-8, 1928 Massachusetts Boys Days

September 13, 1928 Al Mello Defeats Billy Murphy, again (Boxing)

September 22, 1928 College Avenue M. E. Church (Somerville) 3, Center Street Baptist (Jamaica Plain) 2 (1st game) College Avenue M. E. Church (Somerville) 6, Center Street Baptist (Jamaica Plain) 5 (2nd game)

September 29, 1928 Boston College 38, Catholic University 6 (Football)

October 12, 1928 Boston College 19, Duke 0 (Football)

OCTOBER 28, 1928

Duke Eleven Loses to Boston College

NORTH CAROLINA TEAM BOWS BY 19-0 BEFORE 20,000 IN FENWAY PARK CONTEST

Little Paddie Creedon scampered and squirreled on the gridiron at Fenway Park today and with his backfield mates, Smith and Weston, gave Boston College a 19 to 0 over Duke University. A holiday crowd of 20,000 saw the conquerors of the Navy combat the much-heralded forward passing attack of the boys from North Carolina.

November 2, 1928 Boston Tigers Hockey Team Works Out on Fenway's Field

NOVEMBER 12, 1928

Boston College Beats Fordham to Keep Pace with Carnegie

MCKENNEY'S PUPILS ENCOUNTER LITTLE TROUBLE DOWNING NEW YORKERS

Fenway Park was nearly packed with an Armistice Day crowd of 30,000 that welcomed back former Boston College and Dartmouth head coach Frank "The Iron Major" Cavanagh as his Fordham squad face an undefeated Boston College team led by his protégé, former star quarterback Joe McKenney.

McKenney at 22 was the youngest head coach in collegiate football and his team overcame a brief second quarter lapse where Fordham achieved the short-lived distinction of being the only team to have led Boston College during any of their games to date. Their 7-6 lead was soon surmounted as Boston College scored the next thirteen points and finished the game with an interception of a Fordham pass on their 10-yard line in the waning seconds.

November 24, 1929 Boston College 51, Connecticut Aggies 13 (Football)

December 1 , 1929 Boston College 19, Holy Cross 0 (Football)

JANUARY 30, 1929

Boston Mayor Malcolm E. Nichols, the Braves and Red Sox announce a new city ordinance allowing the playing of Sunday baseball. Both teams agree not to raise prices and the Sox pay a $1,000 assessment fee.

FEBRUARY 18, 1929

Sunday baseball denied in Boston despite state referendum because Fenway Park is within 1,000 feet of a church. Revere officials offer blueprints for a 41,000-seat stadium in their city for the Red Sox. Though the American League had given the Sox permission to play Sunday games in Revere Sox President Quinn continues talks with the Braves to use Braves Field for Red Sox Sunday home games.

FEBRUARY 25, 1929

Sox President Quinn discusses leaving Fenway Park for Braves Field as they'd just signed up to play 13 Sunday "home" games at their rival's ballpark.

April 9, 1929 Pittsfield Hillies hold practice session at Fenway Park

April 11, 1929 Pittsfield 7, Boston College 5 (7 innings)

May 26, 1929 War Memorial Service

June 20, 1929 Jake Zeramby Beats Sammy Fuller in Third Round of Featherweight Bout (Boxing)

July 9, 1929 Gus Sonnenberg Defeats Strangler Lewis (Wrestling)

AUGUST 10, 1929

New Bedford Beats Boston Eleven, 3-2

WINS OPENING GAME OF THE AMERICAN SOCCER LEAGUE AT FENWAY PARK

In the opening game of what would be their last full season in the American Soccer League (they'd play 4 games in 1930 before going out of business) the Boston Wonder Workers defeated the New Bedford Whalers in a match that featured all of the goal scoring in the first half. Both squads represented a league that sports historians view as the best yet to play in the USA. Many teams featured international stars from the United Kingdom lured to the states by teams that also arranged for their stars to work for companies affiliated with their owners. Fenway Park was an infrequent venue for the Wonder Workers who also played at the old South End Grounds.

August 17, 1929 Fall River 3, Boston Wonder Workers 1 (Soccer)

August 26, 1929 St. Thomas of Jamaica Plain 11, St. Francis of Charlestown 2

August 27, 1929 South End Athletics 4, Boston Pirates 9

August 29, 1929 Larry "Big Boy" Rawson Knocks Out Bob Mills in 4th round (Boxing)

September 18, 1929 Roslindale 5, Quincy 0

September 28, 1929 Boston College 13, Catholic University 6 (Football)

October 5, 1929 Boston College 42, University of Maine 0 (Football)

OCTOBER 12, 1929

Boston College and Villanova Tie at 7-7

October 18, 1929 Boston College High 21, Boston Latin 0 (Football)

October 26, 1929 Boston College 40, Canisius 6 (Football)

November 2, 1929 Boston College 20, Duke 12 (Football)

November 9, 1929 Fordham 7, Boston College 6 (Football)

November 11, 1929 Holy Cross Freshmen 7, Boston College Freshmen 6 (Football)

November 30, 1929 Boston College 12, Holy Cross 0 (Football)

December 7, 1929 New England Navy Team 14, New England Army Team 12 (Football)

Elise Yawkey and Tom Yawkey view the progress of the re-construction of Fenway Park in March 1934. Note that the rear slats have yet to be added to the grandstand seats.
(Courtesy of the Boston Public Library)

CHAPTER THREE

Reconstruction

"Daddy Warbucks, Santa Claus, Our Rich Uncle"

—NEWSPAPER REFERENCES TO NEW RED SOX OWNER TOM YAWKEY

The thirties represented an era in which Fenway Park remained very much a people's park. It was a venue where Post Office clerks, soda jerks, and inspectors from the Public Works were just as apt to venture as participants as fans. In 1932 alone the park was host to 43 schoolboy football games not to mention the many wrestling, boxing, soccer, and college football dates on the venue's expansive calendar.

It was also home to two pro football teams, the Redskins and Shamrocks. Both won championships in 1936 with the aftermath being the re-location of the Redskins to Washington in 1937 and the financial collapse of the Shamrocks a year later.

In 1933 both the park and the Red Sox were immediately rejuvenated by the arrival of new owner and budding millionaire Tom Yawkey. Within a year of his arrival Yawkey became a hero to working-class Bostonians as his ambitious renovation of Fenway Park hired all union labor and was the second biggest contracting project in Depression-era Boston after the building of the Mystic-Tobin Bridge.

The park's renovation was nothing short of miraculous as a near total reconstruction was completed in five and a half months despite the fact that a full slate of pro, college, and high school football games were played during the early phases of the work.

Thus was wrought the park we know today. The park of the Green Monster and the center field triangle, replete with Updikian nooks and crannies.

An unidentified Red Sox player slides homeward in this 1930 photograph by the legendary Leslie Jones. Note the openings in the rear of the grandstand. They'd soon be covered to block the sun after Tom Yawkey bought the club in 1933. *(Photograph by Leslie Jones, Courtesy of the Boston Public Library)*

Red Sox trainer Bits Bierhalter stokes the clubhouse stove in this 1932 photograph. *(Photograph by Leslie Jones, Courtesy of the Boston Public Library)*

fine rally which gave him that stanza. It was his best of the entire bout and had the affair been of longer duration, he might have nosed into a victory.

September 4, 1930 Agawam A. A. 5, Gurnett & Co. 1

September 11-12, 1930 Rehearsal for Boston Fire Department 150-Man Band and Others

SEPTEMBER 27, 1930

Boston College 54 Catholic U 7

October 4, 1930 Boston College High 7, Boston English 0

October 6, 1930 Boston College 13, U. S. Marines of Philadelphia 7

October 10, 1930 Boston College High 7, Boston Latin 0

October 12, 1930 Fordham and BC Football Teams Practice

October 13, 1930 Fordham 3, Boston College 0

October 25, 1930 Boston College 15, Dayton College 6

November 1, 1930 Marquette 6, Boston College 0

NOVEMBER 8, 1930

Boston College Nipped By Georgetown 20-19

November 22, 1930 Boston College 47, Boston University 7

MAY 30, 1931

Yankees Conquer Celtics at Fenway Park

BILL GONSALVES, NATIVE BORN STAR, SHINES IN 4-3 VICTORY

In one of the few games ever played at Fenway Park where a team named Yankees were the home team, the soccer version of the New York Yankees defeated the legendary Glasgow Celtic FC before 8,000 fans.

Boston Post correspondent observed, "The inimitable New York Yankees registered a brilliant 4-3 triumph over the world-famous Glasgow-Celtic combination in an international soccer game at Fenway Park yesterday afternoon,

Red Sox trainer Bits Bierhalter with assistants Moe Gottlieb and John Orlando in 1932. *(Photograph by Leslie Jones, Courtesy of the Boston Public Library)*

a thrilling conflict featured by the wonderful exhibition of footwork and marksmanship by the skillful native born star, Billy Gonsalves.

Billy was in his element against the Scottish cupholders, the Fall River youth capping one of the greatest exhibitions of forward play ever seen in these parts with three characteristic goals. Gonsalves was the master craftsman afield in this rousing encounter of artistic soccer. Billy manipulating the ball with the skill of a Bobby Walker, while his splendid shooting was altogether too much for the noted Celtic goalie, John Thomson, heralded as the finest custodian in the game today.

A gathering of 8,000 enthusiasts witnessed this stern struggle between the respective champions of America and Scotland and even the most rapid Celtic supporter was forced to admit the Yankees superiority over the invincible Scots-Irish outfit in a fiercely contested game played on a small playing pitch that often marred the combined efforts of the front ranks.

Celtic never looked like the old Celtic teams which made history in Scottish circles some two decades ago, the invaders carrying too many passengers to be rated a first class combination."

(Source, Boston Post, May 31, 1931)

August 21, 1930 Boston Post Office Clerks Local 100 Team 8, All-Boston Police Team 3

September 12, 1930 St. Thomas C. L. A. A. of Jamaica Plain 6, Maintenance of Lines of Edison Light Company 0 (Boston Parks Department Final)

September 26, 1931 Boston College 26, Catholic U 7

October 24, 1931 Marquette Edges Boston College 7-0 Before 5,000 at Fenway

November 14, 1931 Boston College Tips Centre College 7-0

MAY 27, 1932

Finally, Sunday Baseball

Sunday baseball approved at Fenway Park as distance is extended from 500 to 1,000 feet from the appropriately named Church for The Redemption

May 29, 1932 War Memorial Service

May 29, 1932 Boston Shamrock Lacrosse Club Works Out at Fenway

June 2, 1932 Boston Shamrocks 9, New York Giants 5 (Lacrosse)

June 9, 1932 Boston Shamrocks 13, New York Yankees 3 (Lacrosse)

June 15, 1932 Paul Adams Defeats George Myerson (Wrestling)

June 17, 1932 Baltimore 7, Boston Shamrocks 5 (Lacrosse)

June 18, 1932 Boston Shamrocks 12, New York Giants 7 (Lacrosse)

June 22, 1932 Paul Adams Defeats Ted Germaine (Wrestling)

June 28, 1932 Ad Zachrow Defeats Nap Proulx (Boxing)

July 7, 1932 Leo Larivee Wins over Odonne Piazza (Boxing)

July 12, 1932 Paris Apice Defeats Pancho Villa (Boxing)

July 13, 1932 Mephisto of Germany Defeats Steve Passas (Wrestling)

July 14, 1930 All-Scholastics 2, Milford High 2 (Tie)

JULY 19, 1932

Jolley Tumbles Down Duffy's Cliff

Red Sox left fielder Smead Jolley attempted to scale Duffy's Cliff to snare Cleveland pitcher Wes Ferrel's drive only to stumble and fall backwards down the slope. The cliff would soon be leveled when extensive renovations were ordered by new owner Tom Yawkey in the winter of 1933–34.

July 20, 1932 George Myerson Defeats Ted Germaine (Wrestling)

July 26, 1932 Leo Larivee Defeats Odonne Piazza in Rematch (Boxing)

August 2, 1932 Maxey Rosenbloom Retains Light Heavyweight Crown against Joe Barlow (Boxing)

August 10, 1932 Paul Adams Beats Louis Poplin (Wrestling)

August 16, 1932 Nap Proulx Beats Manny Davis (Wrestling)

August 23, 1932 Dave Shade Beats Norman Conrad (Boxing)

August 24, 1932 Mephisto Pins, Defeats Art Flynn (Wrestling)

August 30, 1932 Walter Cobb Knocks Out Jack Sigmore in 4th Round (Boxing)

August 31, 1932 Steve Passas Defeats Sahib Seibeg (Wrestling)

SEPTEMBER 6, 1932

*Sullivan Square Palledoes 5, East Boston Neptunes 2 (Boston Park Department Finals)

*Roslindale Tuskaroras 5, Hyde Park Sunnyside A.C. 2 (Boston Park Department Finals)

*Holy Name Midgets 3, Roxbury Cubs 2 (Boston Park Department Finals)

SEPTEMBER 6, 1932

All Chocolate in Fenway Bout

THE "KEED" COMPLETELY BAFFLES STEVE SMITH BY HIS SPEED – ONLY ONE ROUND EVEN

By Doc Almy

Kid Chocolate of Cuba, making his second appearance in several years in Boston, won as he pleased over Steve Smith of Bridgeport in last night's Argonne A.A. main bout at Fenway Park.

The result was no surprise—they have fought before, with somewhat similar results. At that, Smith tried all the way—did his best. His best, however, amounted to little.

BUSY SIXTH ROUND

The busiest round of the contest was the sixth, in which Smith's two-fisted attack to the body managed to even that stanza. Otherwise, the Keed from Cuba had the battle. It was the case of the colored ringster being too good a fighter—really a great fighter for his 128 pounds for either Smith or any other average opponent.

He met Smith's rushes with jabs, usually blocked or sidestepped the white boy's attempts to slug, and then slung his man hard and often with either straight drives to head, or right hand uppercuts to chin. In one of the later rounds, Steve's left eye went to pieces, while the slams he stopped with his face brought the color to his lips.

It was just as many thought it would be – Smith, a willing performer, up against a chap far and away too smart for him. At that, the bout drew about 4,000 fans, one of the largest crowds the Argonne A.A. has played to this season.

Kid Chocolate Whips Smith

BON BON KID IN BOXING WORKOUT HAS SMITH WOOZY IN 7TH

His Majesty Kid Chocolate, uncrowned, but still the king of the lightweights, flashed a lightning two-fisted barrage of leather into one Steve Smith of Bridgeport, and won the 10-round feature Argonne A.A. bout Tuesday night at Fenway, while a great crowd including two local stars, Andy Martin

World lightweight boxing champion Kid Chocolate headlined a Fenway Park boxing card on the evening of September 6, 1932 and defeated Steve Smith in a 10-round decision. *(Collection of the author)*

April 21, 1932, marked the first Ladies Day at Fenway Park. *(Photograph by Leslie Jones, Courtesy of the Boston Public Library)*

The 1931 season marked the first season the Red Sox sported uniform numbers, and in this photograph outfielder/first baseman Al Van Camp is shown caught in a run down against the Indians. Note the scaled-down version of the left-field wall. *(Photograph by Leslie Jones, Courtesy of The Boston Public Library)*

In their NFL opener at Fenway Park, the newly christened Boston Redskins led by Native American head coach Lone Star Dietz beat the New York Giants by a score of 21-20. *(Photograph by Leslie Jones, Courtesy of the Boston Public Library)*

Boston Redskin Hall of Fame running back Cliff battles was also a skilled concert pianist and a Phi Beta Kappa graduate of West Virginia Wesleyan College. *(Collection of the author)*

and Sammy Fuller, marveled at his speed and skill. Chocolate won without having to loosen his "big guns" and simply set back and gave the tough Mr. Smith a boxing lesson. And what a lesson!

It appears as if Chocolate was out to give the fans a bit of boxing entertainment, and as a result, Smith ate plenty of leather. Chocolate's gloves came in so fast that Steve often wondered who was in back of 'em. But Smith was willing. He gave everything to keep up with the Kid. However, he needed a racing car. The Bridgeport boy could only hope for a K.O. slug. But each time he got

set to deliver, the Cuban would either poke him off balance or smother him like a blanket.

Chocolate worked as if he'd planned his battle. He never wasted a shot, and each blow was a picture. His footwork was brilliant, and the 10-round decision was merely a workout for him. He could have cut Smith up more than he did.

Only in the seventh when the Kid thought Smith was a bit too gay did he shoot the heavy artillery. A beautiful left hook ripped a gash over Smith's eye and up came a jolting right to the jaw. Smith almost went "out."

(The Boston Guardian)

SEPTEMBER 11, 1930

FILENE'S 6, HOUGHTON & DUTTON 3

SEPTEMBER 13, 1932

"Unknown" Winston Floors Cobb Easily

WINSTON STOPS COBB IN SECOND ROUND

DOWNS BALTIMORE CRACKER IN BIG RING UPSET

(The Rover)

Two Nordic boxers "walked out" on Walter Cobb, the Baltimore giant. Mons Dorval got lost in the woods of Maine, and Les Kennedy got lost somewhere between California and Fenway Park. Thereupon, someone was needed to substitute in the both cases, and in both instances, the boxers selected were Negroes.

Sigmore was the first to meet the 206-lb bone crusher and the southern gent was so furious at having to joist with a Negro that he attempted to murder the Cambridge lad after suffering the disgrace of having been dumped on the mat. The Nordic papers went heywire over this new heavy find, and even the "Magic Coin" hombres were picking him to win over the second substitute and an "unknown" at that. Came the opening gong of the fight.

Cobb started throwing punches at the gent who tosses leather under the label of "unknown Winston" and who scales a very capable 190 lbs. The famous Cobb's left hook slammed home repeatedly, and whereas in the past it had had evil

LOCAL BOYS MAKING GOOD WITH PROS

PAIR OF BAY STATE REDSKINS
Ernie Concannon (left), guard from Waltham and N. Y. U., and Flavio Tosi, end from Beverly and Boston College.

Local lads Ernie Concannon (left) of Waltham and Flavio Tosi (right) of Beverly were Redskin fan favorites. *(Collection of the author)*

effect on one Primo Carnera, and our own Jack Sigmore, this large gentleman from Waterbury took them all in good style and continued to waltz in and shoot terrific rights and lefts to face and body. Cobb didn't like it one bit. He figured he'd teach this lesson that he'd never forget. But Winston had other ideas.

The Negro eased in and let fly a driving right that exploded on the beezer of the raging Mr. Cobb and the wine began to flow. The Unknown kept plodding in like the well known Herr Schmelling against one Squire Sharkey. And Cobb, who makes it a business to stay on his dogs was smacked from the vertical to the horizontal pose no less than three times before the first round was completed. Came the second round and the battered cracker who had attempted

to do a "job" on Sigmore recently, lasted just one minute and fifty-five seconds.

Winston whaled Cobb with both hands and the southern giant went down and out when the Connecticut Negro smashed a hard left hook to the body. And with this upset, the fans are curious to know more about this unknown ring phantom and how good he really is. For Tuesday night he looked good enough to give sailor Ernie Schaaf all he could take – and more.

(The Boston Guardian)

(Author's note. The none-too-subtle code language in this piece, printed in the African-American *Boston Guardian* reveals much about the racial climate of the time. It is also interesting to note that nearly thirty years before the Red Sox became the last major league baseball team

to integrate with the arrival of "Pumpsie" Green that Fenway Park was home to both black boxers such as Kid Chocolate and Unknown Winston as well as other noted African-American athletes such as Boston College football player Lou Montgomery and the Harlem Globetrotters.)

September 18, 1932 Post Office Clerks Local 100 Team 9, Old-Timers Team 1

September 27, 1932 East Boston 12, Brighton High 0

September 27, 1932 Roxbury Memorial 6, Charlestown 6

September 29, 1932 Jamaica Plain 7, Mechanic Arts 0

September 29, 1932 Trade School 6, Hyde Park High 0

September 30, 1932 Dorchester High 0, South Boston High 0

October 4, 1932 Charlestown High 0, High School of Commerce 0

October 4, 1932 Brighton High 19, Mechanic Arts 0

October 5, 1932 Hyde Park High 20, Roxbury Memorial 7

October 6, 1932 East Boston 6, Trade School 0

October 6, 1932 Jamaica Plain 6, South Boston 0

October 7, 1932 Boston College High 7, Boston Latin 7

October 12, 1932 Boston Trade School 7, Boston English 0

October 12, 1932 Dorchester High 21, Mechanic Arts 0

October 13, 1932 Hyde Park High 13, Brighton High 0

October 13, 1932 Roxbury Memorial 7, South Boston High 0

October 14, 1932 Jamaica Plain High 20, Charlestown High 0

October 14, 1932 East Boston High 0, High School of Commerce 0

October 21, 1932 Boston English 6,
Roxbury Memorial 0

October 21, 1932 Dorchester 6,
Trade School 0

October 25, 1932 Boston Latin 16,
High School of Commerce 7

October 25, 1932 Hyde Park High 6,
Charlestown High 0

October 28, 1932 Boston English 7,
Charlestown High 0

October 28, 1932 Roxbury Memorial
0, Jamaica Plain High 0

October 31, 1932 Hyde Park High
27, South Boston High 0

October 31, 1932 East Boston High
13, Charlestown High 0

November 1, 1932 Boston Trade 7,
Boston Latin 2

November 1, 1932 Brighton High 0,
Roxbury Memorial High 0

November 2, 1932 Jamaica Plain 19,
Dorchester High 0

November 2, 1932 High School of
Commerce 19, Mechanic Arts 0)

November 4, 1932 Boston English
12, Boston College High 0

November 9, 1932 High School of
Commerce 6, Boston Trade 0

November 11, 1932 Boston Latin 7,
Dorchester High 0

November 11, 1932 Boston English
19, Mechanical Arts 0

November 14, 1932 Hyde Park High
0, East Boston High 0

November 15, 1932 Roxbury
Memorial High 6, Dorchester
High 0

November 16, 1932 Boston Latin 33,
Mechanical Arts 0

November 16, 1932 Charlestown
High 0, Brighton High 0

November 17, 1932 High School of
Commerce 7, Boston English 6

November 21, 1932 Boston Trade
School 7, Mechanical Arts 6

November 22, 1932 South Boston
High 0, East Boston High 0

November 24, 1932 Boston Latin 18,
Boston English 7

New Red Sox owner Tom Yawkey became a folk hero soon after he hired union labor to tackle what turned out to be the second largest contracting project in Depression era Boston after the building of the Tobin Bridge. *(Collection of the author)*

Harsh winter conditions plagued the re-construction of Fenway Park in the winter of 1933-34. (*Collection of the author*)

November 24, 1932 High School of Commerce 12, Dorchester High 0

November 27, 1932 Providence Steamrollers 3, Pere Marquette 0

April 21, 1933 Ladies Day started at Fenway Park

August 5, 1933 New Bedford 6, Springfield 2 (Junior American Legion Semi-Final)

August 9, 1933 Ed Don George Defeats the Black Secret (Wrestling)

August 10, 1933 New Bedford 5, Lowell 4 (American Legion State Final)

August 31, 1933 Ivy Cubs of Roxbury 4, Savin Hill Pirates 0

August 31, 1933 Tuscaroras Cubs (Roslindale) 4, Savin Hill All-Stars 3

October 3, 1933 Boston English 12, East Boston 0

October 3, 1933 High School of Commerce 14, Charlestown 0

October 4, 1933 Memorial High of Roxbury 6, Jamaica Plain High 0

October 4, 1933 Brighton High 0, South Boston 0

OCTOBER 8, 1933

Burly Redskins Beat New York Giants 21-20 in NFL Opener at Fenway Park

Scoring a spectacular opening game victory before 15,000 at Fenway Park, the Boston Redskins effort was marked by a Turk Edwards block of Harry Newman's point after attempt following a Giants third quarter touchdown. This marked the Redskins first game under their new name after having played as the Boston Braves at Braves Field during the 1932 season, their first in the NFL. The Redskins also had the ironic distinction of being led by head coach and Sioux native William Henry "Lone Star" Dietz.

Many claim that team owner George Preston Marshall re-named his club in honor of Dietz while others find it more likely the name change came about due to the fact that Marshall left Braves Field in the wake of many unpaid bills and simply needed a euphemism for Braves with trunks of uniforms

The re-construction of Fenway Park virtually created a new ballpark in a period of just six months. *(Collection of the author)*

emblazoned with the images of native Americans. The latter scenario also seems more likely for an owner who was the last to integrate his team after their move to Washington in 1937.

October 10, 1933 Hyde Park High 8, Memorial High 7

October 10, 1933 South Boston High 15, Charlestown 0

October 11, 1933 Brighton High 7, Jamaica Plain High 0

October 11, 1933 East Boston High 0, High School of Commerce 0

October 12, 1933 Boston English 19, Boston Trade 0

October 12, 1933 Mechanical Arts 6, Dorchester High 0

OCTOBER 15, 1933

Presnell Star as Portsmouth Tops Boston By 13 to 0

The right arm and right leg of Glenn "Press" Presnell provided the Portsmouth (Ohio) Spartans (now the Detroit Lions) with a 13-0 victory over the redskins before a crowd of 10,000 at Fenway Park. Not only did he toss a 48-yard touchdown pass to John Cavosie but he also booted two third-quarter field goals after Boston had stopped them within the 10-yard line.

October 17, 1933 Brighton High 12, East Boston High 6

October 17, 1933 Memorial High

13, Charleston High 0

October 18, 1933 Mechanic Arts 6, Jamaica Plain High 0

October 18, 1933 South Boston High 7, Dorchester High 0

October 20, 1933 Hyde Park High 15, Boston Trade 7

OCTOBER 22, 1933

Redskins Keep the Chicago Spark-Plug Bottled During Game

The Boston Redskins put together a mighty defensive effort to contain Chicago Cardinals star all-purpose

Red Sox General Manager Eddie Collins points out details of the park reconstruction in January 1934 to Elise and Tom Yawkey. *(Courtesy of The Sports Museum)*

Red Sox patch. *(Collection of the author)*

Thomas Austin Yawkey started life as Thomas Yawkey Austin before being adopted by an uncle who owned the Detroit Tigers. Yawkey grew up playing catch with the likes of Ty Cobb, and on his 30th birthday inherited one of the largest fortunes in America. He bought the Red Sox soon afterwards. *(Photograph by Fabian Bachrach, Courtesy of The Sports Museum)*

back Joe Lillard aka "The Midnight Express" (Author's note: Lillard was one of two African-American players in the NFL until Woody Strode and Kenny Washington joined the league after WWII) as they treated 16,000 fans to a 10-0 victory.

The Cardinals un-doing was three interceptions of Lillard passes by the Redskins who scored their lone touchdown and field goal in the third quarter.

October 23, 1933 Brighton High 7, Mechanical Arts 6
October 25, 1933 Dorchester High 13, Memorial High 0
October 26, 1933 East Boston High 13, Charlestown 0
October 27, 1933 Boston College High 7, Boston Latin 6

OCTOBER 29, 1933

Pittsburgh Pirates Beat Boston 16-14

The Redskins lost to the Pittsburgh Pirates (later re-named Steelers) before the smallest NFL crowd of the season (7,500) at Fenway Park. Boston struck first as future Hall of Fame running back, concert pianist, and Phi Beta Kappa member Cliff Battles scored on short yardage. A second-quarter Pittsburgh touchdown and field goal gave the visitors a lead that increased courtesy of a Tony Holm 60 yard touchdown pass to Edgar Westfall. Boston made their last touchdown on a Louie Weller rush, capping an 88-yard drive.

October 30, 1933 Hyde Park High 14, Brighton High 6
October 30, 1933 South Boston High 13, Memorial High 0

November 1, 1933 Mechanical Arts 14, High School of Commerce 2
November 2, 1933 Boston Latin 7, Boston Trade 0
November 3, 1933 Boston College High 14, Boston English 13

NOVEMBER 5, 1933

Boston Hands Bears First Grid Defeat

An enthusiastic crowd of 22,820 cheered their Redskins to victory over the previously un-defeated Chicago Bears. Not only did the Boston defense thwart both red Grange and Bronco Nagurski but Bears end Bill Hewitt twice dropped sure touchdown passes in the end zone supplied by quarterback Johnny Doerhring. The key play of the game turned out to be a Turk Edwards interception of a Red Grange pass that led to a Cliff Battles field goal and a 10-0 lead. (Author's note: Turk Edwards joined the Redskins/Braves in 1932 and was paid $1,500 for the 10-game season. He was elected to the Pro Football Hall of Fame in 1969.)

November 7, 1933 Memorial High 0, East Boston High 0 (Football)
November 9, 1933 Boston Trade 9, High School of Commerce 0 (Football)
November 10, 1933 Jamaica Plain High 33, Charleston High 0 (Football)
November 11, 1933 Boston English 13, Mechanical Arts 0 (Football)
November 12, 1933 Pere Marquette 0, Fitton A.C. 0

(Football)
November 13, 1933 Memorial High 9, Boston Trade 6 (Football)
November 14, 1933 Jamaica Plain High 12, South Boston High 6 (Football)
November 15, 1933 Hyde Park High 13, East Boston High 6 (Football)
November 17, 1933 Boston English 13, Dorchester 0 (Football)

NOVEMBER 19, 1933

Redskins Best Packers 20-7 at Fenway Park

A crowd of 16,500 at Fenway Park saw the burly Boston Redskins thwart the famed Green Bay Packer aerial attack as they closed their National Professional Football League season with a 20-7 triumph. The Redskins dominated for the entire 60 minutes and among their highlights were a 75-yard punt by all-purpose star Cliff Battles that ultimately set up Boston's first touchdown and a third quarter interception by former Stanford star Ernie Pinckert that resulted in his 45-yard scamper for Redskins second td.

November 20, 1933 Brighton High 27, Charlestown 0
November 21, 1933 Jamaica Plain High 0, Hyde Park High 0
November 22, 1933 Boston English 6, High School of Commerce 0
November 23, 1933 Boston Latin 21, Mechanical Arts 7
November 24, 1933 Boston Trade 7, Dorchester High 6
November 26, 1933 Fitton A.C. 13, Pere Marquette 12

were stationed to see that these orders were carried out.

The blaze, which started in the canvas which covered the newly poured concrete in the bleachers, caught the oiled pine board forms holding the concrete and spread with lightning speed. Five alarms were sounded, and damage estimated at $250,000 was caused.

Four workmen who battled to stave the spread of the flames were injured. Hundreds of cars driven into Landsdowne street blocked and delayed the fire apparatus from getting into action.

WORKERS AID FIREMEN

Because of the long delay in getting water on the fast spreading fire, it seemed for a time as though the whole section would go like tinder. When Chief Henry A. Fox arrived the situation was grave. He sounded a fifth alarm, calling apparatus from all parts of the city.

Meanwhile, the first firemen to get into action dragged lines of hose from the Ipswich street side of the park and across the playing field to get to the fire.

An army of workmen fought side by side with the firemen to save as much of the new structure as possible. Joseph Petrozzi, 408 Hanover street, one of the workmen, was badly injured while trying to rip off the burning canvas. In a leap to avoid the flames, he landed on a nail which punctured his foot.

OTHERS INJURED

Philip Fason of East Boston injured his hand in assisting firemen drag in a line of hose. Lawrence Ponciroli, 73 West Canton street, South End, was knocked down while handling a line of hose, and received a badly battered knee. George Ash, 396 Reservoir avenue, Revere, received a lacerated wrist in helping to pull down part of the fence in order that the smoke-eaters could get to work.

Up in the newspapermen's room, another little drama was enacted. Surrounded by pictures of the great and near great players in the history of the Red Sox club, Collins was making his usual frugal lunch of graham crackers and milk when he received the first news of the fire, a few minutes after 1 o'clock.

BAT BOY GIVES ALARM

Johnny Orlando, the bat boy, stuck his head in the door. He was near tears. "Fire," he choked, "fire."

In the building of the Checker Taxi Company at the corner of Ipswich and Landsdowne street, eight cars jacked up for engine repairs were fairly melted by the intense heat.

The Seiberling Rubber Company at 41 Lansdowne street across the street from the ball park burst into flames. The big sign of the roof caught first. Then smoke burst from the roof and through the windows where thousands of dollars worth of tires were stored. The old quarters that once housed the Cotton Club, a former night club of several years ago, caught next, and then the Olds Motor Works and Pontiac Motor Company at 49-65 Lansdowne street burst into flames.

Girls fled from the offices in the building. Walter Musgrave, cashier of the Seiberling Company, had only time to run with the office books and cash.

HOW FIRE STARTED IS MYSTERY

Despite the fact that the wind was blowing against them, the flames clawed the opposite side of Lansdowne street. As paint, oil and tires in the buildings caught, the smoke became even more dense. The streets glazed with ice were especially treacherous. Scores of firemen and workmen were bruised in tumbles.

Just how it started is a mystery. Fire officials were loath to discuss the matter. Building Commissioner Roemer said that it could be partly explained by the conditions. He said that the concrete in the centre section of the bleachers had been poured into the forms on Wednesday and Thursday nights. The east end of the bleachers had been poured about three weeks ago, and the west end about Christmas.

WOOD DRIED OUT

In order to protect this concrete from intense cold, it had to be covered over with canvas and a number of fires built in salamanders, big pipe-like stoves, which kept the temperatures underneath the canvas above freezing. This process is used to dry the water out of the concrete. If it should freeze, the job is spoiled and must be done over.

The heat from these salamanders during a period of weeks had dried most of the wood to a tinder-like consistency. Heightening the inflammable nature of these forms, it had been necessary to coat them with oil. Forms which are not properly oiled leave the concrete filled with small splinters of wood, which engineers say is the sign of a poor concrete job.

YAWKEY NOTIFIED

Collins called Thomas A. Yawkey, owner of the club, at his camp in Georgetown, S.C., and broke the news.

The Detroit Lions (light uniforms) score against the Boston Redskins in their 17-7 win at Fenway Park on October 13, 1935. Note the lone Lions mascot at the far corner of the end zone. *(Courtesy of The Sports Museum)*

The "new" Fenway Park sported many of the biggest billboards in baseball.. More than a few fans observed, "The Red Sox use Lifebuoy ..and they still stink." *(Courtesy of The Sports Museum)*

After the telephone conversation with Yawkey, Collins called the newspapermen together in a much more cheerful frame of mind than before.

Answering a steady barrage of questions, he said that he did not regard the fire as a jinx in the least, and he laughed as he recalled last year's train wreck.

All the construction work is insured, and the fire will cause no financial loss to the club.

Insurance officials said the loss of the park would probably be about $75,000 at a conservative estimate. The value of the park in its present state, they said, is about $500,000, and the insurance on the damaged section will figure about 15 percent of this amount.

1,000 Men Resume Work on Fenway Park Today

More than 1,000 men will start work today, if weather permits, at Fenway Park. General Manager Eddie Collins has instructed the contractors to renew the job at once.

Last week over 750 men were employed at Fenway Park reconstructing the entire layout. Friday fire swept through the park, wrecking the center-field bleachers, which were part-way constructed. The framework and newly laid cement was ruined.

But Collins has received word from Owner Tom Yawkey to go right ahead with the job, no matter how much money it costs or how many men would have to be

Former Providence College star Hank Soar was the quarterback and leading gate attraction for the Boston Shamrocks. *(Courtesy of Bob Walsh)*

employed, so that the park will be ready for the opening game.

In the original plans the remodeling job called for an expenditure of $750,000. Last Friday's fire ruined $150,000 worth of material and labor, which boosts the cost to $900,000.

Yawkey and Manager Bucky Harris are expected to be in Boston some time this week to look over the damage and to make plans for the spring trip. Harris has been at his Washington home, while Yawkey is still gunning on his South Carolina estate.

APRIL 14, 1934

Rebuilding of Fenway Park Was Victory Over Elements

WORLD'S NEWEST BALL PARK A TRIBUTE TO UNTIRING EFFORTS OF GENERAL CONTRACTORS, COLEMAN BROTHERS, AND WORKERS WHO OVERCAME MANY OBSTACLES

Tomorrow, Boston's new Fenway Park will be officially completed. In addition to being the finest baseball park in the country it represents a victory of men, management and materials over fire, freezing cold and snow, and, most important of all time.

To the throngs of fans who will stream into the stands this week for the opening game there will be no evidence of the epic task involved in rushing the project to completion within the short time limit allotted. Instead they will see imposing grandstands, splendidly-engineered, modern buildings, and

in front of them an accurately-surveyed and laid out diamond surrounded by velvety green grass.

STARTED LAST SEPTEMBER

The story of the reconstruction of Fenway Park has already spread far and wide. It began one day last September when representatives of the firm of Coleman Brothers, the contractors, were summoned to the offices of the Red Sox Baseball Club. Present were Tom Yawkey, Eddie Collins, other Red Sox officials and members of an engineering organization from Cleveland. Yawkey showed them the preliminary plans of the work. "Can you do it before the opening game next April?" he asked them.

A consultation followed and after a study of the plans, Yawkey, his officials and the engineers were assured that the job would be completed on schedule if Coleman Brothers could start at once and (another "if") if winter weather conditions were not abnormal.

STAKED REPUTATION ON PROMISE

But here another drawback arose. The field must be used for professional and high school football until the last day of November. The existing grandstand, pavilion and centre field bleachers had to remain in use until that date as their facilities had been engaged previously. Again the representatives of Coleman Brothers went into a huddle.

After considering the date of completion they were satisfied that if the men were allowed to work nights as well as days the job could be done by the time specified in the contract. Should the work fail to be completed on time Coleman Brothers agreed to furnish at their own expense the facilities of Braves

Field for the home games of the Red Sox. Doubtful up to this point, the baseball club officials and the engineers then assented and the deal was made.

Ground was broken on the 25th of September. At that time work was started on the left field grandstand extension and during the football season was pushed to rapid completion.

After the whistle of the closing football game on Thanksgiving, the task was on in earnest. Before the end of the following day the grounds swarmed with workmen, machinery and equipment. The payroll jumped from a few hundred names to more than a thousand. The old wooden bleachers and the pavilion disappeared as if by magic. The seats in the former grandstand were demolished in rapid order. Roof and steel work melted away. Concrete steps were smashed into fragments and carted off. Faster and faster went the pace. Finally all was cleared and the old Fenway Park became a thing of the past.

In its stead wooden forms began to rise for the formation of the new stands. Another landmark disappeared with the famous Duffy Lewis' cliff. Here excavation was started for the new retaining wall along Lansdowne street. Despite snow and freezing weather the work went on.

CONQUERED FIRE OF JAN. 5

Then came the fire – on Jan. 5, two days after the concrete work was completed. Headlines screamed news of the catastrophe to thousands of Hub baseball fans. Fire, starting from an unknown cause in centre field bleachers, raged so fiercely that four alarms were rung. Side by side workmen and firemen battled flames for five solid hours before the fire was under control.

Despite the setback, however, the programme went on unceasingly day and night and in a few days not a vestige of the holocaust remained.

Some idea of the vast amount of supplies used on the job during the past six months can be gained from the following figures:

Cement – 18,000 barrels, or enough to require a 70-car freight train to haul it. Sand and gravel, 18,000 cubic yards or 3,600 large truckloads. Approximately 1,500,000 bricks, or enough to build a wall 12 inches thick, eight feet high, extended almost two miles in length. A million and one-half feet of lumber, or enough to build houses for 100 families. Add to this, 400 tons of structural steel, 200,000 square feet of wire mesh, tons of plumbers' pipe, electric wire, roofing materials and miscellaneous supplies.

WAS HEAVY RESPONSIBILITY

To supervise, step by step, this entire reconstruction programme required no small responsibility. The entire construction programme of Coleman Brothers operations was under the personal supervision of W.R. Coleman with S.R. Berke, chief engineer, and William F. Kearns, superintendent of operations.

To give one an adequate idea of the magnitude of the operations carried on by the firm of Coleman Brothers, here are some of the additional projects which were undertaken simultaneously with the Fenway Park job:

- Construction of the new Mystic River bridge at Medford.
- Charles river development,

grading and beautification.
- Worcester turnpike section between Newton and Brookline.
- Paving of the new East Boston traffic tunnel.

According to William R. Coleman, treasurer of Coleman Brothers, rigid care was exercised in the selection of sub-contractors. Only firms with tried and proven records were employed on the various sub-divisions of the work. Among these were:

The Security Fence Company of Somerville, which supplied wire fences, guards and grilles; the Sawtelle Coal Company, which furnished all the coal and coke used; the American Oil Company, whose Amoco gasoline and oils were used by the large fleet of trucks operated by Coleman Brothers; Field & Cowles, with whom the owners of Fenway Park placed their insurance; D.B. Raymond, who furnished cinders; the Aberthaw Company, M.J. Grady & Co., Frank W. Baldwin, Oliver Whyte Company, Charles J. McCarthy Co., the Eagle Electric Supply Co., all of whose services and materials were up to specifications.

To the Red Sox and their owners, all wish a successful season.

APRIL 17, 1934

"New" Fenway Opens

SENATORS WIN 6-5 IN 11 INNINGS

May 20, 1934 War Memorial Service
June 11, 1934 Golden Jubilee Celebrating Cardinal William O'Connell's Career

June 30, 1934 All-Boston Interscholastic Team 5, All-Springfield Interscholastic Team 4 (10 Innings)
July 5, 1934 Youth Field Day
July 18, 1934 Wrestlers Ed Don George and Jimmy Londos Wrestle to a Draw

---

AUGUST 13, 1934

Vast Fan Army in Good-By to Ruth

BABE WEEPS IN DRESSING ROOM, OVERCOME BY GREATEST OF TRIBUTES – THOUSANDS FAIL TO GET IN

By Paul H. Shannon

Boston fandom, turning out en masse as a farewell tribute to baseball's idol, big Babe Ruth, shattered all Fenway Park attendance records yesterday, when more than 47,000 of the 60 odd thousands who stormed the gates at Tom Yawkey's ball yard gathered to watch the Red Sox break even in the double header which featured the Yankees' final appearance in Boston for the year.

Besieging the entrances 'til the grandstand gates were forced to close a full hour before play was scheduled to begin, packing the pavilions and bleachers with the tremendous overflow of rooters who could find no reserved seat accommodations, overrunning the playing field which finally had to be roped off while mounted police held them in check, more people than this historic park had ever welcomed before, waited, rooted and stood for nearly five hours yesterday as the Yanks and Red Sox divided the laurels, and that colorful figure who made his big league debut here on the same diamond two decades before participated for the last time as an active figure in big league battling in the Hub.

Great a drawing card as this New York team really is, Babe Ruth was the magnet. Who else upon such a cold and gloomy day, with showers imminent at all times, could have packed those ample stands and drawn to the Fenway such a cheering, enthusiastic assemblage as Ruth brought here yesterday? It was "Hail and farewell" for Ruth. It was Boston's emphatic declaration that Ruth has won a place in the affections of local fandom such as no athlete has ever attained before. And likewise the immense gathering was an indication that Greater Boston rooters were all anxious to be in at the death, for even the one time King of Swat himself has acknowledged that he is soon to pass out of the picture.

PACK ROOFS AND BUILDINGS

Fans were massed upon adjoining roofs. Every building in the neighborhood had its quota of rooters who found themselves unable to get admission to the park. Neighboring hotels gave grudging points of vantage to those who were willing to risk life and limb for a last long look at the greatest hero the national game has ever produced. And for hours after the entrances had been closed, indeed even after the second game had been started, thousands lined the sidewalks of Jersey street or sat upon walls or in their machines hoping that some break might come that would permit them entrance to the stands and one farewell glimpse at the man whose name as a baseball idol has now become nearly a tradition.

Boston redskins patch. *(Collection of the author)*

Boston Redskins head coach Red Flaherty stands by while Ernie Pinckert models the new Redskins uniform in 1936. *(Courtesy of Bob Walsh)*

Wrestler Steve "Crusher" Casey was a top drawing card at nearly every Boston sporting venue from the Arena to Braves Field and Fenway Park. The Irish immigrant was also a skilled oarsman and later owned a bar in Boston. *(Courtesy of* The Boston Herald*)*

FOOD & LIQUORS

Meet Me At
CRUSHER CASEY'S
340 Massachusetts Ave.
BOSTON
Jim, Steve, Tom
CI. 7-8315

CLOSE COVER BEFORE STRIKING

Such homage was never paid to a baseball player before. And, very likely such homage will never be paid to one again. Sympathy as well as adulation moved the great assemblage for baseball can ill afford to part with a player of the Babe's caliber and thousands who have put him upon a pedestal are grieved to realize that time has at last taken its toll and the greatest homerun hero of two decades is shortly to yield the field to younger and equally ambitious rivals.

BABE IN TEARS AT GREAT TRIBUTE

That Ruth played the entire first game as well as the greater part of the second was his response to the temper of the fans for in these sad days the aging limbs no longer respond to the impulses and demands of his earlier career. That the tribute paid him by the great assemblage was thoroughly appreciated his teammates will aver, for after leaving the park late in the second contest when more than 40,000 fans rose to voice their sentiments in one great roar of applause and induced even the hard boiled war correspondents to join in the farewell salute, Babe went to the clubhouse and was found by the trainer and some of his closest local friends in tears. Still but a big boy with the heart of a child, and most impressionable of all, he broke down completely. "Tell all my friends I appreciate this sendoff," he said. "It's an occasion I'll never forget."

October 2, 1934 Jamaica Plain
High 13, Mechanical Arts 0
October 3, 1934 Boston English
13, South Boston High 0
October 3, 1934 High School of
Commerce 7, Brighton High 6
October 4, 1934 Roxbury
Memorial 0, South Boston
High 0
October 4, 1934 Boston College
High 0, Dorchester High 0

Red Sox rookie Bobby Doerr sees action at third base in this photo from 1937. *(Photograph by Leslie Jones, Courtesy of the Boston Public Library)*

Long before the light towers were installed, nighttime events were a Fenway staple as temporary kleig lights were brought in to illuminate this 1938 contest between the soon-to-be-defunct Boston Shamrocks and a squad of college All-Stars. *(Courtesy of The Sports Museum)*

OCTOBER 7, 1934

Redskins Fall to the Giants 16-13

A crowd of 17,033 watched the Redskins lose to the New York Giants led by former Michigan All-American quarterback Harry Newman who not only ran back the opening kickoff 93 yards for a touchdown but also booted a 30-yard first quarter field goal. He also dazzled the crowd with two additional field goals to lead the Giants to a come-from-behind win in the final eight minutes of play.

(Source: The Salt Lake City Tribune, page 11, October 8, 1934)

October 10, 1934 Brighton High 6, Roxbury Memorial High 0

October 10, 1934 South Boston High 22, Charlestown High 0

October 11, 1934 Jamaica Plain High 6, High School of Commerce 0

October 11, 1934 Boston College High 0, Boston Latin 0

October 12, 1934 Dorchester High 7, Mechanical Arts 6

OCTOBER 14, 1934

Redskins Whitewash Pittsburgh 39-0

The Redskins climbed to second place in the NFL Eastern Division behind the Giants after blasting the Pittsburgh Pirates before a crowd of 15,515 at Fenway Park.

(Source: Lowell Sun, page 13, October 15, 1934)

October 16, 1934 South Boston High 7, Roxbury Memorial 6

October 16, 1934 Jamaica Plain High 14, Charlestown High 0

October 17, 1934 Boston Latin 6, Mechanical Arts 0

October 18, 1934 East Boston High 19, Brighton High 6

OCTOBER 21, 1934

Cliff Battles Leads Redskins to a 6-0 Win

The Philadelphia Eagles fell victim to a third-quarter touchdown by Redskin all-purpose back Cliff Battles who won the game before a crowd of 10,344 at Fenway Park. The score could have been far more lopsided as two sure Boston touchdowns were called back earlier in the game due to a backfield illegal motion call and a forward lateral to Battles.

October 24, 1934 Hyde Park High 12, South Boston High 0

October 25, 1934 Brighton High 7, Boston Trade 0

October 25, 1934 East Boston High 13, Charlestown 0

October 26, 1934 Boston English 19, Boston College High 0

October 26, 1934 High School of Commerce 6, Mechanical Arts 0

OCTOBER 28, 1934

Chicago Cards Drop Game To Boston 9-0

Former Nebraska star Steve Hokuf not only threw the game's sole touchdown pass but he also kicked the game's only field goal to lead the Redskins to a 9-0 victory before a crowd of 10,000 at frigid Fenway Park. The win kept Boston in second place in the NFL East, a full game behind New York.

October 30, 1934 East Boston
High 6, Jamaica Plain High 0
October 31, 1934 South Boston
High 6, Brighton High 0
November 1, 1934 High School of
Commerce 19, Boston College
High 6
November 2, 1934 Boston English
19, Dorchester High 0

NOVEMBER 4, 1934

Packers Down Boston 10-0 in Hard Rain

Despite a driving rain that pounded the Fenway gridiron a crowd of 18,000 watched their Redskins fall to Green Bay in a sloppy contest hampered by the slippery conditions. Green Bay ace quarterback Arnold "Flash" Herber only completed two of his eight pass attempts, which included a 15-yard touchdown toss to end Lavern Dilweg. The Packer touchdown followed a remarkable 41-yard Green Bay field goal by Clark Hinkle that cleared the cross bar with 10 yards to spare.

Malden Massachusetts native Charlie O'Rourke makes a long gain for Boston College in their 14-0 win over Indiana at Fenway on November 5, 1938. *(Courtesy of Charlie O'Rourke)*

November 5, 1934 South Boston
High 19, Mechanical Arts 2
November 7, 1934 Boston Latin 7,
High School of Commerce 6
November 8, 1934 Hyde Park
High 19, Brighton High 7
November 9, 1934 Boston Trade
19, Charlestown High 0

NOVEMBER 11, 1934

Bears Slam Redskins 21-0

An Armistice Day crowd of 26,000 watched their Boston Redskins fall to Bronco Nagurski and the first place Chicago Bears at Fenway Park by a score of 21-0. It marked the ninth consecutive victory for George Halas's powerhouse squad.

(Source: Charleston (W. VA) Gazette, November 12, 1934)

November 13, 1934 Boston
English 9, Mechanical Arts 0
November 14, 1934 Boston Latin

19, Dorchester High 0
November 14, 1934 Brighton High
18, Charlestown 0
November 15, 1934 High School of
Commerce 19, Boston Trade 0
November 16, 1934 Hyde Park
High 6, East Boston High 0
November 20, 1934 Jamaica Plain
High 0, Brighton High 0
November 21, 1934 Boston Latin
24, Boston Trade 6
November 22, 1934 Boston
English 15, High School of
Commerce 6
November 23, 1934 Charlestown
High 7, Roxbury Memorial 6
November 26, 1934 Jamaica Plan
High 6, Hyde Park High 0
November 27, 1934 East Boston
High 6, South Boston High 0
November 27, 1934 Boston Trade
0, Mechanical Arts 0
November 28, 1934 Boston
College High 6, Roxbury
Memorial 0
November 29, 1934 Boston Latin
13, Boston English 12

DECEMBER 2, 1934

Boston Drubs Brooklyn Dodgers 13-3

A crowd of 13,000 saw the Redskins close out their successful 1934 season with a 13-3 drubbing of the Brooklyn Dodgers at Fenway Park.

May 12, 1935 War Memorial Service

June 12, 1935 Lowell High 2, Mission High of Roxbury 1

June 12, 1935 St. Mary's of Milford 8, Framingham 7

June 13, 1935 Somerville High 7, St. Joseph's of Pittsfield 6

June 13, 1935 Holyoke 6, Taunton 3

June 14, 1935 Lowell High 9, St. Mary's of Milford 8

June 14, 1935 Somerville High 10, Holyoke 4

June 15, 1935 Somerville High 20, Lowell High 8

June 19, 1935 House Republicans 10, House Democrats 6 (Six Innings)

JUNE 27, 1935

O'Mahoney Feared Foe Only Twice

LONDOS' TOE HOLDS HURT – PHONES HIS FATHER

STRONGEST MAN HE EVER HAS FACED, SAYS LONDOS

By Dan O'mahoney
Written Exclusively for Boston Post

In his dressing room following the bout, Londos declared O'Mahoney is the strongest man he has ever met. "I knew after the first five minutes I would have to be lucky to win," Jimmy said. "That kid is green, but with his strength I believe he can beat any man in the world. And when I took the bout in New York people told me I had nothing to fear! I wish I knew as much before I signed as I do now, and this bout would never have taken place tonight."

I hardly know what to say. I have just called my father on long distance telephone in Ballydehob, Ireland, and you should have heard the cheering when I told him I had beaten Jim Londos, whom my father regarded as the world's greatest wrestler. The whole village must have been assembled at the farm judging by the noise that came over the phone.

TOE HOLDS PAINFUL

Only twice did I fear Londos and that was on occasions when he had toe holds on me. They were the most painful I have ever felt and I was careful he didn't get the hold a third time. He might have crippled me.

His punches did not hurt a bit and that is the reason I did not punch back early in the bout. In fact, I don't remember him hitting me at all until just before I won the fall. Then I caught one on the lip and gave a few back.

My tooth was loosened by the final hit he gave me. It was a stiff right directly in the mouth and it was then that I hit him the first real hard one I swung all night. Immediately, I saw that it dazed him and I followed it up. Then it was easy, after throwing him over with headlocks two or three times and using the body scissors. I don't know which weakened him most, the punches or the scissors.

Londos is really a great wrestler, but he is not big enough. I am indeed happy to have beaten him and now I want to get at Ed George. I think I can win the wrestling title outright, and then a long vacation in Ireland.

25,000 See Danno Topple Londos

TAKES LONE FALL AFTER ONE HOUR

By S.J. Mahoney

Dan O'Mahoney, Irish heavy-weight champion, disposed of the chief obstacle in his path to the world's wrestling title last night before 25,000 fans at the Crosscup-Pichon show at Fenway Park, beating Jim Londos in a match that ended in one hour, 16 minutes and 50 seconds, being decided by one fall.

Danno, who has shot to the top of the mat heap in a very short period after coming out of the Irish Free State army, brought the bout to a conclusion with a flying body scissors, indicating that he has been a student of Farmer George McLeod's winning system.

As Referee Ted Tonneman slapped him on the back after determining Londos' shoulders were pinned securely to the canvas, admirers of Danno broke loose with cheers that made the welkin ring for several minutes.

Londos, who is regarded as champion of the world only in New York, Pennsylvania and Illinois, was dazed by the result. He was speechless when he regained his feet.

It was Danno's 55th victory in a row since he came to this country in December, 1934, and proved beyond all doubt that he is one of the greatest wrestlers in the game's history.

Vicious headlocks were Londos' mainstays until Danno pulled his coup and had wrestled the giant Irishman, who weighed 222 pounds to Jimmy's 205, evenly. Twice Londos tossed Danno heavily with body slams but Danno came up fast off the mat.

Because of the threatening weather, which cleared after a light shower, the main bout was started at 9:13.

July 9, 1935 New York Policemen & Firemen 3, Boston Policemen & Firemen 2 (Three Innings – called due to rain)

July 9, 1935 Boston Department of Public Welfare Athletic and Musical Carnival

September 11, 1935 Dan O'Mahoney Pins Ed Don George (Wrestling)

SEPTEMBER 22, 1935

47,000 See Red Sox Lose Twinbill to Yankees, 6-4, 9-0

September 23, 1935 Boston Baseball Writers 16, Fenway Park Front Office 3 (Three Innings)

When Red Sox rookie Ted Williams was told that he should take the time to watch player/manager Joe Cronin and slugger Jimmie Foxx hit, he replied, "They ought to see me hit." *(Courtesy of The National Baseball Hall of Fame)*

SEPTEMBER 29, 1935

25,000 Witness Redskin Win

Led by their new coach, former Harvard star Eddie Casey, the Boston Redskins beat the Brooklyn Dodgers by a score of 7-3 in their home opener at Fenway Park. Their win was sparked by a 65-yard drive capped by Bill Shepard's touchdown pass to Flavio Tosi. The game was saved by Redskins star Cliff Battles who made a game-saving tackle of Bull Karcis after the Brooklyn linebacker had picked off a Redskin pass and made it to the Boston 1-yard line.

OCTOBER 6, 1935

Giants Use Aerials to Down Boston 20-12

Roughly 8,000 fans braved the cold and rain to watch their Redskins fall to a skilled New York Giant aerial attack. Long passes by Tony Sarausky and Ed Donowski set up all of the Giant touchdowns. All in all Giant passers completed six of eight passes for 77 total yards while the Redskins just couldn't connect in the inclement conditions while connecting on only one of eight passes.

OCTOBER 13, 1935

Lions Roar in 17-7 Victory Over Boston

Potsy Clark's Detroit Lions won a hard fought game against the Redskins before 20,000 at Fenway Park on a beautiful fall afternoon. The game was close until the third quarter when Roy Gutowsky of the Lions caught a touchdown pass to increase the Lions lead to 10-0. After Boston cut the lead to three after scoring on a Pug Renter pass to Charlie Malone the Lions sealed their victory with an Ernie Caddell zigzag touchdown run.

October 16, 1935 Dorchester High 13, Mechanic Arts 7

October 16, 1935 Charlestown High 0, Jamaica Plain High 0

October 17, 1935 Boston Latin 19, Roxbury Memorial High School 0

October 17, 1935 East Boston High 7, Brighton High 0

October 18, 1935 Hyde Park High 0, South Boston High 0

October 18, 1935 High School of Commerce 8, Boston Trade 0

October 23, 1935 Roxbury Memorial 13, Brighton High 6

October 23, 1935 South Boston High 10, Charlestown 6

October 24, 1935 High School of Commerce 7, Mechanic Arts 0

October 24, 1935 Dorchester High 12, Boston Trade 0

October 29, 1935 Roxbury Memorial 6, Boston Trade 0

October 29, 1935 South Boston High 14, Brighton High 0

NOVEMBER 3, 1935

Boston Redskins Drop Sixth Game in A Row

The smallest crowd of the Redskins season (9,000) saw the Boston team drop its sixth consecutive game by a score of 7-6 to the Philadelphia Eagles. Former Western Maryland star back Bill Sheperd sent Boston into the lead after scoring on a 42-yard rush off his right tackle, but the Eagles roared back in the second quarter with a touchdown and game-winning extra point by Hank Reese.

November 9, 1935 Rutgers 12, Boston University 6

NOVEMBER 10, 1935

Chicago Bears Hand Boston Seventh Loss

The mighty Chicago Bears proved too much for the Redskins as the perennial NFL powerhouse rolled over the Redskins by a score of 30-14 before 16,000 at Fenway Park.

Chicago took a commanding 27-7 lead by halftime and the Redskins could only manage a last-minute touchdown by Charlie Malone in the second half.

NOVEMBER 24, 1935

Boston Redskins Suffer Eighth Straight Defeat

A shivering crowd of only 5,000 trekked to Fenway Park to see the Chicago Cardinals beat the redskins by a score of 6-0. The field was so slippery and muddy that neither team could muster much of an attack. The Cardinal points came by way of two field goals by former Washington University end, Bill Smith.

DECEMBER 1, 1935

Belated Boston Rally Beats Pittsburgh

A hearty crowd of 5,000 die-hard Redskins fans bundled up at Fenway Park and endured a snowstorm to watch their boys engineer a brilliant fourth quarter rally to beat the Pittsburgh Pirates in their final home game. The Redskins, whose only previous victory came in their season opener in September, waited until the final five minutes of the fourth-quarter to secure victory.

Downing a Pittsburgh punt on their 15 the Redskins surged upfield on three carries by Jim Musick, Ernie Pinckert, and Pug Rentner before Musick ran it in from the 4 and also kicked the extra point. Following the kickoff Turk Edwards recovered a fumble and within a minute Rentner scored on a 19-yard run.

APRIL 26, 1936

Nine Arrested as Police Smash At Gambling at Fenway Park Games

Nine bookmakers were arrested yesterday as police sought to smash baseball gambling with a surprise raid during the game at Fenway Park.

Led in person by Capt. Francis M. Tiernan, newly appointed commander at Station 16, Back Bay, the raid was the biggest ever staged in a Boston ball park and the first in three years.

The raiders, including Sergt. William H. Long, Sergt. Francis I. Mullen, Special Officer Roy Bates and three squads of plain-clothes men posted themselves in various sections of the righ-hand bleachers, focal point of this type of gambling, before game time. There they watched the alleged betting commissioners begin to work.

ODDS OFFERED

The bookies began by offering odds, first of 75 to 100, that the New York Yankees would not score, and various other bets on the innings and outcome of the game.

When the Boston Red Sox scored six runs in the first inning, the odds against the Yankees scoring jumped to 175 to 300. Then New York broke the game wide open by scoring seven runs in the second inning.

As the gamblers began to pay off openly, the raiding squad went into action, but their task was made difficult as the bookies fled among spectators and tried to secrete themselves.

The raiders followed, stumbling over spectators and greeted by cheers and boos. Other spectators thought a small riot had broken out and converged on the two or three knots of struggling men. The majority of the 12,000 fans, in the distant grandstand, forgot the ball game in an attempt to determine that cause of the disturbance.

Cornering the leaders of the betting ring, the police arrested nine. At least six escaped in the crowd, it is believed.

Taken to the Back Bay station, the men all gave names which the raiders said were fictitious. They were held for illegal registration of bets and will be arraigned in Roxbury court today.

The raiders said a large amount of money was in evidence during the payoff and that more than $5000 in cash was found on the nine prisoners. The betting was done, the raiders said, by a deaf and dumb system of showing fingers, to indicate the wagers.

The police said the last raid of this nature was conducted about three years ago at Braves Field, where five men were arrested.

Persistent complaint, police said, that gamblers were making a hangout of the ball parks and were openly soliciting bets brought the squad to action.

May 17, 1936 War Memorial Service

June 16, 1936 Somerville High 10, Milford High 2

June 16, 1936 Lowell High 6, Watertown High 2

June 17, 1936 Somerville High 9, Lowell High 8

June 20, 1936 Templeton High 2, Somerville High 1 (MA State Title Game)

June 25, 1936 Jack Sharkey Defeats Phil Brubaker in 10-Round Match (Boxing)

July 27, 1936 Cottage Court (Waltham) 6, Dorrance A. C. (Worcester) 1

July 27, 1936 Clarmac A. A. (Franklin) 5, Canton A. A. 2

July 28, 1936 Miller Oil (Waltham) 12, Newton Independents 5

July 28, 1936 Baysides (Hull) 11, Smart Oil (Waltham) 6

July 29, 1936 Firestones (New Bedford) 5, Boston All-Stars 2 (Eight Innings)

July 29, 1936 Hall All-Stars (Somerville) 2, Casey Paper

A father and his daughters take in a game in the old chairs that formed the original box seating at Fenway Park. *(Photograph by Leslie Jones, Courtesy of the Boston Public Library)*

Company (Haverhill) 2 (Tie)

July 30, 1936 Currans Express (Milford) 15, St. Therese Baseball Club (Everett) 0

July 30, 1936 Norwood Press 10, Muldoons (Brighton) 5

OCTOBER 4, 1936

Tuffy Leemans' Score Gives Giants Victory Over Redskins

A 20 yard touchdown run by Tuffy Leemans gave the New York Giants a 7-0 win in the Boston Redskins home opener before 15.000 at Fenway Park. The Boston attack was limited almost solely to runs by All-Pro back Cliff Battles.

The game was marred by a torrent of booing as fans jeered the announcement of future games due to the fact that the price of reserved grandstand tickets had been raised and the price of unreserved seats had been raised to the level of last season's reserved seating.

This incident marked the beginning of the end for the Redskins in Boston as owner George Preston Marshall had already started scouting for a new city for his team.

OCTOBER 11, 1936

Boston Shamrocks Beat Brooklyn Tigers 10-6

Former Providence College star and future American League umpire Hank Soar led the Shamrocks to the fourth straight victory over the Brooklyn Tigers at Fenway Park. Soar connected on a long touchdown pass to Don Elser and also made both the extra point and a 42-yard field goal to seal the win.

OCTOBER 12, 1936

Temple Owls Beat BC Eagles 14-0

The Temple Owls, led by legendary head coach Glenn "Pop" Warner spun their wingback magic and gained 380 yards of total offense to just 93 for Gil Dobie's overmatched Eagles and beat the home team before 25,000 at Fenway Park.

Source: Reno Evening Gazette. Page 13, October 13, 1936

October 17, 1936 Boston University 6, Washington University 0

OCTOBER 18, 1936

Only 4,000 See Redskins Beat Philadelphia 17-7

A week following a vocal fan protest at the raising of ticket prices, a meager crowd of only 4,000 ventured to Fenway Park to see the Redskins beat the Philadelphia Eagles by a score of 17-7. Touchdowns by former Holy Cross star Eddie Britt and Charley Malone following a Riley Smith field goal accounted for the Boston scoring.

Source: Fitchburg Sentinel, page 8, October 19, 1936

The Oshkosh Northwestern, page 16, October 19, 1936

OCTOBER 31, 1936

Boston College Tie Michigan State 13-13 Before 10,000 at Fenway

NOVEMBER 1, 1936

Redskins Topple Chicago Cardinals 13 to 10

Hall of Fame back Cliff Battles both passed and ran for touchdowns as the Redskins entertained 7,000 fans at Fenway Park and maintained their lead in the NFL Eastern Division.

Source: The Portsmouth (Ohio) Times, November 2, 1936

NOVEMBER 7, 1936

12,000 SEE BOSTON COLLEGE BEAT NORTH CAROLINA STATE 7-3 AT FENWAY

NOVEMBER 8, 1936

Packers' Aerial Circus Trips Up Redskins 7 to 3

Packer all-time great wide receiver Don Hutson hauled in a 20-yard touchdown pass from Arnold Herber to climax a 55-yard march and send the Redskins to defeat before a crowd of 10,000 at Fenway Park. The game was a preview of the NFL championship game which should have been played at Fenway Park but was instead moved to the Polo Grounds in a fit of pique by Redskins owner George Preston Marshall.

Source: The Oshkosh Northwestern, page 12, November 9, 1936

NOVEMBER 15, 1936

Nagurski and Bears Beat Boston 26-0

One observer likened Chicago Bears back Bronco Nagurski to a wild steer as Nagurski and the Chicago Bears ran roughshod over the Boston Redskins before 12,000 fans at Fenway Park. Only twice during the game did the Redskins manage to make it over midfield as the Bears secured a win that tied them with the Packers for the lead in the NFL Western Division.

Source: The Titusville (PA) Herald, page 6, November 16, 1936

NOVEMBER 22, 1936

Redskins Topple Brooklyn By a Score of 39 to 6

It is a safe guess that few of the 4,200 fans in attendance at Fenway Park for the final regular-season home game of the 1936 Boston Redskins campaign realized they were attending the last game in team history. Despite both their lopsided win over the Brooklyn and clinching of the NFL eastern Division crown the team would move its home NFL title game to the Polo Grounds in New York and later move the entire franchise to Washington DC.

Source: The Portsmouth (Ohio) Times, page 11, November 23, 1936

NOVEMBER 28, 1936

Boston College Rallies to Beat Holy Cross 13-12 In The Snow Before 28,000 at Fenway

In a classic match-up played in a blinding snowstorm, Boston College tipped rival Holy Cross in a game that saw the Eagles outrush their opponents 223 yards to 68 and make 14 first downs to the Crusaders 5. Boston College overcame a 12-0 first-quarter deficit to narrow the margin to 5 points at halftime. Eagle right halfback Fella Gintoff rushed for a touchdown early in the fourth quarter to clinch the 34th meeting of the traditional rivals.

Source: Syracuse Herald, page 3-B, November 29, 1936

NOVEMBER 29, 1936

Redskins Near East Title, Beat Pittsburgh 30-0

The final Redskins game at Fenway Park was a bittersweet contest as Ray Flaherty's men inched closer to clinching a spot in the NFL championship game with their thumping win over the Pittsburgh Pirates by a score of 30-0. However, only 4,000 braved the unseasonably bitter cold weather to attend what would be the last NFL game in Boston until the arrival of the Boston Yanks in 1944. Redskins owner George Preston Marshall not only moved the team to Washington but also moved what would have been the first and only NFL championship game to be played at Fenway Park to the Polo Grounds in New York where his team lost to the Packers by a score of 21-6

Source: Wisconsin State Journal, November 30, 1936

June 6, 1937 Mayo F.C. 17, Massachusetts All-Stars 8 (Gaelic Football)
June 9, 1937 Watertown High 8, Belmont High 0
June 9, **1937** Lynn English 3, Medford High 1
June 10, 1937 Lynn English 4, Watertown High 3 (14 Innings)
June 10, 1937 Lowell High 12, Braintree High 2
June 11, 1937 Lynn English 12, Lowell High 3

JUNE 17, 1937

Al McCoy Defeats Natie Brown (Boxing)

June 29, 1937 Steve Casey Tosses Ed Don George (Wrestling)
July 13, 1937 Natie Brown Beats Tony Shucco (Boxing)

JULY 20, 1937

"Crusher" Casey Wins Over Danno

GAINS ONLY FALL IN 90-MINUTE BATTLE ON MAT AT FENWAY PARK TO COP IRISH MAT TITLE

BY Doc Almy

Ireland has an honest-to-goodness heavyweight mat champion in Steve Casey of Sneem, County Kerry – a wearer of the mantle whose ascent to the throne is not to be disputed.

He was crowned last night at Fenway Park, the result of a victory over Danno O'Mahoney, one-time world's champion – a fellow Irishman and rival for several seasons.

A CLEANCUT WIN

It was a cleancut victory but, due to the 90-minute time limit, but one fall was scored. Casey "copping" that in 60 min., 56 sec., when Danno, missing with his famed whip, was caught with a flying body scissors and brought to grass for the toss. And, as affairs turned out— the loss of all claims to the crown of Erin.

In Steve's winning of the title, there was a lot of action – clean, straightforward wrestling – grim tussling between two closely-matched gladiators with no horse-play and very little of the spectacular in there. From the fact that the ex-fisherman from Sneem was able to register but one fall, it may be gained that Danno, though whipped, was no cinch. Of the pair, the ex-champion was the better grappler, but Casey, though several pounds the lighter man, had the

strength to repeatedly counter and break the holds clapped onto him.

About 8,000 fans, close to the largest gather about a Boston mat thus far this season, witnessed the fray, also the string of attractive preliminary contests underneath

August 6, 1937 Fenway Park Clubhouse Boys 3, Earache Alley unit of the Boston Baseball Writers 2

OCTOBER 12, 1937

Pop Warner Coaches 400th Game at Fenway Park vs Boston College

In a traditional Columbus Day game at Fenway the Temple Owls and Boston College slugged it out for a scoreless tie before 25,000. The Eagles should have won the game as early in the fourth quarter they failed to score a touchdown on four tries from the Owls 5-yard line.

Source: Panama City (FL) News-Herald, page 3, October 13, 1937

OCTOBER 13, 1937

Los Angeles Bulldogs Top Boston Shamrocks . 14-0

In a rare night game at Fenway Park (temporary lighting had to be brought to the park) the Boston Shamrocks finally played their

Tom Yawkey's newly renovated Fenway Park became the venue of choice for most area fans who flocked to see such stars as Lefty Grove, Jimmie Foxx, Joe Cronin, and young phenom Ted Williams. (*Courtesy of the Boston Public Library*)

season's home opener on an evening they were assured was free of competition from the World Series or college football. Members of the media speculated the Shamrocks night game was nothing less than a referendum on whether Boston could support pro football in the wake of the Redskin's recent departure.

Source: Lowell Sun, page 17, October 13, 1937

October 16, 1937 Holy Cross 7, University of Georgia 6
October 17, 1937 Rochester Tigers 6, Boston Shamrocks 0
October 23, 1937 Western Reserve 7, Boston University 0

OCTOBER 23, 1937

7,500 See Detroit Pound Boston College 14-0 at Fenway

OCTOBER 24, 1937

Larry Kelley Fails to Play for The Shamrocks

HINT YALE ALUMNI OPPOSED

A crowd of 7,500 came to Fenway Park expecting to see former Yale Heisman Trophy winner Larry Kelley play his first professional game for the Boston Shamrocks but instead witnessed their hero in street clothes on the sidelines. Kelley reportedly had the flu but news accounts also had the Yale icon being pressured by influential alumni to not enter the professional ranks. On leave from his job as a teacher and coach at The Peddie School in Highstown, NJ, Kelley remarked, "Since I signed contract there has been quite a fuss at school and from Yale alumni."

Apart from posing for photos on the Fenway gridiron this brief appearance was as close as Kelley got to pro football as he declined repeated appeals from the Shamrocks to play for them.

Aside from the distraction of Kelley's appearance, the Shamrocks beat the Pittsburgh Americans by a score of 27-7.

November 7, 1937 Boston Shamrocks 50, Collegiate All-Stars 0
November 11, 1937 Villanova 12, Boston University 0

NOVEMBER 13, 1937

Only 3,500 See Boston College Beat Kentucky By a Score of 13-0 at Fenway

November 20, 1937 Boston University 13, Boston College 13 (Football)

The January 1934 Fenway Park fire that set back construction during one of the worst winters in Boston history. *(Photograph by Leslie Jones, Courtesy of the Boston Public Library)*

NOVEMBER 27, 1937

35,000 See Number 17 Ranked Holy Cross Beats Boston College By a Score of 20-0 at Fenway

May 10, 1938 Out-of-Town Firemen vs. Harvard Varsity Team Postponed

July 26, 1938 Steve Casey Retains Championship over Richard Shikat (Wrestling)

August 1, 1938 Mayor's Field Day Benefit for Special Welfare Fund

August 1, 1938 West Division/ Police Department 4, East Division/Police Department 3 (Three Innings)

August 1, 1938 Boston Fire Department 5, Boston Police Department 2 (Three Innings)

August 1, 1938 Boston City Hall Team 7, State House Team 3 (Three Innings)

September 7, 1938 Joe Cronin Day at Fenway Park

September 14, 1938 College All-Stars 7, Boston Shamrocks 6 (Football)

September 26, 1938 Pittsburgh Pirates 16, Boston Shamrocks 6 (Football)

October 8, 1938 Boston University 19, St. Lawrence University 14 (Football)

OCTOBER 12, 1938

20,000 See Boston College Beat Detroit by a Score of 9- 6 at Fenway

October 15, 1938 Boston University 25, Upsala College 0 (Football)

OCTOBER 29, 1938

EAGLES DOWN GATORS 33-0 BEFORE 7,732 AT FENWAY

NOVEMBER 5, 1938

25,000 SEE BOSTON COLLEGE DOWN INDIANA BY A SCORE OF 14-0

NOVEMBER 11, 1938

BOSTON COLLEGE BEATS BOSTON UNIVERSITY 21-14 BEFORE 15,000 AT FENWAY

November 19, 1938 Villanova 39, Boston University 6 (Football)

NOVEMBER 26, 1938

36,000 SEE 11TH RANKED HOLY CROSS BEAT BC 29-7 AT FENWAY

APRIL 1939

Ted Williams Debut

Ted Williams makes his Fenway Park debut and only manages a single in four trips to the plate. Two days later, he gave fans a glimpse of his genius as he went 4-for-5 against the Athletics, socking a homer, a double, and two singles. The home run was a tape-measure 400' shot that landed in a section of the park reached by only Babe Ruth, Hal Trosky, Bill Dickey, Lou Gehrig, and Charlie Gehringer.

June 4, 1939 War Memorial Service
June 7, 1939 Medford High 3, Maynard High 0
June 7, 1939 Watertown High 7, Attleboro High 0
June 8, 1939 Lynn Classical 9, Somerville High 8 (10 Innings)
June 8, 1939 Norwood High 13, St. Clement 0
June 9, 1939 Watertown High 3, Medford High 1
June 9, 1939 Norwood High 5, Lynn Classical 3
June 10, 1939 Norwood High 7, Watertown High 2
July 12, 1939 National League Old-Timers 8, American League Old-Timers 4
July 12, 1939 Lowell Thomas's Nine of Old men 8, Johnny Lane's Merry Go Rounders 2
August 1, 1939 Boston Park Department Baseball Field Day
September 11, 1939 Washington Redskins 30, Eastern College All-Stars 27 (Football)
October 7, 1939 Boston University 19, Franklin & Marshall 7 (Football)

OCTOBER 12, 1939

FLORIDA EDGES BOSTON COLLEGE 7-0 BEFORE 18,000 AT FENWAY

OCTOBER 21, 1939

BOSTON COLLEGE 19 TEMPLE 0 (ATT 13,300)

NOVEMBER 4, 1939

BOSTON COLLEGE 13 AUBURN 7 (ATT 14,000)

November 11, 1939 St. Anselm 39, Catholic University 13 (Football)

NOVEMBER 25, 1939

BOSTON COLLEGE 38 KANSAS STATE 7 (ATT 11,000)

DECEMBER 2, 1939

BOSTON COLLEGE UPSETS NUMBER 10 HOLY CROSS BY A SCORE OF 14-0 BEFORE 40,432 AT FENWAY

Ted Williams poses for fans in 1942. For a full generation, Williams was both the biggest gate attraction and resident batter/artiste. *(Photograph by Fay Ruby)*

CHAPTER FOUR

Life During Wartime

"Man, what a pitcher's graveyard."

—SATCHEL PAIGE ON FIRST SEEING FENWAY PARK

The forties at Fenway began with a collegiate football clash of undefeated titans, Georgetown and Boston College, that legendary sportswriter Grantland Rice called the greatest game he'd ever witnessed and ended with the desperately heartbreaking conclusion of the epic 1949 pennant race between the Yankees and Red Sox. In between the park hosted yet another pro football team with the improbable name of the Yanks; dozens of collegiate football games featuring Boston College, Dartmouth, Notre Dame, and Boston University; a World Series; an All-Star Game; the first playoff game in American League history; boxing; several war-related charity events; an annual military mass/memorial ceremony; FDR's final campaign speech; and a tryout in April 1945 which included Negro League star Jackie Robinson whose aftermath would haunt the team for decades.

In 1940 Tom Yawkey rewarded his young right, and soon to be left fielder Ted Williams with an unprecedented gift of architecture as the club built their bullpens in a section of the bleachers perfectly suited for the young slugger's tape-measure blasts. This new addition was soon dubbed, "Williamsburg." Lights were added to the park in 1947, and television soon brought the magic of Fenway into homes throughout New England.

How Williamsburg Will Look Next Season

"BOY, WON'T I BE GLAD TO SEE THOSE SHORTER FENCES"—WILLIAMS

Above is a diagram of Fenway Park as it will look in 1940 and as announced by the Red Sox yesterday in confirming a Globe exclusive of seven weeks ago. The blackened spots are the present seats, with the shaded areas the positions where extra box seats and new bullpen will be constructed. The foul line now extends to the 332-foot mark and this will be shortened to 302 feet. The bleacher starts in right field, 402 feet from home plate and the building of the new bullpen there will reduce the home-run range at that point to 380 feet. In center is Teddy Williams, whose batting and home-run marks are expected to soar with the new layout.

The new bleacher and seating configuration added following the 1939 season was soon dubbed Williamsburg as it favored the left-hand power stroke of the Red Sox newest superstar. *(Courtesy of The Sports Museum)*

Ted Williams pitched two innings against the Tigers on August 24, 1940. The former minor-league pitcher allowed just one run on three hits. *(Collection of the author)*

May 19, 1940 War Memorial
Service

June 15, 1940 Belmont High 6,
Turners Falls High 4

August 17, 1940 Boston Park
Department Baseball Field Day

AUGUST 24, 1940

Teddy Ballgame Takes the Mound in 12-1 Tiger Rout

Ted Williams trotted in from left field to face the Detroit Tigers for the last two innings of the Red Sox 12-1 loss to the Tigers at Fenway Park. Pitcher Jim Bagby, Jr. took Ted's place in left field as the slugger allowed one run on three hits. He also struck out future teammate, first baseman Rudy York.

September 10, 1940 Washington
Redskins 35, Eastern All-Star

Collegians 12

October 2, 1940 Columbus Bullies
17, Boston Bears 0

October 6, 1940 Boston Bears 29,
Cincinnati Bengals 7

OCTOBER 12, 1940

Boston College Beats Temple 33-20

In a traditional Columbus Day game 30,000 packed Fenway Park to watch Boston College top the Temple Owls in an entertaining free-scoring melee.

Source: The Charleston (SC) Gazette, page 18, October 13, 1940

OCTOBER 19, 1940

Boston College Trounces Idaho

Boston College maintained its un-beaten status as they continued their

march towards a New Year's Day bowl game with a 60-0 thrashing of Idaho before a crowd of 8,000 at Fenway Park. Boston College head coach Frank Leahy sent in his reserves after his starters had fash-ioned a two-touchdown lead mid-way through the first quarter. The game was so lopsided that Idaho didn't cross the 50-yard line until Ray Davis ran a BC punt back for a 70-yard gain in the third quar-ter. Davis' run was nullified when a teammate fumbled on the Eagles 15 and Idaho never gained any traction against their intersectional rivals.

Source: Nevada State Journal, Reno, page 19, October 20, 1940

October 20, 1940 Boston Bears
20, Buffalo Indians 0

October 27, 1940 Milwaukee
Chiefs 14, Boston Bears 0

NOVEMBER 9, 1940

BOSTON COLLEGE BEATS BOSTON UNIVERSITY BY A SCORE OF 21-0 BEFORE 15,000 AT FENWAY

NOVEMBER 16, 1940

Perfect Football Weather Predicted

TAKE IT FROM THE WEATHER MAN, THIS AFTERNOON IS GOING TO BE FINE FOR FOOTBALL, ESPECIALLY SO FOR THE PLAYERS IF NOT THE SPECTATORS

THERE WILL BE CLOUDINESS, ACCORDING TO THE FORECAST, AND THE AIR WILL BE SLIGHTLY COLDER. WINDS WILL BE GENTLE, ACCORDING

TO THE WEATHER MAN, AND THERE WILL BE NO RAIN.

By Gerry Hern

New England's maddest football fiesta in many a year will get under way this afternoon at 2 o'clock at Fenway Park when the Georgetown University Hoyas throw their undefeated record of 23 games into the same ring with the Boston College Eagles, who haven't tasted defeat since last New Year's Day. Seated around the gridiron will be the largest gathering of football followers that have ever tested the concrete retaining walls of the park. A post-season "Bowl bid" is going to the winning team.

In a form of hysteria that has been almost unknown locally in recent years the general public has stated a weird scramble for every available ticket for this mighty clash between two of the famed Jesuit colleges in the nation. Speculators were asking $12 and $14 a pair for tickets last night and if the weather stays fair through the early morning today that price will move up. The gathering will be something more than 41,000 people.

Based on the same mysterious factors that influence all betting, the price professional book-makers were offering on Newspaper Row at midnight was 100 to 65, which is 10 to 6 ½ in simpler mathematics. Boston College is favored over the mighty Georgtown eleven which has gone undefeated since the middle of the 1937 season but the Blue and Gray operatives from Washington, D.C., are confident that nothing can keep them from the Sugar Bowl or the Rose Bowl.

The program from the game which sports writer Grantland Rice called the greatest he'd ever witnessed. *(Courtesy of Wes Dow)*

White Sox manager Jimmy Dykes made use of a shift against Ted Williams five years before Indians player/manager Lou Boudreau employed the same tactic. Williams is shown batting for the first time against Dykes' shift. He stroked a double to left. *(Courtesy of The Brearley Collection)*

B.C. Stages Motorcade Grid Rally

NOISY DEMONSTRATION BY STUDENTS IN DOWNTOWN

Rampant Boston College students, rallying for victory on the eve of the gridiron struggle between the Maroon and Gold and the visiting undefeated Georgetown team, frolicked in a noisy motorcade from the Newton institution into downtown Boston, tying up traffic and cavorting with merriment through the streets.

Supreme in their confidence that the Eagles would humble the Hoyas today in the "game of the year," the young men, carrying banners proclaiming the invincibility of their alma mater's football team, ended the session by holding an ear-splitting cheering practice at the Parkman Bandstand on the Common.

Nearly 200 cars, gayly bedecked with signs and tin cans that dragged along the road surface, formed the motorcade down Commonwealth avenue to the heart of the city. Without any formal notice, the boys abandoned the machines at Arlington and Beacon streets.

So engrossed were they with the spirit of the evening, they forgot all traffic regulations and, as a result, along the intersection there was unrestrained double and triple parking. This created a traffic snarl that had police busy for nearly an hour. The police, mindful that boys would be boys on the eve of the crucial game, took the law-breaking with good-natured shrugs.

PLENTY OF NOISE

For a time, as the 500 or so students, many of whom had their girlfriends along for the occasion to make up a co-ed delegation, formed a parade, it seemed like a combination of New Year's Eve and the Fourth of July. There were horns and noise makers galore, which, coupled with the bang of firecrackers, echoed in the streets.

Singing, cheering and yelling, they marched along Arlington street and into Park square. At intersections, they paused to give long and lusty college yells that startled and entertained passersby. As they strode along Washington street, near Boylston, a parked "baby" car caught the attention of a score or more.

With a heave-ho, they gave the tiny machine a lift that finally ended with the machine coming to a rest on the sidewalk, there to await the return of a surprised owner. Swinging around to Winter street, they then swarmed to the bandstand, where cheers again resounded in the glare of red torchlights.

LEFTY GROVE SEES VICTORY OF EAGLES

Lefty Grove, the great lefthanded pitcher of the Boston Red Sox, was an interested spectator at yesterday's Boston College–Georgetown game. Lefty came to Boston especially to see yesterday's great football game, and though a resident of Lanaconing, Md., he was rooting for the Boston College Eagles.

FENWAY PARK GOES WILD AFTER B.C. WIN

After the final whistle had blown in yesterday's thrilling Boston College-Georgetown game, Fenway Park was turned into a mad house. The goal posts were floored in a matter of seconds after the game had ended, the Boston College band led one of several victory marches. Although thousands of spectators flocked to the field, some 20 minutes after the game had ended, there were approximately 25,000 people remaining in the stands, making no effort to leave the park.

B.C. Smashes Hoyas in Thrilling Game, 19-18

O'ROURKE'S DAZZLING FORWARDS GIVE EAGLES MOST SENSATIONAL VICTORY OF GRID SEASON – SEE-SAW BATTLE ALL THE WAY, WITH VISITORS GETTING AWAY TO EARLY 10-0 LEAD – CROWD OF 40,000 ON FEET THROUGH ENTIRE 60 MINUTES OF TERRIFIC ACTION – BOTH TEAMS BRILLIANT ON OFFENSE

CLOSING THREAT FOILED AS B.C. DELIBERATELY TAKES SAFETY IN LAST MINUTE OF CONTEST

FOURTH DOWN ON THEIR 9-YARD LINE, 19 YARDS TO GO, LEAHY'S MEN WORK GREAT STRATEGY

By Bill Cunningham

With the blue chips piled Bowl, or $75,000, high, an inspired, but cool and perfectly poised Boston College team, smashed the three-year, 23-game victory run of Georgetown's Hoya Hilltoppers in

Fenway Park yesterday in what accredited experts, many of them syndicate and metropolitan veterans, were unanimous in calling one of the greatest games of college football ever played on any field. The margin of victory was one slender point, 19-18 being the eventual score, but the two last Georgetown digits were a gift through a deliberate safety taken by the Eagle's most scintillant hero, little Charley O'Rourke, to move his team out of a threatening situation in the last minute of play.

Probably never before in the entire history of football have two great teams, undefeated, untied and so highly publicized, lived so thoroughly up to their reputations in a featured head-on collision. And seldom, if ever, has any audience been treated to a more thrilling gridiron spectacle, one in which the lead kept ever changing through spectacularly perfect plays, with suspense electric until the very last whistle and one team then shading the other by the mere width of one point. Yesterday's Fenway Park capacity of 40,000 didn't sit. It mostly stood through 60 playing minutes of truly terrific action. The day was cold, gray and damp but the play was hotter than flame. Despite the week-long rain, the field was firm and the ball was dry.

The game, given added significance and pressure because the golden shadow of a Bowl bid hovered definitely over it, was one of the greatest of all memory because it was a pyrotechnical spectacle of two beautiful and powerful offences breaking over defenses strong enough to stop anything the nations has seen in a great many years. The scoring came quickly and it kept on coming through the day despite some of the most courageous tackling and some of the fastest and airtight pass coverage of any game ever developed.

Georgetown scored a field goal and a touchdown, B.C. a touchdown in the first period. The Eagles scored a touchdown in the second. Georgetown came back to smash out another in the third. B.C. almost immediately responded with another.

The fourth was a thrilling session which saw a powerful offense trying to fight down a desperate, and somewhat flagging defence, with Georgetown ever pressing and the Eagles fighting desperately with beak and talon to protect a slender three-point lead. And then, at the very finish, came of the piece of brilliant generalship that capped it all – O'Rourke's intentional safety that cost his team two points but preserved its slender lead and quite possibly saved the ball game.

WIDE OPEN BATTLE

It was a great game for the spectators because there was practically no piling up in the line. Plays were open and spectacular. The only close line crashing was when the fullbacks were sent ramming for that extra yard for first down. It was a great game for the experts because there was but one questionable bit of generalship in the entire affair. This was a pass O'Rourke flung deep in his own territory once in the fourth period while protecting that slender three-point lead. It was almost intercepted and an interception might and probably would have been fatal.

That was the game's sole mental lapse. There was none of the physical variety. Even the breaks pretty evenly distributed. Hoya rooters might argue B.C. was lucky when Woronicz caught that slapped forward pass for a touchdown and when the pass interference penalty set up another Eagle score, but B.C. rooters can come back with the holding penalty and the blocked kick that led up to the Hoya's first 10 points.

But Georgetown has no reason to be anything but proud in defeat and as for the Eagles, this may prove to be the most important football victory in the history of their institution. They were undoubtedly talking that score over seriously in New Orleans and Pasadena last night. That victory may be the start of the new Boston College Field House. Whatever the future may hold, the past will now hold something real. A victory such as that one was a masterpiece.

NOVEMBER 23, 1940

Unbeaten Boston College Bashes Auburn 33-7

On an afternoon where Bostonians could have availed themselves of a first run screening of Charlie Chaplin's film, *The Great Dictator* they instead came in droves to see their undefeated Eagles. Once again Boston College's talented all-purpose back Charlie O'Rourke ran and passed with reckless abandon as his Eagles entertained 35,000 fans with a decisive 33-7 win over Auburn in their next-to-last home game of the 1940 season.

NOVEMBER 30, 1940

Boston College Noses Out Holy Cross 7-0

Over 30,000 spectators held their breath for nearly three hours as the Holy Cross Crusaders battled courageously against the heavily favored Eagles, yielding only in the fourth quarter when a Joe Osmanski fumble led to the game's lone touchdown on a 2-yard plunge by Dolph Kissell.

The win assured Boston College of a New Year's date with Tennessee in the Sugar Bowl.

May 25, 1941 War Memorial Service

June 11, 1941 Norwood High 11, Chelmsford High 7

June 11, 1941 Braintree High 2, Brockton High 1

June 12, 1941 Somerville High 13, Reading High 3

June 12, 1941 Haverhill High 12, Wakefield High 4

June 27, 1941 Boston Park League All-Stars 2, Army Base 0

June 27, 1941 Massachusetts State Officials 6, Boston City Officials 3

JULY 23, 1941

Dykes Makes First Use of Williams Shift

Five years before Cleveland Indians shortstop/manager Lou Boudreau (and later Cardinal manager Eddie Dyer) would get credit for unveiling a similar strategy, Chicago White Sox manager Jimmy Dykes sought to neutralize the sting of Ted Williams' terrifying line drives by employing a dramatic shift of his defense in a Wednesday afternoon game against the Red Sox at Fenway Park. Deployed in the seventh inning with the bases empty Dykes placed his shortstop to the right of second as a spare outfielder, moving his third baseman to the shortstop hole and sliding the entire outfield to the right with his left fielder positioned just to the left of dead center, center fielder in right center, and his right fielder guarding the line. These measures were meant to nullify Williams power by forcing him to hit to left, where he lacked power. Mostly it was designed to mess with the young slugger's mind. However, upon its first use, it failed miserably as Williams doubled to left as the Sox won by a score of 10-4. The shift was abandoned by Dykes only to be resurrected by his Cleveland counterpart following the war.

JULY 25, 1941

Robert Moses Lefty Grove's 300th victory is Safely in the Records

"DIDN'T HAVE A THING ON THE BALL" SAYS GROVE

By Jack Malaney
Burt Whitman, Boston Herald

"That's the greatest thrill of my career no matter what happened before," proudly declared old Lefty Grove in the Red Sox clubhouse after he had been pummeled on and congratulated by his teammates on achieving his 300th victory.

"It was a poorly pitched game I know, but when we got those four runs I knew we had them licked," he went on.

"It's been my ambition to win 300 games ever since I won my 200th, and now I've got it. Boys! Looks like I'll have to hit out for .500 now."

CURVE DIDN'T WORK

"I didn't have a thing out there today."

"That isn't so," interrupted Jawn Peacock, Mose's catcher. "You may not have had good stuff but you had good control."

"Yeh, I had good control, but that wasn't enough," Lefty answered. "I couldn't throw my curve with anything on it and they belted it all around. And tired–I say–I was so tired that when Walker hit that triple in the seventh and there was an overthrow, if I had left the mound to go over and back up the play I never could have got back to the mound again. I told Joe Cronin that I was petrified out there and I couldn't move."

"Boys, this is great –I've never been so happy in my life, although I didn't think I'd be able to say that after the banquet you people gave me last year."

"I'd like to give Jimmie [Foxx] something for winning the game for me that he could keep forever. But the sonuvagun has got everything. I'd like to give every fellow on the club a present for helping me win that one."

Lefty took quite a beating in a mild way after the game had been concluded. Boudreau made the third out with a fly to Dom DiMaggio.

Lefty Grove warms up prior to a start in his final season in 1941. *(Courtesy of Mike Andersen)*

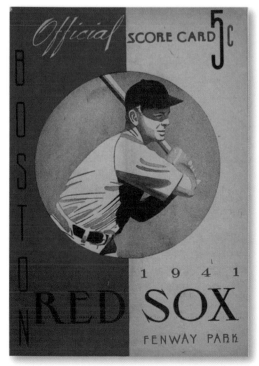

1941 Red Sox scorecard. *(Collection of the author)*

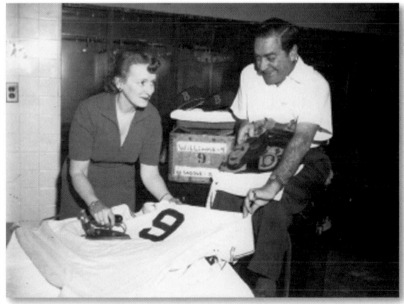

For 59 years, Helen Robinson served the Red Sox as switchboard operator, seamstress, and receptionist extraordinaire. *(Photograph by Dick Thomson, Courtesy of The Sports Museum)*

Ted Williams (left) was the greatest performer in Fenway's first century, and Joe DiMaggio was the most feared opponent. DiMaggio's 29 Fenway home runs top the opponent career home run list at the park. *(Courtesy of Mike Andersen)*

Instinctively, Lefty turned to wait for Dom and the baseball, always his in the winning game. This ball was something else again. Today it will be on its way to the Baseball Hall of Fame in Cooperstown, NY. Lefty has promised that and will substitute another, properly marked, for his own collection. He has a baseball in his home of Lonaconing MD for every victory he has won in major league competition, World Series games included.

As he walked off the mound to await Dom, the fans rushed out of the stands and surrounded him. Men hugged him and patted him on the back. The crowd got bigger by the second, and it took the police to make a path so he could get into the dugout. There, too, the fans had congregated and there was another rush for him.

Lefty finally got started down the under pass to the clubhouse and the love pats of the teammates started. Dom finally reached him and handed him the ball.

RULE SUSPENDED FOR DAY

Photographers and newspapermen were awaiting him in the clubhouse. The rule forbidding anyone from entering the room after a game was taken off yesterday because of the occasion. It was fully an hour before Lefty could get loose so that he could take a shower bath.

He was tired, almost to exhaustion. He was so thrilled and enthused that he hardly realized his own condition. Some of the older Cleveland players came in and congratulated him. Mel Harder came in late but there were so many around Lefty that the quiet Harder backed out. Clint Brown forced his way through to shake the hand of the grand old veteran.

Mighty Tennessee avenged their Sugar Bowl loss to Boston College when they beat the Eagles by a score of 14-7 before 32,000. *(Courtesy of Wes Dow)*

"We counted Grove's pitches. By innings there were: 9, 22, 19, 15, 12, 12, 15, 6, and 11, a total of 121, which is a tremendous afternoon of work for any pitcher, let alone one 41-years-old. And Lefty says the second 300 can't be any harder."

Dr T.K. Richards weighed Lefty. He tipped the scales at 199 ½ lbs. and had lost eight and a half pounds during the game.

The general team reaction to the win was that it will mean as much to the team and Lefty asserts he'll be ready for everything and anytime from here in."

SEPTEMBER 2, 1941

The Doyen of Fenway Park

Red Sox General Manager Eddie Collins hired switchboard operator/seamstress Helen Robinson. Robinson remained a Fenway fixture for the next 59 years during which time she served as Red Sox gatekeeper behind her switchboard. She was also a trusted confidante of Jean Yawkey. It was said of Robinson that she not only knew where all the proverbial bodies were buried at Fenway Park and often wielded great power within the executive suite. Former team President John Harrington relied on her judgment on administrative decisions such as sending workers home on "snow" days. If Helen said to go home the park soon emptied. In her early years Robinson also served as the team seamstress while sewing the numerals on the jerseys shipped to the ballpark from Wilson Sporting Goods.

SEPTEMBER 11, 1941

Chicago Bears Maul All Stars 23-6 Before 38,503

The Chicago Bears dominated a squad of collegiate All-Stars in a game played for the benefit of the American Legion under the auspices of the Crosscup–Pishon Legion post.

A capacity crowd of 38,503 jammed Fenway Park under the glare of temporary floodlights and watched a spectacle that included not only the game but also featured several marching bands, a fireworks display and speeches by amry and navy officials.

It was appropriate that three former New England collegiate stars scored for the Bears as Bill Osmanski (Holy Cross), Ray McLean (St. Anselms), and Gary Farmighetti (BU) tallied for George Halas's team while the lone All Star touchdown came on a Charlie O'Rourke pass to teammate Lou Montgomery.

Bill Wright of the Baltimore Elite Giants was one of the great Negro League stars to play at Fenway Park when his team fell to the Philadelphia Stars by a score of 8-7 on September 8, 1942. *(Collection of the author)*

OCTOBER 11, 1941

Clemson Triumphs Over Eagles 26-13

The Clemson Tigers came from behind to beat Boston College before a shivering Columbus Day crowd of 23,000 at Fenway Park. Walter Payne passed to Joe Blalock for two of the Tiger touchdowns, and backs Charley Timmons and Harry Franklin scored State's other touchdowns.

OCTOBER 18, 1941

The "Other" Ted Williams Leads Boston College Over Manhattan

Boston College fullback and Gloucester native Ted Williams earned many of the same cheers reserved for his Red Sox namesake as he scored three touchdowns, including two off interceptions, to lead the Eagles to a lopsided 26-13 victory over Manhattan. His lone touchdown from scrimmage came in the

Program for the Army Emergency Relief game between the Chicago Bears and an All-Army squad. *(Courtesy of Wes Dow)*

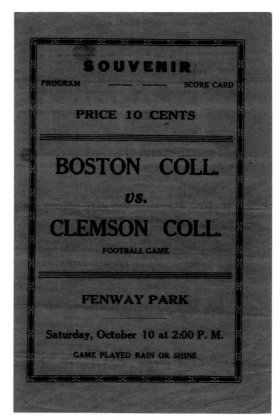

Program for Boston College vs. Clemson game on October 10, 1942. *(Courtesy of Wes Dow)*

third quarter on a 59-yard scamper off tackle. The Jaspers managed a late rally, scoring two touchdowns as the result of a flurry of passes with three minutes to go but couldn't overcome the Eagles big lead.

OCTOBER 25, 1941

Boston College Passes to Beat Georgetown

The Boston College Eagles executed a brilliant passing attack to beat the rival Georgetown Hoyas by a score of 14-6 before a crowd of 20,000 at Fenway Park. Led by the pinpoint passing of Ed Doherty, the other Eagles that enjoyed a banner day were Ed Zabilski, Harry Connolly, and Frank Maznick.

NOVEMBER 1, 1941

Eagles Beat Owls 31-0

The previously undefeated Temple Owls fell to Boston College by a decisive 31-0 before a crowd of 15,000 on a rainy, muddy day at Fenway Park.

NOVEMBER 8, 1941

Boston College Beats Wake Forest By a Score of 26-6

Boston College won its fourth straight game (all at Fenway Park) before a crowd of 15,000 as they whipped Wake Forest 26-6. Ted

Willams was once again the star as his interception late in the second quarter led to the first Eagles touchdown. Wake Forest miscues, including an unnecessary roughness penalty and a fumbled punt, led to two other Eagle touchdowns.

NOVEMBER 15, 1941

Tennessee Topples Boston College By a Score of 14-7

In a replay of January's Sugar Bowl the Tennessee Volunteers exacted revenge against Boston College in front of 32,000 at Fenway Park. Tennessee second string fullback Bill Gold, a native of Brockton,

Mass., helped lead the Vols to victory as he intercepted an Eagle pass with four minutes remaining that set up the winning touchdown, scored on a 4-yard run by Bobby Cifers.

NOVEMBER 22, 1941

Boston College Tops Boston University 9-7

The Eagles never looked back after fullback Adolph Kissel scored a thrilling touchdown on a 96-yard runback of the opening kick-off as Boston College beat their Commonwealth Avenue rivals by a score of 19-7 at Fenway Park.

NOVEMBER 24, 1941

Ted Williams Turns the Trick for Boston College

On the day that former Boston College coach Frank Leahy was named "Coach of the Year" by the *New York World-Telegram* for his revitalization of Notre Dame, 40,000 filled every corner of Fenway Park to watch his former team play Holy Cross. Despite being outclassed by Holy Cross for much of the afternoon, heavily favored Boston College managed to grab a last-minute victory over the Jesuit rivals courtesy of a twisting 22-yard touchdown run by fullback Ted Williams and a game-winning point after by Frank Maznicki. Earlier in the game Maznicki's

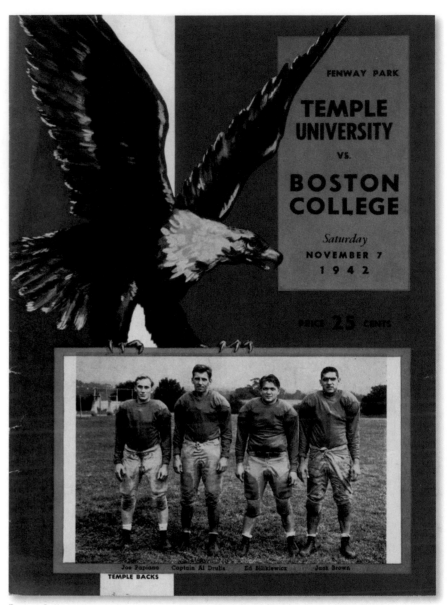

Boston College played all its games at Fenway Park in 1942. *(Courtesy of Wes Dow)*

block of a Crusader extra point set up the Eagle victory.

APRIL 14, 1942

TED WILLIAMS BOOED FOR DRAFT DEFERMENT IN SOX OPENER. SOCKS FIRST INNING THREE RUN HOMER AGAINST PHILADELPHIA AS BOSTON WINS 8-3

In post-Pearl Harbor America even the most beloved celebrities were subject to the scrutiny and judgment

of their fellow citizens when it came to the issue of military. With an overwhelming majority of males between the ages of 18 and 40 eagerly volunteering to join the war effort, performers such as Frank Sinatra and Ted Williams were criticized for their deferment of service.

While Sinatra would never serve and therefore earn the lifelong enmity of many vets, Williams endured a brief period of booing at Fenway Park before enlisting despite the fact he was the sole means of support for his widowed mother.

In time Williams, along with fellow star Bob Feller, became a shining example of the many athlete/warriors who sacrificed a significant portion of their careers to serve America.

May 17, 1942 War Memorial Service

JUNE 20, 1942

Arlington Bows in Final, 5 to 4

TURNERS FALLS WINS BAY STATE SCHOOL TITLE ON WELCOME'S TRIPLE TO FENCE IN THE NINTH

By J.W. Mooney

And the third time didn't fail! Turners Falls High saw to that yesterday at Fenway Park when they snatched off the State high school baseball championship by coming from behind in the last two innings to beat Arlington, Eastern Massachusetts champs, 5 to 4, in the seventh annual tournament final. Twice before the Western title winners came to Boston to play at the big league park, and twice before they were sent home disappointed, first by Lynn English, in extra innings, and then by Belmont, two years ago.

But it was a happy and hilarious crowd of Turners Falls supporters making up a crowd of nearly 3000 who crowded around their youngsters in the last of the ninth when with two away, Catcher Harvey Welcome bashed out a long triple to the centre field fence that scored the deciding run. For Arlington it was a tough game to drop.

September 5, 1942 Fort Devens 6, Fort Terry 2 (First Service Command Championship)

September 8, 1942 Philadelphia Stars 8, Baltimore Elite Giants 7 (Negro National League)

September 10, 1942 Dick Casey Club Defeats Navy Yard A.A. (Boston Park League)

Army, Bears Battle Today

38,000 EXPECTED AT FENWAY CLASSIC

One of the best football attractions ever offered Boston sports fans is scheduled for Fenway Park at 2 o'clock this afternoon when the champions of the world, the eye-filling Chicago Bears, attempt to uphold their prestige against the challenge of the best All-Star football team ever assembled, the Army team drilled by Col. Bob Neyland, which already has beaten the New York Giants, and the Brooklyn Dodgers.

Boston has been the scene of many an important football clash in the long history of the gridiron game but today's billing seems to be the biggest of them all.

The kickoff is scheduled for 2:10 p.m., but there will be exercise of one kind or another from 12:15, just 15 minutes after the gates open, until the whistle blows. Between the halves there will be more ceremonies, highlighted by the appearance of Lieutenant Lyndmilla Parlichenko, the Russian girl sniper, who was credited with personally killing 309 Nazis.

Mighty Bears Beat Army, 14-7

PRO CHAMPIONS TRIUMPH IN ROUGH BATTLE OVER ALL-STARS BEFORE 40,000 AT FENWAY PARK

The mighty Chicago Bears, champions of the National Professional Football League, had the scare of their lives as they eked out a 14 to 7 victory over a great Army All-Star eleven before 40,000 shrieking fans in a rip-roaring, knock-down-drag-out battle at Fenway Park yesterday afternoon.

Only by the grace of a quick break early in the third session and a goal-to-goal march in the final quarter did the proud Bears manage to pull from the fire the most dangerous threat with which a pro championship team has ever been faced. Even at that, they had to abandon most of the tricks in the bag of George Halas and stick to straight football, bulling their way through when everything else had failed.

(Source: Boston Post)

SEPTEMBER 27, 1942

Tony Lupien Day which is also the last day before Ted Williams and Johnny Pesky join the service. 4,293 fans bring 29,000 lbs. of metal scrap for the military effort.

OCTOBER 3, 1942

BOSTON COLLEGE HUMBLES WEST VIRGINIA 33-0 BEFORE 15,000

OCTOBER 10, 1942

**23,400 SEE EAGLES EDGE
CLEMSON 14-7**

OCTOBER 17, 1942

**25, 107 SEE EAGLES CLIP
WINGS OF NORTH CAROLINA
NAVAL FLYERS BY A SCORE
OF 7-6**

OCTOBER 24, 1942

**NUMBER 10 RANKED BOSTON
COLLEGE BEATS WAKE
FOREST 27-0 BEFORE 21,500**

OCTOBER 31, 1942

**EAGLES WHITEWASH
GEORGETOWN 47-0 BEFORE
28,000**

NOVEMBER 7, 1942

**NUMBER 5 RANKED EAGLES
BASH TEMPLE 28-0 (ATT
24,000)**

NOVEMBER 14, 1942

**NUMBER 3 RANKED EAGLES
ROUT FORDHAM 56-6 (ATT
36,300)**

NOVEMBER 21, 1942

**BC BLANKS BU 37-0 BEFORE
10,000 AT FENWAY**

Ted Williams lights Babe Ruth's cigar prior to a 1943 war charity game at Fenway Park. *(Collection of the author)*

Birmingham Black Barons uniform patch. The Barons played Fore River Shipyard at Fenway Park in 1943. *(Collection of the author)*

The program for the famous Boston College vs. Holy Cross duel of 1942 featured a prediction of the upset score as the jerseys of the Boston College co-captains predicted the exact score of Holy Cross's monumental victory. *(Courtesy of Jerry Nason)*

nearly flawless football cascaded sparks all over Fenway Park yesterday afternoon as it pulverized supposedly invincible Boston College, 55 to 12 before a capacity gathering of 41,000 amazed spectators.

In the lush hour of triumph the courageous and talented pupils of Ank Scanlon really turned on the heat to rack up the highest score ever compiled in the historic series between the two famous Jesuit institutions. The one-sided triumph was reminiscent of the Purple triumphs of 41 to 0 in 1921 and 33 to 0 in 1924 during the Cavanagh era.

EIGHT PURPLE TOUCHDOWNS

The Purple unit of 1942 buried hapless Boston College under a blizzard of eight touchdowns, five more than the Eagles' eight previous opponents had been able to register. Three were fashioned in the electrifying third quarter, two were manufactured in the second and fourth periods and the other came in the opening semester. It was a Roman holiday for the boys from Mt. St. James who took complete control of Boston after the final whistle sounded.

NOVEMBER 28, 1942

HOLY CROSS IN ROMP, CRUSHES BC., 55 TO 12

CRUSADERS SCORE EIGHT TOUCHDOWNS, THREE COMING ON FORWARDS, ONE ON INTERCEPTION

8 TOUCHDOWNS CRUMBLE EAGLE BOWL CHANCES

BEZEMES 67-YARD RUN LONGEST OF GAME-GRIGAS SCORES TWICE-EAGLES OUTPLAYED FROM START

By Howell Stevens, Boston Post

Exhibiting the most glittering attack seen here all season, an inspired Holy Cross team playing

408 DEAD, 350 INJURED IN FIRE AT COCONUT GROVE

GAY BOSTON NIGHT CLUB TURNS INTO SCENE OF HORROR AS FLAMES ENGULF STRUCTURE---START STAMPEDE TO ESCAPE---HUNDREDS TRAPPED AT EXITS---RESORT FILLED

WITH NEARLY 1000 PATRONS---MANY HOLDING PARTIES AFTER B.C. GAME DEAD ARE EVENLY DIVIDED AMONG MEN AND WOMEN---MANY SERVICE MEN

(Author's Note: The monumental Holy Cross upset not only cost Boston College a major Bowl bid and a shot at a national title but also included a significant silver lining. For that night the Coconut Grove fire in Boston's south end killed 492 and injured hundreds more in the second worst single building fire in American history. The BC football team had originally scheduled its victory party at the club that night but canceled after their devastating loss.)

November 29, 1942 Charlestown Town Team 7, South Boston Chippewas

---

APRIL 13, 1943

RED SOX CRUSH BC EAGLES 17-2 IN FENWAY EXHIBITION GAME

May 23, 194 War Memorial
Service
July 9, 1943 Fore River Shipyard
3, New York Cuban Stars 0

JULY 12, 1943

Williams Homers to Give Stars Win Over Braves 9-8

By Joe Cashman, Boston Daily Record

Ted the Kid parked one high in the centerfield seats, in the shadow of the flag pole 420 feet away. That settled everything.

Professor Dom tripled and singled. He threw out a daring base

runner. He streaked to the center field wall and pulled down a drive.

Just two of them-Teddy Williams and Dom DiMaggio-were all the Service All-Stars needed to beat the Braves in a Mayor's Field Day game witnessed by some 16,000 at the fens yesterday.

They saw everything they came to see.

They saw Babe Ruth swing and Rabbit Maranville mimic.

They saw old time diamond greats and such modern heroes as Coast Guardsman Babe Young of the Giants, Soldier Skippy Roberge of the Army, Coast Guardsman Jim Hegan of the Indians.

But what they'll remember longest, these customers who contributed approximately $15,000 to a fund for Boston's undernourished and underprivileged children, is that Williams wallop.

The Kid, taking a day off from his studies at pre-flight Naval School at Chapel Hill, hadn't done a thing in his first three times at bat.

KID WAS DUE

He was due up the fourth time in the seventh.

The score was tied at 5-all, due largely to DiMag's triple which knocked in two runs and sparked a four-run rally against Norwood's Ray Martin in the third.

The same Dom drew a walk from Dave Odomafter. Skippy Roberge had singled to open the lucky frame.

So up stepped Theodore.

He watched a strike sail by. He fouled one back into the packed grandstand. He took a pitch in the dirt.

Then came the next Odom serve.

It was fast, about letter high and slightly outside. The Splinter gave it all he had.

On a line screamed the agate as Charlie Workman playing center field for the Tribe yesterday gave chase.

It was a futile gesture on the part of the Braves slugger, who incidentally kept his mates close in the game by rapping out a homer and a triple.

The ball never stopped until it found a parking space about 10 rows in that section of the center field stands which is kept clear for the batter's benefit except on days of over-capacity crowds.

Thus "Ted the Kid" added one more to the innumerable games his mighty wagon tongue has won at Fenway Park.

And this time, when he crossed the plate and smiled up at the cheering thousands in the stands, he tipped his cap.

He was happy to be back.

And were the fans delighted to see him swing once again and to watch DiMaggio do his stuff.

You could hear the spectators say, "No wonder the Sox are in seventh place without these two guys."

It wasn't a great ballgame. But it was interesting all the way and Ted and Dom made it memorable.

Babe Ruth Gets Biggest Reception

By Huck Finnegan

RUTH ARRIVES

"All I've got to say if the Babe at 50 years, without a bat in his hands for a year , can hit one into the right field stands, he's a wonder," said Williams.

And then it happened. In came Eddie Collins leading the Babe by the ear.

"Hiya Kid" boomed the Babe, tanned as an Indian. "A very great pleasure indeed," said Williams in turn gazing with something approaching awe to the man who made the Home Run famous.

They exchanged amenities for a minute and the major popped in. "Boy, they must have a drag to get me up here," boomed Williams, meaning, of course, His Honor.

Ruth, black cigar in his mouth, then went over and sat in front of Bobby Doerr's locker. Dom and Williams occupied Joe Cronin's private cubby. But before Babe had a chance to put on a uniform, he was forced to sign not a dozen but three dozen baseballs, also everything from autograph books to wrapping paper. This he did with a cheery smile,. "Glad to," he said, a cigar still in his mouth, he did his signing right-handed.

Johnny Orlando brought undersocks, undershirt, and the Babe stripped showing the famous "Alderman" he developed in his late baseball years. But, he insisted he weighed only 231 pounds whereas he weighed 247 in 1934, his last year with the Yankees.

It was so hot the Babe sat around in his underthings puffing away at a cigar, cutting up old touchs with Rabbit, Babe Young, and Cy Perkins. He dressed in his old Yankee uniform with the familiar number 3 on the back; Williams was dressed in his Red Sox uniform with number 9 on the back.

Williams was the first to appear on the field. He was given a fine hand but nothing compared to that

Mr and Mrs Satchel Paige at Fenway Park, August 10, 1943 *(Courtesy of the Boston Public Library)*

the Babe received when he ambled out of the dugout at 3:30.

The 16,000 in the stands (not a soul in the bleachers) arose as one and gave the Babe a greeting such as he never received in his playing days.

-ZIP YOUR LIP –SAVE A SHIP-

(Among the baseball dignitaries in attendance were: Fred Parent, Fred Tenney, Hugh Duffy, Fred Mitchell, Joe Wood, Jack Barry, Hal Janvrin, Cy Perkins, Buck O'Brien, Joe Dugan, Red Rolfe, Bump Hadley, Chippy Gaw, Shanty Hogan, Fredddy Maguire, Otto Derringer, and Duffy Lewis.)

AUGUST 10, 1943

Satchel Paige at Fenway Park

The greatest pitcher of all time, Leroy "Satchel" Paige and his world-famous Kanasas City Monarchs will make their only New England appearance of the baseball season at Fenway Park Thursday night, August 12, when they tangle with Jack Burns Fore River Baseball Club in a twilight contest.

Paige comes here from an exhibition last Sunday in Chicago where he wowed 51,000 fans who turned out to see the famous star in action.

Standing 6 ft. 4 inches and weighing 180 pounds, the great Satchel has pitched in 125 games per season for the past seven years. He plays 12 months a year and from all indications he's improving with age. This year, since returning from Puerto Rico where he played last winter Paige has twirled in Kansas City, Denver, Cincinnati, Yankee Stadium, and Comiskey Park with the world champion Monarchs.

Paige still relies on his fastball, which he considers his best pitch. His fast ball is really fast and his curve ball is of the sweeping type. *(Source: Boston Guardian)*

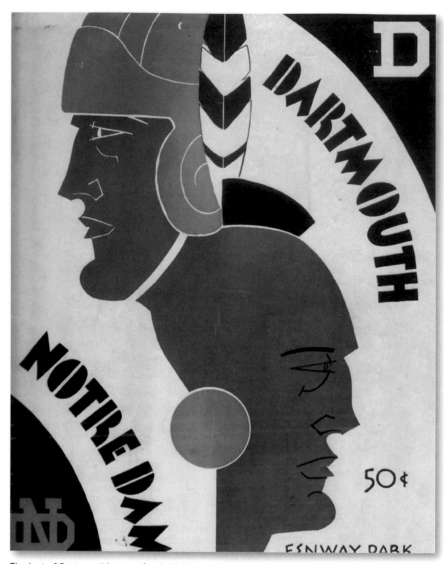

The last of Dartmouth's many football dates at Fenway Park was a disastrous 64-0 defeat before a full house in 1944. *(Courtesy of Wes Dow)*

AUGUST 12, 1943

Paige Features Monarchs' Win

FANS FIRST FOUR FOES DURING THREE FRAME WORK

By Ed Earle, Boston Herald

Loose as ashes and inimitable change-of-pace showman, Leroy "Satchel" Paige, famed Negro of the number 12 size shoes, pleased an appreciative gallery when he worked the first three innings, fanning the first four men to face him and allowing two scattered doubles as the Kansas City Monarchs, Negro major league champions of 1942, belted out three runs in the sixth inning to defeat the star-studded Fore River Baseball Club, 4 to 1, in a tight eight-frame contest last night at Fenway Park before a crowd of more than 8,000.

Booker McDaniels, fast ball pitcher, followed Paige to the mound and held the War Workers to a three hit ration in five innings, Charlie Bird hurled a great game up to the sixth inning as he went the route.

Fore River broke the ice in the first of the sixth when Tony Novello doubled to left, went to third when "Skinny" Graham pounded out to first and scored on Joe Lehan's single to right.

The Monarchs surveyed Bird for two singles and a pair of doubles for three runs in their end of the sixth, featuring Willard Brown's two bagger off the left field fence.

Three singles in a row in the seventh inning by Jesse Williams, spectacular shortstop; Newt Allen and Herb Souell accounted for the Monarch's fourth run.

August 23-29, 1943 Three-Ring Circus

September 2, 1943 Birmingham Black Barons 2, Fore River Shipyard 2

OCTOBER 24, 1943

BOSTON COLLEGE BEATS CAMP HINGHAM (MA) 42-6 (ATT 10,000)

OCTOBER 31, 1943

BROOKLYN COLLEGE FALL BY A SCORE OF 37-6 TO BOSTON COLLEGE (ATT 11,000)

NOVEMBER 7, 1943

BOSTON COLLEGE BEATS ROME AIR FORCE STATION 64-0 (ATT 14,7000)

November 21, 1943 Holy Cross 41, Tufts College 0.

May 8, 1944 Cleveland Indians Intrasquad Game

JUNE 15, 1944

Anybody Home?

Only 770 fans attend a game in which Cecil "Tex" Hughson beats the Athletics by a score of 5-1.

SEPTEMBER 26, 1944

EAGLES PASTE YANKS IN BOSTON DEBUT 28-7 IN NIGHT GAME (ATT 24,000)

OCTOBER 8, 1944

NEW YORK GIANTS TOP YANKS AT FENWAY, 22-10 (ATT 17,000)

OCTOBER 14, 1944

Notre Dame Is Big Favorite

Picked to Win Over Dartmouth at Fenway Today – Over 40,000 Expected to See Game

Notre Dame Heavy Favorite Against Dartmouth

ATTRACTS 40,000 TO BOSTON DEBUT

By Arthur Sampson
(Boston Post)

Boston awaits its biggest football game of the year today when a highly favored Notre Dame team, figured by the experts to be able to name its own score, meets a determined Dartmouth eleven which hopes and expects to make an unexpectedly good showing before a capacity crowd of 40,000 at Fenway Park.

The fact professional gamblers would not even consider taking a small wager against a Notre Dame victory last night, and were offering as high as 40 points to anyone willing to support the Green, was in no way diminishing the number of persons anxious to pay a heavy premium for available tickets.

$130,000 GATE

The tremendous appeal of a Notre Dame football team, performing in Boston for the first time in history, more than overshadowed the fact the Dartmouth eleven appears to be no match for the Irish eleven on the season's performance.

Hotels were jammed to more than the usual capacity, with reservations received months in advance. Extra cots in crowded rooms were worth even more than tickets on the 50-yard line in some quarters. A game which figures to be little more than a Notre Dame exhibition to most of the close followers of the game had a $130,000 gross gate assured weeks ago.

Most of those fortunate enough to be attending this clash made applications for seats early last summer. Thousands who were anxious to attend had ticket money refunded to them. The lure of Notre Dame alone could have filled a park twice as large.

Whether the game develops into the anticipated rout or not depends to a great extent on the ability of an inexperienced and injury-riddled Dartmouth team to rise to the occasion. The young Indians alone, among the huge throng, which will squeeze into Fenway Park this afternoon, are conceding nothing.

Notre Dame Is Victor, 64-0

FOOTBALL SUPER-TEAM ROLLS ALMOST AT WILL OVER DARTMOUTH BEFORE 40,000 AT FENWAY PARK

By Howell Stevens

Immortal Notre Dame, kingpin of the American football firmament for the last quarter of a century, added fresh luster to its gridiron fame in its Boston bow at Fenway Park yesterday, the dazzling, green-shirted dervishes, directed by Texas Ed McKeever, blitzing a game but thoroughly outclassed Dartmouth team, 64 to 0, as a capacity crowd of more than 40,000 spectators watched in awe.

This was the largest score compiled by a Notre Dame team since 1922, when Hunk Anderson's stalwarts buried the Haskell Indians, 73 to 0. It was the most decisive defeat suffered by a Dartmouth team since 1900 when Harvard humbled the Hanoverians by the same count.

The game yesterday wiped out bitter memories of Notre Dame's only other trip to New England. That was in 1914, just 30 years ago, when the South Benders were defeated 28 to 0 by Frank Hinkey's laterally-minded Yalensians in New Haven.

The fabled Irish possessed every attribute of a championship machine yesterday except ability to convert try points. They scored 10 touchdowns, one in each of the first and third periods and four in both the second and final quarters. Only four of the extra points were converted, a negligible factor in the one-sided affray at Fenway Park but possibly of vital importance when the South Benders stack up against such worthy foemen as Navy and Army.

Satisfied Just to See Notre Dame

ONE-SIDED SCORE FAILS TO BOTHER RAIN-SOAKED FANS

By Jack Malaney

Inasmuch as everyone went to see Notre Dame play, it didn't make much difference about the score. They were all satisfied that they had seen one of the great teams of the day, and found that the Notre Dame football tradition was all it was supposed to be.

HOPE GREEN WOULD SCORE

That, at least, seemed to be the consensus of the thousands who braved the elements. Even that woman in Section 15, whose husband insisted on remaining where they were even when the rain was coming down heavily. She seemed to want to favor her beautiful mink coat, but husband insisted she stay. Well, why not, he had to pay for the coat, didn't he?

Even the most ardent Notre Dame rooters were hoping Dartmouth would have the consolation of scoring once anyway. But it was not to be, because those third and fourth string Irish players were looking out for their own reputations.

When Dartmouth's speed king, Newman, caught a pass out in the open, everyone had visions of a Green touchdown. But the fleet

Newman was not as fleet as Boley Dancewicz of Lynn, who gave him a five-yard start and caught him just as the gun sounded ending the first half.

The wounded veterans down at the end of the field seemed to enjoy the proceedings. They had been reading about Notre Dame teams for years, and here was one that lived up to all advance notices. It was a thrill for the veterans who know how to play an even greater game.

OCTOBER 15, 1944

BOSTON YANKS MISS FOURTH QUARTER SCORING CHANCE AND LOSE TO REDSKINS 21-14 (ATT 17,000)

OCTOBER 28, 1944

BOSTON COLLEGE EDGES SYRACUSE 19-12

NOVEMBER 4, 1944

FDR's Final Campaign Speech

(Author's note: A crowd of 40,000, noted in the press as being comprised mostly of women and service men in uniform, packed Fenway Park for the final campaign speech of Franklin D. Roosevelt's career as an additional 15,000 supporters surrounded the park. The park was illuminated by racks of temporary floodlights and a section of the left-field bleachers were covered by canvas as a security measure ordered by the Secret Service. As a haze of cigarette smoke drifted from the grandstands, the crowd, inspired by Roosevelt's characteristic

oratorical reiterations, responded in kind by adding an additional "again" to the Presidents" again, and again and again." Likewise they responded to every rhetorical question with a loud communal roar of "No." This remained the most significant political speech in Boston history until candidate John F. Kennedy spoke at Boston Garden on the eve of the 1960 election and Senator Barack Obama delivered the keynote address at the 2004 Democratic National Convention at the then TD Banknorth Garden.)

PRESIDENT'S SCHEDULE
(From *The Boston Post*)

10:00 AM Arrive Bridgeport for rear platform speech

10:10 AM Leave Bridgeport

11:50 AM Arrive Hartford for 10 minute speech

12 noon Leave Hartford

1:00 PM Arrive Springfield for platform speech

1:15 PM Leave Springfield

2:15 PM Arrive Worcester to pick up U.S. Senator David I. Walsh

5:00 PM Arrive Beacon Yards, Allston

5:30 PM Open Fenway Park gates

6:00 PM Dinner on Presidential train

6:30 PM Start entertainment programme starring Frank Sinatra, Orson Welles, Phil Reagan, Kate Smith, and Morton Downey

8:00 PM Chairman William H. Burke presents State ticket headed by Mayor Maurice J. Tobin for governor for short addresses

8:15 PM President Roosevelt leaves train

President Franklin D. Roosevelt poses in the car rigged with a microphone that he used to give the final campaign speech of his storied career at Fenway Park on November 4, 1944. *(Collection of the author)*

9:00 PM President starts 45 minute speech over nation-wide radio hookup

10:00 PM President leaves Fenway Park

10:20 PM President boards Presidential train in Beacon Yards, Allston, for trip to Hyde Park, N.Y.

Gates to Fenway Park will open at 5:30 and as soon as the park is filled the gates will be ordered closed by the Secret Service. For the entertainment of the crowd previous to the arrival of the President the committee has arranged a programme of entertainment including band music and the appearance of radio stars including Orson Welles, Phil Reagan, Kate Smith, and Morton, Downey. (Author's Note: Frank Sinatra was the surprise performer)

The President arrived at Fenway Park by car through the center field gate and drove up a ramp to a platform erected behind second base for his speech. He gave his speech while sitting in his car.

CLOSE WATCH ON NEWSMEN

Clumping along in a column of squads, without benefit of a band the press was regimented with grim efficiency last night as part of the elaborate Secret Service precautions to protect the President.

Gathered into one group at the taxi-cab garage a quarter mile from Fenway Park, the men and women of the press were tagged, counted, and formed in a column three abreast. A mounted policeman was placed at the head of the column and a dozen officers afoot surrounded the motley news-gatherers as they sauntered sulkily forward, out of step, out of temper and out of patience.

"How many miles to Siberia?" grumbled the anti-New deal segment of the press.

The precautions were taken so that no interlopers with fell schemes against the safety of the president could insinuate themselves into the press rows under the speaking stand.

When the odd awkward squad straggled through the centerfield gate the crowd craned and buzzed expectantly.

"What are they?" everyone wanted to know.

"Inductees", someone shouted, and there was a spatter of applause.

The press grimly took their seats and began belaboring their typewriters.

GREAT ROAR OF WELCOME

When Frank Sinatra, who slipped into the park to avoid a waiting contingent of bobby-sockers, sang the national anthem, there was a typical bobby-sockers squeal of delight. But almost immediately the President's car rolled onto the field and the crowd surged to its feet and loosed a tremendous roar of welcome, drowning out a band striving to play "Hail to The Chief" loud enough to be heard over the roar of the cheers.

Frank Sinatra, bobby-sockers hero, stood in the shadows beneath the flood-lights watching the President as he talked.

"What a guy," he said. "And, boy, does he pack 'em in."

G.O.P. 'Lies" Hit By Roosevelt

PRESIDENT IN FENWAY PARK ADDRESS CHARGES OPPONENT CARRYING ON CAMPAIGN OF DISTORTION AND FALSEHOOD- SEES ATTEMPT TO SPUR RACIAL INTOLERANCE- FIGHTING SPEECH CHEERED BY 40,000

By Wilton Vaugh Boston Post

Acclaimed by a wildly cheering throng of 40,000 that packed flood-lighted Fenway Park for the climax speech of his campaign for a fourth term, President Franklin D. Roosevelt last night accused his Republican challenger of "trying to stimulate racial and religious intolerance" and conducting a campaign of "misrepresentation, distortion, and falsehood."

He told his Boston audience that he was reluctant to run for 16 years in the White House but that because of the character of the campaign staged by his opposition, he really wants to win in Tuesay's national election.

Back in 1928 when he came here to campaign for the "Happy Warrior," he said, "All the bigots were gunning for Al Smith," at that time, he said, he warned about racial and religious intolerance "which was then, as it unfortunately still is—a menace to the liberties of America"

He did not mention Governor Dewey by name, but the Boston audience remembered the speech which the republican Presidential nominee made before a crowd of 15,000 three nights before at Boston Garden. The president took off his gloves and swung with both fists in this, the sixth and final speech of his campaign.

Following Frank Sinatra and other Hollywood stars to the microphone the President seemed to be in better voice than his recent radio talks. The weather was perfect for his outdoor speaking, in contrast to his previous trips to Boston when he usually brought rain, sleet, and hail.

Hinting at the Republican propaganda related to his expectancy of life, the President reminded his audience that when he ran for Governor in 1928 his opponent said his health would not permit him to carry out the duties of Governor. That was the time when the late "Al" Smith retorted that the Governor of New York did not have to be an acrobat.

QUOTATIONS FROM FDR'S FINAL CAMPAIGN SPEECH

"We have nothing to fear but fear itself. We must wage the coming battle for America in association with the United Nations—with the association ever-growing. We must wage a peace to attract the highest hearts and the most competent hands and brains. That, my friends, is the conception I have of the meaning of total victory.

"The memory of our people is not short. The years from 1929 to 1933 are thoroughly and grimly remembered by millions of our citizens-by workers who lost their jobs and their homes, by farmers who lost their crops and their farms, by families who lost their savings. Since those dark days back in 1933 many fortifications have been erected to protect the people of this country, just as we promised there would be.

"These fortifications have provided protection for your bank deposits and your investments—your standard of living—your right to organize unions and to bargain collectively with your employers.

"They protect your soil and rivers and trees—your heritage of natural resources. They provide you with protection against the hazards of unemployment and old age—they protect you against inflation and runaway prices.

"These fortifications are now manned by zealous defenders and these defenders are not communists.

"Can the citizens of the nation now afford to turn over these bulwarks to the men who raised every possible obstacle to their original construction?

"Does the average American believe that those who fought tooth and nail against progressive legislation during the past 12 years can be trusted to cherish and preserve that legislation?

"Can it be that those who financed the bitter opposition to the New deal have made an about face and are now willing to fight for the objectives of the New Deal?"

At the conclusion of his speech, President Roosevelt circled the field in his car with Mayor Tobin, Leader McCormick, Chairman Burke, and National Chairman Robert Emmett Hannegan riding with him, while the crowd chanted wildly, "We want Roosevelt" for fully ten minutes. He then proceeded to the Presidential train in Allston where he departed to Hyde Park, N.Y. where he would remain through election day.

NOVEMBER 19, 1944

YANKS END HOME SEASON WITH WIN OVER BROOKLYN TIGERS BY A SCORE OF 13-6 (ATT 16,487)

APRIL 16, 1945

Black Monday

Even in baseball-mad Boston, the events of April 16th were overshadowed by news of the death of President Franklin D. Roosevelt. Until recently the news pertaining to the saddest and most controversial event in Fenway Park's long history remained, and to a large extent, remain cloaked in obscurity. For the sad result came not from the outcome of a scheduled game but of a forced tryout given to Negro League stars Jackie Robinson, Marvin Williams, and Sam Jethroe while the Red Sox were on a road trip. The now infamous session was arranged due to pressure placed on the team by Boston City Councilor Isadore Muchnick. Muchnick had the support of Wendell Smith, the influential sports editor of the famed black weekly, The *Pittsburgh Courier.* Both men felt strongly that African Americans should be given a shot at the majors in the wake of many social changes, including the valiant service of so many blacks in the second world war. Muchnick also threatened to press for revocation of the team's license for Sunday baseball if they didn't hold the historic tryout.

Several events pertaining to the 16th are irrefutable and they are that the three players were put through their paces by Sox coach and future Hall of Fame inductee Hugh Duffy. Following the workout they were praised by Duffy and asked to fill out information cards. They never heard from the Red Sox again.

Jackie Robinson later wrote, "Not for one minute did we believe the Boston tryout was sincere. We were going through the motions."

Claims have been made but never conclusively proven that a Red Sox executive observing the tryout called out, "Get those niggers off the field."

It would be fourteen long years before the team finally achieved the regrettable distinction of being the last of the 16 major league clubs to integrate.

In 1946 the Red Sox played seven men at third base, one of Robinson's natural positions, as the team lost to the Cardinals by a single run. During that same season Boston's top farm team in Louisville threatened to boycott the minor league Little World Series due to the presence of Robinson on the opposing Montreal Royals.

June 25, 1945 Tami Mauriello First-Round Knockout of Lou Nova (Boxing)
June 28, 1945 Cuban Stars 8, Boston Colored Giants 5
June 28, 1945 Presentation CYO (Brighton) 6, Holy Name CYO (Hyde Park) 1

July 4, 1945 *Here's Your Infantry* Show
September 2, 1945 St. Marguerite (Lowell) 2, St. Joseph's (Needham) 1 (State CYO Title Game)
September 2, 1945 Sacred Heart Malden 2, Sacred Heart of Atlantic 1 (State CYO Title Game)
September 23, 1945 Boo Ferris Day

SEPTEMBER 25, 1945

YANKS SHOW REAL PUNCH, BEAT STEELERS 28-7 (ATT 27,502)

OCTOBER 7, 1945

BOSTON YANKS HAND REDSKINS BITTER PILL IN GEORGE PRESTON MARSHALL'S RETURN TO HUB, YANKS WIN 28-20

NOVEMBER 4, 1945

YANK'S AUGIE LIO MISSES CONVERSION AND BOSTON LOSES BY A 10-9 SCORE TO LIONS (ATT 21,000)

NOVEMBER 17, 1945

PACKERS JUST TOO GOOD, AS YANKS FALL 28-0 BEFORE 35,000 AT FENWAY PARK

November 18, 1945 Green Bay Packers 28, Boston Yanks 0 (Football)
November 25, 1945 Holy Cross 46, Boston College 0 (Football)
April 28, 1946 Boston Braves 6, Philadelphia Phillies 1
April 28, 1946 Boston Braves 2, Philadelphia Phillies 1

JUNE 9, 1946

The Lone Red Seat

The lone red seat in the right field bleachers (Section 42, Row 37, Seat 21), signifies the spot where the longest measurable home run ever hit inside Fenway Park's 1934 configuration landed. Ted Williams hit the home run on June 9, 1946, off Fred Hutchinson of the Detroit Tigers. Williams' bomb was officially measured at 502 feet (153 m)—well beyond "Williamsburg". According to Hit Tracker Online, the ball, if unobstructed, would have flown 520 to 535 feet.

The ball landed on one Joseph A. Boucher, who was supposedly taking a nap at the time, penetrating his large straw hat and hitting him in the head. A confounded Boucher was later quoted as saying,

"How far away must one sit to be safe in this park? I didn't even get the ball. They say it bounced a dozen rows higher, but after it hit my head, I was no longer interested. I couldn't see the ball. Nobody could. The sun was right in our eyes. All we could do was duck. I'm glad I didn't stand up."

No other player at Fenway Park has ever hit that seat since, although on June 23, 2001, Manny Ramirez hit two home runs; one measuring 463 feet and another one that was said to have traveled 501 feet. The 501-foot blast landed somewhere in the Mass Pike/Railroad cut beyond left field and the official estimate deferred to Williams' record, placing Ramirez's home run exactly 1 foot short.

(World Architectural Images)

Jackie Robinson talks with Ted Williams at a Fenway Park gathering following Robinson's retirement. Of his 1945 Fenway tryout Robinson wrote, "Not for one minute did we believe the Boston tryout was sincere. We were going through the motions." *(Photograph by Dick Thomson, Courtesy of The Sports Museum)*

JUNE 14, 1946

Eastern All Star Nine Gains 6-2 Victory Over Mid-Westerners

By Will Cloney

New England collegians, headed by Jerry Daunt of Boston College, held their own with representatives of some 35 other institutions yesterday at Fenway Park as the Easstern All-Stars scored a 6-2 victory over their Mid-Western brethren in the somewhat timid inaugural of what may become an important annual diamond feature.

With the East using 19 players and the Mid-West 22, the cast of characters changed so rapidly that keeping an accurate box score would baffle anyone except a combination certified public accountant and detective. It was a much easier tack to count the paying customers, who couldn't have numbered more than 400, than it was to discover who was playing where when.

JULY 9, 1946

American League Administers Boston Massacre, Beat NL, 12-0

AMERICAN LEAGUE ALL-STAR GAME

After a year's interruption due to war-time travel restrictions, the American League crushed the National League in the most one-sided contest in All-Star Game history, 12-0. Three American League pitchers—Bob Feller, Hal Newhouser and Jack Kramer—combined to hold the National League to three harmless singles.

No fewer than eight members of the host Red Sox were included on an American League team that walloped their counterparts for fourteen hits including two home runs by Ted Williams, the last being a ninth-inning three-run shot hit off an eephus pitch by Pirate junkballer Rip Sewall.

The first All Star Game in Fenway Park history remains the most lopsided contest in the eight plus decade history of the game.

August 10, 1946 St. Paul 5, St. Louis 4 (32nd Annual Union Printers International Baseball Tournament)

August 25, 1946 The town of Gardner Ma brings giant chair to Fenway for Ted Williams.

AUGUST 26, 1946

Splinter Short Stopped

With Ted Williams at bat against the vaunted Boudreau Shift, the entire Cleveland infield was practically on Van Ness Street when dwarf and Vaudeville performer Marco Songini clambered out of the stands, grabbed Sox third baseman Mike Higgins glove and started pounding the leather while standing atop the third base bag. The crowd paused for a few seconds before players, umpires and fans started laughing at the clever stunt. After making his point Songini was boosted over the infield railing by Coach Buster Mills. He then struck a fighting pose on top of the Indians dugout before being escorted from the park. It remains one of the funniest and most offbeat stunts in Fenway history.

OCTOBER 1, 1946

Red Sox Beat All Stars

By Joe Cashman Boston Daily Record

Red Sox pitching was artistic but Red Sox hitting was anemic as our American league champions whitewashed the American league All Stars 2-0 while a scattering of 2,000 fans ran up and down the aisles in an effort to keep warm yesterday.

The All-Stars, represented by such sluggers as Joe DiMaggio, Stan Spencer, Luke Appling, George Stirnweiss and Cecil Travis failed to get a runner to third base as Tex Hughson, Joe Dobson, and Bill Zuber conspired to limit them to four widely separated safeties.

But the Hose hitters were almost as impotent against the southpaw slants of Mickey Haefner of the Senators and "Stubby" Overmire of the Tigers.

The Croninmen deserved only one run. Held to seven hits, they put over their two tallies in the second inning.

Walks by Ted Williams and Rudy York, separated by a Bobby Doerr double, filled the sacks with nobody out in the frame. Mike Higgins followed with a roller to Cecil Travis, who stepped on third for a force out and then tried to double up "Pinky" at first. The peg was wild, the ball hopping over Eddie Lopat and rolling to right field. So York as well as Williams registered.

Thereafter only two of the natives advanced as far as third base. They had a couple of scoring opportunities but tossed them away by hitting into double plays.

If the Sox play the Cardinals in the series, they'll face a flock of portsiders who are rated as effective as either Haefner or Overmire.

Tex Hughson, toiling the first five frames, was sparkling. He yielded only three hits and a walk. His speed handcuffed the All-Stars and they couldn't touch his other stuff either. Tex was fast against the Senators last Friday, striking out eight batters, but his curve and other deliveries were hit solidly by the foe, who fashioned 11 singles.

There was some question after that performance whether he'd get the assignment in the series opener. After yesterday's showing, it seems a safe bet that he'll be the starting slinger.

It wasn't much of a ball game to watch. Neither side appeared to care whether school kept or not. Incentive was lacking. And it was bitter cold.

The change in weather was a bad break for the All-Stars. Their only remuneration is the money taken in at the gates. They won't be able to buy more than doughnuts and coffee with their share of yesterday's receipts.

Williams Injured; Lost to Sox for Week

By Joe Cashman

If the World Series starts before next Sunday Teddy Williams won't be in the Red Sox lineup. The Hose mightiest macer was hit on the right arm by a Mickey "Lefty" Haefner pitch while at bat in the fifth inning of yesterday's Sox All-Star game at the Fens.

X-rays revealed he had escaped a fracture but his right elbow is swollen to the size of a toy balloon and the slightest movement to the arm causes intense pain.

Dr. Ralph McCarthy, club physician, opines that it will be a week before the Kid's throwing arm is back to normal.

The Sox without Williams are akin to a ship without its rudder. He's the big punch. He's the guy who shatters the nerves of opposing pitchers. But he'd be no threat with his arm as badly bruised as it is and he'll be missing from the lineup unless his wing is healed by the time the series starts.

The pitch that struck him looked from the roof like a fastball, well inside. He waited until the last split second, as is his habit, before pulling away from the plate. This time he waited an instant too long. As he turned his body, the ball struck him squarely on the elbow.

He gave no evidence of pain as he ambled down to first base, but an alarmed Joe Cronin lifted him from the lineup at once, putting on Leon Culberson to run, and sent in a hurried call for Dr. McCarthy.

The club physician, after a hasty examination of the injury, rushed the patient to the offices of Dr. Paul Butler for X-rays.

FIRST INJURY

The pictures dispelled fears of a fracture. That was some consolation, but there remained the despair in the Sox ranks caused by swelling and the pain in the stout arm of their slugger extraordinary.

It was the first time this year that Williams had been injured. He'd been out of the lineup a couple of

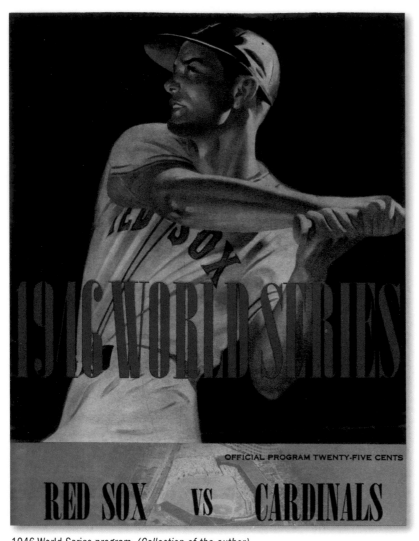

1946 World Series program. *(Collection of the author)*

1946 Fenway Park pass and World Series tickets.
(Courtesy of The Sports Museum)

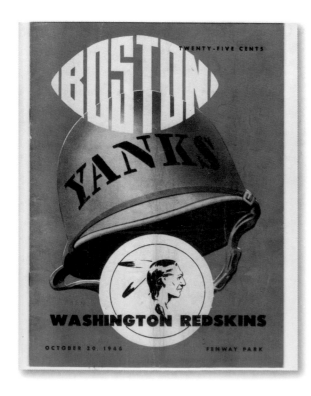

(above) Postcard showing Fenway's newly installed lights, c. 1947.
(Collection of the author)

(left) The Redskins, led by quarterback Sammy Baugh, returned to their
former home and beat the Yanks by a score of 20-0 on October 20, 1946.
(Collection of the author)

Military mass, c.1947. *(Courtesy of* The Boston Herald*)*

Purdue proved a mismatch for the 1947 Boston University football squad as the Boilermakers crushed the Terriers by a score of 62-7. *(Collection of the author)*

Boston University belted NYU by a score of 38-7 before a crowd of 6,000 in 1947. *(Collection of the author)*

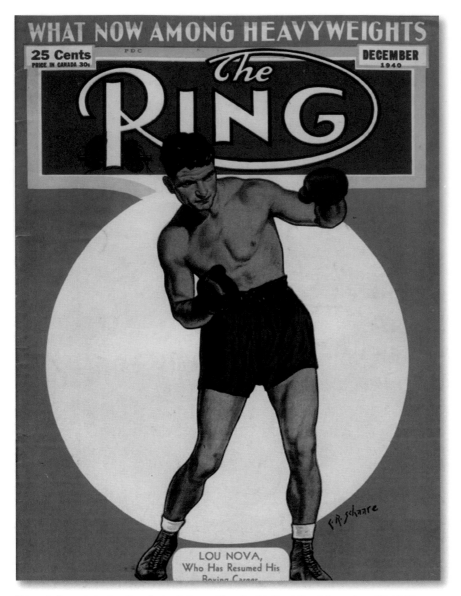

Future Hollywood star Lou Nova lost a first round knockout to Tami Mauriello on June 25, 1945.
(Collection of the author)

times, but those absences were due to an upset stomach. He had been nicked by pitches on two or three occasions but experienced no ill effects.

Ironically enough, Ted has been doing his best throwing of the campaign during the past few weeks; earlier he had been complaining of a soreness in his right shoulder.

But it isn't his throwing the Sox are thinking about. Their thinking is only of his bat swishing and what effect the injury may have on his hitting.

OCTOBER 9, 1946

Ferris Shuts Out Cards, 4-0 as Sox Takes Series Lead

In the first World Series game played at Fenway Park in 28 years, the Red Sox, behind the pitching of 25-game winner Dave "Boo" Ferris shut out the Cardinals by a score of

4-0. Rudy York supplied most of the runs courtesy of his first-inning three-run homer. Fans were also delighted to see Ted Williams bunt for a single with two outs in the third inning against a shift improvised by Cardinal manager Eddie Dyer.

OCTOBER 10, 1946

Cardinals Rout Boston, 12 -3 , Tie Series

Twenty game winner Cecil "Tex" Hughson endured possibly the worst start of his career while giving up six hits and three earned runs in just two innings as the Cardinals romped by a score of 12-3. Future broadcaster Joe Garagiola enjoyed a banner day with four hits and 3 RBIs. Cardinal right-hander Red Munger enjoyed the game of his life while scattering 9 hits and allowing just one earned run while pitching a complete game for his first and only career World Series victory.

OCTOBER 11, 1946

Sox Win 6-3 Behind Dobson, Take 3-2 Series Lead

Red Sox fans had never experienced a World Series loss and departed Fenway Park confident of an imminent title after watching fourth starter Joe Dobson dominate the Cardinals to draw Boston to within a victory of their sixth world championship with a possible two games remaining to be played in St Louis. Dobson earned his first and only

World Series victory by holding the Cardinals to just 4 hits as the Red Sox mounted a balanced attack that included a home run by right fielder Leon Culberson and doubles by Dom DiMaggio and Pinky Higgins.

OCTOBER 20, 1946

SAMMY BAUGH LEADS WASHINGTON REDSKINS TO 20-0 WIN OVER YANKS

OCTOBER 27, 1946

STEELERS THRASH YANKS 33-7

NOVEMBER 3, 1946

CHICAGO CARDINALS BEAT HAPLESS YANKS 28-14

NOVEMBER 24, 1946

YANKS BEAT LOS ANGELES RAMS 40-21

DECEMBER 8, 1946

EAGLES SMOTHER YANKS 40-14 (ATT 29, 555)

JANUARY 4, 1947

LIGHTS INSTALLED AT FENWAY PARK

June 4, 1947 Somerville High 5, Wayland High
June 4, 1947 Newton High, Malden Catholic 6
June 5, 1947 Lynn Classical 12, Boston College High 0
June 5, 1947 Belmont High 9, Norwood High 4
June 6, 1947 Newton High 8, Somerville High 0
June 6, 1947 Lynn Classical 7, Belmont High 5

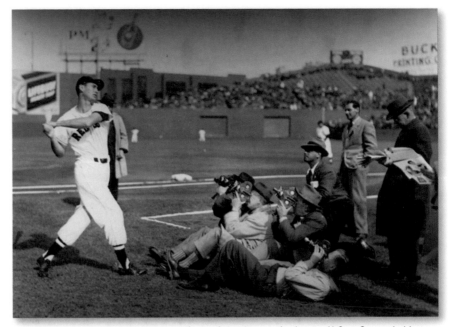

Ted Williams was the major attraction of two of the three major league Al-Star Games held at Fenway Park while walloping two home runs in the 1946 game and bidding a tearful farewell to Boston in 1999. *(Courtesy of Mike Andersen)*

June 7, 1947 Lynn Classical 7, Newton High 6

JUNE 13, 1947

Red Sox Play First Night Tilt

35,000 WATCH SOX WIN , 5-3

Jack Malaney, Boston Post

The lights go at Fenway Park tonight for the first official night baseball game there and the first appearance of the Red Sox at home in over three weeks. And though the Red Sox wobbled all over the American League circuit since they were last seen in Boston, they have lost little of their popularity judging by the demand for reserved seats for the affair.

NO CEREMONIES

Though it is quite an event in the history of the Sox, there will be no special ceremonies or fireworks or vaudeville. It will be just a ballgame with the Sox opposing the Pale Hose of Chicago. At 8:10 as the sun goes down, Old Glory will be hauled down. That will be the lone ceremony.

The lights have been turned on several times in trials. The was a preview of the illumination last night for the press, and the general opinion of all who have seen a demonstration is that they are everything the Sox claim—as good as if not better than any other lights in baseball.

There was a time a few years back when it was a fairly good wager that there would never be lights at Fenway. Tom Yawkey doesn't like that type of baseball and hasn't changed his mind even with the installation of the newest thing in lighting equipment. But he bowed to public opinion and the necessity of being geared to compete with the Braves for football, for instance.

The Red Sox gave an illuminating demonstration that they are on their way back to their former heights when they defeated the Chicago White Sox in the first game played under lights at night at Fenway Park last night, 5 to 3. A capacity crowd of 34,510 highly enthusiastic fans, the second largest turnout of the year at the Sox park, were on hand for the occasion.

AUGUST 2, 1947

BOBBY DOERR NIGHT

**SEPTEMBER 27, 1947
BOSTON UNIVERSITY 45, MOHAWK COLLEGE 7**

SEPTEMBER 29, 1947

GIANTS TIE YANKS 7-7 IN NIGHT CONTEST BEFORE 21,905

OCTOBER 5, 1947

BILL DUDLEY LEADS LIONS OVER YANKS 21-7

OCTOBER 11, 1947

BOSTON UNIVERSITY BELTS NYU FOR 38-7 VICTORY BEFORE 6000 AT FENWAY

OCTOBER 12, 1947

STEELERS BEAT YANKS 30-24

OCTOBER 18, 1947

PURDUE SLAUGHTERS BU, 62-7 BEFORE 11,446 AT FENWAY

NOVEMBER 1, 1947

BOSTON UNIVERSITY 26, FORDHAM 6

NOVEMBER 2, 1947

SID LUCKMAN LEADS CHICAGO BEARS TO 28-24 WIN OVER YANKS

NOVEMBER 15, 1947

BOSTON UNIVERSITY 33, KINGS POINT MERCHANT MARINE 6

NOVEMBER 22, 1947

BOSTON UNIVERSITY CONQUER COLGATE RED RAIDERS, 20-14, BEFORE 15,000 AT FENWAY

NOVEMBER 23, 1947

EAGLES ARE UPSET BY YANKS 21-14 (ATT 15,366)

NOVEMBER 30, 1947

BOLEY DANCEWICZ OUTSLINGS SAMMY BAUGH, LEADS YANKS TO 27-24 WIN OVER REDSKINS

JUNE 16, 1948

Brockton Gains Eastern Title

CLASSICAL FALLS BY 4-2; MILFORD DOWNS CASE, 13-3

By Ralph Wheeler

Brockton High won the Eastern State interscholastic baseball championship by dethroning the defending champion, Lynn Classical, 4-2, and Milford High walloped previously undefeated Case High of Swansea, 13-3, to annex the championship of the first annual small schools' tournament at Fenway Park yesterday afternoon.

BROCKTON IN FINAL AT HOLYOKE SATURDAY

Brockton, which last won the Eastern State title in 1939, will play Cathedral High of Springfield for the state championship at Holyoke next Saturday afternoon.

The Shoe City nine, coached by Charley Holden, richly deserved its title yesterday, since its two pitchers, Eddie Pellegrini and Warrin Boutin, restricted Lynn Classical to three scattered singles. Boutin, a southpaw, enjoyed the distinction of having finished up all three games played by Brockton in the tournament, being credited with victories in the quarter-final and semi-final rounds.

Armand Colombo's sensational glove-hand catch of George Bullard's fly at the foot of the left field wall, with the bases loaded and Brockton nursing a 4-1 lead, in the seventh inning, saved the day for the South Shore entry.

The brilliant quarterback of the Brockton football team, lost his balance as he was moving up the slight incline in left field but he threw up his hand just as it seemed that the ball was going to hit the wall, for the most spectacular play of the tournament.

Case, which had gone through the regular season undefeated in 15 games, fell apart entirely, making nine errors, while its two pitchers were giving up eight bases on balls. Joe Stoico, Milford first baseman, hit a triple and a single to drive in three runs in the nine-run fifth.

July 13, 1948 Mayor's Charity Field Day: New England Hoboes 2, Dick Casey Club 0

Congressional candidate John Fitzgerald Kennedy made a campaign appearance at Fenway in 1946 with (left to right) Ted Williams, Eddie Pellagrini, and Hank Greenberg. *(Collection of the author)*

SEPTEMBER 17, 1948

GREEN BAY RUNS WILD AT FENWAY, BEAT YANKS 31-0

SEPTEMBER 23, 1948

SWIACKI STAR AS N.Y. GIANTS BOMB YANKS 27 -7 BEFORE 7,428 AT FENWAY PARK

OCTOBER 4, 1948

Indians Knock Red Sox Out of Series, Feller to Pitch Against Braves' Sain

DEFEAT STUNS SOX ROOTERS

FANS "DISINTERESTED" IN SERIES CLASH NOW

By Arthur Stratton

A young woman with two tiny red socks pinned to the lapel of her jacket dropped a noise maker and three unopened packages of confetti to the floor of the grandstand at Fenway Park at 4:00 yesterday, and with these useless articles also fell the emotions of 33,957 persons that may never again be aroused to such a pitch by baseball.

LOSS INCREDIBLE

To that partisan Red Sox crowd, this week's world series, even with their friends the Braves as co-participants, won't be anti-climactic, it will be a wake. Or, as one member of the dejected Fenway faithful expressed it: "I shall be a disinterested spectator at Braves Field Wednesday."

To be awakened at all from the fantastic dream that saw its club

The Bears edged the Yanks by a score of 28-24 on November 2, 1947. *(Collection of the author)*

Fans enjoy a front row view of the heroes. *(Photograph by Leslie Jones, Courtesy of The Boston Public library)*

Boston University (striped helmets) faces off against St. Bonaventure at Fenway Park on November 19, 1949. *(Photograph by Dick Thomson, Courtesy of The Boston Public library)*

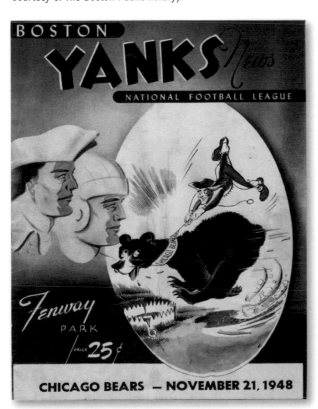

In their second-to-last ever home game, the Boston Yanks lost to the Bears by a score of 51-17. *(Collection of the author)*

Boston University, led by triple-threat quarterback Harry Agganis, beat NYU by a score of 38-0 at Fenway in 1949. *(Courtesy of the Agganis family)*

first deadlock the pennant race and then provide what could have been the game of games, with the whole American League pot at stake, was disconcerting enough, but then to have their hopefuls turn it into a nightmare was incredible.

It was difficult for this crowd to accept the realization there still wouldn't be another chance, even after the victor-crazed Indians carried the five-hit Gene Bearden off the field on their shoulders. So many times their Sox had come through like true baseball thoroughbreds that it was not until long after the last player had left the field did it dawn on the bulk of the crowd that the blank space under "Here Tomorrow" truly meant there would be no more games at Fenway this year.

But one could sense after that horrible first of the fourth, when Ken Keltner neatly spanned the uprights of the arc light structure in left field with a three-run homer, that the partisans had begun to entertain the possibility that this game could be lost. Never again were our spirits as high.

NOT BASEBALL WEATHER

From the standpoint of good baseball, it wasn't worth staying up all night or risking life and limb to get a ticket. Certainly it wasn't baseball weather, as the shivering crowd gave plain evidence. But no real Red Sox fan could afford to confess he didn't see this unprecedented playoff.

It was a challenge to the VIPs, too, to be seen at Fenway yesterday, and from the turn-out of those in the political, theatrical and baseball worlds, these big sports event regulars made good. The short notice given them, however, made many content with $1.80 seats far up in the grandstand instead of the towel-covered chairs of the front boxes.

Undoubtedly the most crowded area of Fenway Park just before game time was at the so-called press gate. Thousands of friends of friends of some individual with influence milled around the mounted policemen, but so far as could be observed along about the third inning, they all got inside.

"You wouldn't think it was a working day," observed one woman to another as they pushed their way into the grandstand.

Thousands came equipped for a roaring victory celebration. They carried cow bells, horns and other racket makers, but they began to disappear steadily as the Indians' leader Lou Boudreau and Keltner sent those long ones over the fence and as our side couldn't seem to get into the spirit of things.

In the late stages of the "struggle," when the visitors appeared on their way to make the score something like 18 to 3, instead of 8 to 3, many of the home folks began to accept the disaster philosophically. When a Cleveland batter began shelling the short stands in back of third base, near left field, with hard-driven fouls, a number of white handkerchiefs began waving.

This gesture of surrender did not manifest itself elsewhere in the park on any large scale, but it was what many were thinking before the game was much more than an hour old.

OCTOBER 17, 1948

YANKS BLAST PITTSBURGH STEELERS OUT OF 1ST PLACE, 13-7, BEFORE 7,208 AT FENWAY PARK

OCTOBER 22, 1948

BOSTON UNIVERSITY 28, NEW YORK UNIVERSITY 7

OCTOBER 30, 1948

BOSTON UNIVERSITY 12, SYRACUSE 7

NOVEMBER 7, 1948

SAMMY BAUGH TOSSES 2 TDS TO LEAD REDSKINS TO 23-7 VICTORY OVER YANKS BEFORE 13,659 AT FENWAY

NOVEMBER 21, 1948

CHICAGO BEARS MAUL YANKS 51-17 BEFORE 18,048 AT FENWAY

DECEMBER 3, 1948

Champ Eagles Upset By Last-Place Yanks, 37-14, at Fenway

A crowd of 9,652 saw both the greatest and last game in the short history of the Boston Yanks as the underdogs upset the NFL East Champion Philadelphia Eagles by a score of 37-14. Following the game Yanks owner Ted Collins remarked, "I guess we'll move," but added, "I don't know for sure yet and I may be back again next season. It's strictly an economic situation." (Author's note: Collins moved the team to New York the next season where they played as the New York Bulldogs. Later the franchise shifted to Dallas where they played as the Dallas Texans in 1952. Ultimately they moved to Baltimore where they became the Colts who now play in Indianapolis.)

Source: The Berkshire Daily Eagle, page 16, December 6, 1948

OCTOBER 14, 1949

AGGANIS SPARKS BU TO VICTORY OVER WEST VIRGINIA 52-20 BEFORE 19,300 AT FENWAY

OCTOBER 22, 1949

BU REMAINS UNDEFEATED, BEAT NYU, 38-0 AT RAIN SOAKED FENWAY

OCTOBER 29, 1949
BOSTON UNIVERSITY 46, SCRANTON 6

NOVEMBER 12, 1949

MARYLAND STOPS B.U. 14-13

TOPPLED IN FOURTH QUARTER

TERRAPINS' 81-YARD DRIVE SNAPS SIX-GAME STREAK

Boston University's splendid football team stumbled on the threshold of its cherished pot of gold yesterday. After outplaying a powerful University of Maryland eleven most of the way, the Terriers were nipped, 14-13, before a crowd of 30,263 at Fenway Park when an 81-yard fourth-period march by the Terrapins overcame a six-point B.U. lead.

Three breaks enabled the visitors from College Park, Md., to stay in the game and at the same time prevented the home team from running up what could easily have been a 20-point lead." (Boston *Post*)

Harry Agganis, playing the entire game, did a good job, but was prevented from taking a sensational part in the play by the way the Maryland players checked the B.U. ends on the line of scrimmage and then heckled them down the field... George Sulima was well-covered throughout the afternoon... The attention he received didn't prevent him from being one of the stars of the game, but it did keep him from getting loose for any long touchdown heaves.

Agganis completed eight of thirteen passes, but most of them were short ones into the flat, and they produced only 65 yards. If the officials, who were so sure they saw a few other vital plays correctly, had wanted to watch the attention Sulima was getting illegally, as well as the legitimate meat-grinding he was forcing his way through, perhaps Agganis would have been able to find an uncovered pass receiver more often.

Since the score of this game was virtually a tie, and each team has lost one game, some Bowl committee might do worse than schedule a play-off on January first... It will probably be New Year's Day before some of the Maryland students who first ripped down one set of goal posts and then attacked the B.U. bandsmen near the opposite posts, are ready for another post-game brawl.

(Author's note: This game also marked the first play-by-play broadcast assignment for 21-year-old Fordham graduate Vin Scully. Scully has gone on to become the legendary voice of the Dodgers, both in Brooklyn and Los Angeles, where he now enters his seventh decade of service to the team.)

November 19, 1949 St. Bonaventure 19, Boston University 0 (Football)

AT BAT | STRIKE | BALL | HIT | ERROR | OUT | INNING | VISITORS | BOSTON

Hall of Fame shortstop Joe Cronin and Mike "Pinky" Higgins were the principal members of a Red Sox brain trust that saw the Red Sox finish out of the money and attain the dubious distinction of becoming the last major league team to integrate, some $2^1/_2$ seasons after Jackie Robinson retired. *(Courtesy of The Boston Public Library)*

CHAPTER FIVE
Twilight Time

"Then here's to the City of Boston, The town of the cries and the groans,
Where the Cabots can't see the Kabotschniks, And the Lowells won't speak to the Cohns."

—FRANKLIN P. ADAMS

The promising postwar Red Sox faded quicker than a December sunset as Fenway Park began a slow decline through the fifties. Sure, Teddy Ballgame made things interesting in between flying combat missions and throwing temper tantrums. And for all his drama, Ted Williams was one of the most compelling solists since Jascha Heifetz. For when one ponders his single-minded devotion to, and perfection of, the art of hitting while playing for the dreary also-ran Red Sox of the fifties, one comprehends why he'd tossed a bat or occasionally spit at the press box.

Following the departure of the Braves in 1953, not only did Boston miss the arrival of Henry Aaron by a season, but the Red Sox also adopted the Jimmy Fund from their former Back Bay neighbors. In due time the only billboard allowed at Fenway would trumpet the Jimmy Fund as team owner Tom Yawkey along with

Ted Williams would help raise millions for the fledgling charity.

On the field the team that missed signing both Jackie Robinson and Willie Mays finally integrated in 1959 when Elijah "Pumpsie" Green made his debut in 1959. This was a full two and a half years after both the retirement of Robinson and the NHL debut of Bruin Willie O'Ree as the league's first black player.

As television tightened its grip on Greater Boston's leisure hours, the sheer number and variety of activities at Fenway changed as apart from the rare Field Day, Mass, Globetrotter game, or college gridiron clash, the park was mostly silent following baseball season. The only consistent sporting tenant of the park, apart from the Red Sox, were those candlepin bowlers lucky enough to discover the alley hidden in a basement snug underneath the Jersey Street ticket offices.

One of the great hallmarks of Ted Williams legendary career was that he was named "Player of The Decade" by *The Sporting News* during the fifties while playing for non-contenders. *(Photograph by Leslie Jones, Courtesy of The Boston Public library)*

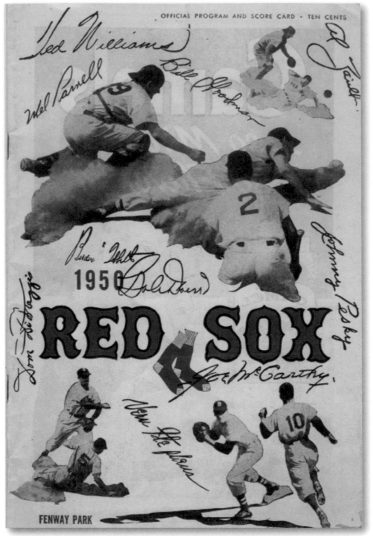

The 1950 Red Sox were a team of bashers while leading the league with 1,027 runs and batting .302 as a team. Iffy pitching saw them finish in third, four games behind the Yankees. *(Collection of the author)*

Cigarettes were very much a part of the 1950's ballpark ambience as broadcaster Jim Britt hawked Chesterfields in the company of a Fenway Park vendor *(Collection of the author)*

APRIL 16, 1950

CITY SERIES, RED SOX 3, BRAVES 1

Braves rookie right hander and future Atlanta Braves broadcaster, Vermont native Ernie Johnson, surrendered a 3-run homer to Ted Williams in the eighth inning before a crowd of 15,203.

JUNE 8, 1950

Red Sox Beat St. Louis Browns 29-4

SOX SHATTERS RECORDS, BELTING BROWNS, 29-4

By Joe Cashman

Ruth and Gehrig and the rest of the old Yankees, they only busted the ball. Cobb and Crawford and the others of those old Tigers, they swung toothpicks.

The Red Sox, my friends, yesterday climaxed a week of unprecedented slugging by unleashing the mightiest offensive seen on a diamond since baseball was invented more than a century ago.

They beat the Browns from St. Louis by a score of 29-4 by way of demonstrations to a house of 5,105 that they had been only warming up when they walloped the visitors 20-4 the day before.

SIZZLING DAY

That run total was the highest compiled by one club in one game in the major league since 1900. The previous high was 28 by the Cardinals of 1929. The American League mark was 27 by the Cleveland Indians in 1923.

That was only one of several records shattered by the Hose on this sizzling afternoon as they cut loose with a bombardment that contained three home runs by Bobby Doerr, and two each by Ted Williams and Walt Dropo.

The two consecutive game run total of 49 was a new major league high. An old Pirate team had scored 45 in two games running; the Red Sox of '40 and the Yanks of '36 had scored 40 in two consecutive contests.

Twenty-eight hits popped off Sox bats, which was two shy of the record for one game, but those 28, added to the 23 of the bad day before, gave the McCarthy men credit for 51 safeties in two straight games, and that was a new mark. A Pittsburgh club had made 49 hits in two straight games, while the A.L. record had been 46.

DOUBLE MARK

The seven Boston home runs in one game was one short of the major league in that respect, but these round-trippers helped hoist the Sox total base figures for the day to 60, another all-time high. Back in the prehistoric past, the Cincinnati club had made 55 total bases. Since 1900, the highest T.B. mark had been 53 by the Yankees in '39. When the game was over, a writer's scorebook was of minor importance. A record book was all-important.

Clyde Vollmer, Sox lead-off man, got his name in the book by going to bat eight times in a nine-inning game. Since 1900, nobody else had ever stepped to the plate more than seven times in a regulation contest. Clyde was up eight times in eight innings. He swung

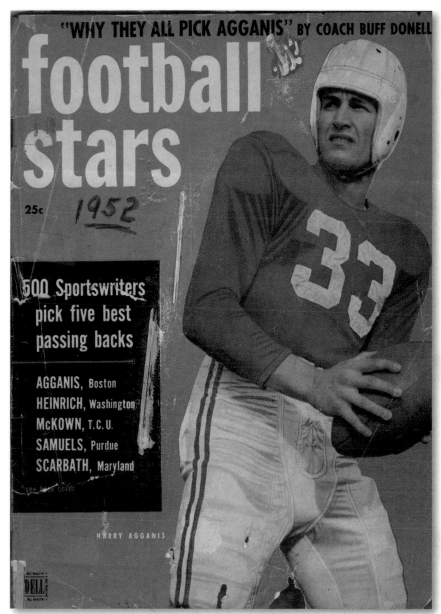

Lynn Massachusetts native Harry Agganis rejected scholarship offers from schools like USC and Notre Dame to remain in Boston where he starred as a triple-threat performer (quarterback, defensive back, and punter) for Boston University. (*Courtesy of The Sports Museum*)

once in seven different frames and got to bat twice in the third.

In three consecutive innings, the Sox more than batted around.

Al Zarilla tied a record by getting four doubles in one game and also picked up a single. Johnny Pesky got five hits. Chuck Stobbs drew walks on four successive trips to the platter, which must be a record for consecutive passes received by a pitcher, as well as a record for ineffectiveness on the part of the

pitchers against a pitcher at the plate.

Getting three homers in the one afternoon, Doerr fashioned as many as he had in 43 previous games this season. Bobby knocked in eight runs.

Dropo, hitting his 13th and 14th homers, rescued seven tallies and now has an RBI mark of 52 for 36 games. Williams, hitting homers 15 and 16, knocked in five runs.

Superfan "Megaphone" Lolly Hopkins was a fixture at both Braves Field and Fenway Park for two generations. *(Photograph by Leslie Jones, Courtesy of the Boston Public Library)*

INCREDIBLE .313

Verne Stephens, the Sox and the league's leader in the RBI department, chased home three tallies with a triple, double and single, and now has rescued 61 runs in 49 games.

For the day, the Hose batted .538. Their team average for the season is an incredible .313.

The game never has witnessed such tremendous sustained power as the McCarthymen have exhibited in the seven games of this home stand.

In those seven contests, the Back Bay boys have scored 104 runs, which is an average of virtually 15 a game. That's fantastic.

The highest number of runs ever scored by a Sox team in the past was 29 by the 1940 club against the Senators.

Yesterday the natives reached that total in seven innings. Then they added five runs in the eighth.

SOFTEST JOB

Their big inning was the second wherein they scored eight times

against Cliff Fannin. Williams hit a three-run homer high in the centerfield stands and Dropo dropped one into the left-field nets with one on during that explosion.

The third inning saw them tear into Clarence Marshall for five runs. They scored seven in the fourth, when Doerr delivered the first of his homers and Stephens tripled. Marshall was in the showers before little Sid Schacht could check the conflagration. The latter was a victim of what cannonading the Hose did thereafter.

Doerr's second homer came in a two-run seventh. His third followed the second round-trippers of the day by Williams and Dropo in the eighth.

Stobbs, with little incentive to bear down, gave up eight hits and seven walks and hit a batter in annexing his fourth win.

Wouldn't you like to be pitching for these Red Sox? That's the softest job in baseball these days.

BATTING AROUND

Twelve Sox went to the bat in the second inning, eleven in the third, and eleven more in the fourth...Thirty-four batters in three successive innings... It's a safe bet that's a record.

If this keeps up, it will require a certified public accountant as well as a baseball writer to cover a game...The Hose made six hits in three different innings; got one hit or more in every stanza.

The sun scorching, bleacherites were invited to move into the grandstand soon after the game started... Not all accepted the invitation.

Williams is running ahead of his home run pace of last year, when he hit 43...He didn't hit his 16th until June 17 in 1949.

CLIMB TO .384

Dropo may well be the leader among the Big Six batters when he enters the final game of this series with the Browns this afternoon... The big fellow climbed to .384 by getting four blows in six tries yesterday...Zarilla moved up to .367, Pesky to .358.

Maurice McDermott is down to face the lowly invaders this p.m.... Ned Garver, the Browns' one effective pitcher, will see what he can do about cooling off the Sox sticks.

June 12, 1950 Tufts College Baseball Team Workout (The '50 Jumbos made it all the way to the College World Series

July 11, 1950 Mayor's Charity Field Day: New England Hoboes 3, Philadelphia Colored All-Stars 3

August 13, 1950 St. Anthony's (Everett) 20, St. Theresa's (West Roxbury) 1 (CYO Game)

OCTOBER 13, 1950

**ST. BONAVENTURE 25,
BOSTON UNIVERSITY 21**

OCTOBER 28, 1950
**SYRACUSE 13, BOSTON
UNIVERSITY 7**

NOVEMBER 4, 1950
**BOSTON UNIVERSITY 16,
WILLIAM & MARY 14**

NOVEMBER 11, 1950
**BOSTON UNIVERSITY 41,
NEW YORK UNIVERSITY 13**

NOVEMBER 18, 1950
**UNIVERSITY OF IDAHO 26,
BOSTON UNIVERSITY 19**

APRIL 15, 1951
**CITY SERIES, RED SOX 6,
BRAVES 3 (WINNER, MAURY
MCDERMOTT)**

MAY 15, 1951:

Years Turn Back at Fenway Park Today

OLD-TIMERS HELP RED SOX MARK A.L.'S ANNIVERSARY

By Jack McCarthy

They were sitting around the lobby of the Kenmore, re-living the old days to the hilt. It had been forty years since they had barbered in a hotel lobby, longer since some of them had seen one another. They were the men who had been playing baseball in 1901, the first year of the American League.

DAYS OF SPITTER, SHINE BALLS RECALLED

A few starry-eyed schoolboys were moving among them, getting autographs, even though these men were mere names of whom their grandfathers had talked. There were

The railroad tracks at the back of Fenway Park remain to this day. More than a few home run blasts bounced their way onto the rail bed. *(Photograph by Leslie Jones, Courtesy of the Boston Public Library)*

Connie Mack, Charley Hemphill, Fred Mitchell, Cy Young, Harry "Kid" Gleason, Hughie Duffy, Lou "Sport" McAlister, Bill "Boileryard" Clarke, and Harry Howell, to name a few.

Today they'll help the Red Sox celebrate the 50th anniversary of the League. They'll parade to the State House, City Hall, through Scollay Square and finally stand once again at home plate prior to the Red Sox–Chicago game, and hear the cheers they've missed for nearly a half century.

Yesterday was a time for memories and tall stories of when baseball was in swaddling clothes; stories of themselves, of the days of the spitter, the shine ball, the emery ball.

Mr. Mack was the last one in, unmistakable in the high celluloid collar – Mr. Baseball. The ol' timers walked up to him with a sort of reverence, and shook his hand,

and he, slowly peering from under white eyebrows, identified them all. That is, they all were reverent except Harry Howell, the old Baltimore spitball pitcher.

Harry wrung Connie's hand heartily, slapped him on the back and bellowed, "Connie, I played baseball for 100 years and made $1,000,000. I'm gonna take that million and build an old-ball-players' home. And the first one I'm gonna want to take in will be you."

The old Oriole didn't play quite 100 years, for he's only a mere 77, and he didn't make a million, either, but he has an inexhaustible fund of stories of baseball, and he brought them all with him from Spokane, Wash.

SEAWEED-CHEWER BANE OF HITTERS' EXISTENCE

He's quite a guy, this Harry Howell. He uses two canes only because he

Fans wait patiently in a line at the Jersey Street ticket windows in 1955. *(Photograph by Leslie Jones, Courtesy of the Boston Public Library)*

split his kneecaps a few years ago while working as a steam-fitter. His booming voice attracts attention throughout the lobby as he tells his tales, but he disappears every now and then – and sneaks off to the Marine Room to play the piano.

"Got to have a half-hour practice every day, or I'll get rusty," he says.

They used to call him Handsome Harry when he was with the Orioles and the St. Louis Americans. He had his own distinctive pitch, "the seaweed spitter." Instead of using saliva or tobacco juice, he'd chew the seaweed, and "inside of an inning, I'd be frothing at the mouth like a racehorse, and so would the batters. Nobody could hit that spitter when I was right. Although some days I wasn't right. Threw it into the grandstand near third base once."

"I remember once I was pitching a tight game against Rube Waddell, and who was the hitter but Nap Lajoie. Threw him two

spitters, and he almost broke his back. Then I decided to dust him. It went right down the middle and Larry hit it off the center-field fence, and lost me the ball game. But I was a control pitcher, not like that kid I watched yesterday (Chris Van Cuyk of Brooklyn)."

"That boy reminds me of Waddell. He could be a great pitcher, but he doesn't know how to pitch. He said to me last night, 'Show me what I'm doing wrong.'

"We only had a few minutes to talk, but I told him to start throwing with his body, not his arm. I wish I had him, I wish they had the spitter back. Then I'd be able to teach them something and home-run hitters would disappear from baseball.

"In my day (1901-1910), the spitter kept 'em from getting set and taking that full cut. They got so they hunched up and started trying to punch it to get a good piece of it, instead of hitting on top when it broke down. It was hard to hold, too."

"I remember once when this skinny kid named Branch Rickey said he could catch me. He stayed in there for nine innings – he was game – but he hadn't caught one yet. It was hitting him on the wrists, the arms and the chest. Yes, sir, it was hard to hold."

"You're not kidding!" broke in Sport McAlister. "I used to catch spitball pitchers, and look at these fingers." Sport used to catch without a glove, sometimes with a piece of steak on his palm, wrapped in canvas. Harry, Sport, and the rest of them, will be out there tomorrow, in a big-league park once again, in front of the crowd. Wonder what they'll be thinking of?

Old Timers Score Indifferent Attitude of Modern Day Stars

By Murray Kramer

Baseball is still a grand old game, but 28 veterans who helped write American League history in 1901, feel that the major leaguers of today are just a bit too mechanical and lack the pep and fire of the past.

Taking part in the Red Sox Golden Anniversary celebration yesterday, these 28 stars of yesteryear who were in the A.L. the year of its founding, were having themselves a wonderful time.

On the day that Ted Williams bid Boston farewell prior to entering the Marine Corps for his second hitch, the slugger was honored in a pregame ceremony that included both the Tigers and Red Sox assembled in a "wing" formation for the playing of the "Star Spangled Banner." *(Courtesy of Fay Ruby)*

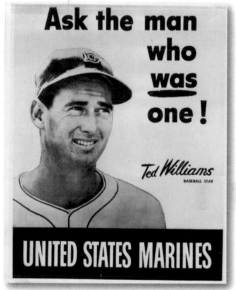

Ted Williams served in the Korean conflict in a unit that also included future astronaut/politician John Glenn and New York Yankee second baseman Jerry Coleman. *(Collection of the author)*

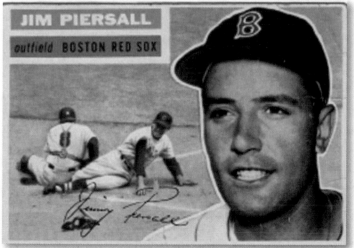

Waterbury, Connecticut, native Jimmy Piersall was an instant fan favorite at Fenway. Not only was he a dazzlingly talented center fielder but he also battled Yankee second baseman Billy Martin in a memorable brawl on May 24, 1952. *(Courtesy of The Sports Museum)*

Bill Bradley, Bill Hoffer, Pat
Livingston, Earl Moore, Oliver
Pickering, Frank Schelbeck
DETROIT – Louis McAllister
MILWAUKEE – William Conroy,
Hugh Duffy, Bill Friel, Bill
Maloney, George McBride
PHILADELPHIA – Dave Fultz,
Tom Leahy, Connie Mack

The big day started at 10:30
a.m. when the 1901 veterans were
greeted by Gov. Paul A. Dever...
They then paraded through downtown Boston in 1901 vehicles, stopping off at City Hall to be welcomed
by Mayor John B. Hynes...The parade route was down Washington
St. to Scollay Sq., up Tremont St.
to Boylston and down as far as
Charles St....Thousands lined the
course to pay tribute to these grand
old men of baseball.

A buffet luncheon at Fenway
Park followed... The stars of 1901
were then driven on the field in the
same 1901 vehicles in which they
rode for the parade and gathered at
the home plate... Curt Gowdy, Sox
baseball broadcaster, introduced
each of the 28 players and most of
them said a few words...

Cy Young, Connie Mack,
Hugh Duffy and Clark Griffith
received royal welcomes... Harry
Howell made a hit when he said,
"I hope the Sox win the pennant
by 10 games."...Charles Hemhill,
Sox outfielder in '01, and Bill
Clarke, Washington catcher of that
era, both accepted invitations, but
didn't make it... The only other
living pitchers from 1901 not on
hand were Bill Clingham, Jim
Jackson, Nap Lajoie and August
"Cannonball" Weyhing.

The windup was a big dinner
at the Kenmore last night... The
grand old guys will start scattering

New York Giant center fielder Willie Mays calls out to a teammate prior to The Jimmy Fund
game on August 16, 1954. Mays should have signed with the Red Sox in 1950 but was passed
over in what was one of the more egregious examples of mis-management in franchise
history. *(Photograph by Dick Thomson, Courtesy of The Sports Museum)*

to all parts of the nation today... It
was a day for them... As one said,
"It's probably the last time we'll
ever be together again."

Gov. Paul A. Dever headed
a list of speakers which included
Connie Mack, Clark Griffith,
William Harridge, president of the
American League, Cy Young, and
Lou Bremer, representing Mayor
Hynes at the breakup party...

Billy Dale Goodman shared
some of the glory with the Old
Timers before the game... While
the veterans of ol' were still gathered around the home plate,
Will Harridge, president of the
American League, presented
Goodman with the "Bud" Hillerich
Memorial Award – a sterling silver
replica of his own bat for having
won the American League batting
championship last year.

June 4, 1951 Camp Lejeune
Marines 4, Boston College 3
(Navy Relief Society Benefit)
June 6, 1951 Somerville High 11,
Melrose High 4
June 6, 1951 Haverhill High 3,
Natick High 1
June 7, 1951 Mission High 7,
Hyde Park High 1
June 7, 1951 Durfee High 2,
Newton High 1
June 8, 1951 Somerville High 2,
Haverhill High 0
June 8, 1951 Mission High 11,
Durfee High 9
June 9, 1951 Somerville High 6,
Mission High 4 (Eastern Mass
Schoolboy Tournament Title
Game)
June 9, 1951 Hudson High 6,
Scituate High 0 (Eastern Mass
Schoolboy Tournament "Small
School" Title Game)
June 28, 1951 Sandlot Baseball
Championship

Ted Williams celebrates his return to Boston in 1953 following combat duty in the Korean conflict. *(Photograph by Leslie Jones, Courtesy of the Boston Public Library)*

APRIL 30, 1952

Sox Win 5-3 on Ted's HR

KID BIDS HUB ADIEU, PART II FAREWELL BLAST RUINS TIGERS

Joe Cashman, Boston Record

Ted Williams said his second baseball farewell in 10 years with a game-winning, two-run homer yesterday to give the Boston Red Sox a 5-3 victory over the Detroit Tigers.

Williams' first 1952 four-bagger, the 324th of his major league career, strengthened the Red Sox' hold on first place as he left them

to rejoin the U.S. Marines for a 17-month tour of duty as a flyer.

Making his first appearance in the starting lineup since the opening game in Washington, during which he pulled a leg muscle, Williams drove one in to the right field stand against Dizzy Trout, with Dom DiMaggio on base in the seventh inning to break a 3-3 tie.

Hollywood End Provided By Ted

By Murray Kramer

"A script writer couldn't have provided a more perfect setting," yelled Manager Lou Boudreau, as the Sox happily stormed into their dressing room yesterday. "What a grand way for the big guy to bow out."

And it was a script writer's dream.

It was Ted Williams' last time at bat – the score was tied 3-8 in the seventh – 24,764 fans had turned out to pay tribute to The Kid – they had lavished him with gifts before the game, ranging from a gold tie clasp to a robin's egg-blue Cadillac – Ted was leaving.

TOWERING DRIVE

He came through. A towering home run into the centerfield bleachers off Dizzy Trout scored the two runs that meant victory.

It gave him tremendous satisfaction, yet Ted admitted after the game that the home run still didn't thrill him as much as the All-Star homer he belted off Claude Passeau in Detroit back 11 years ago. "Maybe it's because I was younger then," he added.

"Actually," said Ted, "that foul ball I hit off Trucks in the third (the ball went over the right field roof) was better hit than the homer in my mind."

USUAL SELF

All in all, Ted was his usual self for the most, yelling, ribbing and a few ribald remarks.

It seems the perfect way to bow out.

And yet there is a chance that yesterday's windup may be anticlimactic. Ted will be at the park today, as there are many, many details he must clear up before leaving Boston.

If he can, he will play.

Ted was the "Big Guy" in every sense of the word today.

ROAR OF HOUSE

When he stepped up to the "mike" before the game, he responded to the roar of the house by waving his cap at full arm's length at two

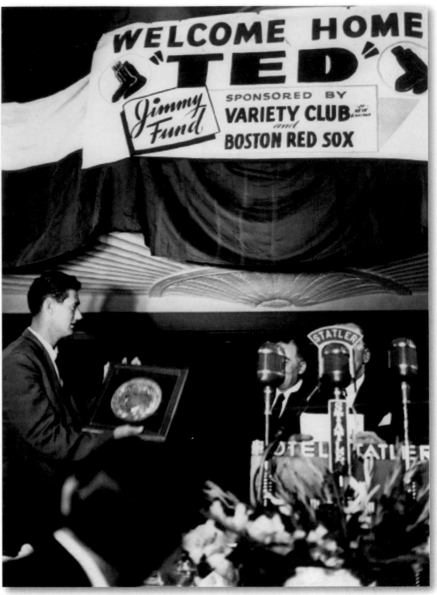

Ted's return from Korea prompted a Jimmy Fund fundraiser. *(Courtesy of The Sports Museum)*

grandstand sections and then out to the bleachers.

The town was his.

But during the game, he reverted right back to old practice, and wouldn't tip his cap after the home run.

When asked why, Ted simply shrugged his shoulders and then said, "I just don't do it."

But that made little difference yesterday.

New England went all out and Ted answered:

"I've always believed that one of the finest things that could ever happen to any ballplayer was to have a day for him," said Ted, "and my being so honored today with such little advance fanfare makes me feel humbly honored.

"Little did I realize in 1938 that I was joining such a wonderful organization, and that I was to be with so grand an owner.

"I wish I could remain all summer, for I feel sure the Sox will surprise a lot of people. I do hope you fans stick with them.

"This is a day I'll remember as long as I live, and I want to thank you from the bottom of my heart."

With the conclusion of these words from Ted, the Tigers and Red Sox players joined hands extending across the field to the stands where spectators clasped hands with the players. Ted was in the middle and in his way, he "shook hands" with everybody in the park.

As for the gifts – they were many.

The presents included:

Flowers from Sidney Hoffman which were wired to Mrs. Ted Williams and Ted's mother; Evans bag for Mrs. Williams from Evans Mfg. Co.; jewel box for Mrs. Williams from Farrington Mfg. Co.; two-wheel bike and doll carriage from Hedstrom-Union Co. of Fitchburg for Barbara Williams; gold razor and blades from Gillette Safety Razor Co.; a sporting print from Joe and Frank Stevens, park concessionaires; gold cufflinks with No.9 from Filene's; solid gold tie clasp and baseball bat from Swank; New England food basket from S.S. Pierce; personal gift from the family of the late doctor Joseph Shortell; portable typewriter from Remington-Rand; Memory Books with the names of 13,000 Ted Williams fans; messages from the New England governors; a scroll presented by Gov. Paul A. Dever; a portable radio from the Red Sox office staff; a plaque with the signatures of every Sox player presented by Dom DiMaggio; a solid silver replica of the Paul Revere bowl presented by Mayor John B. Hynes on the part of the City of Boston; oil painting from the Manchester Union-Leader; a plaque from St. Vincent DePaul Infant Asylum in Providence; a trophy from the Bourne selectmen; an electric razor from Wes Palmer of Rochester, N.H.

The climax came when the robin's egg blue "Caddy" was driven to home plate – a personal gift from Ted's intimate friends.

Ted Masks Feelings As He Departs Boston

By Alex MacLean

Farewells said, and wanting no sad songs, Ted Williams leaves his baseball career behind him for the second time, as he returns to an active duty status with the Marine Corps. Baseball's most controversial figure leaves Boston this morning – perhaps for the last time – with Ray Sisk, a fellow Marine captain who is likewise recalled from an inactive status, but with much less clamor and commotion.

They are driving from Boston to Willow Grove, Penn., where they will fly S.N.J. training planes, and perhaps, some operational aircraft, for eight weeks during a refresher course, after which they will report to M.C.A.S. Cherry Point, N.C., for operational assignment.

TOO MANY DETAILS

What Williams' true feelings were as he visited Fenway Park to pick up his gloves, spikes and other sundry personal effects were masked. He said he had too many late details for which to care and that they prevented him from playing yesterday. He answered a battery of interviewers who wondered about his greatest thrills, his favorite or most respected opponents, and a few hundred other questions that he answered time and again.

What went on in his mind only he knows, but it is likely that he anticipates his return to the Marine Corps with more excitement than he had admitted. It has been a cruel blow to his earning power and his baseball career, but Williams adjusted himself with remarkable poise to military life during World War II, was respected by everyone with whom he was connected, and probably worked harder than most who graduate in the upper segment of his class at Pensacola into the Marine Corps.

RESPECT WINGS

He has as much respect for his gold wings as he has for his bat or his bone fishing tackle.

Cadets and officers who flew with him or associated with him during World War II respected him. He, without the preparatory school or college education that most others had, worked harder, studied harder, and fought a harder fight to become an aviator.

It was not his doing that he spent most of time instructing cadets at Pensacola, Fla., for he never accepted the Marine Corps or his aviation program as a shield. He considered his training a weapon he wanted to employ more vigorously than the Marine Corps let him.

LOVES TO FLY

He loves to fly and he worked as hard to be a good pilot as he did to develop himself into one of baseball's greatest hitters. The spark probably has started to re-kindle. Now that it is so definite that he must return to flying, he will probably fling himself into a Marine

On the day that Harry Agganis graduated from Boston University he also hit a game winning home run against the Tigers prompting a teammate to observe he was the only player to hit a home run at Fenway park and celebrate at Braves Field, the location of the graduation ceremonies. *(Courtesy of Boston University)*

career with the same determination which he has always marked everything he has done.

AUTOMOBILE AMONG GIFTS TO WILLIAMS

Among the gifts received by Ted Williams yesterday were flowers, a jewel box and a handbag for Mrs. Williams, a two-wheel bicycle and doll carriage for his daughter, a razor and razor blades, a sporting print, an oil painting, gold cufflinks, a gold tie clasp, a gift bucket of New England food, a portable typewriter in case he wishes to become a sports writer in his spare time, a souvenir presentation from Gov. Dever, a portable radio from the Red Sox office staff, silver bowl from the City of Boston presented by Mayor Hynes, and an automobile.

MAY 24, 1952
BILLY MARTIN V. JIMMY PIERSALL BRAWL

JULY 7, 1952
CHARITY FIELD DAY, GEORGIA CHAIN GANG VS. VALLEYFIELD CHIEFS

OCTOBER 10, 1952
BOSTON UNIVERSITY 9, MIAMI UNIVERSITY 7

OCTOBER 18, 1952
AGGANIS HURLS 4 TDS, LEADS BU TO 33-28 VICTORY OVER WILLIAM & MARY (ATT 15,885)

NOVEMBER 1, 1952
MARYLAND CRUSHES BU, 34-7, FOR 19TH STRAIGHT WIN (ATT 32,568)

NOVEMBER 8, 1952
BOSTON UNIVERSITY 14, TEMPLE 14

NOVEMBER 15, 1952
BOSTON UNIVERSITY 14, NEW YORK UNIVERSITY 7

Prince of The City, Part I

Not only was Harry Agganis the greatest high school football prospect ever scouted by Notre Dame football coach Frank Leahy, the Lynn Classical product was also a first-rate baseball and basketball player as well as a talented student of dramatics. He was also described

Globetrotters owner Ape Saperstein with players prior to his team's Fenway Park debut. *(Courtesy of Bob Walsh)*

In a battle of Commonwealth Avenue rivals, Boston College edged Boston University by a score of 7-6 on November 13, 1954. *(Courtesy of Wes Dow)*

The Globetrotters returned to Fenway Park on August 25, 1955 when they beat Honolulu Surf Riders by a score of 43-38. *(Collection of the author)*

as the nicest young man most people could remember and he spurned nearly one hundred college scholarship offers to remain in Boston in order to look after his widowed mother.

Long before he joined the Red Sox for a $50,000 signing bonus, Agganis filled Fenway Park as a triple-threat left-handed quarterback who also punted and played defensive back for the Boston University Terriers. Under coach Buff Donelli, Agganis and his teammates played a first-rate schedule playing national powerhouses such as the University of Maryland.

Against all odds the hometown favorite achieved unprecedented national recognition at a school known more for its great men's hockey teams. Before long he was featured on the cover of *Sport* magazine and was selected to several All-Star squads. By the end of his collegiate career he'd also been selected as the best college quarterback in the country in a poll conducted with 500 sportswriters for *Football Stars* magazine.

Red Sox manager Mike "Pinky" Higgins watches his team from the dugout in 1955. *(Courtesy of the Boston Public Library)*

Left-hander Mel Parnell pitched his first and only career no-hitter at Fenway Park on July 14, 1956. *(Photograph by Dick Thomson, Courtesy of The Sports Museum)*

Edward Coveney of South Boston and J. Herman of Dorchester watch the game from out in the bleachers in 1951. *(Photograph by Leslie Jones, Courtesy of the Boston Public Library)*

Boston native and undisputed World Welterweight Champion Tony DeMarco fought twice at Fenway Park, in 1954 and 1956. *(Collection of the author)*

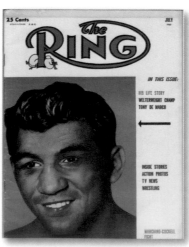

Even when the Red Sox had invariably slipped out of contention, Fenway Park was the place to be in Boston simply for the fact that you never knew what Ted Williams might say or do. *(Courtesy of Fay Ruby)*

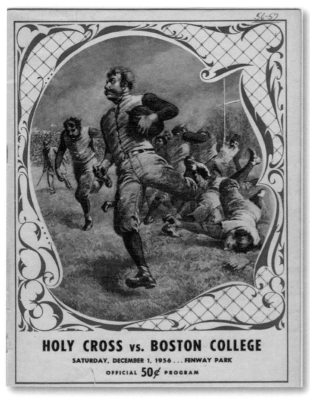

Program for the last Boston College/Holy Cross game played at Fenway Park. *(Courtesy of Wes Dow)*

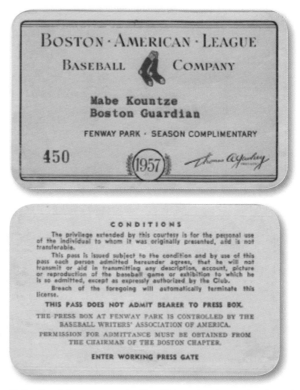

Mabe "Doc" Kountze was the first African-American writer issued a press pass by the Red Sox in 1957, two years before Pumpsie Green became the team's first African-American player. *(Courtesy of The Sports Museum)*

As he pondered offers baseball contract offers from the Phillies, Tigers and Yankees, he was also approached by Paul Brown with an offer of $100,000 to sign for the Cleveland Browns where'd serve first as understudy and heir apparent to the great Otto Graham.

As with his college scholarship offers, he chose instead to remain near his family and friends in Boston and became a major leaguer in his second best sport within a year of signing with the Red Sox.

APRIL 20, 1953

10:15 Start is Earliest in Big League History

The Sox 10:15 AM start is the earliest in major league history for the traditional Patriots Day game as the BoSox played a morning/afternoon separate admission doubleheader on a day where only 5,385 fans bundled in blankets and overcoats to watch the Red Sox beat the Senators by a score of 4 to 2 in the first game behind 2 home runs by first base man Dick Gernert.

May 24, 1953 American Legion Memorial Mass

September 26, 1953 Boston College 14, Clemson 14

October 11, 1953 Boston College Loses to Villanova, 15-7 Before 11, 901 at Fenway

October 31, 1953 Richmond Spiders Best Boston College, 14-0 Before 6,167 at Fenway

November 7, 1953 Eagles Beat Wake Forest, 20-7, Before 3,273 at Fenway

November 15, 1953 Detroit Falls to BC, 33-20, Before 7,628 at Fenway

November 28, 1953 Boston College Edges Crusaders 6-0 Before 37,000 at Fenway

JUNE 6, 1954

Agganis Socks Game Winning Homer on Graduation Day

On the day he was slated to graduate from Boston University the great Harry Agganis added to his considerable legend as he insured he'd get to the ceremonies by socking a fifth inning two-run homer that not only broke a 4-4 with the Tigers but also scored the game-winning runs.

Sportswriter Hy Hurwitz would describe it as "one summa cum laude swing of his bat," and teammate Del Wilbur joked, "It's the first time anyone ever hit a home run at Fenway Park and had to go to Braves Field to celebrate." (Author's note: Boston University had just bought the former home of the Braves and used it for their graduation exercises.)

In a scene from a movie Agganis, clad in his cap and gown, ran the mile between the ballparks through the post-game crowds and just made it in time. The next day's front page *Boston Globe* proclaimed "Harry's Heyday."

In a little more than a year, over 40,000 crowded along the route of his funeral procession in nearby Lynn as the 26-year-old was laid to rest after dying of complications from a blod clot. At the time of his death he was batting .313 and was

planning on pursuing a two-sport career after having had his pro football rights transferred to the Baltimore Colts.

JUNE 12, 1954

MAYOR'S CHARITY FIELD DAY

JULY 12, 1954

NORTH END WELTERWEIGHT TONY DEMARCO TKOs ARAUJO IN 10TH ROUND UNDER THE LIGHTS AT FENWAY BEFORE 9,781

JULY 29, 1954

20,000 May See Bevo, Trotters Play Tonight

Boston Post

The fabulous Harlem Globetrotters aided and abetted by such publicized figures as Bevo Francis and Ronnie Perry hope to break all Boston basketball attendance marks tonight at Fenway Park. The four-hour combination of court artistry and pantomime starts at 7:15.

Francis, the man who changed the Rio Grande from a river to a college, will lead a team called the Boston Whirlwinds against some bearded gentry reportedly from the House of David in the opening game.

Then the Trotters, just back from another of their triumphal European tours, take on the United States Stars, the team that has been traveling with the dark magicians. Paul Arizin and Bob Davies, the NBA standouts who have bulwarked the Stars, will get some local help from Perry and his erstwhile Holy Cross teammate, Togo Palazzi as well as from the Kentucky trio of Lou Tsiropolulos, Frank Ramsey, and Cliff Hagan, who someday may be wearing Celtics suits.

The Trotters have Sweetwater Clifton back at center to go along with Goose Tatum, the game's top clown. When the Trotters made their only Boston appearance last season, Goose was out with a bad back, but he's supposed to be ready for another of his provocative performances tonight.

Vaudeville acts will take up the slack between games and the Trotters will stage their usual comic warm-up drills. The Stars may take some of the play away from them, though, because veterans like Davies are fancy on the court, too.

This will be the first major outdoor basketball production in Boston, although the Trotters have been successful in other major league ballparks for the last two years. With a break in the weather, the doubleheader may draw as many as 20,000 to Fenway Park.

THE COLONEL SAYS:

WORLD'S GREATEST IN HUB HOOP ACTION

(Dave Egan, Boston *American*)

"There will be basketball under the beam of the lights and the twinkle of stars at Fenway Park tonight, and if you have even an academic interest in sports you owe it to yourself to attend, if only to see the new race of men that America has grown since the economic collapse of a century ago. The advisors of heavyweight champion Rocky Marciano have had the good sense never to permit him to pose with a professional basketball player, and come to think of it, I do not recall

For many years the Jimmy Fund billboard and clock were the only advertisements allowed in Fenway Park. *(Courtesy of The Sports Museum)*

ever having seen a picture of Ted Williams or Stan Musial craning their necks and gawking up at the pleasant and intelligent features of man-and-a-half-Mikan."

13,344 Fens Fans Roar As Tatum Paces Trotters

By Leo Monahan

Reese "Goose" Tatum, the basketball buffoon, was at his inimitable best last night as he frolicked with the Harlem Globetrotters to a 61 to 41 victory over the United States Stars at Fenway Park. A crowd of 13,344 chuckled at the comedy capers.

Clean-shaven Bill Spivey, a ringer with the bearded House of David five, pumped in 27 points in a losing cause in the companion piece. The

hirsute hoopsters lost 47-46 to the Boston Whirlwinds, whose affiliation with Boston is purely nominal.

Bevo Francis, the 19-year-old beanpole from Rio Grande who swapped his textbooks for a chunk of Abe Saperstein's greenbacks scored 21 points for the Whirlwinds.

Tatum, an impish double jointed character who has more tricks than Dady and Jacks was the whole show against the Stars who played it by the book for a while then decided to string along with the Trotters and take a gander at the goose.

Five Celtic chattels were in the Star cast. Togo Palazzi and Ronnie Perry of Holy Cross and three Kentuckians, Cliff Hagan, Frank Ramsey and Lou Tsioropolous who transplanted to the bluegrass region from Lynn. Palazzi and Ramsey impressed in the serious phases of the feature. Ramsey dunked in eight points including four free throws.

Legendary Red Sox broadcaster Curt Gowdy poses with pitcher Hersh Freeman in the Red Sox dugout in 1955. *(Photograph by Dick Thomson, Courtesy of The Sports Museum)*

When they were buckling down, the Rotters proved they can play the game straight, too. Tatum, for example scored 18 points to lead the Harlem club while Sweetwater Clifton, the New York Knick star who summers with the Trotters because he has no aversion to money contributed 14 and set shooting Clarence Wilson had 11.

ARIZIN GETS 11

Paul Arizin, the Philly NBA ace recently sprung from the Marines, had 11 points only other U.S. player besides Palazzi to hit double figures.

The House of David–Whirlwind prelude was interesting, but looked like it was right from Saperstein's script. The Whirlwinds, aided by the addition of Bob Davies, the Rochester Royals backcourt specialist, were 30-21 in the van at intermission, but the bearded boys pulled abreast only to lose in the finals seconds.

AUGUST 16, 1954

JIMMY FUND GAME FEATURES RED SOX AND NEW YORK GIANTS 37,710 WATCH AS FRANK BAUMANN AND TED LEPCIO LEAD SOX TO 6-5 WIN

OCTOBER 9, 1954

BOSTON COLLEGE SPANKS VMI, 44-0, BEFORE 7,941

OCTOBER 23, 1954

SPRINGFIELD FALLS TO BOSTON COLLEGE, 42-6, BEFORE 5.400 AT FENWAY

OCTOBER 31, 1954

XAVIER NIPS BC, 19-14 AT FENWAY BEFORE 4,972

Palazzi was high for the All Stars with 14 points. Arnold Auerbach was on hand to give his protégés a look-see and he must have been pleased with Togo. He looks like he's got the stuff. In fact, it'll require only a little alteration to make him a true Hibernian indeed. Just spell it Tog O'Palazzi and he'll be in the clan.

BAG OF TRICKS

But back to Goose and you can't deny that he's most of the Trotter show. He's got more moves, maneuvers than Molotov at a UN conference and most of 'em he trotted out for the amusement of the 13,344 in the audience. The crowd was only 565 short of the Garden maximum but Walter Brown's midsummer night's dream. January in July was more pleasing under the Fenway areas than it would have been in the sticky North Station emporium.

Tatum as usual saved most of his legerdemain for the finale, the last five minutes. He feigned injury after a foul called under the basket and careened over to the bench, supposedly for repairs. When he returned for his foul shot he had rung in a ball with an elastic attached to a king sized yo-yo which had the fans in stitches. Subsequently, he tried the shot with an off-center ball.

Ted Williams was the chief reason the Red Sox and not the Braves remained in Boston. His at bats prompted silence at Fenway Park as fans recognized they were witnessing an artist at work. *(Collection of the author)*

NOVEMBER 7, 1954
CORK ALL-IRELAND HURLING CHAMPIONS 37, AMERICAN HURLERS 28 (HURLING)

NOVEMBER 7, 1954
CONNAUGHT 5, MUNSTER 5 (GAELIC FOOTBALL EXHIBITION)

NOVEMBER 13, 1954
BC EDGES BU, 7-6, BEFORE 40,542 AT FENWAY

NOVEMBER 27, 1954
BC POUNDS HOLY CROSS, 31-13, BEFORE 40,642 AT FENWAY

JUNE 28, 1955
MAYOR'S CHARITY FIELD DAY: GEORGIA CHAIN GANG 3, PARK LEAGUE ALL-STARS 2

AUGUST 15, 1955
STATE OF MAINE DAY NORM ZAUCHIN WINS A BEAR CUB!

AUGUST 25, 1955
HARLEM GLOBETROTTERS 43, HONOLULU SURF RIDERS 38 (BASKETBALL)

OCTOBER 8, 1955
BOSTON COLLEGE BEATS VILLANOVA, 28-14, BEFORE 10,102

OCTOBER 15, 1955
EAGLES WHITEWASH DETROIT, 23-0, BEFORE 6,428

OCTOBER 21, 1955
MARQUETTE TIES BC, 13-13 BEFORE 18,224 AT FENWAY

NOVEMBER 26, 1955
EAGLES CRUSH CRUSADERS 26-7 BEFORE 37, 235

JUNE 16, 1956

Welterweight Tony DeMarco Wins 10 Round Decision Over Vince Martinez at Fenway Park

MARTINEZ BEATEN IN SIZZLING FIGHT

By Bill Cunningham

"Bewildered, bothered and jabbed jauntily for the first half of a

Red Sox owner Tom Yawkey (left) looks on as Massachusetts Governor Christian A. Herter tosses out the first pitch of the 1955 season. *(Courtesy of The Sports Museum)*

furious contest, former world welterweight champion Tony DeMarco of Boston's North End came from behind to roar his way to a unanimous 10-round decision over the fancier, flashier, but obviously lesser-fire-powered Vince Martinez of Paterson, N.J., at Fenway Park last night.

The margin of the scoring cards was narrow but unanimous, Judge John Norton rating it 98 to 95, Judge Joe Santoro 91 to 87, and Referee Jimmy McCarron 96-93.

VICTOR'S WELTERWEIGHT STOCK RISES

The victory moved DeMarco back high up in the welterweight picture, and probably saved high-powered fighting in this vicinage for the immediate future, at least.

A crowd of 10,832, who made a gross gate of $88,440, and took advantage of the cooling break in the weather raised a roar of delight at the end of the fray that must have been audible all the way down to the victor's home neighborhood in Fleet Street.

But they must have known how close they came to tears instead of cheers. The fight was close on the officials' cards and it actually was close in the aggregate, but there were some very nervous moments en route for both camps.

It was a slam-bang mambo from the rap of the gong and it went the distance at top speed, even without blood being drawn from either gladiator and without any knockdowns. That latter was a surprise, since both men can hit. In fact, DeMarco can bomb, and did on several occasions in the later stanzas of the fray.

It seemed for a moment in the 10th that DeMarco would knock him out. In a terrific two-fisted barrage, he rushed the tiring Martinez on the ropes and caught him with a terrific right to the jaw. There's no question about the fact that it hurt. Martinez made no effort to disguise it. His face plainly showed it. But the New Jersey man has never been knocked off his feet in 52 fights, or so his publicists have proclaimed. He must be a hard man to drop, and he refused to drop now.

That was practically the end of it although there was possibly a minute left in the round. Both seemed to realize they'd done all they could on this particular night, and while they whaled away they were obviously waiting for the bell.

As the officials ruled it, it was close. But it was actually two fights, with Martinez winning the first half, DeMarco the second. The nod went to DeMarco because he won his half bigger.

Johnny Saxton, Rocky Marciano, sundry managers and ring officials from many parts of the country made a semblance of ring royalty at the ringside. All seemed agreed it was "a great fight," and that DeMarco, the victor, is now very important again.

(Bill Cunningham, Boston Herald*)*

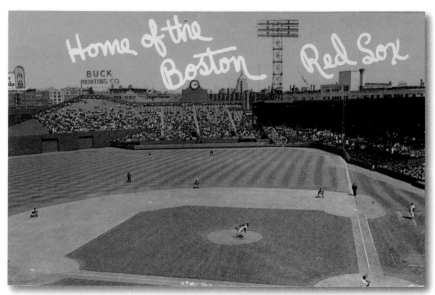

This postcard from the 1950s shows a Boston skyline marked only by the old John Hancock tower and nothing else. *(Collection of the author)*

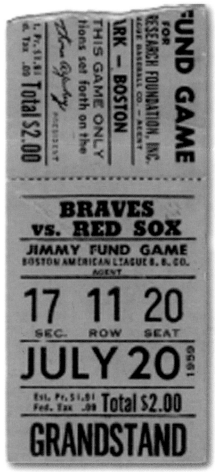

The Braves returned to Boston for several Jimmy Fund games in the 1950s and 1960s. *(Collection of the author)*

JUNE 25, 1956

Mayor's Charity Field Day, Georgia Chain Gang vs. McGuire Air Force Base

JULY 14, 1956

Parnell's No-Hitter Secures $500 Raise for 34-Year-Old Souhpaw

Mel Parnell was just two walks and one error away from perfection as he pitched a rain delayed (68 minutes) no hitter against the White Sox at Fenway Park. A ninth-inning base on balls made it possible for Boston second baseman Billy Goodman to make a force out on what likely would have been a base hit by Luis Aparicio. Parnell grabbed former teammate Walt Dropo's groundball and tagged first for the final out.

NOVEMBER 2, 1956

BC EDGES VILLANOVA, 7-6, BEFORE 13,275 AT FENWAY

NOVEMBER 10, 1956

QUANTICO MARINES CLOBBER BC 20-6 AT FENWAY BEFORE 7.404

NOVEMBER 18, 1956

BC 13, BU 0 (ATT 15,077)

NOVEMBER 24, 1956

EAGLES WALLOP BRANDEIS, 52-0 BEFORE 5,458 AT FENWAY

DECEMBER 1, 1956

HOLY CROSS 7 BOSTON COLLEGE 0 (ATT 34,176)

MAY 21, 1957

The Boy's Club

Writers voted to exclude women from Fenway press box after Cleveland writer Doris O'Donnell seeks credentials. It was in 1957 that Medford native Mabere "Doc" Kountze of The Negro Associated Press and National Negro Association of Sports Editors" became the first African-American to receive full accreditation from the Red Sox for the Fenway Press Box.

Elijah "Pumpsie" Green made history when he became the Red Sox's first African American player in 1959 as the team became the last to integrate. *(Courtesy of Jerry Nason)*

MAY 24, 1957

Williams Bats Cleanup In Fenway Pigeon War

Whether he uses a bat or a shotgun, Ted Williams is the big game man of Fenway Park. The Red Sox batting star put in a couple of leisurely Thursday hours defending Fenway Park from pigeons.

Apparently naming each pigeon for a sportswriter, Williams slaughtered between 30 and 40 of the birds, some on the wing and others just standing or sitting.

He sat on a chair in front of the Red Sox bullpen in right center, waiting with a double-barrel shotgun. With Sahib Williams on this pigeon-safari was his close friend, John Buckley, but John had to leave the Back Bay jungle and head for his Cambridge movie theater.

The sit-still safari is one Williams often stages when the Sox have an open date and nothing is scheduled for either the squad or

Ted. Observers of Williams' keen marksmanship included trainer Jack Fadden, pitcher Willard Nixon, General Manager Joe Cronin and Manager Mike Higgins. None of these spectators cared to watch the proceedings very long.

TED MAY BE A 'DEAD PIGEON'

A full-scale probe of Ted Williams' reported shooting of "30 to 40 pigeons" at Fenway Park was launched yesterday by the Massachusetts Society for the Prevention of Cruelty to Animals.

"We're going over there and thrash it out with them," declared MSPCA Chief Prosecuting Officer Herman N. Dean.

He indicated he would be at Fenway Park on Monday – when the team arrives home from its brief road trip to Baltimore – ready and waiting for a full explanation of the matter.

Ted, ordinarily a fishing enthusiast, was reported to have sat in a chair near the Red Sox bullpen with a double-barreled shotgun on Thursday. Any unsuspecting pigeon which happened into range – a somewhat shorter distance than the famed left-field wall – was blasted.

Reportedly, the Park authorities have a permit to protect the stands and playing field, and Ted was the man to do it.

MSPCA Officer Dean said, however, he checked with police, and they reported no such permit had been issued.

City Ordinances specifically ban the firing or discharge of a "cannon, gun or fowling-piece within the limits of this city except at a military exercise or review," but the ordinances do not apply to

Workers set up speakers for the Boston Jazz festival in August 1959.

(5.39) Dakota Staton was one of the many performers at the Boston Jazz Festival. Other star attractions included Ray Charles, Coeleman Hawkins, Thelonius Monk, Dave Brubeck and Dizzy Gillespie among many others. *(Collection of the author)*

"persons engaged in a trap or target-shooting on the grounds of a gun club licensed for such purposes."

Violations are subject to a penalty of up to $20 in fines.

Another ordinance cites that anyone who "uses any live bird to be shot at either for amusement or as a test of skill in marksmanship" could be "punished by a fine of not more than $50 or by imprisonment for not more than one month, or both."

A spokesman for the Red Sox declined to take any part in the matter, simply stating, "No comment," when queried on the shooting and the report that a permit is in their hands to allow the shooting.

The smoke has cleared out of the Fenway Park outfield, but there definitely will be a cloud over the front gate on Monday.

(Arthur Siegel, Boston Traveler)

JULY 22, 1957

BRAVES RETURN TO BOSTON FOR JIMMY FUND GAME, WHIP RED SOX 13-4

MAY 18, 1958

BOSTON SPORTS LODGE, B'NAI B'RITH PRESENTS THE 25 OUTSTANDING RED SOX PLAYERS OF THE YAWKEY ERA

JUNE 23, 1958

MAYOR'S CHARITY FIELD DAY, GEORGIA CHAIN GANG VS. UNKNOWN OPPONENT

JULY 20, 1958

DETROIT PITCHER JIM BUNNING HURLS A NO-HITTER AT FENWAY PARK

SEPTEMBER 21, 1958

Temper Temper

In one of the more notorious examples of Ted Williams' often childish antics the All-Star left fielder tossed his bat some 75 feet in the air after taking a called third strike and hit

Gladys Heffernan, Joe Cronin's housekeeper, on the head. As Williams stood mortified Heffernan asked the medics who brought her to a waiting ambulance, "Why are they booing Teddy?" Luckily for Williams no charges were filed. The incident reminded many of a similar display of anger that saw Williams toss his bat on the backstop screen during batting practice. On that occasion Manager Joe Cronin made his star climb the backstop in spikes to retrieve his bat.

NOVEMBER 28, 1958

Carl Yastrzemski visits Fenway Park for the first time and remarks to his dad, "I think I can hit in this park."

JANUARY 28, 1959

GOODWILL DINNER FEBRUARY, 1959 FENWAY PARK SERVES AS TEMPORARY HOME FOR AMERICAN LEAGUE HEADQUARTERS

JUNE 22, 1959

MAYOR'S CHARITY FIELD DAY, GEORGIA CHAIN GANG VS. UNKNOWN OPPONENT

JULY 20, 1959

MILWAUKEE BRAVES WIN JIMMY FUND GAME, 7-3

JULY 24, 1959

Pumpsie Green arrives in Boston three nights after his major league debut in Chicago.

AUGUST 21-23, 1959

Boston Jazz Festival

In August, a three-day jazz festival presented by music promoter and producer George Wein took place at the park. Performers included Ray Charles, Pee Wee Russell, Dakota Staton, Dukes of Dixieland, Coleman Hawkins, Dizzy Gillespie, Thelonious Monk, Dave Brubeck, the Modern Jazz Quartet, Duke Ellington, Dinah Washington and Oscar Peterson.

SEPTEMBER 30, 1959

Clubhouse man Johnny Orlando fired by Red Sox after having worked for the team for 35 years.

Jim Lonborg is besieged by jubilant fans following the Red Sox victory over the Minnesota Twins on October 1, 1967. The win assured the Red Sox of at least a tie for the pennant. Later, the team assembled in the clubhouse to listen to the radio broadcast of the back end of the Angels/Tigers double-header. The Tigers loss brought Boston its first American League championship in 21 seasons. *(Courtesy of The Boston Herald)*

CHAPTER SIX

Redemption Song

"There's nothing in the world like the fatalism of the Red Sox fans, which has been bred into them for generations by that little green ballpark, and by the Wall, and by a team that keeps trying to win by hitting everything out of sight and just out-bombarding everyone else in the league. All this makes Boston fans a little crazy, I'm sorry for them."

—BILL LEE (RED SOX 1969-1978)

The irony of ironies in the long curious history of Fenway Park was the fact that in its most glorious summer of 1967, and in the midst of the greatest pennant race in American league history, owner Tom Yawkey, always reticent towards the press, practically begged in print for the authorities to assist him in bulldozing a place New England and America would soon rediscover and recognize as nothing less than a baseball version of Westminster Abby or the Alamo.

To many, Fenway Park had become a dump in the semi-endearing way that much of Boston had become decrepit by the early sixties. This was the age of urban redevelopment, the razing of the west end, and the building of a new city hall and a new stadium seemed a sure bet. Proposals were even floated for a super stadium to be constructed on land near the Neponset River in Dorchester where all four major teams would play in a facility that was two parts Astrodome and one part Shopper's World.

As talk of a new stadium continued, the sixties marked the last decade in which Fenway Park was used as Boston's one true all-purpose facility. Not only had Boston College built a new football stadium but the entire world of sports and entertainment had undergone a shift from purely spectator-driven events to televised games from all corners of the nation. Fans who would have braved the cold to watch a local high school game at Fenway were now seated in their living rooms watching the college or pro Game of the Week, likewise for amateur baseball or other local teams. However, the Patriots did call the park home for six seasons, the fifth and last pro football team to do so. For a single season in 1968 the Boston Beacons of the fledgling North American Soccer League played in the shadow of the Green Monster. And Presidential candidates Barry Goldwater and Eugene McCarthy jousted windmills there, as well.

The competitive, financial, aesthetic, and spiritual re-birth of Fenway coincided with, and was driven by, a similar renaissance for the Red Sox. Simply put, 1967 saved Fenway Park and the Red Sox and made the park a single-attraction venue soon after.

A crowd of only a little over 10,000 attended Ted Williams' last game and witnessed him socking a home run off Orioles pitcher Jack Fisher in his final at-bat. *(Courtesy of The National Baseball Hall of Fame)*

1961 All-Star Game scorecard. *(Collection of the author)*

GOODWILL DINNER

MAYOR'S CHARITY FIELD DAY, MAJOR LEAGUE ALL-STARS VS. GREATER BOSTON COLLEGE ALL-STARS GAME CANCELED

BIBLE RESEARCH AND TRAINING ASSEMBLY OF JEHOVAH'S WITNESSES

Homers in First, Last Hub Games

TED DEPARTS AS HE ARRIVED

On September 28, 1960, the third ranking slugger in baseball history arrived on the field at Fenway Park barely a half hour before game time and played catch with teammate Pumpsie Green as reporters awaited word regarding his pending retirement.

Following a brief ceremony in which Boston Mayor John Collins

presented the slugger with a proclamation declaring it to be "Ted Williams Day," the Red Sox did nothing as a check for several thousand dollars was presented to the Jimmy Fund in Ted's name by adoring fans. On the field broadcaster Curt Gowdy observed, "I don't think we'll see another like him."

Williams' remarks were brief and pointed, "Despite the fact of the disagreeable things that have been said about me—and I can't help thinking about it—by the Knights of the Keyboard out there, baseball has been the most wonderful thing in my life. If I were starting out and someone asked me where is the one place I would like to play. I would want it to be Boston, with the greatest owner in baseball and the greatest fans in America. Thank you."

Hitless until his final at bat in the eighth inning Williams waited for a two-minute standing ovation to subside as he dug in. He took a ball for the first pitch and swung at a fastball for the strike one. On the next pitch, almost identical to its predecessor, Williams walloped the ball into the bullpen in deep left center for his 2,645th hit, and 521st home run.

Circling the bases with his head bowed slightly, Williams crossed the plate and shook the hand of teammate Jim Pagliaroni and disappeared. No tip of the cap. No acknowledgment of the crowds echoing chants of "We Want Ted! We Want Ted!"

In the manner of countless landmark Boston sporting events, including the epic 8th and concluding game of the 1912 World Series, the final game of the 1918 World Series, and most of the Celtics regular-season home games during the matchless Cousy/Russell/Havlicek years, Ted Williams' final game was witnessed by a crowd that didn't fill half the stands on a dreary Wednesday afternoon.

Luckily writers John Updike and Ed Linn were among the meager crowd as they penned much-anthologized pieces documenting Williams artistry and the drama attendant to his final at bat. Of course, it marked the third time he'd accomplished that feat in a game slated as possibly his last, only this time it was.

It was appropriate that the man who aspired to be the greatest hitter in baseball history end his career with this singular exclamation mark. Over parts of four decades and following service in two wars, Ted Williams was the primary reason fans flocked to Fenway Park and most likely the primary factor the Braves and not the Red Sox left Boston for greener pastures. His every at-bat was a compelling solo, like those of his beloved jazz musicians Dave McKenna or Errol Garner, compelling, memorable and often perfect.

Fenway Park as it appeared in 1961 with the Cities Service sign forming the backdrop over the Green Monster. *(Courtesy of the Croteau family)*

JANUARY 25, 1961
GOODWILL DINNER

JUNE 20, 1961
MAYOR'S CHARITY FIELD DAY

JULY 31, 1961

All-Stars Fit to be Tied, 1-1

The second of the two major league All-Star games of 1961 promised to be a home run filled classic played in ideal conditions and instead became a forgettable pitchers' duel halted by rain after a 21-minute delay with the score locked at 1-1 in the ninth inning.

The game's only home run and the American League's lone run came from a Rocky Colavito shot over the left-field wall off Reds starter Bob Purkey in the first inning. The National League scored their run in the sixth inning after Bill White stroked a single off Red Sox rookie Don Schwall that scored former Boston Brave Eddie Matthews.

American League starter Jim Bunning of the Tigers picked up where he left off in the first All-Star of 1961 played in San Francisco where pitched two perfect innings with three additional perfect innings. The crowd, however, saved it's biggest ovation for former Boston Brave favorite Warren Spahn, who'd only just won the 298th victory of his career the day before. Red Sox broadcaster Curt Gowdy and former Boston nemesis Joe Garagiola announced the game on NBC.

It would be only the second All Star Game ever called on account of rain and the first to end in a tie.

AUGUST 21, 1961

Braves Whip Sox, 4-1; 19,773 Fans Defy Rain

SPAHN PITCHES PERFECT INNING FOR JIMMY FUND

Nearly a decade after they'd left Boston the Braves returned to Fenway Park for another in a series of Jimmy Fund games and beat the Red Sox before 19,773 as future Hall of Famer Warren Spahn pitched a perfect inning as Hank Aaron and Joe Torre both singled home Eddie Matthews for two of Milwaukee's runs in the 4-1 victory.

Not only did Spahn receive the night's biggest ovation but he retired the Red Sox on only 11 pitches in the first inning as he struck out Chuck Schilling and Carl Yastrzemski before making Pete Runnels ground out to second.

May 19, 1962 Armed Forces Day: 100 New Englanders Inducted Into US Air Force

June 19, 1962 Mayor's Charity Field Day

JUNE 26, 1962

Fast Balls Key To Earl Wilson's No Hit Gem

6'4" Right-hander Earl Wilson closed his eyes and threw his best fastball to Los Angeles Angels first baseman Lee Thomas and froze for a split second as Red Sox center fielder Gary Geiger made the routine catch to finish both Wilson's first complete game of the season and the first no-hitter by an African-American pitcher in American League history.

As teammates surrounding the burly former Marine, Wilson kept saying "I can't believe it, I can't believe it."

Of the game's final out Wilson observed, "I was a little worried when I heard Thomas hit that ball. I thought it might hit the wall, but then I saw Geiger in front of it and everything went blank." The former catcher helped his effort with a third-inning home run off Angels

Carl Yastrzemski shown in a Fenway Park presentation in 1961. When Yastrzemski first visited the park with his father several years earlier, the elder Yastrzemski remarked, "I think you can hit here." *(Courtesy of The Sports Museum)*

starter Bo Belinsky who'd later comment, "I won't know for a couple of days whether I'm glad he did it. Cripe, right now all I know is I pitched a helluva game and all I got out of it was beat."

Following the game Red Sox owner Tom Yawkey made a rare clubhouse appearance and was so elated that he tore up Wilson's contract and presented him with a new one that included an immediate $1,000 raise.

JANUARY 5, 1963

Boston Patriots agree to play at Fenway Park. Patriots partner and former Red Sox outfielder Dominic DiMaggio assists with this agreement.

JUNE 3, 1963

RED SOX BEAT BRAVES 5-2 IN JIMMY FUND BENEFIT

July 1, 1963 Mayor's Charity Field Day

August 23, 1963 Harlem Globetrotters vs. US All-Stars (Basketball)

OCTOBER 11, 1963

Pats Top Raiders, 20-14 in Fenway Debut

By Joe Cashman (Boston Daily Record)

Bob Dee, Larry Eisenhauer, Houston Antwine, Ross O'Hanley, "Chuck" Shonta, Nick Buoniconti.

Those are the "Monsters" who made it possible for the Patriots to christen their new Fenway home last night with a 20-14 win over the Oakland Raiders, even though the box score shows that Jimmy Colclough and rookie Tom

Neumann, catching touchdown passes from Babe Parilli, and Gino Capaletti, kicking two field goals and two points after, scored all the Boston points.

The Pats were a sluggish and looked like a beaten club until their defensive geniuses set the stage for a thrilling victory fashioned before an enthusiastic crowd of 26,494.

Down 3-7 at the half and 3-10 at the nine-minute mark in the third period, the Pats then began their gallant comeback.

Parilli, who looked rusty during the first half, wherein he completed only two passes, suddenly got hot.

He completed a 15-yarder to Capaletti to put the ball on the Boston 40. Two plays later, he really put a charge into a throw from his 43.

Down near the 15 was Colclough. Jimmy, with an heroic reach, pulled in the ball which was slightly over-thrown. He stumbled and fell to his knees on the seven, but bounced up and went on to score.

From then on, the Boston defensive unit stole the show and soon had stolen the ball game from the Raiders.

After the kick-off following the Pats' first TD, the Raiders moved out to their 40.

At that point, Dee and Eisenhauer put the blitz on Tom Flores, who was Oakland quarterback on all but one of its offensive plays in the game.

Dee knocked the ball loose from the hostile pitcher and Eisenhauer fell on the leather on the Oakland 25. Now the Oakland defense got stubborn and the Pats had to settle for a 33-yard field goal by Cappy, who had kicked one 37 yards for the game's first score in the opening period.

Earl Wilson became the first African-American in American League history to pitch a no-hitter on June 26, 1962, as he shut out the Los Angeles Angels by a score of 2-0. *(Courtesy of* The Boston Herald*)*

So the Pats were close, but they still trailed by one.

The defense quickly took care of that.

On the second last play of the third period, the Raiders took a touchback and put the ball on play on the 20. On the next play, Antwine was roaring in to knock the ball loose from Bo Roberson's grasp and recover on the 15.

On the first play of the final quarter came the payoff maneuver.

Parilli looked like he was trapped back on the 30 for a big loss. Somehow or other, the Babe, with a small army chasing him, managed to elude all grasping arms as he ran thither and yon until he saw Neumann in the clear around the two and hit him waist high. It

took the rookie only two steps to reach pay dirt.

The defense overshadowed the offense on both sides from start to finish of the battle.

In the first period, O'Hanley intercepted a Flores pass on the Boston 33, and ran it back to the Oakland 6. A moment later, Jim McMillin was intercepting a Parilli pass in the end zone.

Shortly after that, the same McMillin pulled a pass out of Cappy's arms and meandered 47 yards to a touchdown unmolested.

Before the half was over, the Pats were short-circuited again by an interception, this one by Arch Matzos deep in Oakland territory, while both O'Hanley and McMillin chipped in with second interceptions.

The Harlem Globetrotters made their third and final appearance to date at Fenway Park on August 23, 1963. (*Collection of the author*)

The only sustained offensive march by the Raiders came when they moved eighty yards to their third period T.D.

On the drive, Flores threw a 42-yard pass to Ken Herock. That put the ball on the 30. Two more passes moved it to the 11.

Here, Flores was shaken up. Cotton Davidson, who had been expected to start the game, came in. He rolled out, kept and scored on the only play he called during the evening.

Parilli completed only five passes but two of them were very big ones. The Pats had the edge in rushing, the Raiders the edge in the air.

Larry Garron ran well at times. So did Neumann. Parilli was better than the statistics might indicate. Two or three times he hit receivers in the open, only to have the catchers drop the ball.

But the stars of the Pats' first game in Fenway Park were Dee, Eisenhauer, O'Hanley, Buoniconti and Antwine.

OCTOBER 18, 1963

Patriots Drub Denver Broncos, 40-21

Gino Cappelletti booted four field goals and caught a touchdown pass to increase his AFL scoring lead as the Patriots rocked the Broncos in front of 25,418 at Fenway Park.

NOVEMBER 1, 1963

Pats Sink Oilers, 45-3

The Patriots achieved a tie for the AFL East lead with a decisive win over the Broncos that included six interceptions of future Hall of Fame quarterback George Blanda in front of 31,185. This was also the most lopsided of the sixteen regular season victories the Patriots won at Fenway Park from 1963 to 1968.

Source: 2009 NE Patriots Media Guide

NOVEMBER 10, 1963

Chargers Edge Boston, 7-6

A crowd of 28,402 was treated to a preview of the AFL title game as the high flying San Diego Chargers just barely beat the Patriots 7-6. The Patriots had also lost a narrow 17-13 decision to the Chargers in the second game of the season at Balboa Stadium.

Source: 2009 NE Patriots Media Guide

The Boston University/Boston College matchup, scheduled for November 23, 1963, was to have been the last college football game played at Fenway Park but was canceled in the wake of the assassination of President John F. Kennedy. *(Courtesy of Wes Dow)*

The Mayor's Field Day was a longtime Fenway Park staple that featured music, exhibition baseball, and youth activities. *(Collection of the author)*

The football field at Fenway Park as it looked just prior to the Patriots home opener in October 1963. Football had long been a staple at both Fenway Park and nearby Braves Field. *(Courtesy of the Boston Public Library)*

Revere native and St. Mary's of Lynn graduate Tony Conigliaro was the shining star of the Red Sox of the mid-sixties as he possessed the best right-handed home swing since Jimmie Foxx. Conigliaro reached the 100 home run plateau faster than any batter in American League history. *(Courtesy of The Sports Museum)*

Nicknamed "The Monster," 6' 6" 230-pound Dick Radatz was the best relief pitcher in the American League in the mid-1960s while toiling for the perpetual basement-dwelling Red Sox. The powerful right-hander once struck out the Yankee trio of Mickey Mantle, Roger Maris, and Elston Howard on eleven pitches to notch a save. *(Courtesy of The Sports Museum)*

Former University of Kentucky quarterback and Bear Bryant protege Vito "Babe" Parilli fires a pass against the Chargers at Fenway Park. *(Photograph by Jerry Buckley, Courtesy of Al Ruelle)*

NOVEMBER 17, 1963

Chiefs Catch Patriots for 24-24 Tie

The Fenway Park crowd of 17,500 roared when Patriots back Larry Garron raced 47 yards for the touchdown to put the Patriots ahead of the Chiefs by a score of 24-17 but slumped in their seats when Chiefs rookie quarterback Eddie Wilson, in his first pro start, tossed a late TD to Curtis McClinton to set up the equalizing point after.

Source: The Bennington (VT) Banner , page 6, November 18, 1963

DECEMBER 1, 1963

Pats Corral Buffalo, 17-7, Before 16, 981 at Fenway Park

Patriots head coach Mike Holovak had enjoyed fame at Fenway Park as an All American back in the glory days of Frank Leahy in the late 1930s early 1940s. His Patriots won perhaps their most significant game in their short stint at Fenway when they beat the rival Bills in front of a relatively small crowd of a little less than 17,000. Following the win Holovak observed, when asked of his team's title hopes, "It's up to us now. We just got what we asked for and now we can win it all by ourselves. It's up to us."

The Patriots split their last two regular-season games on the road against the Oilers and Chiefs but beat the Bills in an extra division title deciding game played in swirling snow and icy conditions at War Memorial Stadium in Buffalo. They ultimately were crushed by the Chargers in the AFL title game by a score of 51-10.

Source: The Bennington (VT) Banner, page 6, December 2, 1963

January 29, 1964 Goodwill Dinner

Program for the Patriots/San Diego game of October 9, 1964. *(Collection of the author)*

Goldwater campaign pin from 1964. *(Collection of the author)*

APRIL 17, 1964

Celebrities See Hose Win, 4-1

SOX TRIBUTE TO KENNEDY NETS LIBRARY $36,818

TONY C 1ST HR

By Arthur Sampson

A glamour-packed pre-game ceremony, a 4-1 Red Sox victory over the White Sox, and Tom Yawkey's contribution of $36,818 to the John F. Kennedy Memorial Library Fund, which represented his proceeds from the 20,213 in attendance, made yesterday's Fenway Park opener a never-to-be-forgotten occasion.

MUSIAL REPRESENTS PRESIDENT JOHNSON

This 64th Red Sox opener was dedicated to the late President John Fitzgerald Kennedy who was born a short distance from the scene of yesterday's festivities.

The performance of the Hose, while winning their second straight opener this year, would have thrilled not only the late President, but his maternal grandfather, Honey Fitz, who organized the Red Sox Royal Rooters organization more than a half-century ago.

Joe Cronin, American League President, touched off the speaking part of the pre-game ceremonies when he said while addressing the audience, "Never before has baseball been so proud of Tom Yawkey as we are today."

"The American League in particular commends Mr. Yawkey for

On a day that the Red Sox donated the gate proceeds from their home opener to the John F. Kennedy Library Foundation, Tony Conigliaro socked a home run in his first Fenway Park at bat off Joel Horlen of the White Sox. *(Courtesy of* The Boston Herald*)*

his cooperation with the Trustees of the Kennedy Memorial Fund. We in baseball, in turn, thank the Trustees of the Memorial Fund for giving us the opportunity and privilege of cooperating with them in this memorial effort. All of us in baseball are honored indeed to pay tribute in this manner to the late President John F. Kennedy."

Other celebrities who addressed the audience before the game included Gov. Peabody; Mayor Collins; Robert Kennedy; United States Attorney General; and Stan Musial, representing President Lyndon B. Johnson.

Gov. Peabody said the Red Sox tribute to the late president was typical of Tom Yawkey. He added that the Red Sox were as much a part of Boston as Bunker Hill, Old Ironside, and the Navy Shipyard.

Mayor Collins thanked everyone present and the millions throughout the country who were

making possible the erection of the memorial library in this area.

Attorney General Kennedy said, "On behalf of all the members of the Kennedy family, Mrs. Kennedy, the Trustees of the Library, I want to take this opportunity to thank Tom Yawkey and all of those who are here for making this day possible. We thank the people of Boston, which is our home, and thank all the fans of the Redskins. (Author's note: when this slip produced a loud roar, he commented, "That's what happens from living in Washington so long.")

DEMPSEY-TUNNEY ON HAND

Musial, after stating that he would feel more at home if he had a bat in his hand instead of a microphone, said that he wanted to announce that President Johnson intended to continue the national physical fitness program that was started by the late President Kennedy. "My job as Chairman of the Physical Fitness Program is to carry on the ideas instigated by President Kennedy," he said.

* * *

Other members of the Kennedy family who were introduced included Senator Edward 'Ted' Kennedy, Mrs. Jean Smith and Mrs. Pat Lawford.

Other notables introduced were Jack Dempsey and Gene Tunney, former heavyweight boxing champions, Carol Channing, star of Broadway musical comedy *Hello, Dolly*, the producer of that show, Charles Lowe, Frederick March and Frank Fontaine.

* * *

The festivities opened with a concert by the excellent Harvard University Band. The band saluted the late president by playing a medley of his favorite Harvard songs. Then they played the "Navy Log," recalling President Kennedy's first service to the nation, and finished with "Anchors Aweigh," which was one of the late president's favorites.

* * *

During the game, most of the celebrities present appeared with Gowdy during the radio-TV broadcast of the contest.

The sponsors gave up their commercial spots so that the notables could make an appearance on TV.

* * *

Tony Conigliaro, an amazing 19-year-old rookie, slammed the first pitch served by righthander Joe Horlen high and deep to left center, and his Fenway debut became historic as the ball sailed completely over the screen atop the left-field wall and plunked out on Lansdowne street.

The Patriots missed out on a re-match with the Chargers in the AFL title game (and home-field privileges) when they lost to the Bills on a snowy afternoon at Fenway Park on December 20, 1964. *(Collection of the author)*

"I'll celebrate that with a real Italian dinner tonight," he quipped later. "What'll it be? Everything: lasagna, spaghetti, chicken, the works. No, I wasn't looking for anything special, just a good ball to hit, and it was there, a fast ball. I thought it might be off the wall or even in the nets but I never dreamed it'd clear everything, though I hit it good."

"Nervous? No, I wasn't nervous like I was yesterday in New York. I only saw two fast balls after that and they were bad. Yeah, my folks and brothers were here and I guess everybody I ever knew. I could hear them yelling to me from the stands, especially in the bleachers."

May 20, 1964 Massachusetts Democrats 8, Massachusetts Republicans 7

June 3, 1964 Northeastern University 9, University of Maine 5 (NCAA Division One Finals)

June 3, 1964 Northeastern University 4, University of Maine 2 (NCAA Division One Finals)

June 15, 1964 Mayor's Charity Field Day, Northeastern vs. Boston College Baseball Game

SEPTEMBER 23, 1964

Capacity 35,000 to Hear Goldwater at Fenway Park

By Paul W. Costello

Massachusetts backers of U.S. Sen. Barry Goldwater are confident that even if Boston is pelted with rain tomorrow in the backlash of Hurricane Gladys, a capacity crowd of 35,000 will turn out for the big Republican presidential rally in Fenway Park at 8 p.m.

TICKETS VIRTUALLY IMPOSSIBLE TO FIND

Boston Police Commr. Edmund T. McNamara apparently shared this view, as evidence by the fact that McNamara has assigned 234 police to crowd details inside the park.

Another 50 have been assigned to keep spots along the route Goldwater will travel in a motorcade from Logan Airport at 6 p.m. into Boston, as well as for the trip by limousine at 7:30 p.m. from the Ritz Carlton Hotel to Fenway Park.

Goldwater is scheduled to speak approximately 30 minutes at the rally. Then the candidate will attempt to meet personally as many of the persons who jam into Fenway Park as possible before returning to the Ritz Carlton at 9:45 p.m.

While no figures on the sale of the $1 per head Goldwater rally tickets have been announced since Sunday when sales stood at 25,000, tickets were virtually impossible to find yesterday.

The first inkling that the Goldwater rally would be a sellout came last week when Goldwater coordinator Lloyd B. Waring of Rockport ordered the rally shifted from Commonwealth Armory to Fenway Park, when 10,000 tickets were sold within 24 hours after they were offered to the public.

Goldwater and his wife, Peggy, are scheduled to arrive by chartered plane at Logan Airport tomorrow at 5:45 p.m., accompanied by 75 newsmen from all sections of the nation.

Former Gov. John A. Volpe, GOP U.S. Senate nominee Howard Whitmore, Republican State Chairman Frederic C. Dumaine, Jr., as well as other GOP leaders will greet the Goldwaters when they debark at the American Airlines Maintenance Hangar.

Republic Presidential candidate Barry Goldwater made his plea for "peace through strength" at a well attended rally on September 23, 1964. *(Courtesy of* The Boston Herald*)*

Goldwater Asks For Peace Through Strength Attacks 'Curious Crew' Seeking Disarmament

BIG CROWD AT FENWAY HAILS BLAST

Barry Goldwater came to Boston last night as a "peacemonger" preaching the "cold, hard, ugly, dirty fact of life" that only through strength could the United States keep the peace in the world.

STEPS UP ATTACK

To his New England partisans gathered in Fenway Park – park officials said 18,000 to 20,000 of them, Goldwater people 25,000 to 30,000, with the truth somewhere in between – the Republican candidate for President lashed out at "the strange, curious crew abroad in our land" calling for disarmament as a way to peace.

While Goldwater spoke to cheers inside the park, a nearly endless line of pickets from the Committee Against Political Extremism circled the park in silence, to protest the candidate's stand on civil rights.

Police reported no incidents, and the picket line gave way, quietly, as those bearing the $1 admission tickets to the rally made their way inside.

With his audience making up in enthusiasm what it may have lacked in the hoped-for sellout of 35,000, Goldwater quickened the pace of his attacks on President Johnson and dealt in detail with his denunciation of crime in the streets as evidence of "the law of the jungle."

But it was his ad-lib remarks, given at the end of a 30-minute prepared text that Goldwater struck back hardest at those who have criticized him as "trigger-happy" and careless of the way strength is handled.

"We will be attacked the minute our enemy thinks he can whip us," he said, adding later:

"And we can find peace if we want to put our tail between our legs and lie down."

(W.J. McCarthy, Boston Herald *)*

SEPTEMBER 27, 1964

SPIRITED PATS PUNCTURE JETS BUBBLE, 26-10 BEFORE 22,716 AT FENWAY

OCTOBER 1, 1964

Monstrous

On the day that pitcher Dick Radatz made his record breaking 79th appearance the Sox played before just 306 fans. This also capped one of the greatest single season performances in club history as the towering right-hander led the majors with 29 saves and won 16 more for the eighth place 1964 Red Sox. Following each Fenway triumph Radatz exhulted in his trademark gesture of raising both arms over his 6' 6" 240-lb. frame in the knowledge a cold one awaited him in the clubhouse.

OCTOBER 9, 1964

Chargers Top Pats, 26-17

The largest crowd to yet witness an AFL game in Boston, 33,096, saw their Patriots fall to the Chargers in a Friday night game while snapping a four-game win streak. Former Kansas All-American quarterback John Hadl came off the San Diego bench late in the first quarter to rally his team to victory.

OCTOBER 16, 1964

Patriots and Raiders Tie 43-43

It was safe to say that most of the 23,379 fans that bit their nails through this wild Friday night game went home smiling as the Patriots overcame a 20-point deficit to take a slim three-point lead only to see the game end in a tie with the Al Davis–coached Oakland Raiders. Patriots quarterback Babe Parilli enjoyed a career day while tossing for an even 400 yards and four touchdowns while back Larry Garron also chipped in while scoring three TDs.

OCTOBER 23, 1964

Patriots Battle for Division Lead and Beat Chargers 24-7

The Patriots improved their record to 5-1-1 with a resounding Friday night victory over the Kansas City Chiefs in front of 27,400 at Fenway Park. Former Boston College star wide receiver Jim Colclough was the star of the game as he made the most of his three receptions as they covered 95 yards and accounted for two of the Patriots' three touchdowns.

NOVEMBER 6, 1964

Gino Kicks, Pats Win, 25-24 Over Oilers

The spotlight shone brightly on All-Star kicker/receiver Gino Cappelletti as his last-second field goal capped a hard won 25-24 win before 28,161 at Fenway Park. It was the fourth field goal of the night for Cappelletti in the "must win" game for Boston.

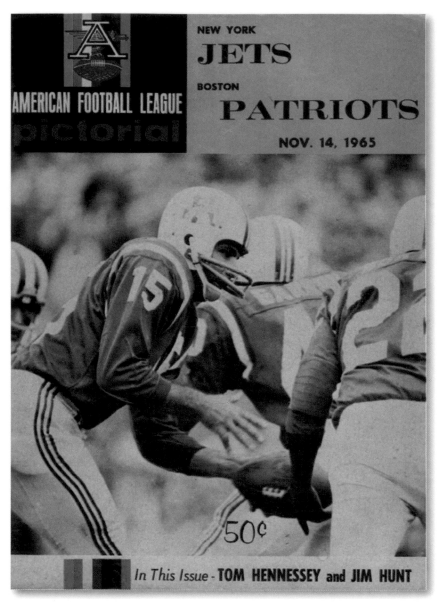

NEW YORK
JETS
AMERICAN FOOTBALL LEAGUE
BOSTON
PATRIOTS
pictorial
NOV. 14, 1965

50¢

In This Issue - TOM HENNESSEY and JIM HUNT

Program for the Patriots/Jets game of November 14, 1965, that saw quarterback Joe Namath make his Boston debut for New York in the Jets 30-20 victory. *(Collection of the author)*

NOVEMBER 20, 1964

Patriots Salvage "Must Win" Over Broncos, 12-7 before 24,979

Gino Cappelletti did everything but sell programs at Fenway Park as the All-Star kicker/receiver scored a touchdown, kicked a field goal, and made an extra point conversion as the patriots hung on to beat Denver to keep their playoff hopes alive.

DECEMBER 20, 1964

38,021 See Bills Bomb Patriots, 24-14 in Snowstorm

The start of the most important game in the Patriots six-year tenure at Fenway Park was held up for 45 minutes as fans tossed snowballs at a group carrying a sign that said "South Buffalo Irish-Dump Patriots," and crews cleared the field of protective hay and a tarpaulin. Once the game got underway, future congressman and Presidential hopeful Jack Kemp gained revenge for the previous season's playoff loss by scoring two touchdowns and passing for a third as Buffalo's pass defense thwarted the Patriots at every turn.

June 3, 1965 University of
Connecticut 7, Holy Cross 4
(NCAA District One Finals)
June 3, 1965 Holy Cross 5,
University of Connecticut 0
(NCAA District One Finals)
June 4, 1965 University of
Connecticut 7, Holy Cross 0
(NCAA District One Finals)

SEPTEMBER 16, 1965

Higgins Fired

MOREHEAD FIRES GEM, SOX WIN 2-0

On the day Tom Yawkey fired Pinky Higgins as General Manager and hired Dick O'Connell as his replacement 22-year-old right-hander Dave Morehead pitched a near perfect no-hitter against the Cleveland Indians and Luis Tiant before a crowd of only 1,247. Outfielder and clubhouse jester George Thomas socked a Tiant fastball for a solo home run to help the Red Sox to a 2-0 win. Little did the small crowd realize but their owner had made the best executive decision of his long tenure as they cheered for the third no-hitter by a Red Sox pitcher in three seasons.

SEPTEMBER 24, 1965

Pats Bombed by Broncos, 27-10

The booing cascaded throughout Fenway Park as a Friday night crowd of 26,782 (roughly 25,000 more fans than had watched Red Sox pitcher Dave Morehead's Fenway no-hitter against Cleveland just eight days earlier) saw their team sink to an 0-3 record by way of a 27-10 rout by the Denver Broncos. Babe Parilli received the lion's share of catcalls as the result of his connecting on only seven of twenty pass attempts.

OCTOBER 8, 1965

Pats Become AFL Patsies, Lose 5th Straight, Bow to Oakland 24-10

The Raiders formidable passing combination of Tom Flores and receiver Art Powell (2 touchdowns) humbled the Patriots before a Friday night crowd of 24,824.

OCTOBER 17, 1965

Pats, Chargers in 13-13 Tie

The Patriots battled heroically to achieve a tie against the AFL's lone undefeated team before 20,924 at Fenway Park. Despite being held to just 71 yards rushing, the Patriots led the game 7-3 until John Hadly hit Lance Alworth for an 84-yard

Dave Morehead scrambles to make a key out in his no-hitter versus the Cleveland Indians and Luis Tiant on the same day that owner Tom Yawkey fired Pinky Higgins as general manager. *(Courtesy of the Boston Public Library)*

touchdown midway through the second quarter. The Patriots had to scramble in the second half and gained the tie by way of two Gino Cappelletti field goals, the final one coming after the Chargers had stopped the Patriots on their 4-yard line.

NOVEMBER 7, 1965

PATS LOSE 7TH GAME AS BUFFALO GAINS 23-7 VICTORY BEFORE 24,415 AT FENWAY

NOVEMBER 14, 1965

Jets Top Pats, 30-20

All Patriots head coach Mike Holovak could say following his team's 8th loss was, "We just give these games away and early, too. I think we've given every game away, but one, to San Diego." The Jets highly publicized $400,000

quarterback, former Alabama star Joe Namath, went the distance while tossing two touchdowns to wide receiver Don Maynard. Boston's Babe Parilli also threw two touchdowns and was more than a match for the man for whom he'd soon serve as a backup.

NOVEMBER 21, 1965

PATS NAB A 10-10 TIE WITH CHIEFS BEFORE ONLY 13,056 AT FENWAY

DECEMBER 18, 1965

Cappelletti Stars in Pats 42-14 Win Over Oilers

Gino Cappelletti scored 28 points while catching two touchdowns, kicking four field goals and four points after conversions to take over the lead for AFL scoring as the Patriots scorched the Houston

Hometown hero Tony Conigliaro receives a portable TV as a gift in this Fenway Park ceremony from the mid-sixties. *(Courtesy of The Sports Museum)*

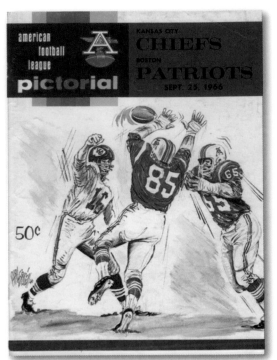

Program for Patriots/Kansas City Chiefs game of September 25, 1966. *(Collection of the author)*

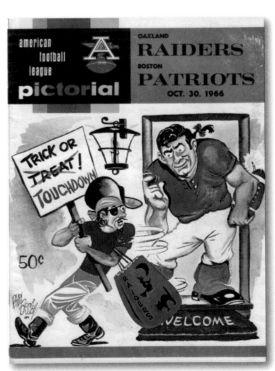

(above) Program for the Patriots/Oakland Raiders game of October 30, 1966. *(Collection of the author)*

(left) Future Red Sox manager Dick Williams and son Rick at Fenway's "Fathers and Sons Game" in 1964. *(Courtesy of Bob Walsh)*

Manager Dick Williams and owner Tom Yawkey confer at Fenway Park. In the midst of the greatest season, Yawkey made headlines when he made the threat of possibly moving the team within five years if the city didn't help him build a new stadium. *(Courtesy of The Sports Museum)*

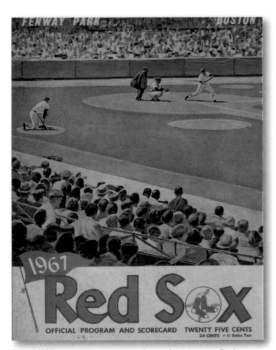

The 1967 season represented an phenomena Red Sox will likely never experience again, namely their storied franchise overcoming odds of 100/1 to win the American League pennant. *(Collection of the author)*

At 8:42 PM on the night of August 18, 1967, time literally stopped for Red Sox fans as star right-fielder Tony Conigliaro was struck in the left eye by a Jack Hamilton fastball. Conigliaro would miss both the balance of the pennant-winning season and the following season as he endured grueling rehabilitation. *(Courtesy of Dan Desrochers)*

Fenway Park in 1967 experienced a re-birth from a competitive, economic, aesthetic, and spiritual standpoint as the winning ways of the Impossible Dream Red Sox transformed the once-decrepit ballyard into a charming and eccentric landmark. *(Courtesy of Dan Desrochers)*

Red Sox fans returned to Fenway Park by the busload in 1967. *(Courtesy of Bob Walsh)*

were treated to a brilliant performance as Larry Garron caught two touchdowns from Babe Parilli and rushed for another as the Patriot defense held the vaunted Charger offense to just 40 yards of rushing yardage to counter the two touchdowns scored by All-Star receiver Lance Alworth.

OCTOBER 30, 1966

Nance Guides the Pats to a Big Win Over Oakland, 24-21

Fullback Jim Nance not only scored two touchdowns but bowled over Oakland for 208 yards, including 150 in the first half alone to lead the Patriots to victory before 26,941 fans at Fenway Park.

NOVEMBER 6, 1966

BRONCOS DOWN PATRIOTS 17-10, BEFORE 18,154 AT FENWAY

NOVEMBER 13, 1966

Gino Cappelletti Scores 21 in Pats 27-21 Win Over Houston

Gino Cappelletti delighted the Fenway crowd of 23,426 with an epic performance that included corralling two Babe Parilli touchdown passes while also booting two field goals and three points after conversions to lead the Patriots over the Oilers by a score of 27-21.

Oilers by a score of 42-14 before 14,508 at Fenway Park.

January 26, 1966 Goodwill Dinner

June 7, 1966 Boston College 8, University of Massachusetts 5 (NCAA District One Finals)

June 8, 1966 Northeastern 5, Colby College 4 (NCAA District One Finals)

June 9, 1966 Northeastern 10, Boston College 2 (NCAA District One Finals)

August 6, 1966 Boston Typos 5, Washington 0 (National Union Printers Championship)

August 8, 1966 The infamous FOG game.

SEPTEMBER 25, 1966

PATS LOSE HOME OPENER TO CHIEFS 34-24 BEFORE 27,255

OCTOBER 2, 1966

Namath and Jets Rally to Tie Patriots, 24-24

Joe Namath rallied the Jets from a 17-point fourth-quarter deficit to stun a Fenway Park crowd of 27,255. The former Alabama star hit on 14 of 23 passes including two fourth-quarter touchdowns as well as setting up Jim Turner's game-tying field goal.

OCTOBER 23, 1966

Pats Execute Perfect Game Plan to Down Chargers, 35-17

The largest crowd (32,371) to view a Patriots game since the snow game against the Bills in 1964

Red Sox fans raced onto the field in a torrent of joyful chaos following the final out of the game on October 1, 1967. *(Courtesy of Dan Desrochers)*

Ticket stub from the pennant clinching game of October 1, 1967. It is a toss up whether this game, the eighth game of the 1912 World Series, Game 6 of the '75 World Series or Game 4 of the 2004 ALCS is the greatest Red Sox game in Fenway Park's first century. *(Courtesy of Dan Desrochers)*

DECEMBER 4, 1966

Record Crowd of 39,350 Cheers Pats to 14-3 Win Over Bills

After his Bills had fallen to a resurgent Patriots team, their owner Ralph Wilson called his rivals the best team in the division despite the fact Buffalo had one more win for the season. Boston quarterback Babe Parilli had a great day scoring one of the Patriots two touchdowns on a 3-yard run. The win left the Patriots atop the AFL east with two road games remaining.

January 25, 1967 Annual
Goodwill Dinner

Opening Day 1967

By Leigh Montville

I will not deny the excitement that buzzed through my head and body like so much happy static on the morning of Apr. 11, 1967, when I stepped off the train at Back Bay station, my Olivetti Lettera 32 portable typewriter swinging from my right hand, my shoes shined, sport coat buttoned and heart pure. I was 23 years old. I was first time in the big time.

"Fenway Park," I told the driver as I slid into the back of his cab.

"Why're you going there?" he asked.

"I'm a sportswriter," I explained. "I'm here from the New Haven, Connecticut, *Journal-Courier* to cover Opening Day. I'm a journalist."

I could have explained more, of course, about how I was the new star on the horizon, a certain future great in the field of American sports letters, a master of simile and metaphor, a different voice, an intrepid reporter and all-around great guy, but I held my tongue. Modesty was the best approach.

"Called off," the cab driver said.

"Called off?" I said.

"Postponed."

"Postponed?"

"Too cold."

The day was a bit nippy, to be sure, but the sun was shining. Maybe 35 degrees. This was a crisp, New England spring day. An Opening Day. Button up your overcoat. Normal stuff. Called off? Who could have predicted this?

American League MVP Carl Yastrzemski (left) and owner Tom Yawkey celebrate the 1967 American League pennant. *(Courtesy of The Boston Public Library)*

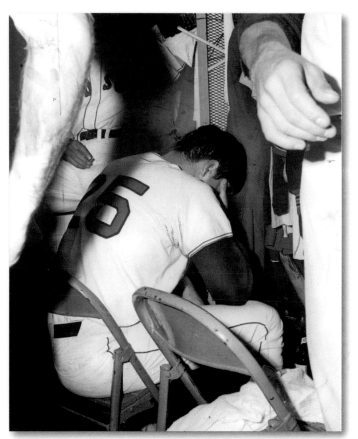

Injured outfielder Tony Conigliaro cries tears of anguish in the Red Sox clubhouse following the news his team had clinched the pennant after the Tigers had lost. Conigliaro missed out on what would have been his only World Series. *(Courtesy of Dan Desrochers)*

"What do you want to do?" the cab driver said.

"Take me to the ballpark anyway," the new star on the horizon, master of simile and metaphor, replied in an uncertain voice.

Oh, my.

No other civilians were in the Red Sox clubhouse when I arrived. The other sportswriters apparently had done their work and left. A few baseball players were still wandering around in various stages of undress. I recognized faces from bubblegum cards. It is a good frame of reference, bubblegum cards. I never before had been in a major-league clubhouse.

This was a one-shot deal. The sports editor in New Haven had thrown me this small reward, a round trip to Fenway, one day

among the bubblegum cards before my fast return to the other end of the food chain covering high school sports and testimonial dinners and writing headlines with active verbs like 'rip' and 'blast' and 'destroy.' This was my big chance to show what I could do.

Postponed?

That never had been part of my planning.

I gulped hard and somehow found the manager's office. Dick Williams was in residence in his underwear. I think he just had taken a shower. He was on his first regular-season day of this new job, but already had a no-nonsense reputation as a tough guy with a brush cut and the attitude of a Marine Corps drill instructor. True to this reputation,

he looked like a man who would ask you to do 20 push-ups before any conversation started.

"Mr. Williams?" I said from his office doorway.

"What do you want?" he said from beneath the brush cut.

"I'd like to ask you some questions."

The memory of the interview pretty much has disappeared. I know that I asked my questions, somehow forcing out actual words from an uncertain mouth. I know that Dick Williams was very nice. I know that I wrote down every word as if it were part of The Sermon on the Mount. I can't remember anything else.

Back in the clubhouse, I know that I talked to a couple of

Fans from Bridgewater Massachusetts cheer for their Red Sox against the St. Louis Cardinals outside the Fenway Park ticket office. *(Courtesy of the Boston Public Library)*

players. The only one I remember was Reggie Smith, a rookie, scheduled to open the season at second base. He also was very nice, providing more words from that Sermon on the Mount. I scribbled fast. I thanked him, I am sure, with disproportionate gratitude, as if he had given me keys to a new car or the secrets of eternal life.

I was sweating when I left the clubhouse. Exhilarated. Exhausted.

There was a press room at Fenway, up on the roof, where all the other sportswriters no doubt were typing out their compositions, working in efficient luxury, but I did not know this existed. I figured I had to find a quiet spot somewhere to work. I found the Pennant Grille on the corner of Landsdowne Street and Brookline Ave. It was a bar.

Now known as the Cask n' Flagon, the Pennant Grille at that time was a seedier incarnation of a

watering hole. A few old timers at the bar watched a game show on the black and white television. A few black and white pictures of former Sox greats hung on the walls. A thin layer of cigarette smoke hung over the proceedings. Perfect.

I asked the proprietor if it would be all right for me to type in a booth in the corner. He had no problem with the idea and I bought a beer, simply because it seemed to be the right thing to do. I unsheathed the Olivetti Lettera 32. I sat down to compose the greatest baseball story that ever had been written.

Stuck for a beginning to this story, rejecting a few stumbling attempts, I finished my beer and bought another beer. The words began to flow. I bought another beer and maybe another while I typed and thought, typed and thought. I bought another beer in celebration

at the end. It helped as I dictated the important words to the greatest baseball story ever written to a copy boy back in New Haven from the pay phone in a corner of the Pennant Grille.

Done!

I had a wonderful feeling of relief from confronting my great test, slaying the beast, surviving. I bought a beer. I had about six beers in me. I was buzzed.

The beer-filled thought that soon arrived, with time to kill before the return train to New Haven, was that *Boston Globe* sports editor Ernie Roberts once had told me to give him a call if I ever were in town. Hey, I was in town. I called him at his office. Hey, he told me to take a cab over to Morrissey Boulevard. Hey, I did.

It turned out that this was my job interview. Roberts introduced me to a dozen different Globe poobahs. I met them all from my cloud of Pennant Grille affability. I laughed easily. I talked forcefully. I was far from nervous.

I remember my meeting with Thomas Winship, the editor of the *Globe*. He was a very bright, very bouncy character with horn-rimmed glasses, a bow tie and suspenders. He would have terrified me into class-conscious silence on most days, but now we sat and chatted in his glass-walled office as if we both were members of one of his exclusive Brahmin clubs. Hah. We both knew the future of sports journalism.

"I think we're going to be doing more and more stories about participatory sports," Winship said. "Are you active in participatory sports?"

Hah.

I told him I loved to ski. (I never had skiied in my life.) I sailed.

1967 World Series Program. *(Courtesy of Dick Casey)*

(I never had been on a sailboat in my life.) I hunted, I fished, golfed, played tennis. (Never, never, a few times, not really.) The conversation went well, very well, and Winship said I certainly should be hearing from him one of these days. Roberts told me that I'd made a good impression.

Hah.

I returned to New Haven that night, common sense, sobriety and dread settling in together for the ride somewhere near Pawtucket. What was I thinking? There was a very good chance that a career,

mine, had ended almost before it started.

Common sense, sobriety and dread told me what a fool I had been.

The Red Sox, of course, started their season the next day, Dick Williams leading them on their Impossible Dream course to the pennant and the World Series, laying the groundwork for all the historical stuff that has happened for the franchise in the past 40 years. I didn't see one game that season except on television. I worked far away from the bubble gum cards,

covering my high schools, writing my headlines with the active verbs.

It wasn't until December that Ernie Roberts called.

I began work at the Boston Globe in January of 1968. *(Author's note: Leigh Montville was a sportswriter and columnist at the* Boston Globe *for 21 years, a senior writer at* Sports Illustrated *for 12. He presently writes books. Among them are* The Big Bam, The Life and Times of Babe Ruth *and* Ted Williams, The Biography of an American Hero. *He lives in the Boston area.)*

May 5, 1967 Atlanta Chiefs 3, Toronto Falcons 1 (National Professional Soccer League Benefit Game)

JUNE 20, 1967

Sox Must Leave Fenway – Yawkey

The Red Sox will not be playing baseball at Fenway Park five years from now, according to Red Sox millionaire owner Tom Yawkey. And if the city doesn't have a new stadium, the club may not be in Boston at that time, Yawkey indicated Tuesday.

"We've been losing money," said Yawkey. "You can't go on forever. It's got to stop somewhere. I don't intend to bankrupt myself."

Yawkey clearly indicated, "This is not a threat. Merely a statement of fact."

"I'm losing money with the Red Sox. No person – unless he's a damn fool – likes to lose money," he said.

Restricted parking and limited seating have been mainly

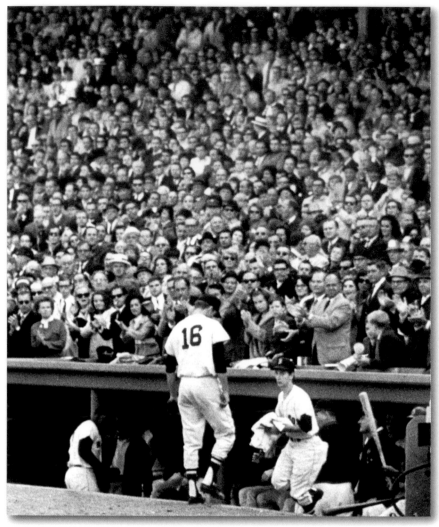

Jim Lonborg enters the Red Sox dugout in the midst of his one hit, 5-0 shutout of the Cardinals in Game 2 of the 1967 World Series. *(Courtesy of the Boston Public Library)*

Stadium Absolute Must, Says Yawkey

By Joe Cashman, Boston Record-American

The Red Sox presently are not for sale, but Tom Yawkey doesn't promise to hold on to them indefinitely regardless of what it might cost him in terms of dollars and cents.

"Love for baseball," Yawkey says, "was my only reason for buying the Boston franchise in 1933. Love for the game is the only reason I still own the club 34 years later. If I had become a club owner in the hope of making money, I'd have sold out long ago. Most of the years I've had the club it has cost me considerable money to operate it.

"I don't know how much longer I can afford to take the losses, which I think will be inescapable as long as the Red Sox must play in Fenway Park.

"I'm not going to move the club. The day may come, though, when I feel compelled to sell. In that event, I suspect the new owners will move to some other city in a hurry unless they can be guaranteed a new stadium in Greater Boston to rent."

TO REMAIN A MAJOR SPORTS CENTER

"If this city is to remain a major sports center, a new stadium must be built somewhere in this vicinity. Otherwise, it appears inevitable the city will lose both its American Baseball League and American Football League clubs."

General Manager Dick O'Connell of the Red Sox has said

responsible for the monetary losses suffered by Yawkey in his 35 years as Red Sox owner. He's puzzled at the endless delays in the new stadium issue.

"It's hard to believe that so many stadiums can be built around the country," Yawkey said. "All that has been done here is talk and more talk.

"Sometimes I wonder why I've continued to take those losses as long as I have. You can only live with a bad situation so long. I've come to this realization and I hope Boston does before it's too late.

"There was lots of talk about the Braves leaving town for Milwaukee, long before it took place. Nobody paid any attention, remember? Then suddenly they were gone.

"The ones that suffer most are the fans of Boston. Personally, I think they're great. They support their major sports teams excellently. If we [Red Sox] go, they are the ones who will lose most. And this would be the same for the football [Patriots] club. If they left, the fans would be the ones that suffered the most," said Yawkey.

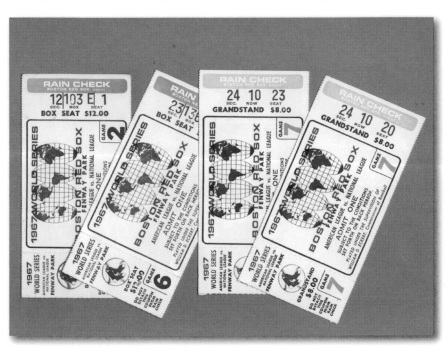

Tickets to the 1967 World Series were the hottest item in town since those for the Kennedy Inauguration seven years earlier. *(Collection of the author)*

he favors a suburban, rather than a downtown Boston site for a new stadium.

"I personally have no preference as to location," says Yawkey.

"Neither do I care whether the plant has a dome or retractable roof, or no overhead cover. I'm not interested in whether it's built by City, County, State, an Authority or a private syndicate. All I want to see is the project get off the ground."

While a new Boston stadium has been under discussion, new sports plants have been erected in several cities, including New York, Atlanta, St. Louis, San Diego, Oakland, Houston and Anaheim. Others are under construction.

Why all the hemming and hawing with nothing happening in this neck of the woods?

"I don't know," answers Yawkey. "It may be a case of too many cooks spoiling the broth. There's one fact which is generally overlooked. Boston is the only state capitol city with an American

League club. Stadium proposals in other cities have only to clear a city hall hurdle. Here such a proposal must clear a state house hurdle as well. That may be the answer to so much stadium talk, and so little stadium action."

Yawkey may have something there.

EDITORIAL: BOSTON TRAVELER, JUNE 22ND

Fenway Facts

For whatever good it may do, Red Sox owner Tom Yawkey deserves credit for jabbing a pin into the slow-motion planners who talk about building a Boston stadium.

He has given them a statement of fact to think about. The fact is, says he, that the Red Sox will not be playing baseball at Fenway Park five years from now. And since the property is his, and the financial losses are his, the decision to move whenever he feels like it is also his.

If the stadium-talkers can work up enough initiative to become stadium-builders, the chances are that the Red Sox will still be around five years from now, playing in a new major league structure. But unless there's a new stadium here, they'll be playing their home games in some other city.

The future of the Boston Patriots is also linked to this, for with Fenway gone, and no stadium taking its place, the Patriots will have no choice but to move to another city.

As Yawkey points out, Boston should have learned its lesson when the Braves moved to Milwaukee in 1953. There was a lot of talk about holding them here, but no action until it was too late.

Yawkey has been generous enough to state the facts in time for constructive action. That means it's time to stop talking about stadiums and build one.

July 7, 1967 Baltimore Bays 4, Chicago Spurs 1 (Soccer)

AUGUST 18, 1967

Fallen Hero Prince of the City, Part 2

"SHOW ME A HERO AND I'LL WRITE YOU A TRAGEDY"
F. SCOTT FITZGERALD

Anthony "Tony C" Conigliaro
Boston, AL, 1964-1985
Outfielder/designated hitter who hit 522 career home runs. Four – time American League home run champion. 1974 American League Most Valuable Player. Led Red Sox to world championships in 1967,

Following the 1967 the Fenway turf was replaced with new sod. The Red Sox shipped the turf from left field to Carl Yastrzemski for placement in the yard of his suburban Lynnfield home. *(Courtesy of Dan Desrochers)*

1974, and 1975. With teammates Carl Yastrzemski, Jim Rice, Fred Lynn and Dwight Evans formed one of the most potent batting orders in the modern era.

(Inscription on the plaque that would have hung in the National Baseball Hall of Fame in Cooperstown, N.Y. had Conigliaro not been beaned by Jack Hamilton on the night of August 18, 1976.)

The digital center-field clock read 8:42 on a warm Friday night in which Fenway Park was both engulfed in the haze of a smoke bomb and the instantaneous shock that

overwhelms and silences a crowd when they've witnessed something very disturbing and very sad.

For sprawled in the dirt near home plate lay Tony Conigliaro, the dynamic slugging wunderkind of the newly re-born Red Sox. The East Boston native had grown up in nearby Revere and gone to high school at St. Mary's in Lynn. Not only had he reached the 100 home run plateau faster than anyone in American League history but he also was helping the 100/1 shot Red Sox contend for the first time in nearly a generation.

The Jack Hamilton fastball exploded up into his face, hitting Conigliaro squarely under his left eye. The baseball rolled past the batter's box as teammate Rico Petrocelli raced to his side and medics scrambled to grab a stretcher. Even fans listening to the game on the radio swore they heard the ball hit the young slugger's face.

Like an American matador Tony Conigliaro faced his opposition with a stance that both crowded the plate and challenged pitchers to either brush him back or try to sneak one past him. Possessed of one of the greatest right-handed power strokes in American League history, Conigliaro was that rarest of Red Sox and Boston stars, a home-grown prodigy who embraced the spotlight and once bragged he wanted to be remembered as a better hitter than Ted Williams.

Not only did his beaning cost him the rest of the 1967 season but the entire '68 campaign as well.

And while the remainder of his career had glorious moments such as his game-tying home run on Opening Day in '69 and his 36 home run season in 1970, his budding Hall of Fame career ended on the night of August 18, 1967.

In a rare piece of film located in the archives of The Sports Museum in Boston, Conigliaro is shown a month and a half after sustaining the injury that nearly cost him an eye. In the first part of the clip he is shown singing acapella with teammates Mike Ryan and Rico Petrocelli in the clubhouse celebration at Fenway Park following the Red Sox clinching of their miracle American League pennant. The last segment of the grainy color footage shows the young slugger seated alone in front of his locker, head in hands, weeping.

AUGUST 27, 1967

On the day of the famous Jose Tartabull play in Chicago, Red Sox General manager Dick O'Connell remarks that the Red Sox are looking for a new state-funded stadium.

August 27, 1967 American
Legion Drum and Bugle Corps
National Championships
September 5, 1967 Mayor's
Charity Field Day

SEPTEMBER 30, 1967

Sox Win 6-4 to Force AL Tie

The most improbable championship run in Boston baseball history since that of the 1914 Braves and the best pennant race in American League history continued before a sellout crowd that contained Vice President Hubert Humphrey, Senator Ted Kennedy as the Twins sought to win their second pennant in three seasons on a brilliantly sunny Saturday afternoon at Fenway Park.

The Red Sox lucked out as Twins starter Jim Kaat left the game with a pulled tendon in his elbow in the third inning. In the fifth Reggie Smith led off with a double followed by Dalton Jones who hit a soft grounder to Rod Carew at second only to take a bad hop. With both runners safe Boston starter Jose Santiago and second baseman Mike Andrews struck out before third baseman Jerry Adair chipped a single that tied the score at one run apiece. Carl Yastrzemski then hit a roller that Twins first baseman Harmon Killebrew missed and Carew scooped only to discover that pitcher Jim Perry had neglected to cover first as Jones scampered home with the go-ahead run.

With the season on the line Yastrzemski once again came through following a Zoilo Versalles muff of a sure double play grounder. On a 3-1 count he crunched a three-run homer into the visitors bullpen sending the Sox on the way to a 6-4 win and one-game lead with but one game to play and two teams to beat, the Twins and Tigers.

OCTOBER 1, 1967

Sox Barely Escape Screaming, Streaming Fans

By Bud Collins

As the ball came down in Rico Petrocelli's glove for the last and final out, the town went up in the air like a beautiful balloon. Perhaps it will never come down. Red Sox euphoria is a gas that can keep you higher than helium. Or pot.

For an instant Petrocelli looked at the baseball. Then he began to run as though he were Chaing Kai-shek in Peking because he could hear the shrieking mob behind him.

It was the Red Sox Guard charging across the Fenway playing field Sunday afternoon, and the old ball park suddenly became a newsreel from Hong Kong, the Red Guard storming the British embassy. These were the zealots, thousands of them from the congregation of 35,770 at Fenway Park, which was packed tighter than the Black Hole of Calcutta.

They leaped the fences and streamed onto the field, screaming the Red Sox Guard oath, "We're Number One!" and displaying their banners.

They made Mao Tse-Tung's gang look like peace marchers, yet this was a frenzy of love, not hate.

Respectable people who had left their homes placidly, if nervously to attend the pennant-deciding rites indulged in by Our Old Town

Team had become fanatics celebrating a holy war triumph.

"Is Yaz God?" asked one of the banners.

It was an interesting theological question in the light of the miracles achieved by Carl Yastrzemski. Certainly he and his fellows are the children of the gods in this year of 1967.

Karl Marx, who said religion is the opiate of the people, would have revised himself had he watched the Red Sox unite to throw off their ninth-place chains. The Red Sox are the opiate right now, Karl, baby, although you might classify them as a religion.

"Just like '46!" proclaimed another banner. "Next Stop St. Louis!" "Spirit of 67!" "Go Sox!" "Wipe Out The Cardinals!"

The banners were waving and the mob advanced, and pitcher Jim Lonborg stood on the mound savoring it all, ready to be hailed as a conquering hero.

"Then it became a mania, and I was scared to death," Lonborg recalled. He didn't mind being raised to the sky by admirers, but not by 5,000 of them, each wanting a piece of him as a relic of their religious experience. He was sucked into the crowd as though it were a whirlpool, grabbed, mauled, patted, petted, pounded and kissed.

"This made Roxbury look like a picnic," said Patrolman John Ryan, a riot veteran who was one of Lonborg's rescuers. "Jim could have been hurt bad. We barely got him out of there."

Lonborg emerged nearly in tatters. His buttons were gone, and though his uniform shirt was still on his back his undershirt had disappeared. Nevertheless his right arm still dangled from his shoulder and

his fingers were intact. He would pitch and win again, although his 5-3 decision over Minnesota seemed enough forever at the moment.

Growing more fervent, the crowd spilit into platoons. One attacked the scoreboard, ripping down signs and everything else that could be lifted for souvenirs. Others looked elsewhere for loot. The fervor had begun to degenerate into the ugliness of vandalism. And the fever in some had become a mood of recklessness that endangered. Twenty or so kids climbed the screen behind the plate like monkeys. Several nearly fell to the concrete 40 feet below. The screen sank ominously beneath their weight as the people in the seats below looked up helplessly.

Nobody seemed to want to leave the park. A few firecrackers went off, and horns blew endlessly. On the field, most of the Red Sox Guard had settled into a milling pattern, wandering about the diamond, dazed at the wonder of it all, ecstatic to be treading on hallowed ground.

Joe Tierney led a group of ushers who stood on the mound protecting that rise from the human bulldozers. A man named Ray Copeland from Wellesley stooped at the edge of the mound, scooping up a palmful of dirt and pouring it into a small box. "Going to take it back to England," he said. "I've been working in Boston a year, became a Red Sox fan, when I go back, some of the old soil of Fenway goes with me to London."

Kris Becker, a college girl from Worcester, plucked a handful of grass from along the third baseline. "Not sure what I'll do with it yet. Maybe frame it."

Only the cops prevented the mob from removing the left field wall.

Last year on the last day of the season the Red Sox choked; they won and blew 10th place by a half game. Sunday it was altogether something else. "You respond differently when you're in first place than when you're in ninth," said Yastrzemski.

Lonborg set the faithful to chanting and clapping with his bunt single that opened the sixth. The Red Sox, behind 2-0 devoted 24 minutes to their half of the inning and the Minnesotans began to feel the mysterious power of Our Old Town Team. They threw to the wrong base, made wild pitches, an error, and put the ball over the plate to Yastrzemski. It meant five runs for Boston, the team that is today's American Dream. The inning ended with John Kiley, the Fenway organist, playing "The Night They Invented Champagne." It was a hymn to the day and to the evening to come when Uncle Tom Yawkey poured for Our Old Town Team.

They drank champagne the way people drink it when it is free, and many of them probably have heads resembling the Goodyear blimp today.

The players will sober up by Wednesday, but it will take the town much longer to get over its Red Sox high.

And now, on this day of revelation we know what Billy Joe and his chick were throwing off the Tallahatchie Bridge: World Series tickets printed in Detroit, Minneapolis, and Chicago.

Bud Collins has written sports for six decades for both The Boston Herald *and* The Boston

Fans of Ken Harrelson react to his 1969 trade to Cleveland with displeasure. *(Courtesy of the Boston Public Library)*

Globe. *Before he became known internationally for his tennis writing and broadcasting, Collins covered a variety of sports in Boston, including a stint on the Red Sox beat.*

Gibson Bests Santiago, Sox, 2-1

Fresh from the greatest pennant race in modern memory the Red Sox faced the mighty St. Louis Cardinals and ace pitcher Bob Gibson in the first World Series game played at Fenway Park in 21 years. Unlike the Red Sox the Cards had plenty of time to secure their rotation and Gibson would prove to be the best pitcher they'd faced all season. The imposing right-hander who once played for the Harlem Globetrotters scattered six hits, including a home run by Jose Santiago that accounted for Boston's lone run.

Lonborg Shuts Out Cards 5-0, One Hitter

The Impossible Dream was jump started anew as Gentleman Jim Lonborg pitched his second consecutive masterpiece while holding the Cardinals to just a single hit (Julian Javier double in the 7th) as Carl Yastrzemski resumed his duties as hero-in-residence with two home runs and 4 RBI to lead Boston to a 5-0 win. Lonborg appeared un-hittable as he retired the first 20 batters he faced. The series shut-out was Boston's first since Boo Ferris had beaten the Cardinals 4-0 in game three of the '46 Fall Classic, also at Fenway Park.

Unheralded Waslewski Tosses Gem, Sox Win 8-4, Tie Series

Red Sox manager Dick Williams made the bold decision to start 26-year-old rookie Gary Waslewski despite the fact the right-hander had won just two games during the regular season. Williams's faith was rewarded as Waslewski pitched 5 1/3 strong innings allowing only four hits and two earned runs. Sox bats boomed as Joe Foy's seventh inning double broke a 4-4 tie and supplemented home runs hit by teammates Rico Petrocelli (2) and Yastrzemski and Reggie Smith. Former Negro League pitcher John Wyatt picked up the victory on the basis of his inning-and-two-thirds stint in relief of Waslewski.

Gibson Leads Cardinals to Series Triumph, Beats Sox, 7-2

The headline of the morning *Boston Record-American* proclaimed "Lonborg and Champagne," and more than a few members of the St. Louis Cardinals made sure to bring copies to their clubhouse as they faced Boston's Impossible Dreamers led by ace Jim Lonborg who'd pitch with just two days rest.

Lonborg had pitched masterfully while notching wins in games two and five. In fact he'd given up just 4 hits over eighteen innings with a microscopic 0.050 ERA.

The matter of two days rest as well as his first head-to-head duel with Bob Gibson made the game the most compelling in Fenway's modern history.

Lonborg pitched heroically for four innings, allowing only two runs but tired by the fifth when he served up a home run to Gibson as the Cardinals went on to win by a decisive 7-2 score. It marked the second time in four seasons that Gibson had pitched a complete game victory in a Series deciding game. With a 5-1 won/lost record, a 2.00 ERA, and 57 strikeouts in 54 innings, Gibson had established himself as one of the best pitchers in World Series history.

OCTOBER 15, 1967

Parilli Paces Pats to 41-10 Win Over Dolphins

Fenway Park had only just played host to the 1967 World Series when the Patriots played a late home opener before a crowd of 23,955. They got their money's worth as 37-year-old Patriots quarterback Babe Parilli tossed five touchdown passes to lead to Boston to its second win of the season.

OCTOBER 22, 1967

OAKLAND CRUSHES BOSTON, 48-14 BEFORE 25,057 AT FENWAY

NOVEMBER 5, 1967

19,422 AT FENWAY SEE PATRIOTS HERO CAPPELLETTI EJECTED AS BOSTON BEATS HOUSTON, 18-7

Patriots ace receiver/kicker had already booted three field goals before he was ejected in the fourth quarter for fighting with W.K. Hicks of the Oilers in the Patriots 18-7 win.

NOVEMBER 12, 1967

CHIEFS BOMB BOSTON, 33-10 BEFORE 23,010 AT FENWAY PARK

NOVEMBER 19, 1967

Patriots Bow to Namath and Jets in Thriller, 29-24

Journeyman quarterback Don Trull nearly led the Patriots to the greatest comeback in club history as he sparked the home team to three fourth-quarter touchdowns as the Patriots nearly erased a 26-point Jet lead halfway through the final quarter. A crowd of 26,790 held its breath as Mike Holovak's tried mightily to counter a Jet team led by Namath's 297 passing yards.

NOVEMBER 25, 1967

The Red Sox raise their ticket prices on reserved tickets from $2.25 to $2.50 while maintaining their general admission prices ($1.50) and bleacher price ($1.00).

DECEMBER 9, 1967

BILLS BOMB PATS 44-16 BEFORE 20,627 AT FENWAY

April 23, 1968 Boston Beacons 3, Detroit Cougars 0 (Soccer)

April 26, 1968 Los Angeles Wolves 4, Boston Beacons 0 (Soccer)

May 10, 1968 Atlanta Chiefs 1, Boston Beacons 0 (Soccer)

May 21, 1968 Cleveland Stokers 4, Boston Beacons 1 (Soccer)

May 26, 1968 New York Generals 1, Boston Beacons 1 (Soccer)

June 21, 1968 Chicago Mustangs 6, Boston Beacons 5 (Soccer)

June 25, 1968 Boston Beacons 3, Washington Whips 1 (Soccer)

JULY 8, 1968

18,431 See Beacons Bow, 7-1

PELE GOAL WINS

A crowd of 18,431 delighted in watching the incomparable Pele as the 27-year-old Brazilian superstar led Satos FC to a decisive 7-1 rout of the host Boston Beacons. Trailing 1-0 after Lloyd McLean scored for Boston, Santos proceeded to take apart the Beacons defense as Pele scored what proved to be the winning goal at the 35-minute mark on a 30-foot drive that sliced through the legs of Beacons keeper Walter Tarnowsky.

The second half brought an avalanche of Santos goals as Pele scored once more as part of a five-goal onslaught. Following the game he and his teammates celebrated by tossing flowers to the women in the crowd from the bouquets they'd

The Boston Beacons of the North American Soccer League called Fenway Park home for their one season of existence in 1968. *(Courtesy of The Sports Museum)*

been presented prior to the match. More than one Boston sportswriter compared Pele to Bob Cousy as he helped set up each of the goals he didn't score himself. Much was also made of his reported $341,000 annual tax free salary that made him the highest paid athlete in the world. Would that anyone would have expected less of the only athlete ever declared a "natural resource" by his homeland.

July 12, 1968 Boston Beacons 3, Vancouver Royals 2 (Soccer)

July 16, 1968 Boston Beacons 1, Houston Stars 0 (Soccer)

July 23, 1968 Toronto Falcons 2, Boston Beacons 2 (Soccer)

JULY 25, 1968

Largest Crowd of '68 Campaign Jams Fenway

35,875 HAIL SENATOR EUGENE MCCARTHY

Following the assassination of Democratic Party presidential candidate Robert F. Kennedy, the campaign and anti-war crusade

of Minnesota senator Eugene McCarthy received a pre-convention boost as not only a full house, but 10,000 gathered outside Fenway Park greeted the poet and former semi-professional baseball player. McCarthy, whose campaign came out of nowhere to force President Johnson from the race with a strong showing in the New Hampshire primary and a solid victory in Massachusetts, thrilled a crowd of mostly students and young voters.

Addressing the packed ballpark from a platform over second base, McCarthy evoked the spirit of the 100-1 Impossible Dream Red Sox of the previous season when he remarked, "America has talked about freedom for almost 200 years. We should not be surprised that 1968 is the year of manifestation of freedom. We shall win in Chicago, and in November and it will not be a new America, but the old America of openness, confidence, and trust. I have not yet despaired of success"

July 26, 1968 Boston Beacons 1, Baltimore Bays 1 (Soccer)

August 6, 1968 Atlanta Chiefs 2, Boston Beacons 1 (Soccer)

August 9, 1968 Boston Beacons 2, New York Generals 2 (Soccer)

August 20, 1968 Boston Beacons 1, Dallas Tornadoes 1 (Soccer)

August 23, 1968 Washington Whips 4, Boston Beacons 1 (Soccer)

September 8, 1968 Boston Beacons 1, Baltimore Bays 0 (Soccer)

OCTOBER 13, 1968

HOUSTON'S BOB DAVIS LEADS OILERS OVER PATS, 16-0, BEFORE 35,502 AT FENWAY

OCTOBER 20, 1968

Taliaferro Leads Patriots to 23-6 Victory Over Buffalo

Quarterback Mike Taliaferro fired a pair of TD's to Jim Whalen and Gino Cappelletti and Cappelletti also booted three field goals to lead the Patriots to victory at Fenway Park before a crowd of 21,082.

Source: The Bridgeport Telegram, page 9, October 21, 1968

NOVEMBER 3, 1968

Fans Jeer as Pats Lose to Broncos, 35-14

Head coach Mike Holovak took all the blame and admitted he'd supplied all the plays as rookie quarterback Tom Sherman completed 11 passes including a touchdown in the Patriots humiliating loss. With middle linebacker Nick Buoniconti injured, the Patriots defense was shredded by both the running of Bronco back Floyd Little and the passing of Steve Tensi. Many among the crowd of 18,301 booed the Patriots off the field at the conclusion of the game.

Source: Newport Daily News, page 17, November 4, 1968

NOVEMBER 10, 1968

CHARGERS HANG ON TO BEATS PATRIOTS, 27-17 BEFORE 19,278 AT FENWAY

NOVEMBER 24, 1968

GRIESE PASSES DOLPHINS OVER HAPLESS PATRIOTS, 34-10 BEFORE 18, 305 AT FENWAY

DECEMBER 1, 1968

Pats Win One, 33-14

The final football game of the hundreds played to date in Fenway Park's long history ended with the Patriots decisive 33-14 victory over the Cincinnati Bengals before 17,796. Rookie quarterback Tom Sherman led the Patriots to a 26-0 half-time lead as he tossed touchdown passes to Jim Whalen (2) and Gino Cappelletti as the Patriots broke a five-game losing streak while bidding farewell to the second of their six home stadiums.

(Author's note: The Bengals game marked the end of the Patriots six-year stay at Fenway and the end of six decades and several hundred pro, collegiate, and schoolboy games of football at the park.)

January 29, 1969 Goodwill Dinner

JUNE 28, 1969

Bruno Displays Quality of Mercy at Fenway

DECKS KILLER BEFORE 12,000 MAT FANS

By Jack McCarthy

Bruno Sammartino showed the quality of mercy last night at Fenway Park. He thoughtfully refrained from breaking Killer Kowalski's squash with a chair, merely denting it as he beat the huge Pole into the canvas to become the heavyweight champion of the Back Bay and lower Beacon Hill.

This was the feature attraction of the first outdoor wrestling carnival staged in a Boston ball park since the 1930s and palmy days of Danno O'Mahony.

Although it was a hot, steamy night, an early estimate put the crowd, which paid a $10 top for ringside, at 12,000 esthetes. The ring was set up between shortstop and the mound and if promoter Abe Ford sold all those $10 ringside, he did alright.

The rain providentially held off and the only moisture apparent was the perspiration of the gladiators and the red corpuscles of one Victor Rivera. Victor was rammed into the ring post by one George Steele.

This enraged the cognoscenti, causing some stirring among the 36 Boston police stationed in the park. Steele, however, escaped in a hail of paper cups and flash cubes.

This was one of the more enlightening events of the highly cultural evening, which was highlighted by a debutante cotillion featuring the perennial debutante, Slave Girl Moolah. She was accompanied by Toni Rose and Donna Christanella in a tag-team triumph over the Boucher Sisters, Betty and Rita, and Vivian Vachon.

This match featured almost as much as Ricky Sexton displays. Sexton at one time was thought to be unconscious in his match with Duke Savage but since his hair covered both the back and front of his head the refs could not tell and the match continued. Sexton wears a leopard-skin bathing suit, which rumor has it is worn daily by promoter Ford at Revere Beach.

The referees included Tom McNeeley, John Stanley and Eddie Santamaria, the Cambridge Comet. Eddie had the toughest chore of the evening, trying to outtalk the six women.

Moolah and her court, by dire and devious means, managed to circumvent Santamaria with some nifty ends around and win three out of five falls.

The crowd was a typical wrestling group—all subscribers for the Boy Scout code. As the blocky Sammartino held the chair high over the fallen Kowalski, Bruno asked the crowd for their verdict. Some stood and gave the thumbs down signal and one at ringside yelled, "Break the chair."

Sammartino, fearful of losing his clientele, proceeded to belabor the Killer to roars of approval. Much of this main bout was held outside of the ring in the general area where Rico Petrocelli charges ground balls.

So the diamond belt went to Sammartino, whom I would want gladly back in a head-on smash with a freight train. Kowalski may have beaten him before, but in a no-holds barred, no referee match, last night was not his night.

A good time was had by all, I think, and Ford could count his promotion a success. And Abe can count.

The only thing not in the script, I think, was a further humiliation of the huge Kowalski. As McNeeley and Stanley carried him from the ring on a stretcher, as per the rules, they dropped him.

Sic Semper Tyrannis.

Democratic Presidential hopeful and anti-war crusader Eugene McCarthy packed Fenway Park for a pre-convention rally on July 25, 1968. *(Courtesy of The Boston Herald)*

Carlton Fisk tags out his rival and
Yankee counterpart Thurman Munson
in a jarring home-plate collision in
1973 that did everything to re-kindle
the heated rivalry between the teams.
(Photograph by Mike Andersen)

CHAPTER SEVEN
Extra Innings

"Here is the American Dream, the one that populated the sleep of all those durable Seperatists who incorporated this old town 350 years ago. The dream assumed the possibility of self-creation through hard work and an unremitting exercise of will. Yaz is a visible expression of that dream. Forty years of age at this writing, but with a new stance, Yaz continues as he always has done, carrying in his person the collective aspirations of our city. He is, I think, heroic. When his virtues come to seem old fashioned—only then will Boston itself grow old.

—ROBERT B. PARKER, C.1979, ON THE MAN WHO PLAYED THE MOST GAMES IN FENWAY PARK'S FIRST CENTURY.

The seventies in Boston started with Bobby Orr scoring the goal of goals and ended with Yaz changing his stance for the umpteenth time and stroking his 3,000th hit against the team that made him dress in the batboys locker room during his tryout at Yankee Stadium a generation earlier.

Fenway Park again was the star of not just the franchise but for all of baseball as America fell in love with the Green Monster for four magical days in October 1975 when anything seemed possible, be it the arrival of Luis Tiant's parents from Cuba or the twin blasts by Bernie Carbo and Carlton Fisk that led the Red Sox to victory on an evening simply referred to as "Game Six" for generations. "Where were you for Game Six?" became a time-honored ice-breaker for New Englanders that was even immortalized in the award winning film, *Good Will Hunting*.

Following the Impossible Dream season in 1967, Red Sox attendance took off as fans filled Fenway in numbers comparable to those that watched the great teams of the late forties. *(Courtesy of The Sports Museum)*

January 20, 1970 Goodwill Dinner
July 9-12, 1970 Jehovah's
Witnesses Gathering
January 27, 1971 Goodwill Dinner

MAY 28, 1971

Sox Chase Blue, Siebert Wins, 4-3

The shadows of 1912 crept over Fenway Park as an overflow crowd filled the park on the Friday night of Memorial Day weekend 1971. Nearly 59 years after his famous duel with Walter Johnson Red Sox legend Joe Wood sat in his Hamden Connecticut home and listened along with an untold multitude of Red Sox fans to the radio broadcast of the most highly anticipated Red Sox regular season game since the final weekend of the '67 pennant race. Wood could easily identify with both Boston starter Sonny Seibert and Oakland fireballer Vida Blue as the 21-year-old visitor came to Boston riding a wave of publicity while defending a personal 10-game win streak as Seibert also enjoyed an undefeated record of 8-0.

The game more than lived up to its advance billing as Rico Petrocelli smashed two homers, a two-run job in the first and a solo shot in the sixth and George Scott singled home the winning run in the eighth with his third hit to send Blue and former Red Sox manager Dick Williams packing.

For his part the 34-year-old Seibert scattered 6 hits including 3 solo home runs to Reggie Jackson, Dave Duncan, and Sal Bando and came within 2 pitches of hurling a complete game. For with two out in the ninth the eccentric right-hander (his baseball glove was covered with

handwritten instructions on how to pitch certain batters) was lifted to a standing ovation and watched as reliever Bob Bolin took over with a 3-1 count on A's catcher Dave Duncan and watched nervously as Bolin surrendered two booming and slightly foul Lansdowne St. shots before finally notching a strikeout and securing the dramatic win.

SEPTEMBER 2, 1971

Sonny Siebert socks two home runs against Baltimore to back his 3-0 shutout of Baltimore (he is the last AL pitcher to hit 2 hr in a game)

May 25, 1973 Northeastern 3, Providence College 2 (NCAA District One Finals)
May 25, 1973 Harvard 4, University of Massachusetts 2 (NCAA District One Finals)
May 26, 1973 Providence College 8, U Mass 7 (NCAA District One Finals)
May 26, 1973 Providence College 5, Northeastern 4 (NCAA District One Finals)
May 26, 1973 Harvard 11, Northeastern 1 (NCAA District One Finals)

JULY 27, 1973
(From an advertisement for Atlantic Records in The Boston Phoenix:)

Newport News

Newport Jazz Festival-New England will be held Friday and Saturday, July 27-28 at Fenway Park in Boston.

George Wein, producer of Newport Festivals for the past 19

years, announced that the two-day program will feature a mix of soul and jazz. "It will be equivalent to two Saturday nights in the old Festivals at Newport, Rhode Island," he said.

Among the Atlantic-Atco performers, past and present, who will be appearing are Ray Charles, ("Ray Charles Live"), Rahsaan Roland Kirk ("Prepare Thyself to Deal with a Miracle"), Herbie Mann ("Hold On I'm Comin'"), David Newman ("The Weapon"), and Donny Hathaway ("Roberta Flack and Donny Hathaway").

Rowdyism Mars Jazz at Fenway

Logistical issues in Newport, Rhode Island, sent their fabled Jazz Festival to Fenway Park in 1973 for the first and likely last time as performances on the last night of the festival were marred by spectators who rushed the field and disrupted the show. The highlights of the weekend festival were a rousing Friday night set by War and B.B. King the following night.

The trouble started on Saturday night when a horde of young spectators clambered onto the field following performances by Charlie Mingus and King just prior to a set by singer Donny Hathaway. Apart from the confusion on the field many of the crowd of 20,000 filed reports of pickpocketing and open robbery with Boston police. Unfortunately B.B. King wasn't the only one singing "The Thrill is Gone."

AUGUST 1, 1973

Munson-Fisk Scrap Provokes Free-For-All; Lyle Beaten Again

SOX KO YANKS IN BRAWL, 3-2

The semi-dormant tong war between the Red Sox and Yankees flared with the intensity of a blue flame in the top of the ninth inning of a Wednesday afternoon game in which the tenor of the fabled rivalry would be established for the next four decades.

With the score tied at 2 and Yankee catcher Thurman Munson on third with one out and Gene Michael at bat, the Yankees attempted a suicide squeeze only to have Michael miss the bunt, refuse to move as Red Sox catcher Carlton Fisk shoved him aside to make the tag on the charging Munson who sent Fisk airborne with the force of their collision.

Fisk then leapt up with the ball, looked to first to hold base runner Felipe Alou before being sucker punched by Munson.

In the melee that followed many of the plot lines that characterized the sizzle of the Yankee/Red Sox wars of the seventies surfaced. First and foremost was the battle of catchers. The athletic and almost patrician Fisk pitted against the scrappy un-shaven Munson. The pinstripe banjo hitter be he named Michael or Dent making his presence felt. And most dramatically, the fierce spontaneity of the key

The Red Sox front office of the early 1970s as imagined by sports cartoonist Vic Johnson. *(Collection of the author)*

play that becomes a conversation topic forty years later.

Oh, the Red Sox won courtesy of a two-out single by Mario Guerrero off loser and former Boston reliever Sparky Lyle. The loss also knocked the Yankees out of first place for the first time since July 1.

SEPTEMBER 28, 1973

Harper Breaks Sox 62-Year-Old Season Steal Mark

The spirit of the long forgotten Red Sox Speed Boys of the dead ball era was revived at Fenway Park when leftfielder Tommy Harper was honored with the presentation of the base he'd stolen during a pause in the Red Sox win over Milwaukee

Brewers. His 53rd steal surpassed the mark of 52, set by Hall of Fame center fielder Tris Speaker in Fenway Park's inaugural season of 1912.

APRIL 8, 1975

Ovation for Tony C. Rocks Fenway as Sox Win, 5-2

On a day in which the legendary Duffy Lewis returned to Fenway Park to toss out the first ball of the Red Sox 75th season, Boston also welcomed back favorite son Tony Conigliaro to the home team as well as cheering home run king Henry Aaron, once a farmhand of the Boston Braves and now a 41-year-old outfielder/DH for the Milwaukee Brewers.

Conigliaro was afforded two standing ovations of roughly a minute each as he stroked a single in four at bats. Aaron walked and then went hitless in three additional at bats, never hitting the ball beyond the infield. The afternoon's biggest star was Luis Tiant who had the Brewers lunging at off-speed stuff while retiring 11 straight Brewers after giving up a home run to Robin Yount and a single to Bob Coluccio.

JULY 21, 1975

CAPE COD LEAGUE ALL-STARS BEST ATLANTIC COLLEGIATE BASEBALL LEAGUE ALL-STARS AT FENWAY BY A SCORE OF 1-0

Kent Seaman of Yarmouth got the win and Steve Tipa of the ACBL was named game MVP.

OCTOBER 4-5, 1975

Yaz Dazzles in Return to Left, Sox Take Two From A's

Due to a season-ending wrist injury to rookie sensation Jim Rice, Carl Yastrzemski returned to his familiar post of left field and turned back the clock as Boston won the first two of their three-game sweep at Fenway Park over the defending World Champion Oakland Athletics. Yaz later remarked of the series to *The Boston Globe*. "I had the homer off Vida Blue when we were down 3-0. Even though I hit .455 in the series, hit homers and so forth, what I remember most is going out after not playing left field most of the season

(8 games total). I went out there and made all the defensive plays. I threw out Campaneris and Bando at third in the second game, then Jackson twice at second in the clincher. I remember Jackson hitting a ball in Oakland to the line. I backhanded it and threw him out at second. Then there was the play in the eighth, diving for Jackson's ball to hold him to a single. The tying run stayed at first—I don't remember what made me dive, but I had to keep him at second. Then Drago got the next batter, Joe Rudi, to hit into a double play, and we won it, 5-3. The thing I remember most is defense."

OCTOBER 11, 1975

El Tiante Scores 6-0 Win Over Reds In Series Opener

Thanks to the combined efforts of several U.S. Senators and Secretary

of State Henry Kissinger, the first game of the 1975 World Series took on extra meaning at Fenway Park as the parents of Boston ace Luis Tiant were allowed to leave Cubs to watch their son in his hour of glory. The elder Tiant already knew of Fenway Park having pitched for the New York World Series opener features Luis Tiant pitching in front of his parents who are brought to America from Cuba by Ted Kennedy and Henry Kissinger. Bill Lee observed, "During the pre-game festivities, the elder El-Tiante walked out to the mound and threw the ceremonial first ball to Fisk. He threw a strike. The he threw another strike, followed by still another. I'll tell you something, he was in great shape. Every pitch he threw has mustard on it and he probably would have kept throwing if someone hadn't led him off the mound. I swear he could have gone nine."

Once the game started, his son Luis embraced the spotlight. Not only did he stroke a memorable seventh-inning base hit but also scored

The bullpen cart was as much a part of the seventies at Fenway Park as doubleknit uniforms and two-tone caps. *(Collection of the author)*

the first of Boston's six runs while out-dueling Reds ace Don Gullett while tossing a five-hit complete game.

OCTOBER 12, 1975

Bench leads Reds To Ninth Inning Rally and 3-2 Victory

In Game 2 of the '75 series the Red Sox started 17-game-winner Bill Lee against Jack Billingham.

In his book *The Wrong Stuff* Lee wrote of the game, "While warming up, I noticed the Reds watching me from their dugout. They couldn't believe what they were seeing. I was throwing so much junk. Most of them were laughing, and I thought they were going to knock each other over,

racing to the plate to hit against me. Pete Rose was their lead-off hitter, and I struck him out. I didn't hear too many peeps out of them for the rest of the afternoon."

Lee was working on a masterpiece until rain delayed the game in the sixth. Once back on the mound Lee maintained his dominance until the top of the ninth. If only someone had told him that during the lengthy rain delay Reds catcher Johnny Bench had told 65 million television viewers he hoped to take Lee to the opposite field then Lee might not have thrown the low sinker the Reds catcher hammered to right for a leadoff double. Thus ended Lee's afternoon as reliever Dick Drago retired the next two batters before surrendering a game-tying single to Dave Concepcion. He then stole second and scored what proved to be the game's winning run on a double by Ken Griffey, Sr.

All Bill Lee could say in a postgame interview to a reporter who asked his impressions of the Series to date was, "It's tied."

OCTOBER 19, 1975

Fenway Measures Down

THE BOSTON GLOBE USES AERIAL PHOTOGRAPHY TO MEASURE THE LEFT FIELD LINE AND FINS IT TO BE 309 FT..LATER TEAM PR DIRECTOR AND ART KEEFE MEASURE IT WITH A TAPE AND FIND IT TO BE 304 FT..NOT THE ADVERTISED 315 FT.

Moments in the Seventies

By Luke Salisbury

I moved to Boston the day in October 1972 Luis Aparicio fell down rounding third in the first inning of a crucial game against the Tigers. It choked off a rally—Yaz had just hit what should have been a run-producing triple—but—you can guess—the Sox didn't get to Mickey Lolich early, he settled down—we lost. This was an appropriate welcome for a Red Sox fan who had just moved from the Bronx. It was 1972. Because of an early-season work stoppage, the Red Sox played one less game than Detroit and lost the Division by one game. So be it. I was in Boston where one could get as much of the Red Sox as one wanted. One could get many things one wanted in Boston. Boston is a great city to be twenty-five. It's a great place to be a Red Sox fan, especially if you're an

Charlestown, New Hampshire, native Carlton Fisk is separated by teammate Doug Griffin as he prepares to go after Thurman Munson following a home-plate collision. Fisk was the standard bearer for New England-born players for a generation and one of a handful of most popular players in Fenway's first century. *(Photograph by Mike Andersen)*

Opening Day 1975 saw Tony Conigliaro's return to the Red Sox and Henry Aaron's first regular-season appearance at Fenway Park. It marked the 11th anniversary of Conigliaro's home run in his first Fenway at bat and reminded many that Aaron had signed his first professional contract with the Boston Braves. *(Collection of the author)*

as the game started at 1:00 PM Eastern Standard Time. Who was the first DH? The Yankees' Ron Blomberg. The day was cold, wind blew, Reggie Smith made an error in the first when the Yankees scored 5 runs off Tiant. The Sox came right back with 8 runs and won the game 15-5. It was another epitomizingly iconic Red Sox afternoon. It was that particular Boston dance of good, bad, unexpected, and doubt. Doubt as in beat the Yankees on Opening Day, let's see you beat them with the season on the line.

Now the Red Sox have won a World Series in our lifetimes (Good Lord, they hadn't won in my parents' lifetimes!), the quality of rooting has altered. It's not that the passion and frustration isn't intense, but the over-arching back-story of inevitability, of getting close and succumbing—either by managerial stupidity (journeyman Denny Galehouse starting the one-game playoff in 1948; taking Jim Willoughby out of the seventh game of the '75 World Series) or an inevitable lack of clutch (two losses in Yankee Stadium with a one-game lead to end the '49 season)—has finally receded into a history that isn't always biting us in the ass. We aren't battling fate, we're rooting.

Fate came calling most deliciously in 1975. Opening Day was the most memorable I've attended with the possible exception of 2005 when the humbled Yankees stood on the top step of the visiting dugout and saluted the new World Champions. Tony Conigliaro and Hank Aaron played that day. They were DHs, so the invisible hand of greed (baseball as dollars, not tradition) gives and takes. Tony C, the greatest might-have-been of his Red

outsider. When the club loses, the natives act like they've been beaten up by their older brother.

Following the Red Sox from another city had its advantages. I was like the hero of the Japanese novel *Snow Country* by Yasunari Kawabata, who loves Occidental ballet because: "A ballet he had never seen was an art in another world. It was... a lyric from some paradise... He preferred not to savor the ballet in the flesh; rather he fancied the phantasms of his own dancing imagination... It was like

being in love with someone he had never seen." By October 1972, it was time to look my beloved in the face, and I got Luis Aparicio, the best American League base runner of his generation, falling down in the most important game of the year.

Having always wanted to follow the Sox in Boston, I waited a long New England winter, went to Opening Day in '73, and have been to every Fenway Opening Day since. That opener lives in trivia. It was the first appearance of the DH. The literal first appearance

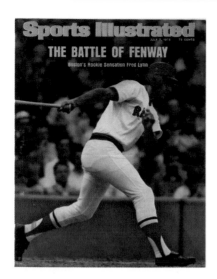

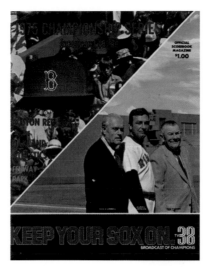

(left) Fred Lynn was half of the rookie combo known as the "Gold Dust Twins" that helped Boston to both a Division title and pennant. *(Courtesy of* Sports Illustrated*)*

(right) American League Championship Series Program *(Collection of the author)*

The rivalry between Fisk and Munson was a compelling subplot to the tong war between the Red Sox and Yankees. *(Photograph by Mike Andersen)*

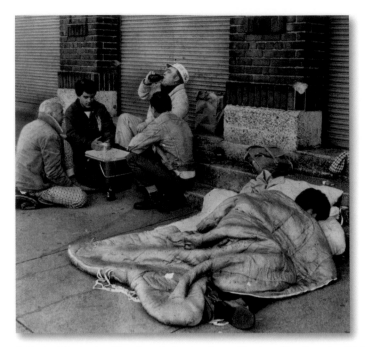

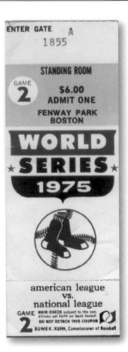

In the best Boston tradition, fans slept out on Jersey Street awaiting the sale of tickets to the 1975 World Series. *(Courtesy of The Boston Herald)*

Luis Tiant gets used to the unfamiliar confines of the batters box in his first World Series at bat. His single led to the first run of his 6-0 shutout of the Big Red Machine. *(Photograph by Mike Andersen)*

Secretary of State Henry Kissinger, Mrs. Kissinger, Baseball Commissioner Bowie Kuhn, and Carl Yastrzemski gather prior to the first game of the 1975 World Series. Kissinger had just helped convince Cuban President Fidel Castro to allow Luis Tiant's parents to travel to Boston to watch their son pitch in the series. *(Courtesy of The Boston Herald)*

Sox generation, and Hank Aaron, who was everything a man and athlete should be, both played in a regular-season game at Fenway. It was a fine start to a fine season. In '75, you could still go to any regular-season games by buying a ticket the day of the game. Going to Fenway wasn't a fashion or corporate statement, it was baseball. I saw Tiant outgun Vida Blue in June, and Tiant beat Jim Palmer in September. A pitchers' duel in Fenway is special as lack of foul territory means extra hacks for hitters and the Wall gives no pity for pitchers. Dwight Evans won the June game with a homer down the right-field line, a rarity for him, and I believe Rico Petrocelli won the September game with a shot into the screen.

The '75 World Series has rightly gone into legend—a legend I savor more after 2004. Whether the sixth game was the greatest game ever played (we have one of those every few years) or maybe the greatest game played at Fenway (perhaps), it was the greatest I ever saw in person. My brother and I were two rows below the old scoreboard atop the right-field bleachers. We weren't close but we were there. Until Bernie Carbo's miraculous pinch homer in the eighth, it certainly wasn't the greatest game ever played. Tiant gave up runs, Fred Lynn crashed into the center-field wall, and the Sox were losing. After Carbo's game-tying homer, it was a great game. Fisk's homer is celebrated because of the TV coverage. Home runs are militant simplifiers, and a game-winning simplifier, with beseeching pirouette and victory hand clap, belongs to the ages. We have seen it, will continue to see it, but we see it from the same angle.

Carlton Fisk connects with the Pat Darcy pitch he sent into the night, which grazed the left-field foul pole and sent Boston and all of baseball into a frenzy, capping the best baseball game in modern memory. *(Photograph by Mike Andersen)*

Dwight Evans' ninth-inning catch off Joe Morgan was the greater spectacle in person. From where we sat, high in the right-field bleachers, it looked like a home run off the bat. I've seen the TV footage. It looks like Evans just has to gallop back and get it. He runs, leaves his feet, which he doesn't have to, and puts up his glove. From where we sat Morgan's drive looked like a comet headed for the bull pen. Evans seemed far away. The ball was hit so high, so hard. It was flying, Evans running, base runners scampering. The catch looked impossible, and high in the bleachers, we were in the air, in the ether, in the moment of supreme action when action stops, "the still point in the turning world," the timeless moment before fate and reality intervene. You can't get this on television. You can't get it in the virtual world. You get it being there. It's flying, love, the whisper of immortality, the place of no death. And it's over in seconds. It's

not transcendence—such a moment has no religious dimension. It's not an epiphany—that's too literary. It's not philosophical. It isn't life-changing. It just is.

And Evans caught the ball.

Fisk's twelfth-inning homer was marvelous but the Red Sox were not going to lose. You could feel it. For once the energy was on our side. It didn't last. The next night the Sox lost a lead, Willoughby got lifted ... inevitable ... inevitable. Other things happened in the 1970s—the '78 collapse, the partial resurrection and otherworldly intense playoff game; the pleasure of watching an outfield of Rice, Lynn, and Evans; flashes of Yastrzemski; the example of Fisk—but that moment, that game, that night, are my pinnacle. As Kawabata says, "There was a quiet, chilly loneliness in it, and a sort of voluptuous astonishment."

May we all have such moments.

OCTOBER 21, 1975

Tiant, Carbo, Fisk Lead Boston To Victory in "Greatest Game"

The memories of this game come in kaleidoscopic fragments. Luis Tiant rocking, swerving backwards, hesitating for a split second before delivering one of his countless pitches, a human metronome designed to destroy the timing and anticipation of enemy batters. Fred Lynn dashing back to the center-field wall only to crash into the concrete base before crumpling silently as trainers and teammates rushed to his side, pinch hitter Bernie Carbo following the worst two-strike foul ball anybody could ever recall with a mammoth game-tying 3-run shot into the center field bleachers, Dwight Evans measuring his backpedaled steps while reaching up to save the game with an epic 11th inning catch off future Hall of Famer Joe Morgan then doubling off Ken Griffey and raising his fist in triumph just as the ump makes the call.....all these memories are joined by the near hieroglyphic body english of Carlton Fisk as he willed his towering 12th inning fly ball fair as it ricocheted off the foul pole atop the Green Monster to send Boston into apoplexy and baseball back to the forefront of American major league sports.

NBC baseball producer Harry Coyle conveyed the drama masterfully as he placed cameras in many of the nooks and crannies of the

Fenway Park organist John Kiley had just started playing Handel's "Hallelujah Chorus" as Fisk wheeled and gyrated down the baseline, offering the all the body english he could muster to will his fly ball fair and the series tied. *(Collection of the author)*

old ballyard including, most memorably, in the belly of the left field scoreboard. It was this camera that captured the tortuous choreography of Carlton Fisk's victory trot as he tracks the flight of his game winning home run. It remains the most replayed highlight in baseball history.

OCTOBER 22, 1975

Sox Lose 3-0 Lead & Series, 4-3

Less than 24 hours since the best Red Sox game played at Fenway Park since the legendary eighth game of the 1912 World Series, the Red Sox prepared to play the third consecutive seventh game of the three World Series they'd played since last winning the world championship in 1918. Once more, Bill Lee was asked to confound the

Reds with his portfolio of curves, drops, spins and changes of pace.

Lee said of the game in *The Wrong Stuff*, "I felt I would pitch well in the seventh game. I had crazy rushes of energy surging through my body, but my mind was mellow and in complete control of the rest of me. I would be starting against Don Gullett. Prior to the game, Sparky Anderson, the Reds manager, had announced, 'Don't know about the fellah for the Red Sox, but sometime after this game, my boy's going to the Hall of Fame.' Upon hearing that remark, I replied, 'I don't care where Gullett's going, because after this game, I'm going to the Eliot Lounge."

After Boston scored three runs in the third, Gullett stopped 227 miles short of Cooperstown while heading toward the shower in the visitors clubhouse while Lee held the Reds at bay until fate and an ill-timed eephus pitch changed things. With Pete Rose on first and

On Saturday June 18, 1977, a national television audience was treated to a dugout altercation between Yankee manager Billy Martin and resident superstar Reggie Jackson. They were eventually separated by Yankee coach Elston Howard. *(Photographs by Mike Andersen)*

one out, Lee got Johnny Bench to hit into what should have been a sure double play. However second baseman Denny Doyle had played Bench deep in the hole and had to race to second for shortstop Rick Burleson's throw. Darting across the bag Doyle's nabbed Rose but his throw to first sailed into the stands. Lee was left with Bench on second and Reds RBI machine Tony Perez coming to bat instead of being out of the inning.

Lee had enjoyed success tossing his slow curve to Perez on other occasions and did so once more. Years later Lee wrote of Perez's game altering home run, "He counted the seams of the ball as it floated up to the plate, checked to see if Lee MacPhail's signature was on it, signed his own name to it, and then jumped all over it. He hit the ball over the left field screen and several small buildings."

With the score. 3-2 in favor of the Red Sox, nearly every diehard Boston fan waited for the other shoe to drop. Lee fell victim to a burst blister on his index finger in the seventh and gave way to Rogelio Moret who allowed the tying run to score.

Jim Willoughby replaced Moret and managed to get Boston out of the seventh and pitched superbly in the eighth but was removed for a pinch runner due to the fact that the designated hitter rule was not yet adopted for World Series play.

It became the most debated managerial decision in team history since Denny Galehouse was selected to start the ill-fated '48 playoff.

Not only did the Sox not score in the eighth but Willoughby's replacement, rookie Jim Burton will forever suffer the stigma of defeat despite pitching well. He walked Ken Griffey, Sr. who was sacrificed

to second. After retiring Dan Driesson he then walked Pete Rose. The next batter, future Hall of Famer Joe Morgan, blooped a perfectly thrown low slider to left center and Griffey scored what proved to be the series-winning run.

Before the final headlines were printed it was clear that the series was not only the best in years, but perhaps the best ever. It was also clear the series assured Red Sox fans that Fenway Park would remain around for years to come. Once again, the ballpark was the star in a drama that had older fans comparing Lynn to Speaker and Tiant to Wood. Same as it ever was.

JUNE 18, 1977

Billy Martin and Reggie Jackson Battle in Yankee Dugout

If the Bronx was burning back home in New York, then surely the Back Bay was simmering on the afternoon of a nationally televised game that had the Yankee soap opera ready for prime time as Yankee slugger Reggie Jackson and manager Billy Martin nearly came to blows. The near brawl came after Martin pulled Jackson from the game mid-inning after he felt his star hadn't hustled properly for a hit by Jim Rice. As Paul Blair trotted out to take his place, Jackson returned to the dugout and was immediately lambasted by Martin who had to be restrained by coaches. It remains one of the most unusual and discussed chapters of the team's intense rivalry.

JULY 4, 1977

Bombs Away

The image of Fenway Park as a launching pad is cast in chiseled in granite as the BoSox set a major-league record by blasting eight home runs against the fledgling Blue Jays. Included in this epic slugfest were Fred Lynn and George Scott with two homers apiece with solo shots by Bernie Carbo, Butch Hobson, Jim Rice and Carl Yastrzemski. Oh, and in a score typical of the era, the Sox scratched out a 9-6 victory.

AUGUST 1, 1977

CAPE COD BASEBALL LEAGUE ALL-STARS ROUT ATLANTIC COLLEGIATE LEAGUE ALL STARS 8-3 AT FENWAY PARK

Future Red Sox pitcher Brian Denman (1982) of the Cotuit Kettleers got the win, and future Yankee and Royals first baseman Steve "Bye Bye" Balboni of Yarmouth Dennis was named the game's MVP.

August 11, 1977 Eastern League All-Stars 5, Bristol Red Sox 3

SEPTEMBER 7, 1978

Massacre

To any Red Sox fan over the age of 45, the word massacre conjures up memories of a four-game series against the Yankees in the heat of the 1978 pennant race that echo like successive hammer blows on an anvil.

The start of this infamous series could not have been more ominous. For the Red Sox sat atop the American League Eastern Division with a lead of four games albeit a margin that had been whittled down by a full ten games in a month and a half by the resurgent Yankees, led by new manager Bob Lemon. If the summer had been a marvelous joy-ride that prompted comparisons with the equally joyful summers of '46, '67, and '75, more than a few jaded fans heard the sound of footsteps that characterized the lost seasons of '48, '49, and '74. With no wild card to save the Sox, the Yankee footsteps that haunted Boston soon became

Carlton Fisk scores in one of the many epic Red Sox/Yankee games that characterized the revitalization of both clubs during the seventies. *(Photograph by Mike Andersen)*

footprints before the series ended with the teams tied and Fenway smoldering in figurative ruins.

The opener was over before it started. Mike Torrez departed after two innings and Catfish Hunter dispatched Sox batters with ease while the Yankees surged with 13 hits by their first 22 batters. They led by 7-0 after three innings and 12-0 after four. Only diehards and vocal Yankee fans remained until the end of the 15-3 debacle.

And it only got worse the next night as Portland, Maine, native Jim Beattie carried a shutout into the ninth inning as the Yankees crushed Boston 13-2.

Game 3 featured a dream match-up between Dennis Eckersley (16-6) and Ron Guidry (20-2) and Boston started quickly with first-inning singles by Burleson and Rice but failed to score as Guidry retired Yaz and settled into cruise control. Eckersley could only make it to the fourth before he fell apart as the Yankees scored seven two-out runs to rout Boston as Guidry became the first left-hander in 4 seasons to record a shutout against the Red Sox at Fenway.

In the final game of the series and the most important game of the season, Red Sox manager made the worst pitching selection since Joe McCarthy tapped journeyman Denney Galehouse to face the Indians in the '48 playoff game.

With noted Yankee killer Bill Lee banished to the bullpen and Luis Tiant pleading to pitch on three days rest, Zimmer instead selected rookie lefthander Bobby Sprowl to face the Yankees. Shortly after, Zimmer remarked, "The kid has icewater in his veins," the Sunday afternoon crowd held their breath as Sprowl didn't even make it out of the first inning as New York won by a score of 7-4 and tied their rivals for first.

The final tally for the series had the Yankees outscoring Boston 42-9 as the Sox made 11 errors on a weekend where everything bad seemed possible at a ballpark that was never so shell shocked, before or since.

OCTOBER 1, 1978

Fit To Be Tied

Baseball is a game of rotations, be they of sliders, curves and cutters as well as pitching staffs. And on the last day of the 1978 regular season, the once-dominant Red Sox were fortunate their rotation called for Luis Tiant to face the Toronto Blue Jays in a must-win game on a Sunday afternoon in which the Yankees had to lose to the Indians at Yankee Stadium to force a one-game playoff at Fenway.

For most of us in attendance it was inconceivable we were being treated to El Tiante's final game for Boston as he dazzled a capacity crowd while shutting out Toronto by a score of 5-0 as Boston won its eighth straight game. The afternoon was marked by cheers for both the game at hand and the periodic scoreboard updates of the Indians improbable 9-2 win over New York as many fans left early to stand in line for tickets to the next day's playoff.

OCTOBER 2, 1978

Dented

Sad to say, but nobody loves Fenway Park more than Russell Earl "Bucky" Dent. On a day in which the Hollywood script called for the Red Sox, led by Carl Yastrzemski's scorching first-inning home run off Ron Guidry, to win the comeback of comebacks, the Yankees beat both the home team and Fenway Park to claim their prize.

There is a small library of books written about the psychological. sociological and mystical ramifications of this game, but the central painful images for Boston fans are nothing less than an anthology of the reasons players and fans have secretly hated the place for generations.

Leading by a score of 2-0 in the bottom of the sixth inning, Fred Lynn laced what he later thought could have been a double or triple only to be robbed by Yankee right-fielder Lou Piniella, who'd moved toward left center as he watched Guidry tire. His gamble paid off as Boston entered the seventh with a two-run and not a three- or four-run lead.

With nine outs separating the Red Sox from redemption, Torrez set down Craig Nettles then surrendered successive singles to Chris Chambliss and Roy White. After pitching carefully to pinch hitter Jim Spencer and retiring him on a fly out, up stepped Bucky Dent.

Batting only .246 and a mere .140 over the last 20 games of the season, Dent was the least likely of heroes. Torrez zeroed in on his former teammate and got two quick strikes, including a foul that sailed off his left foot.

As Dent bounded out of the batter's box and hopped on one leg, it looked as if Bob Lemon would have to go to his bench for a pinch hitter to face two strikes and play somebody, perhaps Craig Nettles or Paul Blair out of position.

As Torrez watched from the mound, Dent shook off his injury as teammate Mickey Rivers, who noticed Dent's bat had chipped on the foul, replaced it as his teammate returned to the plate.

Choking up a full 2 inches on the new lumber, Dent swung under a Torrez fastball and watched as Carl Yastrzemski drifted momentarily under what he knew would be a routine out in any park but Fenway. Yankees 3, Boston 2.

The visably shaken Torrez then walked Mickey Rivers before being taken out for Bob Stanley. Rivers then stole second and was driven home on Yankee captain Thurman Munson's wall-scraping double.

Right-hander Dennis Eckersley arrived via trade from the Indians at the start of the 1978 season, won 20 games, and nearly helped lead the club to the World Series. He later made a career-altering shift to the bullpen and forged a Hall of Fame career with the Oakland Athletics. He returned to Boston in 1998 where he finished his 24-season career. *(Photograph by Albie Walton)*

By the top of the eighth Reggie Jackson once again reminded despairing Sox fans of his nickname "Mr October" while hammering a Stanley slider into the center-field bleachers to make the score 5-2. With six outs to go, a Yankee victory seemed inevitable until Boston, in a microcosm of their season, roared back.

Jerry Remy led off the eighth with a double and was driven home by Yaz with one out. Then Fisk and Lynn singled to score Yastrzemski and suddenly the ballpark exhaled collectively as the score stood at 5-4 with Hobson and Scott set to face Goose Gossage.

The best fastball pitcher in baseball cranked it up a notch while popping up Hobson on a high hard one and striking out Scott with the same.

After setting down the Yankees with ease to start the ninth, the Red Sox sent up pinch hitter Dwight Evans, who, still woozy from a late-season beaning, was retired easily by Gossage. Rick Burleson then worked a walk and should have made it to third but for another right-field miracle by Piniella.

Fenway's right field is usually a chamber of horrors for opposing fielders and thus would have been the case had Piniella not blindly stabbed at Remy's hit which miraculously found the webbing of his glove as Burleson scurried to second. Jim Rice followed with a deep drive to left center that would have tied the game under normal circumstances but merely deposited Burleson on third with two outs and Yastrzemski digging in for the most important at bat of his 23 year career.

Simply seeking to drive a ball through the open right side of the infield for a game-tying single, Yaz took a low pitch for ball one. Gossage's second pitch was right down the middle of the plate and exploded on the left-fielder who could only manage a pop-up to Craig Nettles to end the game of games in a ballpark whose slogan could well be, "The wall giveth, and the wall taketh away."

May 29, 1979 Division Two & Three All-Stars 3, Division One All-Stars 2

July 3, 1979 Burger King Pitch, Hit & Run Competition

JULY 30, 1979

CAPE COD LEAGUE ALL-STARS EDGE ATLANTIC COLLEGIATE LEAGUE ALL-STARS, 6-5

Former Braves pitcher Ed Olwine represented Hyannis while securing the victory, while teammate Ross Jones was named MVP.

SEPTEMBER 12, 1979

The Yaz Watch

Sometimes the best moments at Fenway Park come when you least expect them. The buzz on the night of September 12, 1979, should have been exclusively devoted to Carl Yastrzemski and his quest to become the first player in American League history to get 3,000 hits and 400 home runs. Mired in the throes of a mini-slump, the 40-year-old future Hall of Famer was faced with the pressure of getting his coveted hit in the Sox last home game prior to a lengthy road trip.

Luck would have it that he'd need to gain the hit against the

Luis Tiant owned Fenway Park and the City of Boston during his eight seasons with the Red Sox. Not only did he win 20 or more games on three occasions, but his colorful mound antics, including his completing a backward glance at the bleachers before making a pitch, endears him to Red Sox Nation to this day. *(Photograph by Albie Walton)*

Fenway Park has rarely been more silent than at the moment the Yankees captured the one-game playoff game that finished a heroic 1978 season. Both during the season and during the game, the Red Sox clawed back to the brink of a championship only to lose to their hated rivals. Goose Gossage never jumped higher in his life. *(Photograph by Mike Andersen)*

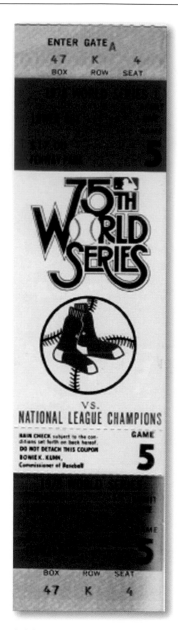

A ticket to the World Series that never was at Fenway Park. Imagine paying just $17 for a lower box seat to the 1978 World Series. *(Collection of the author)*

Yankees, the team which made him dress with the batboys at Yankee Stadium for a tryout 21 years earlier. Duly under-whelmed at his treatment the Long Island native and his father departed the Bronx before later signing with Boston.

As my friends and I sat in the bleachers and talked about our memories of Yaz and the discouraging aftermath of the '78 season, a remarkable event took place. As soon as Yankee starter Jim "Catfish" Hunter lifted the latch on the bullpen door to head to the Yankee dugout, a ripple of applause started in the bleachers, and spread through the park so that by the time the Red Sox nemesis reached the infield he was engulfed in a standing ovation.

It was then I remembered the papers had mentioned this was to be Hunter's last start in Boston before retiring at season's end. Only at Fenway Park would you have more than 30,000 partisans offering their respectful cheers for the man that not only turned down Boston's generous free-agency offering but also beat the Red Sox on a maddeningly consistent basis.

The only similar cheer was that given the Philadelphia Seventy Sixers in 1982 to "Beat LA" as they downed the defending NBA champs at Boston Garden.

The more predictable standing O's later erupted for Yaz who finally broke a 12 at-bat drought with an eighth-inning seeing-eye single off Jim Beattie that just squirted under the glove of Willie Randolph.

As the packed house screamed, clapped and chanted, "Reggie Jackson," the game was then temporarily halted as fans were treated to a 20-minute ceremony that included the slugger's 18-year-old son

and his dad. Addressing the crowd from a microphone set up behind first base, Yastrzemski remarked, "I know one thing. This was the hardest of the 3,000. I took so long to do it because I've enjoyed all those standing ovations you've given me the last three days."

Following the game he told the press, "I've been in pennant pressure, playoff pressure, and World Series pressure situations, but nothing like this. I think it was how the fans reacted the last three days. I wanted to get that hit for the fans, and I came out of my realm of hitting and thinking. I was chasing pitchers' pitches. I was anxious. Normally I wouldn't have swung at some pitches that I have the last three days."

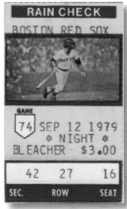

Yastrzemski breathes a sigh of relief as he addresses the media after making his 3,000th career hit off Yankee reliever Jim Beatty in his final at bat in the final game of a home stand against the Yankees. Local newspapers had tabbed the long-awaited accomplishment "The Yaz Watch." *(Photograph by Tom Hunt)*

At the conclusion of nearly every season, Fenway Park undergoes some degree of refurbishment or renovation. Such was the case following the 1979 season as the streets surrounding the park were repaved and the bricks on the park's historic façade were repointed.*(Courtesy of* The Boston Herald*)*

Carl Yastrzemski takes a lap of honor and greets fans in celebration of his 23 years as a member of the Red Sox on the day prior to his retirement in 1983. *(Photograph by Richard Pasley)*

CHAPTER EIGHT
Monster Mash

*As I grew up, I knew that as a building Fenway Park was on the level of Mount Olympus, the
Pyramid at Giza, the nation's capitol, the czar's Winter Palace, and the Louvre — except, of
course, that it is better than all those inconsequential places."*

—BASEBALL COMMISSIONER BART GIAMATTI, C.1981

The eighties at Fenway Park were 99 percent Red Sox and began with the tearful farewell of Carl Yastrzemski
and ended with the ascent and budding superstardom of Roger Clemens and Wade Boggs. As with many of its
predecessors the Red Sox of the eighties delighted fans with virtuoso solo efforts such as Clemens' 20K game
and Boggs' 240-hit season and the crushing heartbreak of losing it all while one strike away in October 1986.

An aerial view of Fenway Park
in 1981. Note the tight parking
and narrow streets. *(Photograph
by Albie Walton)*

Jim Rice carries Jonathan Keane from the field after the five-year-old was injured by a foul ball that rocketed off the bat of Dave Stapleton into the Fenway grandstand. *(Courtesy of* The Boston Herald*)*

Cape Cod League All-Stars 4 Atlantic Collegiate Baseball League All-Stars 4

The game was a welcome respite from the Major League strike until the rains came after a single pitch in the tenth. For one beautiful afternoon the grass was trimmed and the hot dogs steaming at Fenway Park. And the seating was practically first come, first serve. For those who forsook the beach, their Cape Cod League All-Stars maintained their un-beaten record at Fenway Park with a tie against the Atlantic Collegiate League All-Stars before a crowd of scouts, executives, and diehards. Orleans star and future major league utility player Wade Rowden was the game's MVP.

MAY 1, 1982

First Fenway Old Timers Game in Modern Era Features Teddy Ballgame

OLD TIMER'S DAY
by Donald Hall

When the tall puffy figure
wearing number nine
starts late
for the fly ball,
laboring forward
like a lame truckhorse
startled by a gartersnake,
—this old fellow
whose body we remember
as sleek and nervous as a filly's
— and barely catches it
in his glove's tip,
we rise and applaud weeping:
On a green field
we observe
the ruin of even the
bravest body,
as Odysseus wept
to glimpse among shades
the shadow of Achilles.

MAY 4, 1982

Twins Eisenreich Driven From Field By Bleacher Boo Birds

In one of the most disgraceful episodes in Fenway Park's long history, Minnesota Twins rookie outfielder Jim Eisenreich, whose courageous

Ted Williams patrolled his old stomping grounds in left field in several Old Timers Games starting in 1982 when he made the most notable catch of his "career." *(Photograph by the author)*

The D'Angelo Twins pose in front of the headquarters of their souvenir empire. Their story is the embodiment of the American Dream as they built both their store and manufacturing arm from scratch. *(Courtesy of The Boston Herald)*

battle against Tourette's Syndrome made for compelling if not inspirational reading was booed off the field at Fenway Park by hundreds of fans who mocked and derided the young outfielder. At the time Eisenreich was batting .310 but was also forced to leave his fifth game in a row.

AUGUST 8, 1982

Rice To The Rescue

Jim Rice was to Fenway Park what Ralph Kiner was to Forbes Field, Hank Sauer to Wrigley, and Mel Ott to the Polo Grounds. He was the most feared batter in the American League and the slugger best suited to his home park for a dozen seasons from 1975 to 1986.

The tales of his strength echo those once told of Ruth, Foxx and Josh Gibson. The best being that of the bat he broke on a check swing. Imagine that.

Rice was not without his antagonists in bussing-era Boston and more than a few fans chanted 'Uncle Ben" from the anonymous safety of their cheap seats. Rice was also often indifferent to and, at times, antagonistic towards the large local media contingent. As friendly as Fenway's dimensions proved to be for his slugging the fishbowl effect of the crowd at baseball's equivalent of Shakespeare's Globe Theater never quite suited the big guy.

However, on the afternoon of August 8, 1982, Rice emerged as something akin to an African-American Clark Kent/Superman when he immediately went to the aid of a fan, five-year-old Jonathan Keane, who'd been hit in the face, bloodied and knocked unconscious by a foul ball off the bat of Dave Stapleton. Rice carried the stricken child to the first aid station as fans gasped at the sight of the blood that covered his jersey as well as the boy's shrouded face. It was later determined that Keane suffered a fractured skull. However he later recovered and has kept up with Rice over the years.

It is this image, that of the responsible caring father and citizen coming to aid of a child, that many carry in their hearts and minds when they think of the big guy. Number Fourteen.

JUNE 6, 1983

CIVIL WAR

TIME FOR FENWAY FOLLIES AS BUDDY PLAYS THE KING

On the day the Red Sox had designated to honor fallen hero Tony Conigliaro, who'd suffered a heart attack and stroke just months earlier, team partner and former trainer Edward G. "Buddy" LeRoux forever cast himself as a Boston sports villain by attempting a takeover of the team that same day.

THE BOSTON HERALD OBSERVED,

"The move was tasteless, ill-timed and revolting in every sense of the word, but if it works I suppose Buddy LeCoup, whoops, LeRoux, will be forgiven all that, and more.

Jim Conely of Boston's Ironworker's Local 7 carries pipe for the construction of the park's luxury suites in February 1982. *(Photograph by M. Leo Tierney, Courtesy of* The Boston Herald*)*

"What their one-time trainer did yesterday was declare himself King of the Red Sox, although not in so many words.

"He actually named himself the club's new Managing General Partner, but that title doesn't sing like Buddy I, nor does it define his astounding powers. For his opening number,for example, Buddy I relegated his one-time co-owners and General Partners, Mrs. Jean R. Yawkey and Haywood Sullivan, to the bullpen, so to speak.

"Then Buddy I brought back Dick O'Connell, Harwood's predecessor and Mrs. Yawkey's nemesis, as general manager. And finally, Buddy I named Judge Samuel Adams the club's new counsel. Buddy I didn't specify *which* Samuel Adams, but nothing would surprise us at this point."

Sadly, LeRoux's press conference was held just as players from the 1967 Impossible Dream team came to honor their stricken teammate. Later,

former Cy Young award winner Jim Lonborg arrived by helicopter after attending his Tufts University Dental School graduation.

What should have been a joyous celebration of a great team and their hometown hero instead became a farce known forever as "Coup LeRoux."

JULY 25, 1983

Cape Cod League All-Stars 6 Atlantic Collegiate Baseball League All-Stars 2

Future Dodger farmhand Dennis Livingston pitched the Cape Cod League All-Stars to a 6-2 win over the Atlantic Collegiate League All-Stars at Fenway Park as Jamie

Sims of the ACBL captured MVP honors.

OCTOBER 1, 1983 TO OCTOBER 3, 1983

Farewell Yaz

I'd waited in line on Yawkey Way for about an hour back in March 1983 for two tickets apiece for each of the season-ending three games against the Indians. We all knew that Yaz was retiring at the end of the season and before I'd even made it in the doorway of the ticket office most of the section boxes on the wall-mounted season schedule were X'd out and unavailable.

Luckily I was able to grab decent seats for each game with roof boxes for the finale. After all, Yaz had taken me from kindergarten in his rookie season to the heartbreak of his popping up against Goose Gossage in game 163 of the 1978 season just months after my

The bronze plaque placed adjacent to Fenway Park's office entrance in 1934 bears witness to the renovations of the early 1980s. *(Photograph by the author)*

Carl Yastrzemski is feted on the final weekend of his career. Broadcaster Ned Martin is at the microphone as Yastrzemski greets Governor Michael Dukakis and broadcaster/friend Jess Cain. *(Photograph by Richard Pasley)*

Carl Yastrzemski acknowledges the standing ovation that followed his farewell speech. *(Photograph by Richard Pasley)*

Carl Yastrzemski's Fenway Park locker. *(Photograph by Albie Walton)*

The construction of luxury suites was one of the more ambitious renovation projects undertaken at Fenway Park since the massive reconstruction of 1933-34. *(Courtesy of* The Boston Herald)

The 1980s were a decade that featured many memorable Old Timer's Days at Fenway Park. This gathering of Red Sox opponents is from 1986 and includes Joe DiMaggio (fourth from left, back row) and Vince DiMaggio (far left, top row), who faced their brother Dom in the game that followed. *(Photograph by the author)*

graduation from college. His singular achievement during the 1967 season, where his performance combined elements of Faust, Roy Hobbs, and Gil Thorpe cemented my love of the team and most especially Fenway Park.

As the Farewell weekend loomed I took great care in inviting friends to the games and shared a wonderful Saturday with my longtime friend Walter as we watched the formal Yaz Day ceremonies while recalling when we'd begged our parents to buy loaves of Arnold's "Big Yaz" bread. We laughed as Jess Cain sang the Yaz song for his buddy and cheered as Yaz trotted around the perimeter of the park to thank and touch hands with a crowd that years before also booed him on more than a few memorable occasions.

However on his day, all was forgiven as we all knew we'd witnessed the symbolic end of an era. I forget the final score or even any details from the game.

Likewise the next day my father drove down from New Hampshire and we met for a bowl of fish chowder at Legal Sea Foods in Park Square before walking up the quintessentially Bostonian Commonwealth Avenue to the ballpark. As we strolled I reminded him of our first game back in 1968 when he dashed to pick me up from school, completing an operation at Worcester's Memorial Hospital on a day he wore a pinstriped suit to our dollar bleacher seats behind the visitor's bullpen on an sunny weekday afternoon in April 1968.

Yaz played in that game as well as the one in which we saw him play left field one last time, stroke his final hit, a single, and leave the field, unbuttoning his

Tickets from the historic game of April 29, 1986, in which right-hander Roger Clemens became the first major-league pitcher to record a record-breaking 20 strikeouts in a nine-inning game. *(Collection of the author)*

uniform and tossing his cap to a young fan as he left the field for the final time.

It was also the last time my dad and I went to a game for just the two of us. Our conversation on the ride home was nearly identical to those we'd had after every baseball game, namely a rumination on the superiority of baseball to all other games and an oft-repeated recollection of the few times he'd sneaked off to watch the Yankees and DiMaggio

during his time as an intern at Bellevue before the war.

Baseball as a bond between fathers and son, is often overstated in the most maudlin of terms but for us was just another cherished plot of common ground, not unlike politics, literature, art, and family history. A simple gift enjoyed on the best of days.

May 27, 1984 Old-Timers Game

July 6, 1984 U. S. Olympic
Baseball team 17, Park League
All-Stars 2

JULY 23, 1985

Cape Cod League All-Stars 12 Atlantic Collegiate Baseball League All-Stars 9

University of New Haven star Mark Hatje pitched the Cape Cod League All-Stars to a 12-9 win over the Atlantic Collegiate League All-Stars at Fenway Park as future Phillie Ken Jackson of the ACBL captured MVP honors.

APRIL 29, 1986

Clemens K's 20 to Set Record

Joseph Hickey

The talk on the radio was almost all regarding Larry Bird and the '86 Celtics or the Patriots' likely selection with the 26th pick in that evening's NFL Draft as I drove down to Boston from my home in rural New Hampshire on the afternoon of April 29, 1986.

The Red Sox had been my team since I was six when my Dad took me to Fenway to witness consecutive home runs by Williams, Stephens, and Doerr. Fast foward to 1985 when my wife Barb and I went as photographers on the inaugural Red Sox Cruise. That experience opened new contacts with many Sox players and coaches and led to me being able to purchase a single front row season seat for the 1986 season.

Photographer Joe Hickey captured the exact moment Clemens 20th strikeout was called by home plate umpire Vic Voltaggio. Note center fielder Steve Lyons lifting his arms in celebration as the scoreboard informs fans that history is being made. *(Photograph by Joe Hickey)*

Soon after Clemens made history, these fake $21 bills were printed in tribute of Boston's newest superstar. *(Collection of the author)*

Natick native Walter Hrniak was a Fenway Park fixture as the Red Sox bullpen and hitting coach from 1977 to 1989. Hrniak worked tirelessly with batters, pitching batting practice until his shoulder finally gave out. *(Photograph by the author)*

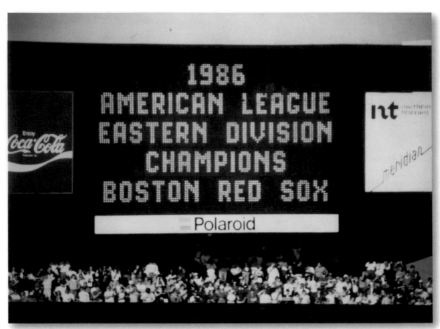

The Red Sox clinched their first division title since 1975 on September 28, 1986, as Oli Can Boyd beat the Blue Jays by a score of 12-3. *(Photograph by the author)*

Fenway erupts in celebration of the Red Sox's first division title in eleven seasons. *(Photograph by the author)*

April 29, 1986, was a cold and raw night and was not the prime Boston sporting event of the evening. The Celtics were playing Atlanta at the Garden and the NFL Draft was also being held in town. Most of the local media photographers took their required shots very early in Roger Clemens' start against the Seattle Mariners and left for warmer venues. By the time "Rocket" Roger was catching fire and mowing down the Mariners, it was too late for the pros to get back to Fenway for any late-inning happenings.

His pitches started sounding like cannon balls hitting Gedman's mitt and his control was masterful. The crowd came to life and the 14,000-plus fans sounded like a sellout as Rog neared the record. I just prayed that I didn't run out of film, and had the old Nikon in sharp manual focus, timed the exact moment because I had no motordrive, and got the full background as home plate umpire Vic Voltaggio called that third strike on Bradley. I was at the right place at the right time and got *the* perfect shot as Clemens got his 20th K and went into baseball history. The image was later printed in *Sports Illustrated* and is on display at The National Baseball Hall of Fame and Boston's Sports Museum. As Woody Allen once remarked, "Seventy per cent of life is showing up."

May 17, 1986 Old-Timers Game

Former player and team broadcaster Bob Montgomery gets a beer shower in the Red Sox clubhouse following the team's division-clinching win over Toronto. (*Photograph by the author*)

SEPTEMBER 4, 1986

Jimmy Fund Exhibition a Showcase for The Mets

With the Mets magic number at 10, the *New York Daily News* hailed the game as a "Monster" preview of the World Series as the Mets and Red Sox squared off at Fenway Park for a rare exhibition game whose proceeds would benefit both The Jimmy Fund as well as the Mets Sandlot Baseball Fund. Apparently the game was originally supposed to feature a Mets/ Yankee matchup but Yankee principal owner George Steinbrenner nixed the idea. Little did he know that the Mets gained an ever-so-slight advantage over Boston as a result of seeing Fenway and dominating a pre-game home-run hitting contest as sluggers like Gary Carter took aim at the Green Monster.

A sold-out park saw the Mets hammer Red Sox reliever Joe Sambito for six runs in the eighth as former Boston minor-league pitcher John Mitchell recorded his first "unofficial" major-league win. The Mets not only made themselves at home at Fenway but also made a few friends while heading out of town. When the team bus broke down at the entrance to the Sumner Tunnel, those players unable to hail cabs stopped passenger cars and received lifts to Logan Airport from surprised motorists. Within six weeks many of those same drivers cursed the day they displayed such hospitality.

JULY 10, 1986

Boyd Storms Out of Fenway After All-Star Snub

Dennis "Oil Can" Boyd had worked hard in 1986 and by the All-Star break had an impressive 11-6 won/ lost record. Despite his record Boyd was left off the All-Star roster by manager Dick Howser who'd selected Charlie Hough of the Rangers and Brent Strom of the Indians because each team had to have a representative on the squad. After learning the disappointing news Boyd sat in his car in the Fenway parking lot and exclaimed to reporters, "I want my reward and I want it today...I've got a good mind to go back to Mississippi I have had it with this town...I'm an angry young man."

At the time Boyd was torn by personal crisis with his finances in such disarray that his phone had been shut off. If anyone needed the $25,000 All-Star bonus it was Boyd. Instead his tirade brought the young pitcher a three-day suspension.

Following his apology to the team Boyd was suspended once more after he was rousted by undercover police near his home in Chelsea. Both the team and the Boston press speculated openly that Boyd had a drug problem.

After a brief hospitalization Boyd finally made it back to the rotation and eventually was on the mound when the team clinched the American League Eastern Division title in September.

Sox Clinch AL East With Win Over Blue Jays

On the eve of the Red Sox division clincher the decision was made for the Boston Police to deploy 15 mounted police officers not to mention another 60 in a supplemental foot patrol to avoid the kind of on-field destruction that had taken place at Shea Stadium two weeks earlier when the Mets clinched their division title.

In the end the horses served only as a welcome mount for the pride of Katy Texas, Roger Clemens, as he celebrated the Red Sox 12-3 win and first division title in 11 seasons.

Dennis "Oil Can" Boyd spent most of the afternoon channeling his inspiration, Satchel Paige, as he scattered eight Blue Jay hits over a complete game for the dramatic win. Referring to his mid-season break down Boyd later remarked, "I got to block that out. My teammates don't want me to dwell on that. They say, 'Can, you get back to business and we'll all get back to business.' My little adversity I went through-all that now is abolished. They said, 'You come back and we'll do something special,' and that's what we did today. This is called, 'You can't keep a good man down and when the going gets tough, I get going.' I just wanted to go out and do what I do best—win for the Red Sox. I'm a good man and you know I have a strong will and mind."

After Jim Rice hoisted Roger Clemens atop a police horse named Timothy the crowd roared at a scene

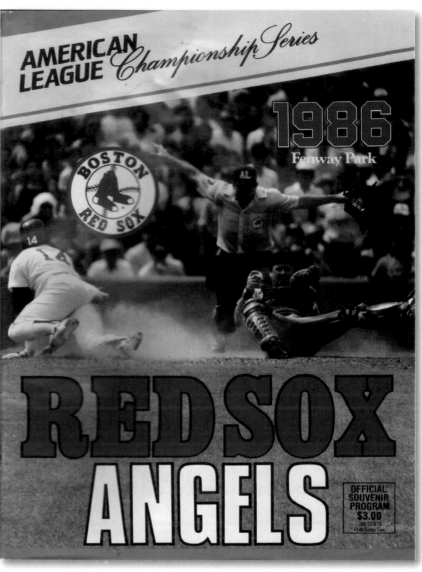

Program for the 1986 ALCS with the California Angels. *(Collection of the author)*

that would have been easily recognized by "Nuff Ced McGreevey and any of his Royal Rooters. Rice later observed, "I just thought he'd look good on the horse. I thought it'd be good for the city, for the people. Good for him. Good for the horse. Good for everyone."

"The smell of victory," remarked third baseman Wade Boggs to reporters, "It's awesome."

Clemens KO'd by Angels, 8-1

Hurst Shines, Red Sox 9, Angels 2

As six small planes circled dangerously over Fenway Park towing advertising signs of Sunday widths, lengths, and messages over the capacity crowd, the only thing to crash and burn was the Angels composure on an afternoon that saw them commit three fielding errors and a costly base-running error by Bobby Grich.

BOSTON
RED SOX

1986 AL CHAMPIONS
0
OCT 22 NY METS 825
OCT 23 NY METS 835

Budweiser
KING OF BEERS

Boston mounted police take to the field to maintain order when the Red Sox clinched the 1986 American League championship. *(Photograph by the author)*

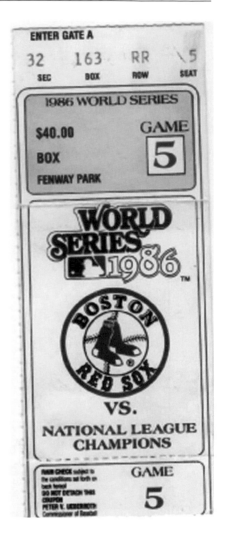

1986 World Series ticket. *(Collection of the author)*

Many of the players had complained of the 3:00 PM start time prior to the game as the bright October sun possessed the power to wreak havoc on the game. Former Red Sox shortstop Rick Burleson summed it up when he cracked, "It's all for TV and they make it difficult for us."

All three Angel errors came in the seventh as hard-luck starter Kirk McCaskill was touched for three unearned runs on just one hit. Hurst, on the other hand, scattered 11 hits while walking none and striking out four in his complete game effort.

The Sox bats exploded for thirteen hits that included a home run for Rice and doubles for Barrett and Evans. Despite stranding nine runners they took advantage of every Angel miscue, prompting Angel manager Gene Mauch to observe, "In the 45 years that I have been in the game, I've never seen a man pitch as well as Kirk McCaskill did and give up six runs. There were all kinds of mistakes, and there is no use discussing it. I don't understand it. We were terrible on ground balls . Maybe

it goes back to when I saw Mildred Cronin [Joe Cronin's widow] come to the park in a green dress. I said to myself that I hoped she didn't bring any of the gremlins with her."

OCTOBER 14, 1986

Sox Continue Comeback Against Angels, Win 10-4

The Red Sox continued the comeback sparked by Dave Henderson's miracle HR in Anaheim as they beat the Angels 10-4 behind Dennis "Oil Can" Boyd. Boyd was in vintage form and spent of his post game interview remarking how he channeled the great Satchel Paige once again.

He exclaimed to reporters, "I was Satchel Paige from the 40s and 30s. That's who I wanted to be. Yeah, man, new socks. I took the stripes off my shoes and I was possessed by Satchel tonight, man, that's who. I had to be, man,

because I didn't want to give those guys any sort of mental edge or this-guy-is-showing-us-up or any of that stuff. I just wanted to let a sleeping dog lie."

Boyd settled down after a rocky first inning in which he allowed two runs on hits by Jackson, DeCinces, and Schofield. He shut down the Angels for the next five innings as his teammates scored two runs in the bottom of the first and a whopping five runs off Angels starter Kirk McCaskill in the third inning as the Red Sox climbed to within a game of their fourth American league pennant since 1918.

Bruce Hurst is embraced by fellow pitcher Al Nipper after the ace left-hander had won Game 5 of the 1986 World Series to take the Red Sox to within a game of an ever-elusive world championship. Other teammates pictured include (l-r) Bill Buckner, Mike Greenwell, and Dennis "Oil Can" Boyd. *(Photograph by Rick Sennott, Courtesy of* The Boston Herald*)*

When asked about whether the Red Sox had gained the series momentum after their second consecutive win he replied cryptically to reporters, "The first six letters of momentum will tell you all you need to know about that word."

OCTOBER 15, 1986

Sox Close Comeback Against Angels and Capture Pennant

The seventh game of the 1986 ALCS had an eerie feel from the beginning. Many of the fans trudging to the park had followed the Astros Mets game that was heading into extra innings and sent many into neighborhood bars before adjourning to Fenway. There was even a rumor circulating that Angels DH Reggie Jackson was asked by a fan in a Back Bay bookstore how he thought his team would do and replied, "We're done man, we're done."

All of which seemed plausible in a game that ended nearly as soon as it started as the Red Sox scored three second-inning runs off starter John Candalaria and added another four in the third as the Red Sox steamrolled the Angels for the first American League pennant clinched at Fenway Park since the Impossible Dream of 1967 both beat the Twins and waited in their clubhouse for the Angels to beat the Tigers.

Sox ace Roger Clemens cruised to victory while scattering four hits over seven innings as his former Texas Longhorn teammate Calvin Schiraldi closed out the win and savored the moment of victory.

Clemens wiped off champagne as he exclaimed to reporters, "This one is for the fans and for managment. I get satisfaction looking around and seeing [pitching coach] Bill Fischer happy, Seeing skipper McNamara happy, Joe Morgan. Walter Hrniak, all the coaches smiling and having fun, making their jobs that much more secure."

Left-hander Bruce Hurst pitched the best baseball of his career in the '86 postseason while crafting a perfect 3-0 record with two wins coming in the World Series. *(Photograph by the author)*

At least one optimistic vendor produced uniform patches proclaiming the Red Sox as 1986 World Champions. Games 6 and 7 at Shea Stadium ended the dream as an almost surrealistic horror played out over three unforgettable days. *(Collection of the author)*

The line at the phone booth adjacent to the Salvation Army Building on Brookline Avenue across from the ticket office was five deep as many pumped quarters into the box just to have the chance to tell relatives they were there to see the Sox win their fourth pennant since World War One. Reggie Jackson was unavailable for comment.

OCTOBER 21, 1986

Boyd Quotes Haunt Sox as Mets Can Boston, 7-1

The unfortunate headline from the morning sports section was posted on the bulletin board of the visitor's clubhouse long before the first pitch. It simply read, "I feel I can master these guys." Dennis Boyd. Boyd went on to remark, "I pitch real well here. I feel comfortable here. I'm going up against a former teammate, Bobby Ojeda, and I'm sure he's going to pitch a good ballgame, but I really think I can get him here because he's not real confident out here."

When asked of the looming Green Monster, Boyd observed, "I've learned to pitch at this ballpark. I've pitched my best games here. The fans have a lot to do with it, I think. I get into those fans, they get into me. I don't worry about that Wall."

Sadly Boyd was forced to eat his words as the Mets, bolstered by his pre-game bragging beat Boston 7-1 in a game they had to win. Boyd barely made it out of the first inning surrendering four runs (including a leadoff home run by Lenny Dykstra) on five hits while struggling though 33 pitches. He settled down while only giving up another four hits and two runs over the next six innings but his teammates did little against Ojeda, managing only one run on five hits.

Met catcher Gary Carter took a poke at Boyd when he remarked to a reporter after the game, "Ojeda was a master out there tonight," to which teammate Lenny Dykstra chimed in, "We didn't take too kindly to that. The only one that got mastered was him [Boyd] tonight."

OCTOBER 22, 1986

Carter Slays Monster

METS TIE SERIES AT TWO GAMES APIECE

To anyone that witnessed Gary Carter's virtuoso performance in the home run hitting contest that preceded the September 4th exhibition game between the Red Sox and the Mets, his two-home-run performance to boost the Mets to a series tying 6-2 victory came as no surprise. Al Nipper gamely held the Mets at bay, allowing only three runs through six innings but was done in by the fact that not only did

Fenway receives some needed sprucing up prior to the 1987 home opener. *(Photograph by Albie Walton)*

Right-fielder Dwight Evans put up Hall of Fame offensive numbers over the second half of his career while helping lead the Red Sox to division titles in 1986 and 1988. *(Photograph by the author)*

Roger Clemens picks up his 1986 American League championship ring from league President Dr. Bobby Brown on Opening Day 1987 at Fenway Park. *(Photograph by the author)*

Dwight Evans looked like Tom Selleck, hit like Carl Yastrzemski, and was acknowledged as the best defensive right fielder in Red Sox history. *(Photograph by the author)*

his teammates strand 16 base runners on the night but reliever Steve Crawford had a miserable two-inning stint that also allowed three earned runs to score.

Following the game Met pitcher and Milbury, Massachusetts, native Ron Darling was asked to explain why both the Red Sox and Mets could lose their first two games at home. The Yale man paused and explained, "I guess it's just another sign of why baseball makes no sense."

OCTOBER 23, 1986

Hurst Beats Mets, Sox Just One Win Away

Boston fans could sense that Bruce Hurst had been in the proverbial zone since returning from the injured list in the heat of the summer's pennant race. The left-hander was already being compared to the great Mel Parnell and many also thought his post-season success was nearly identical to that of the Astros Mike Scott.

In the Red Sox first home World Series game since the unforgettable sixth game of the '75 Series, Hurst once again was at his cagey best while scattering 10 hits in a complete game win that saw the Mets scratch out single runs as Hurst tired in the eighth and ninth innings. Mets ace Dwight Gooden lost his second game of the Series while lasting only four innings during which time he gave up three earned runs on nine hits.

In the jubilant clubhouse Hurst remarked, "I really feel comfortable. It's just a lot of fun for me. I just want it to go on. I didn't feel I was at my best tonight.

I didn't feel I had my best stuff. I felt like I was getting too many of my pitches up."

As fans exited the park they were greeted by vendors selling T-shirts that proclaimed the Red Sox as "1986 World Champions," while inside Fenway's press box *Boston Globe* columnist Dan Shaughnessy wrote a column whose first sentence is now hauntingly prophetic, "Is this the threshold of a dream or the eve of destruction?"

May 23, 1987 Old-Timers Game

JULY 13, 1987

CAPE COD LEAGUE ALL-STARS 10 ATLANTIC COLLEGIATE BASEBALL LEAGUE ALL-STARS 1

MAY 21, 1988

Red Sox Retire Doerr's Number One in Pre-Game Ceremonies

It was a ceremony befitting the man: quiet, dignified and classy. Robert Pershing Doerr was afforded the ultimate honor by the Red Sox when his number one was retired by the team and hoisted to the right-field facade where it joined those of teammates Joe Cronin and Ted Williams. Not only was Doerr the captain of the great Red Sox postwar teams including the 1946 pennant winners but was also the batting coach that worked with Carl Yastrzemski during his 1967 Triple Crown season of seasons.

Throughout every renovation, architect James E. McLoughlin's masterpiece has endured, even with a new roof whose design imitates the park's famous exterior Yawkey Way facade. *(Courtesy of the Red Sox)*

Bob Guarino of American Plumbing and Heating works on the construction of the 600 Club and new media quarters in February 1989. *(Photograph by Jim Davis, Courtesy of* The Boston Herald*)*

AUGUST 13, 1988

Number 24 Propels Sox to 24th Straight Home Victory

Dwight Evans socked two home runs and a bases-loaded triple to lead the Red Sox to a 16-4 win over the Tigers. It is their 24th consecutive home victory, an American League record. By now it was clear that the word interim had vanished from Joe Morgan's job title as the former snowplow driver and minor-league stalwart had already lent his name to a phenomena called "Morgan's Magic." By September 4th his team would move into a tie for first with the Tigers and within the month would edge out the surging Brewers in a close AL East race.

OCTOBER 5, 1988

Sox Drop Playoff Opener to Oakland, 2-1

On the day that Billy Sullivan sold the Patriots to razor magnate Victor Kiam and Doug Flutie was named Patriots starting quarterback by head coach Raymond Berry, the Red Sox dominated the news.

Despite the fact that Bruce Hurst pitched as well if not better than he did in the '86 post-season, the A's proved once again that great pitching nearly always beats great hitting as the Red Sox fell by a score of 2-1 in their playoff opener at Fenway. Hurst made only a couple of mistakes on the afternoon, one of them being Jose Canseco's fourth-inning solo home run and the other surrendering the game-winning RBI single to former teammate and Boston folk hero Dave Henderson in the eighth.

OCTOBER 6, 1988

A's Best Clemens 4-3 to Take Two Game Advantage

The Athletics sucked the life out of Fenway Park and perhaps the entire miraculous season as shortstop Walt Weiss singled home the winning run in the top of the ninth inning after catcher Ron Hassey

The removal of the old press box and broadcast booth left quite a gap in the facade of the ballpark prior to the construction of the 600 Club. *(Photograph by the author)*

Throughout every renovation the James E, McGloughlin's classic original facade has endured. *(Photograph by the author)*

had led off with a single and been moved to third on a one-out single by Tony Philips. With two out Weiss won the game.

AUGUST 6, 1989

Yaz's Number Eight Retired in Fenway Park Ceremony

Just following his induction to the National Baseball Hall of Fame in Cooperstown, Yaz is honored at Fenway Park with a number retirement ceremony.

It had been 52 seasons since Ted Williams first tipped his cap to fans at Fenway Park from his rookie perch in right field when he grabbed a cap from Red Sox reliever Jeff Reardon on his way out to ceremonies honoring the 50th anniversary of his .406 season on May 11, 1991. His gesture prompted a sustained standing ovation. *(Photograph by the author)*

CHAPTER NINE
Gray Garden

"A jai alai court with foul lines."

—WILLIAM LEGGETT

"It's like a huge pinball machine designed by a mad sculptor."

—DONALD HALL

APRIL 9, 1990

Buckner, Gets Opening Day Standing Ovation in Return to Sox

Opening Day 1990 was both a time for both renewal and forgiveness as the banner draped from the upper deck said it all, "Welcome back, Billy Buck, It's OK."

The applause cascaded from the bleachers to the boxes the instant public address announcer Sherm Feller said, "Number twenty two (pause) Bill Buckner."

Columnist David Nyhan observed, "Bill Buckner, won't you please come home? First base beckons. New England doesn't forget. But New England forgives. You are us. We are you. Only by forgiving you do we forgive ourselves. That's why it was so important that you made it back. One thing more, William: on a ground ball hit straight at you, make sure you

touch your glove-tip to the earth before you come up on it. Now, go get 'em."

Roughly two weeks later the final home run of Bill Buckner's storied career was highlight-reel material as Kansas City Royals right fielder Claudell Washington fell into the stands while misplaying Buckner's drive into a memorable inside-the-park home run. Buckner's dodgy ankles barely made the trek as the aging slugger slid into home and baseball eternity with homer number 174.

April 18, 1990 Boston College 4, Northeastern 1 (Beanpot Semi-Finals)

April 18, 1990 Harvard 6, Boston University 0 (Beanpot Semi-Finals)

April 19, 1990 Boston College 6, Harvard 3 (Beanpot Championship)

April 19, 1990 Northeastern 12, Boston University 3 (Beanpot Consolation)

May 19, 1990 Old-Timers Game

OCTOBER 3, 1990

Brunansky Helps Sox Grab East Title, Beat White Sox, 3-1

When the Red Sox beat Chicago at Fenway by a score of 4-3 on Monday, October 1 they clinched at least a tie with the Blue Jays as Toronto lost with but two games to play. In typical Sox fashion they made fans squirm while losing to Chicago in extra innings on Tuesday night hours after the Blue Jays had beaten the Orioles.

On a night that Roger Clemens watched his teammates on TV from a hotel room in Toronto due to the fact he'd start the one-game division-deciding play-off game at Skydome should Boston lose, the division title came down to one game. It was also a night in which the Red Sox set a Fenway Park attendance record of 2,528,986 as they played to roughly 92 percent

Red Sox partners Haywood Sullivan and Jean Yawkey visit the Yawkey MBTA station in February 1991. *(Courtesy of The Boston Herald)*

of capacity for the entire season. Game 162 also came down to one play as with two outs in the top of the ninth Chicago shortstop Ozzie Guillen, who had broken Boston hearts the night before with a game-winning hit, stroked a sinking line drive toward the tricky right-field corner that Tom Brunansky raced for and made an outstretched leap worthy of Harry Hooper or Dwight Evans while snaring an out that took umpires a few moments to confirm. Brunansky immediately popped up and held the ball aloft in

triumph as Boston secured its third post-season berth in five seasons.

OCTOBER 6, 1990

OAKLAND BOMBS BOSTON AS STEWART BESTS CLEMENS AND INEPT SOX BULLPEN, 9-1

OCTOBER 7, 1990

WELCH, A'S BEST BOSTON, 4-1 TO LEAD SERIES, 2-0

May 1, 1991 Harvard 15, Northeastern 1 (Beanpot Semi-Finals)

May 1, 1991 Boston College 5, Boston University 1 (Beanpot Semi-Finals)

May 2, 1991 Northeastern 11, Boston University 1 (Beanpot Consolation)

MAY 2, 1991

HARVARD 12, BOSTON COLLEGE 9 (10 INNINGS) (BEANPOT CHAMPIONSHIP)

MAY 11, 1991

Ted Tips Cap as Boston Re-Names Lansdowne Street, "Ted Williams Way"

The Upper Deck Old Timers Game proved the perfect setting for a gathering of the Boston baseball tribe to honor it Chieftain, Ted Williams, on the 50th anniversary of the glorious season in which he became the last batter to hit over .400 for the season. It was a day that saw old friends and hardball royalty such as Bobby Doerr, Johnny Pesky, Joe DiMaggio and Curt Gowdy flock to the side of the man who simply wanted to be known as the greatest hitter that ever lived.

Gowdy's introduction of his fishing buddy prompted a standing ovation from the capacity crowd as the pre-game ceremony was brief and elegant. First, Williams was presented with a replica of the street sign bearing the script, "Ted

Former Red Sox broadcaster Curt Gowdy introduces his longtime pal and fishing partner Ted Williams at the ceremonies held in the slugger's honor on May 11, 1991. *(Photograph by the author)*

MAY 17, 1992

BOGGS BECOMES SIXTH RED SOX PLAYER TO GET 2,000 HITS IN BOSTON

JULY 1992

Rock Music Replaces Organ Music at Fenway

Move over John Philips Sousa, slide down Richard Rodgers, see ya later Mr. Gershwin. The Red Sox are playing rock music at Fenway Park? What in the name of John Kiley is going on? Shortly after the death of principal owner Jean Yawkey, the Red Sox made the decision to make Fenway sound like all the other ballparks and arenas on the continent. Not that the organ was left at the curbside on the corner of Brookline Ave. and Yawkey Way. Instead, the sound of the park changed forever as the team replaced a portion of the soothing tinny strains of John Kiley's organ music with a mixture of oldies rock that included hits by The Lovin' Spoonful, Stevie Wonder, the Monkees and Tommy James and the Shondells among others.

Reaction was mixed as Wade Boggs loved it and Pittsfield native, Jeff Reardon, echoing the response of many New England traditionalists, remarked to writer Dan Shaughnessy, "Why did they do it, to change things?" Many also speculated the new tunes provided a welcome distraction from the worst Sox team in a generation. Where fans used to expect "Some Enchanted Evening," they now sought "The Last Train to Clarksville."

Williams Way," that would soon hang under that of Lansdowne Street just beyond the edifice of the Green Monster. Other gifts included a shadow box documenting his legendary baseball, fishing and military exploits as well as a check for his favorite charity, The Jimmy Fund.

Just prior to mounting the steps of the Red Sox dugout prior to his remarks, Williams grabbed a cap from relief pitcher Jeff Reardon and soon doffed it in a grand gesture that reminded one and all of the fact that Williams never ever removed his cap to acknowledge the fans following his rookie season as Boston's right fielder in 1939.

The gesture was pure Williams, spontaneous, heartfelt, and marked by the passion that allowed him to achieve his dream in baseball's most intimate setting.

April 21, 1992 Northeastern 6, Boston University 4 (Beanpot Semi-Finals)

April 21, 1992 Boston College 5, Harvard 4 (Beanpot Semi-Finals)

April 22, 1992 Harvard 14, Boston University 2 (Beanpot Consolation)

April 22, 1992 Boston College 3, Northeastern 1 (Beanpot Championship)

In 1992 Wade Boggs reached the 2,000-hit plateau after playing just a little more than 10 full seasons for the Red Sox while becoming only the sixth player to reach that mark for the franchise. *(Photograph by the author)*

SEPTEMBER 24, 1992

"Father" Guido Sarducci Performs Fenway Exorcism

For the record, the alleged "Curse of The Bambino" was removed a full fourteen years before the team acknowledged the feat by winning the World Series.

In a clever promotion Boston's FM powerhouse, WBCN, located just a block from Fenway Park secured the services of comedian Don Novello, aka Father Guido Sarducci, of *Saturday Night Live* fame. For dramatic effect the faux padre and WBCN "Rock Babe" Michelle were hoisted above the ballpark in a cherry picker parked adjacent to Gate B on the corner of Van Ness and Ipswich Streets. Once aloft, Novello loudly remarked, "What am I doing up here?" before sprinkling 'holy' water and asking those in the crowd that had gathered to administer self-inflicted noogies to shake out the evil spirits.

As water droplets descended, Novello proclaimed, "The Curse of the Bambino is about to hit the road."

April 21, 1993 Boston College 8, Northeastern 7 (Beanpot Semi-Finals)
April 21, 1993 Harvard 14, Boston University 1 (Beanpot Semi-Finals)
April 22, 1993 Boston College 14, Harvard 5 (Beanpot Championship)
May 29, 1993 Old-Timers Game

JULY 15, 1993

Kiley Played for Them All

Long before ballparks, arenas and stadiums morphed into noisy TV studios filled with blaring rock music and jumbotronned ads, there was once a time when the only sound beside that of a PA announcer was that of the organist. Show tunes were the standard and Boston's John Kiley played them before appreciative crowds for two genrations both on the radio and most notably at games for the Braves, Bruins, Celtics, and Red Sox. He was a favorite of Red Sox owner Tom Yawkey for whom he often perform the Rodgers and Hart standard, "Where or When," a favorite of Yawkey's wife, Jean.

Former center-fielder Dominic DiMaggio was a fixture at nearly every Old Timer's game at Fenway Park. Nicknamed "The Little Professor," DiMaggio nearly bought the team in 1976 with the millions he'd earned as a successful businessman. *(Photograph by Leland Campbell)*

On September 24, 1992, comedian Don Novello in his guise as Father Guido Sarducci held an exorcism at Fenway Park to rid the Red Sox of the Curse of the Bambino. He is shown accompanied by Michelle, "The Rock Babe," of event sponsor, WBCN-FM. *(Photograph by Brian Walski, Courtesy of The Boston Herald)*

Known for his laconic nature Kiley possessed nimble fingers that could play the "Star Spangled Banner" in roughly 50 seconds. He started as a professional musician at the age of 15 while performing as an organist for the silent films that played at The Criterion Theater in Roxbury. During his career he played nearly every nightclub and restaurant in Boston that featured music and was a Sunday fixture at St.Catherine's Church in Somerville.

Red Sox fans fondly recall his traditional songbook of familiar tunes, such as "Everything's Coming Up Roses," "Stout Hearted Men," and most memorably his rendition of George Fredric Handel's "Hallelujah Chorus" following Carlton Fisk's epic home run to win Game 6 of the 1975 World Series.

JANUARY 27, 1994

Sherm Feller, Songwriter, Radio Host, and "The Voice of Fenway Park" Dies

To many Sherm Feller wasn't just the public address announcer at Fenway Park. To many he was simply the voice of Boston. His greeting of "Ladies and gentlemen, (long pause) boys and girls..(longer pause) Welcome to Fenway Park," was as much a part of the New England experience as Indian pudding, Mike's cannolis, or rush-hour traffic on the expressway

Boston was and is a city of famous voices. It was home to the distinctive lilt of Julia Child, the witty

Organist John Kiley was the answer to the corniest trivia question in Boston namely, "Who played for the Braves, Red Sox, Bruins, and Celtics?" Kiley was a particular favorite of longtime owner Tom Yawkey and entertained generations of fans with old standards and show tunes. *(Courtesy of the Red Sox)*

inflection of JFK, the raspy brilliance of Johnny Most, the widely imitated delivery of Kevin White, and the list goes on with the likes of Fred Allen, Jay Leno, Conan O'Brien, Bob Wilson, Fred Cusick, and Mike Wallace, to name just a few of the more famous characters who've made a living with their vocal chords. And yet with all their fame and notoriety, it was Feller who topped them all with the understated baritone and quirky timing that marked his 25-year tenure at Fenway Park.

The Roxbury native was a Boston original who was also a noted composer of both classical and pop music with such standards as "Snow, Snow, Beautiful Snow," (Fred Waring Orchestra), "It's Easter Time" (Vaughn Monroe) and the classic "Summertime, Summertime"

(Jay and The Jamies) to his credit. The Fenway gig was one of the many jobs held by the former radio talk show host, milkman, and disk jockey. When he started in 1967 the position paid just twelve dollars per game. In a story recounted in his Boston Globe obituary his sister recalled pointing out to him that the round trip cab fare from his home in Milton was costing him two dollars per game to which he replied, "But I see the games for nothing, It's great."

The Red Sox preserve his memory with a recording of his stentorian ballpark welcome as a fixture on their website and for fans above the age of 40 a Sherm impression remains nothing less than a necessary rite of fandom.

April 26, 1994 Northeastern 4, Harvard 1 (Beanpot Semi-Finals)

April 26, 1994 Boston University 9, Boston College 4 (Beanpot Semi-Finals)

April 27, 1994 Harvard 7, Boston College 7 (Beanpot Consolation)

April 27, 1994 Northeastern 10, Boston University 3 (Beanpot Championship)

July 21, 1994 Boston Park League All-Stars 6, Colorado Silver Bullets 0 (The Bullets were a women's All-Star team sponsored by Coors Brewery.)

April 19, 1995 Northeastern 5, Boston University 3 (Beanpot Semi-Finals)

April 19, 1995 Boston College 12, Harvard 3 (Beanpot Semi-Finals)

April 20, 1995 Northeastern 7, Boston College 3 (Beanpot Championship)

April 20, 1995 Boston University 7, Harvard 1 (Beanpot Consolation)

OCTOBER 6, 1995

Indians Clobber Sox, 8-2, Sweep Series

The Sox went zero for three and the muscular duo of Canseco and Vaughn went 0-for-27 as Boston's post-Buckner postseason blues continued in earnest at the Indians pasted them by a score of 8-2 to sweep their ALDS series.

April 18, 1996 Northeastern 9, Boston College 5 (Beanpot Semi-Finals)

April 18, 1996 University of Massachusetts 13, Harvard 2 (Beanpot Semi-Finals)

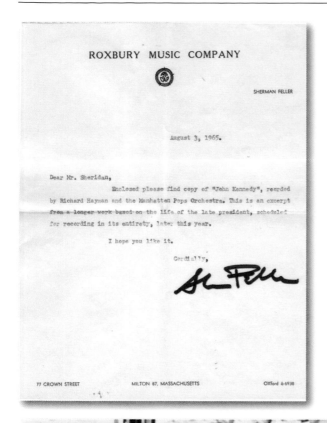

Fenway Park public address announcer Sherm Feller was a Runyonesque character whose eclectic occupations included stints as one of America's first talk show hosts, composer, milkman, and disc jockey. Feller's raspy voice can still be heard on the Red Sox webpage with his trademark greeting of "Ladies and gentlemen, boys and girls.... welcome to Fenway Park." *(Photograph Courtesy of the Red Sox, Artifacts from the collection of the author)*

Fans camp out to purchase tickets for the 1993 season and ask that General Manager Lou Gorman consider signing Pirate free agent Barry Bonds.

(Photograph by Jusine Ellement, Courtesy of The Boston Herald)

Fenway Park themed holiday cards have long been a tradition of the Red Sox. *(Collection of the author)*

April 23, 1996 University of Massachusetts 1, Northeastern 0 (Beanpot Championship)

APRIL 13, 1997

Wally Makes Fenway Debut to Cascade of Boos

The now-beloved Wally The Green Monster mascot made his Fenway Park debut on Kid's Opening Day to a cascade of loud booing prior to a Sunday matinee with the Seattle Mariners. One sportswriter remarked that Bucky Dent and Mike Torrez would have received a better reception that fateful afternoon. Wally, who started life as the central character in a charming children's book, ("The Legend of Wally The Green Monster") was said to be a benevolent creature who'd lived within Fenway Park's famed left field wall for the past 50 years, was brought to life through the efforts of Red Sox Vice President Larry

in the days of Teddy Ballgame and Lefty Grove.

Cancro. The booing, which was especially loud during his 7th inning rendition of "Take Me Out to The Ballgame" was soon drowned out by the cheers for Tim Naehring's grand slam, as the Red Sox beat Seattle by a score of 7-1. Before long Wally became a staple of Red Sox Nation as broadcaster Jerry Remy regaled fans with humorous stories about the mini-version of Wally that sat beside him in the booth in a teeny Adirondack chair.

April 22, 1997 University of Massachusetts 1, Northeastern 0 (Beanpot Semi-Finals)

April 22, 1997 Harvard 9, Boston College 2 (Beanpot Semi-Finals)

April 24, 1997 University of Massachusetts 11, Harvard 4 (Beanpot Championship)

MARCH 19, 1997

Three 25' High Coke Bottles Attached to Green Monster Light Towers

As the Red Sox spoke to both the city and state while exploring the possibility of expanding and possibly replacing Fenway Park, they unveiled their latest ballpark ad in the form of gigantic fiberglass Coca-Cola bottles attached to the prominent light towers atop the Green Monster. Many self-described traditionalists chided the move, conveniently forgetting the fact the left field wall had served as a giant billboard for sponsors such as Gem blades and Lifebuoy back

---

APRIL 10, 1998

Good Friday Turns into Great Friday on Vaughn Walk-Off Slam

The tickets were secured after making a series of phone calls that required my cashing in a pile of chits accumulated over a couple of years. Opening Day. Nothing like it.

The build-up to the 1998 season was considerable as star slugger Mo Vaughn had flipped his pickup truck on a memorable and well-reported trip to the Foxy Lady strip club in Providence. He claimed he liked to eat breakfast with the girls. Soon the club would launch an "eggs and legs" special as Vaughn

By the mid-nineties many in the Red Sox organization felt Fenway Park had become economically obsolete despite the fact the team played to capacity crowds every game. *(Courtesy of Mike Andersen)*

counted his blessings while dropping an astonishing 28 pounds over the course of spring training.

As my friends and I took our seats in section 29 we spied documentary filmmaker Ken Burns clad in a scarf, touque and snappy replica of the Sox wool 1938 warm-up jacket replete with leather sleeves. I made a silent note to monitor just how long our famous colleague might stick around on the bitterly cold afternoon. After all, most celebrities were sampling shrimp and spinach pies in Luxuryville up yonder.

My friend Fred pointed out Burns to me and remarked he'd heard he was a big fan, not just another of the growing and annoying tribe of celebrity Sox followers who wouldn't know Carmen Fanzone from Bizet's Carmen.

This particular Opening Day was noteworthy as the club announced it would not sell beer out of respect for the Good Friday holiday. Not to worry as my buddy John handed around a flask of brandy after the Seattle Mariners took a commanding 7-2 lead into the eighth inning with the Nosferatu-like Randy Johnson pitching a two-hitter.

However, before the silver flask made its second trip around our small group, I looked up to see if our esteemed documentarian remained in his seats and to my delight I saw that he was keeping the faith in shivering silence with the rest of us. Of the original sold-out ballpark it was possible that roughly 9,000 remained.

Much to our delight Johnson tired and was replaced by a conga line of four Mariner relief pitchers

who though asked to close out the game, never recorded a single out as Boston scored seven times, capped by Mo Vaughn's walkoff grand slam home run.

As we all jumped up and down in celebration we waved toward Burns who made fleeting eye contact with us and looked as if he'd just been awarded another Emmy.

The walk home up Commonwealth Avenue took me over to my friend Luke's "secret" parking apace just over the BU Bridge in Cambridge. We laughed like little kids and compared Opening Day notes and I admitted it would be hard to top the '75 Opener he'd witnessed that included the return of Henry Aaron and Tony Conigliaro. However, this came very close, very close indeed.

April 21, 1998 Harvard 11,
Northeastern 0 (Beanpot Semi-
Finals)

April 21, 1998 University of
Massachusetts 7, Boston
College 2 (Beanpot Semi-
Finals)

April 23, 1998 Boston College
9, Northeastern 8 (7 innings)
(Beanpot Consolation)

June 24, 1998 Massachusetts
High School All-Stars 2,
Connecticut High School All-
Stars 1

OCTOBER 2, 1998

**NAGY BESTS SABERHAGAN
AND SOX, 4-3**

OCTOBER 3, 1998

**SOX TIPPED 2-1 BY INDIANS
AND COLON**

MAY 10, 1999

Garciaparra Socks 3 Homers, 2 Grand Slams to Lead Sox Over Seattle

It was a game that equaled the feats of such Boston legends as Tris Speaker, Ted Williams, Yaz, Fred Lynn, or even Clyde "Clutch" Vollmer, Norm Zauchin or Jim Tabor. On the evening of May 10, 1999, Nomar Garciaparra enjoyed the game of games while leading the Red Sox to a 12-4 win over the Seattle Mariners. For the fidgety 25-year-old shortstop hit three home runs, including two grand

The introduction of three 25' tall fibreglass Coke bottles to one of the left-field light towers prompted some purists to cry foul while others pointed out that the park's expansive left-field wall had been a massive billboard for 35 years, from 1912 to 1947. *(Photograph by Jim Dow)*

slams while knocking in 10 runs. He later told the media, "I never hit three home runs in a game, not even Little League. I'm glad I waited until the big leagues to do it. When you're swinging well, good things happen. Today, things felt pretty good."

April 29, 1999 Boston College 4,
University of Massachusetts 2
(Beanpot Championship)

April 29, 1999 Harvard 7,
Northeastern 1 (Beanpot
Consolation)

MAY 15, 1999

Red Sox Announce Plans for New $545 Million Fenway Park

The op ed piece was missed by many *Boston Globe* readers who immediately grab the sports section or scan the front page and Metro section. However on the morning of

Though now a beloved part of the Fenway Park experience, Wally The Green Monster was treated to a chorus of boos and catcalls on his Fenway debut in April 1997. *(Courtesy of the Red Sox)*

the ground and create a new and stronger foundation." He went on to describe a scenario in which any substantial renovation would incur both major financial losses as well as potential hazards for fans.

His conclusion was that only a new park, designed by Camden Yards architects, HOK, would insure a healthy future in which the club maintained and enhanced its competitive and financial standing.

Within weeks fans were presented with site plans and elevations for a new Fenway Park that included many of the distinctive architectural features of the old park (left-field wall, center-field bleachers) while having a full upper deck and many more luxury suites.

Most fans, including the great Ted Williams, groaned when they heard of the plans with Williams even expressing the sentiment that many of the quirks that made Fenway distinctive also made life miserable for many ballplayers.

However, by October many in the media had embraced the new plans even as skeptics wondered aloud if any state or city funding would be requested. Even more pressing was the issue of real estate in space-strapped Boston. The new park required 14 acres to operate as opposed to the 8 acres on which old Fenway stands.

(Author's note: With the one cardinal rule in Boston and Massachusetts sports being that there will never ever be a publicly funded stadium or ballpark built in Boston, there are no plans for a new Fenway Park as the old ballyard has been fully renovated and stands as the venue most new ballparks aspire to be.)

May 15, 1999, Red Sox CEO John Harrington informed fans that the team had decided that Fenway Park was obsolete and that the club would explore building a new home in Boston.

Harrington wrote of the old ballyard, "When our engineers looked at our physical structure, down to the cement pillars and footings, concluded definitively that we cannot add the weight of more seats or an upper deck on top of the existing foundation. The only way to add additional seats in significant numbers is to go down into

Grounds crew member John Stone preps the hand-operated scoreboard in left field. *(Photograph by Ted Gartland, Courtesy of* The Boston Herald*)*

JULY 11, 12 ,13, 1999

All-Star Festivities Marked by Williams Welcome and Martinez Heroics

Most fans who attended the 1999 All-Star Game have likely forgotten the score of the game, however, nobody who was there will ever forget two things. The first being the sustained standing ovation given Red Sox legend Ted Williams as the last player introduced in a star-studded array of baseball greats assembled as an All-Century Team of living players.

As Williams emerged from the bowels of the center-field bleacher on a golf cart driven by Fenway lifer Al Forester, the park erupted as fans paused only to wipe tears from their cheeks as the 80-year-old slugger waved his cap while being driven to home plate to toss the ceremonial first pitch.

Once his cart stopped near the pitcher's mound, the entire gathering of superstars inched then strode to where Williams held court. As major-league officials scurried to try to break up the spontaneous celebration, Williams sought out such sluggers as Mark McGwire and Sammy Sosa and basked in their adoration. Cleveland's Jim Thome

observed, "It was like something out of *Field of Dreams.*"

Williams appearance reminded old timers of his 4-for-4 performance including a towering home run hit off Rip Sewall in the 1946 All-Star Game at Fenway.

After the field was finally cleared Pedro Martinez re-focused the crowd with a dazzling performance that included a Carl Hubbell–like outing that featured his striking out of Barry Larkin, Larry Walker, and Sammy Sosa to start the game, and his doing the same with Mark McGwire and Jeff Bagwell in the second. Electrifying stuff that even had Williams shaking his head as he took in the game from Luxury Box L-22.

For the record the final score was American League 4, National

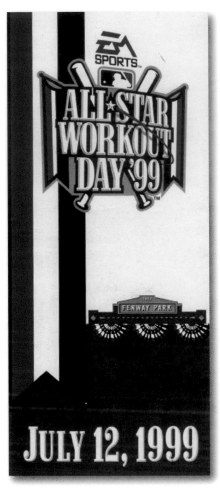

1999 All-Star Game Workout Day Program.
(Collection of the author)

League 1 on a night where Boston bid farewell to Williams while celebrating the feat of its best pitcher since Cy Young.

SAVE FENWAY PARK

Prior to the All-Star Game, the Save Fenway Park activists won much support as they distributed bumper stickers and flyers to those fans lucky enough to attend the game. Among the points group organizer Kimberly Konrad argued was that their proposal would both renovate the park and save taxpayers $90 million. She remarked, "If taxpayers are expected to help foot the bill, they should demand that the money benefits the community at large. Spending tax dollars on a

new stadium for the Red Sox, which would devastate the Fenway community and subsidize the needless destruction of a national treasure, would be the worst kind of corporate welfare."

Team official Jim Healey replied, "The re-build on site plan costs more money and it preserves less of Fenway Park than our plan does. It does not work, and we are not going to pursue the idea any further."

INSIDE THE GREEN MONSTER

Major League Baseball was re-born in the shadow of Fenway Park's Green Monster in the early morning of October 22, 1975. At precisely 12:34 a.m. millions of bleary eyed television viewers across North America fixed their gaze upon the imposing left-field edifice as Carlton Fisk's eleventh-inning home run arched above the landmark and struck the upper reaches of the foul pole to conclude one of the greatest games in baseball history. The Red Sox, faced with elimination in the sixth game of the series, had come back for the second time in a game that was nothing less than an anthology of great plays and clutch hitting.

Not only was the Green Monster the backdrop for this historic moment, but it was also the unconventional staging area for perhaps the most dramatic vignette of video footage ever taken of a home run. For it was through a portal cut into the lower reaches of the hand-operated scoreboard portion of the wall that NBC TV director Harry Coyle decided to place a camera during the series. In fact a new ground rule was created for this opening calling for any ball hit into

the wall on the fly or on a bounce to be ruled a double!

As Coyle's cameraman prepared to shoot the eleventh inning of the sixth game, he found himself startled and temporarily frozen with fear when cornered by a rat. As a result his camera position was inadvertently fixed upon the exact spot where Carlton Fisk gyrated then leapt for joy as his towering drive was signaled as a home run. Coyle, directing his crew from a broadcast truck, wisely aired this serendipitous shot and thus was made baseball's finest televised moment.

The Green Monster. At first sight it is unforgettable. As the most distinctive landmark in American sports it is a functional relic; an integral component of many of baseball's most storied events. For seven decades this most eccentric of barricades has defined both the ambiance of Fenway Park and is proof positive that architecture is destiny. Such has been the tortured (but never dull) history of the Red Sox.

Located a mere 309 feet from home plate, the 37-foot high left field wall is an inviting target for any right handed batter. Just ask Carlton Fisk or Bucky Dent. All Red Sox fans have lived with the painful truth that, "The wall giveth' and the wall taketh away." Hence the birth of the nickname, the Green Monster. Has any fan over the age of twelve ever doubted that they, too, could sock one over, or at least against its green facade? It is a landmark that connects us intimately and immediately with our own history.

In Boston it is impossible to view the game at hand as an isolated event; one instead experiences it with a tribal knowledge, passed down through the generations, of those

Ted Williams appearance at the 1999 All-Star Game was a magnificent farewell as the slugger greeted fans in the adoring company of a pantheon of All-Stars, past and present. *(Courtesy of the Red Sox)*

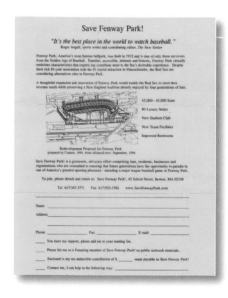

The "Save Fenway Park" effort reached fever pitch following the team's announcement of plans for a new ballpark. In the end their message was heard loud and clear and embraced by fans as well as the new owners in 2002. *(Collection of the author)*

In 1999 these stickers were distributed to fans by Red Sox management. *(Collection of the author)*

games witnessed at Fenway by our parents and grandparents. Want to start a conversation at Fenway Park? Just ask the stranger next to you to relate their most noteworthy Green Monster anecdote and be prepared for a lengthy chat.

Many stories have taken on the guise of legend such as the one connecting Ted Williams to the wall and his love of ice cream. It seems Williams exited the park through an opening in the Green Monster between games of a doubleheader in the late forties and walked into the nearby Pennant Grille on Brookline Avenue and ordered an ice cream soda which he consumed while sitting at a counter stool in his uniform and spikes. After signing autographs for several lucky fans he returned to the game via the same left-field entry and never missed a pitch!

Likewise many fans will never forget the night of August 19, 1963, when Red Sox slugger Dick Stuart added to his league-leading homer and RBI totals with a third inning inside-the-park home run of courtesy of the Green Monster and Cleveland righthander Pedro Ramos. Stuart's drive struck a ledge on the scoreboard portion of the Monster in left center and caromed sideways, striking left fielder Vic Davalillo in the head before rolling into the left-field corner. Fans watched in disbelief as Stuart, all 6' 4" and 220 pounds of him, rounded the bases before sliding home for his 31st home run of the season. Stuart would later add to his improbable heroics by socking a more conventional ninth inning homer which sailed 20' over the Green Monster and onto Lansdowne Street.

At ground level the Green Monster seems even larger and more imposing than from the grandstand. The 275-foot length of the wall nearly matches its distance from home plate. The only remotely human dimension of this Goliath is the tiny 5' x 2' foot door leading into the scoreboard portion of the wall, a dark submarine-like chamber that is the belly of the beast.

It is through this door that every Red Sox left fielder since 1934 as well as hundreds of other major leaguers have ventured to greet the scoreboard operators and sign their names on the interior concrete wall. The wall is a veritable baseball encyclopedia scrawled in varying degrees of legibility in everything from felt tip pen to the scratching of an ice pick! Among the more noteworthy inscriptions are a detailed listing of Ted Williams's home runs, home and away, for the 1950 season as well as the signatures of fellow left-field legends Carl Yastrzemski and Jim Rice. Also prominent are signatures from such Boston greats as Jimmy Piersall, Dave "Boo" Ferris, Mel Parnell, Tex Hughson, and Mike Greenwell.

For years Ted Williams engaged in a running dialogue with scoreboard operator Bill Daley regarding the baseball news of the day. As Daley received regular phone calls from the press box, he would relay choice informational tidbits to Williams who was especially interested in the feats of rival hitters. During Joe DiMaggio's legendary 1941 batting streak, Williams would first learn of DiMaggio's exploits before passing the news to DiMaggio's brother, Red Sox centerfielder Dom DiMaggio.

William's successor and fellow Hall of Famer Carl Yastrzemski also enjoyed interacting with the scoreboard operators. Former scoreboard operator and former Red Sox Vice President Jim Healey recalls that, "Yaz would always

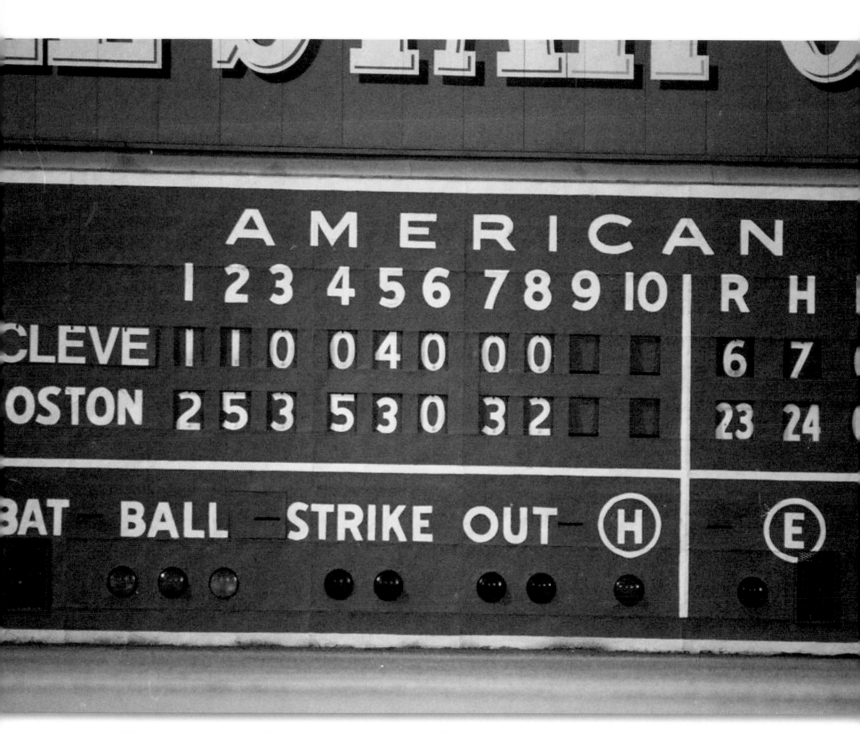

Hidden behind the trademark left-field wall, scoreboard operator Chris Elias has been with the Red Sox nearly as long as Tim Wakefield. *(Courtesy of the Red Sox)*

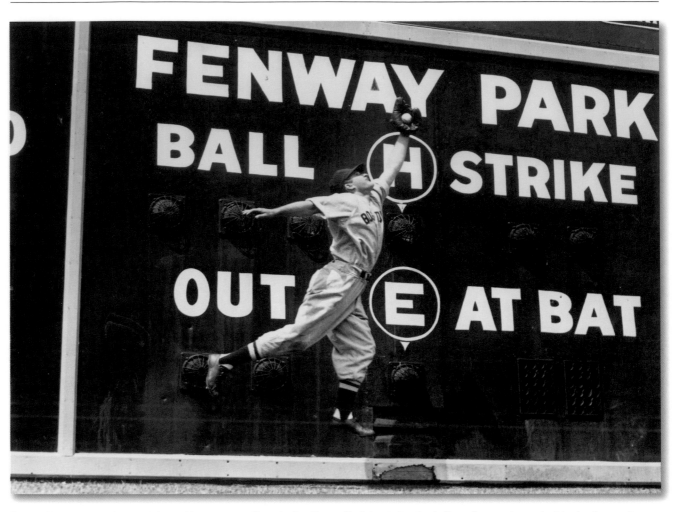

The old Green Monster included the park's name as well as the familiar traffic lights indicating balls, strikes, and outs. In this classic posed publicity shot outfielder Leon Culberson leaps to make a garb against the fabled backdrop. *(Courtesy of Mike Andersen)*

find a time to pound on the wall when you least expected it he'd pound his fist and shout, 'Wake Up,' which always made me jump! The loud bang he'd make against the metal was duplicated only when he crashed into it while making a play."

In his autobiography titled, *Baseball, The Wall and Me* Yastrzemski descibed the wall as follows: "Whenever I'm out at Fenway, someone asks me about it and somehow I wind up walking back there, explaining what life in left field was like under that thing. It's sort of like seeing an old friend, or maybe an old enemy that you've come to have a civilized

relationship with. There is nothing like it in baseball. The wall could make you feel as if you had never played baseball before. The old tin section of the wall would drive you crazy. Whichever batter hit the wall, it would bounce differently off the rivets sharply one way or the other. Then you also had to make a decision as soon as the ball was hit whether it would hit the cement or go above it to the tin. The wall did a lot of things, affected a lot of games and played tricks with people's minds."

The caretaker/operators of the oldest hand-operated scoreboard in baseball for the past decade are Christian Elias and Rich Maloney.

The space in which they work is located under the sidewalk level of adjacent Lansdowne Street and approximates the space of a slightly elongated Boston subway car. The temperatures within this dimly lit poorly ventilated space vary from near freezing in April to higher than 100 degrees in the dog days of summer. Despite these conditions Maloney and Elias are the envy of millions of baseball fans. Not only are they paid to watch every Red Sox home game from these often dank or broiling confines but they do so from the best seats in the house. Their perspective approximates that of most left fielders. Their concrete bunker is also the most historic site in Boston not open to the general public. It is the baseball equivalent of the space shuttle cabin or Oval office; namely a place with which we are all familiar but never experience.

When asked about his job Elias is quick to remark that, "The bottom line is that this is one of the great jobs in baseball; in fact I don't consider it to be work at all. After years of paying to go to games at Fenway Park I feel privileged to be paid to watch the Red Sox."

Elias, who serves as the Assistant Athletic Director and baseball coach at Emerson College, is a student of the game who finds his Fenway Park job has given him a deeper appreciation of the game he has played and watched for three decades. Subtleties

such as pitch selection and outfield positioning are amplified when watching the game from a player's perspective free of the distractions inherent in a ballpark.

Elias especially enjoys the informal relationship he shares with the players. Former Red Sox left-fielder Mike Greenwell would often visit the inside of the wall during his decade with the team, treating the space as a de-facto office. His trips often coincided with a pitching change and would include his taking a bottle of water from a styrofoam cooler and talking informally about everything from politics to baseball before re-joining the game. In similar fashion many visiting players such as Tim Salmon and Chuck Knaublauch visit the

wall during their first Fenway visit of the season and make sure to introduce rookies and new teammates to the Green Monster experience. Invariably each will sign his name or scratch his initials next to those of Williams, Yastrzemski, and Rice.

Elias laughs as he recalls the day Ken Griffey, Jr. switched the city plates on the scoreboard portion of the wall during a game, "We were waiting out a lengthy pitching change and while I was hunting for the right number to formally announce the new pitcher, the crowd has already seen and applauded what Rich and I couldn't imagine; namely that Ken Griffey, Jr had used the down time to shuffle our city plates to new slots, indicating bogus games. More than one phone

Fenway Park in a soaking rain, c.1946. *(Photograph by Leslie Jones)*

The holiday season at Fenway Park always means a cheery park-related card and at least one major free agent signing. *(Collection of the author)*

call was placed from the press box to our scoreboard "hotline" to inquire as to which schedule we had consulted prior to our scoreboard setup. Griffey laughed and pointed at us during the following inning when we hustled from the Green Monster to re-position the plates to their proper places. To this day Griffey waves to us when he sees us at the park."

Despite their occasional encounters with superstars, the pair toil in a working space as humble as any in Boston. Notwithstanding the funky charm of the graffiti, the space is as bare as a tool shed. Not only is there no bathroom, but the Spartan quarters contain only the aforementioned cooler, a wastebasket, a broken space heater, a wall of obsolete electronic controls, and a 4-1/2 inch black and white TV set topped with a radio; an arrangement Elias jokingly calls their "entertainment center." However the five 10-inch by 1-1/2-inch eye slits through which Elias and Maloney view the game afford nothing short of the most spectacular view imaginable of baseball's most treasured park.

Above them is an additional 19' of wall, a framework once constructed of railroad ties and tin but now covered with fiberglass. Above this additional expanse of wall is another 23' 4" of netting first purchased from former Red Sox pitcher Howard Ehmke and installed by Tom Yawkey in 1937 at the behest of Lansdowne Street shopowners tired of replacing windows shattered by the blasts of slugger Jimmie Foxx.

There is more than a little irony in the fact that left field at Fenway Park was once thought to be the Red Sox prime defensive asset. Instead of a Green Monster the team built a less-than-imposing wooden scoreboard fronted by a 10' high embankment known as "Duffy's Cliff" in honor of left fielder George "Duffy" Lewis. Not only was Lewis the master of his "cliff" but the dead-ball era sluggers had all they could do to even reach the cliff, never mind the wall behind it. When journeyman first baseman Hugh Bradley of the Red Sox socked the first home run over the left-field wall on April 26, 1912, one newspaper account described the blast as "being so powerful as not to be human."

This, of course, is roughly the same wall over which such superb Red Sox right-handed sluggers as Foxx, Conigliaro, Rice, Evans, and Ramirez have socked countless homers while contributing to sometime pinball-like tallies. Ironically it is also the site of the most infamous (if you root for the Red Sox!) or famous 310' home run in baseball history. This, of course, was struck by Bucky Dent in the one-game "winner take all" American League East playoff game on October 1, 1978, and stands as the most prominent evidence of the old Fenway adage, "the Wall giveth, and the Wall taketh away."

Is it any wonder that experienced fans never leave Fenway Park until the final out has been recorded. Chris Elias particularly enjoys the electricity of any Yankee series that nearly approximates his all time favorite experience, namely the clinching of the 1995 American League title. He will never forget standing on the warning track as Mo Vaughan mounted a Boston Police horse and rode around the park waving to the cheering crowds.

Elias is quick to remark that come July he will probably have a new all-time favorite Fenway experience once the All Star week is completed. He smiles when he says, "I've already lost count of the number of people who have begged me to get them All-Star tickets or, at the very least, sneak them into the Green Monster. Why, we have even had fans yelling at us after a game offering cash for scoreboard numbers and that sort of thing; it can be crazy at times." He laughs at such lunacy while pondering his good fortune and remarks simply, "I can't imagine not being here."

OCTOBER 9, 1999

Ramon Martinez, Sox Beat Indians, 9-3 for First Post-Season Win in 13 Years

In order for the Red Sox to win their first post-season game in 13 years, Ramon Martinez had to pitch like his kid brother Pedro. And Lou Merloni had to play like his buddy Nomar Garciaparra when pressed into service to substitute for his injured pal at shortstop. Both came through along with John Valentin (tie-breaking 2-run double and home run) and Brian Daubach (3-run homer) as the Sox nailed down a series-extending victory as Derek Lowe got the win in relief.

OCTOBER 10, 1999

Red Sox 23, Indians 7 as Boston Ties Series

Fenway Park more than lived up to its reputation as the world's largest pinball machine as the Red Sox established a new major-league record for runs scored in a post-season game with 23 as they crushed the Cleveland Indians to tie their ALDS at two games apiece.

Not only did their win set a single-game record but the total number of runs, but according to The Boston Herald eclipsed the total number of runs scored by the team is five different World Series 1915 (12), 1916 (21), 1918 (9), 1946 (20), and 1967 (21).

OCTOBER 16, 1999

Martinez Wins Duel of Cy Young Winners as Sox Beat Clemens/Yanks 13-1

Fenway hadn't seen anything like it since the legendary pitching duel between Walter Johnson and Smoky Joe Wood back in September 1912. The match-up was classic, Pedro Martinez vs. Roger Clemens in the daylight of a Saturday afternoon playoff between the Yankees and Red Sox. Cy Young vs. Cy Old. The scalpers could now pay for their timeshares and tuition bills as tickets for the duel became the most sought after since the Patriots last Super Bowl.

The sustained roar of the Fenway crowd surely stirred the ghosts of the long-departed Royal Rooters as Martinez pitched brilliantly, setting a team postseason strikeout record with 12 while besting Clemens who could only make it to the fourth inning. Boston's offense was led by John Valentin's 5 RBI, Brian Daubach's 2-run homer, and Nomar Garciaparra's 3-run blast that sent Yankees reeling in a game in which the crowd never stopped cheering.

A Paean to Pedro

By Luke Salisbury

Between 1997 and 2003 Pedro Martinez was the greatest pitcher of all time. The reasons are simple and the argument is incontrovertible. Pedro faced men of color at the height of the Performance Enhanced Era (PEE, an apt acronym), and he faced the Designated Hitter. Pedro was the uber dominant pitcher during the greatest power surge in the history of baseball. If, as Red Sox General Manager Theo Epstein has said, baseball changed about 2005 with drug testing, there will never be another so blatantly unregulated chemically enhanced time. Señor Martinez dominated hitters during the most unrestrained, pharmaceutically assisted offensive era in baseball history. And he did it in Fenway Park, a notorious hitters' park, with its small foul territory and pop fly (Bucky Dent) left-field wall. He did

being 5' 9" tall, and weighing 155 pounds. He did it with brains and he did it with guts.

When talking baseball, we talk numbers, and baseball's numbers have also been enhanced. Reviewing baseball Internet sites reveals so many statistics, the old (home runs, RBIs, average, wins, ERA etc.) and the endlessly computer-generated new (R*bat*, R*baser*, R*roe*, R*rep*, RAR, WAR, oRAR, oWAR, dWAR) one feels lost in *The Matrix* where behind "reality" are computer-generated walls of numbers. Let's use the old statistics.

Pedro's Red Sox won-and-lost record is 117-37 as a Red Sox, which is the highest winning percentage (.760) for any pitcher with over 100 wins on one team. This includes his subpar year of 2004 when Pedro was only very good at 16-9 with a whopping (for him) ERA of 3.90. During this seven-year stretch ('97-'03, he was with Montreal in '97), Pedro won five ERA crowns, two Cy Young Awards, and led in strikeouts three times. In 1999 he won the pitcher's Triple Crown, leading in wins, ERA, and strikeouts.

Fenway Park has been more conducive to great hitters than great pitchers. There are exceptions who make the rule interesting—Luis Tiant, Roger Clemens, Smokey Joe Wood. Before Pedro, Wood was the best short career Red Sox pitcher. In nine years, Wood was 116-57, including the nonpareil year 1912 when he was 34-5 and beat the Giants three times in the World Series. His ERA was 1.91. Like Wood, Pedro threw hard. Very hard. That is part of mastering Fenway Park. If hitters can't make contact, the dimensions don't help. But there is more to winning in Fenway than velocity. It has been a

graveyard for many a fastball pitcher. Fenway demands guile. It demands change of speed and control (a very bad place to issue walks). Luis Tiant was a master of deception from wind-up to velocity—and guts—but Tiant didn't have Pedro's control. Whether Pedro was blowing a 97-mph fastball by a hitter, dropping in an 82-mph change-up, or pinpointing a nasty (the current epithet is filthy) curve, he could be simply unhittable.

Best pitcher of all time for a four- to seven-year period is a good measure of peak performance. It's different from greatest season. Joe Wood only won over 20 games only once other than 1912. Wood pitched in the dead ball era when winning 30 or having an ERA under 2 was as common as hitting 50 home runs in the PEE. Dizzy Dean had four dominant years in the wild swinging '30s, the other comparable era to the PEE, but Dean's winning percentage and strikeouts are lower than Pedro's. Lefty Grove, 1928-33, is comparable, better in wins and winning percentage, not as good in ERA and strikeouts. In 1930, when the American League hit .288 (the whole league!), Grove was 28-4 with a 2.54 ERA. The National League hit .303. This was indeed the lively ball era. Apparently the seams on the balls were low in 1930 and it was difficult to throw a curve. Like Pedro, Grove was a fireballer. Wood, Dean, and Grove, of course, did not face men of color, unless in exhibition games, where, from what we can reconstruct, the men of color frequently did quite well. Wood, Dean, and Grove didn't face the DH.

The best comparison to Pedro is Sandy Koufax. Koufax's run between 1962-66 is statistically more impressive than Pedro's. He lead in ERA every year, strikeouts three times, wins three times, pitched in more World Series. Every baseball fan I know who saw Koufax says he was the best they ever saw. But what are the differences? Koufax was big and never threw at no one. Pedro was small and would throw at anybody. Which you prefer is a matter of taste. Koufax pitched in Chavez Ravine when it was definitely a pitchers' park. Koufax threw from a higher mound. He faced men of color but not as many as Pedro. Koufax did not face men whose bodies were so chemically jacked they resembled cartoon characters or NFL players. Koufax didn't face the DH. The strike zone was bigger (has it ever been smaller than the last 15 years?). Sandy gets the edge in quality of wins. He pitched in the insane NL pennant races of 1963, '65 and '66, where given the hitting behind him, there was little room for error.

To have seen Pedro Martinez pitch in Fenway Park was a gift. To see Pedro in 1999 was divine. That blinding speed, intimidating inside lightning that kept right-hand hitters off the plate, the high fastball left-hand hitters could neither lay-off nor hit, the breaking pitches slicing the corners, or the ridiculously unhittable change-up that might as well have come from another dimension—Pedro was the master and Fenway his palette. At the All-Star Game, at Fenway, and memorably attended by Ted William, who was wheeled out in a cart, Pedro fanned the first five NL hitters: Barry Larkin, Larry Walker, Sammy Sosa, Mark McGwire, and Jeff Bagwell. The National League needed the cart. Pedro might as well have fanned Dow Chemical

and Balco Labs. His most dominant performance, however, was in Yankee Stadium. On September 10, 1999, he one-hit the Yankees 2-1. The hit was a homer by Chilli Davis. Pedro struck out 17. That Yankee club won 114 games. I saw the game on TV, and I've never seen a good, maybe great line-up, so dominated. From the 5th inning on the Yankees seemed to be conceding their trips to the plate. They stood, watched, sat down.

Pedro's finest moment was the deciding playoff game with the Indians in '99. He entered the game in the third with the score tied 8-8. Pedro wasn't supposed to be able to pitch. He was suffering with a bad back. The man could barely raise his arm over his shoulder. He proceeded to pitch six hitless innings against a line-up that included Kenny Lofton, Robby Alomar, Manny Ramirez, and Jim Thome. (How much Dow and Balco we can only speculate.) Pedro looked like Pedro at half speed, or one should say, his body was at half speed, his mind and his guts were still Pedro. The Red Sox won 12-8.

His lowest moment, one that dogs his legacy, is Game 7 of the ALCS in 2003. After pitching seven innings and leading the Yankees 5-2, no one, apparently not even Pedro, thought he would pitch the eighth. Grady Little, another in the long line of non-genius Red Sox managers, decided he should. As the inning worsened, Little made Hamlet-like trips to the mound, finally taking Martinez out too late. The Red Sox lost in extra innings. The silver lining was Little got fired.

In 2004 Pedro was not the Pedro of the previous seven years. It was, however, the Red Sox year of curse-breaking, destiny, and redemptive

Yankee crushing. Pedro's last game as a Red Sox was seven shutout innings against the Cardinals in the Sox four-game sweep. The Master finished his magnificent Boston career with a World Championship.

For seven years no man ever pitched so well, with so much against him, as Pedro Martinez.

OCTOBER 17, 1999

SUNDAY NIGHT BLUES, YANKEES 9, RED SOX 2

OCTOBER 18. 1999

YANKEES CLOSE OUT SOX/ SERIES WITH 6-1 WIN

Pedro Martinez is one of the five greatest pitchers in Fenway Park history along with Joe Wood, Lefty Grove, Luis Tiant, and Roger Clemens. *(Courtesy of the Red Sox)*

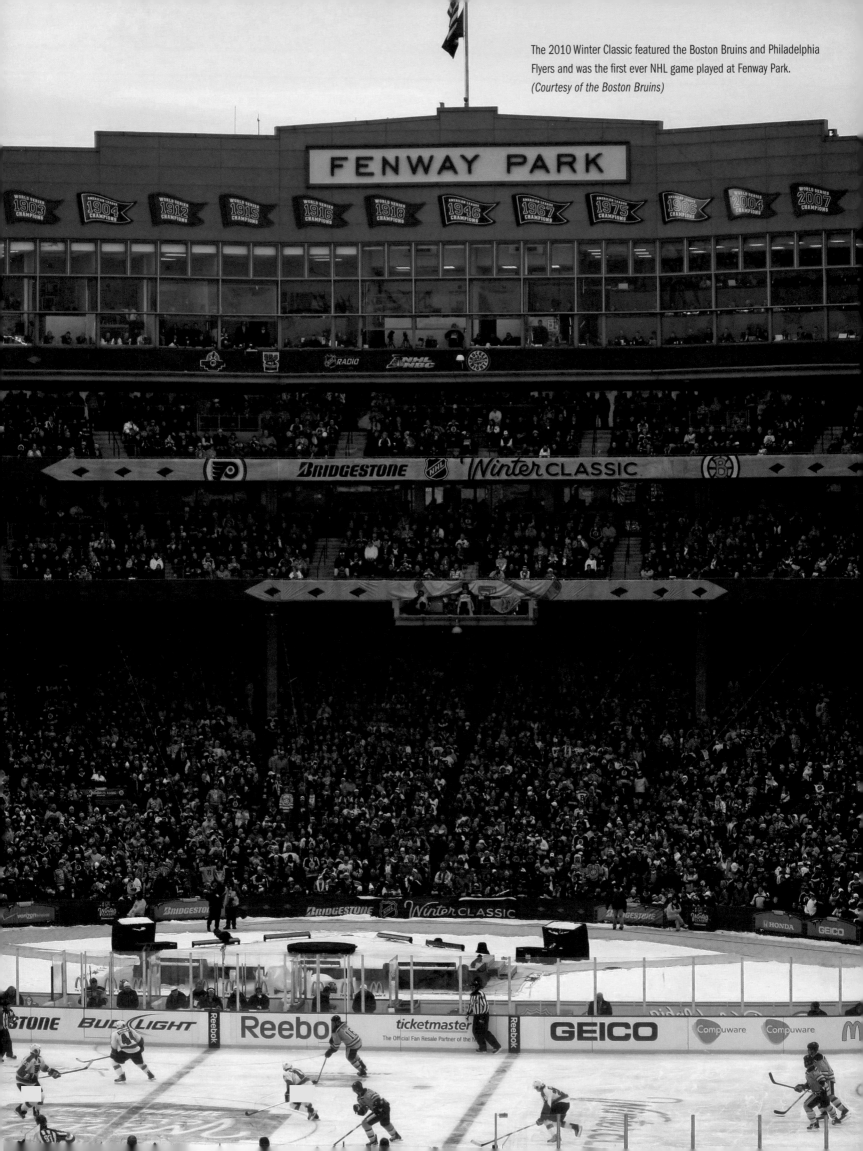

The 2010 Winter Classic featured the Boston Bruins and Philadelphia Flyers and was the first ever NHL game played at Fenway Park. *(Courtesy of the Boston Bruins)*

CHAPTER TEN
RENAISSANCE

"There's no place like it, and it's ours."

—STEPHEN KING ON FENWAY PARK

The new owners not only elevated the Red Sox to Major League preeminence but also restored a semblance of Fenway Park's role as a multi-purpose facility. And while we'll never re-live the days of the park as a regular schoolboy and collegiate venue, we will continue to see the ballyard rock out for the likes of Aerosmith and the Stones and play host to clever one-off extravaganzas such as European club soccer and the host of special events anticipated in celebration of the park's centennial.

Elizabeth "Lib" Dooley was a loyal presence at more than 4,000 Red Sox games at Fenway and often brought players cookies and candy.
(Courtesy of Bob Walsh)

Charlestown, New Hampshire, native Carlton Fisk lived the dream of every New England kid that yearned to wear the hometown uniform. He was the first New England native to have his jersey retired by the team. *(Courtesy of the Red Sox)*

Her seats were the best in the house, Box 36-A. Players and coaches routinely came to chat her up before games, and rookies often received their initiation to her company by munching on the Oreos and Starbursts she'd dispense from her carryall.

Lib was a throwback to the days of the famed Royal Rooters, of which her dad John was a member. The Rooters, lived and died with their Red Sox and Braves and often became personal friends with the players and their families.

Likewise superfan 'Megaphone Lolly' Hopkins cheered for her boys at both Braves Field and Fenway Park while calling their names through her distinctive megaphone.

The spirit of Dooley and the Rooters lives on with the BoSox Club as well as the countless fans who've had their season tickets for generations.

SEPTEMBER 4, 2000

NATIVE SON: FISK'S NUMBER 27 RETIRED

May 2, 2001 Boston College 10, University of Massachusetts 5 (Beanpot Championship)

May 2, 2001 Northeastern 7, Harvard 2 (Beanpot Consolation)

June 19, 2001 Massachusetts High School All-Stars 7, Connecticut High School All-Stars 2

APRIL 3, 2002

SOX PLAYERS GREET FANS AT TURNSTILES

April 16, 2002 Northeastern 8, Harvard 4 (Beanpot Semi-Finals)

April 25, 2000 University of Massachusetts 13, Northeastern 8 (Beanpot Championship)

April 25, 2000 Boston College 8, Harvard 5 (Beanpot Consolation)

JUNE 19, 2000

LIB

The Dooley family has been synonymous with Boston baseball and the Red Sox in particular for much of the past century. For much of that time its most conspicuous member was Lib, who presided over more than 4,000 Red Sox games starting in the 1920s and continuing in earnest after she bought her first season ticket during WWII.

Dolley counted Ted Williams among her best friends and in 1996 he recalled, "Forever, she's the greatest Red Sox fan there'll ever be. Every time I get a chance to get around here. I like to do it because she's really a big-league gal."

On a broiling hot July evening, a near full house gathered at Fenway Park to honor Ted Williams as a ballplayer, solider, philanthropist, and citizen. Among the night's speakers were Dominic DiMaggio, Ned Martin, and Senator John Glenn. *(Courtesy of the Red Sox)*

April 16, 2002 Boston College 7, University of Massachusetts 5 (Beanpot Semi-Finals)

April 23, 2002 Northeastern 7, Boston College 6 (Beanpot Championship)

April 23, 2002 University of Massachusetts 5, Harvard 3 (Beanpot Consolation)

APRIL 27, 2002

Derek Lowe Fires First Fenway No-Hitter Since Morehead in '65

Redemption was never so sweet for any Red Sox player in recent memory as it was for Derek Lowe

on the afternoon of April 27, 2002, as the once-reviled relief pitcher found new life while not only pitching his first complete game but also tossing the first no-hitter at Fenway Park since Dave Morehead turned the trick in 1965. Since his move from the bullpen Derek Lowe found his groove as one of baseball's ultimate groundball pitchers on a sunny Saturday during which the Devil Rays chopped grounder after grounder in their 10-0 loss to Boston.

Lowe, who despite leading the league in saves in 2000 became a hated figure in Boston, savored the moment after inducing Jason Tyner of the Devil Rays to ground out to second base for the final out. Following the game he received the game ball on a silver platter presented by teammate Jose Offerman.

He later remarked to reporters, "It's surreal. I still don't think I did what I did, as crazy as that sounds. I still think it happened to somebody else because you don't ever think something like this can happen to you."

JULY 22, 2002

Ted Williams Memorial Celebrates Life of Sox Slugger

The death of Ted Williams marked the passing of an era not just for the Red Sox but for baseball. However, in the days following his death at age 83, the circumstances surrounding the issue of his final wishes became fodder for public ridicule as it

The construction of the monster seats symbolized the new ownership's embracing of the traditional ballpark while enhancing its function. *(Courtesy of the Red Sox)*

was revealed the slugger's body had been moved to Arizona for freezing at a cryogenics facility. As his oldest daughter Bobby Jo cried foul, son John Henry produced a rumpled handwritten note that alleged his father requested the chance at literal immortality. As his children battled in the glare of the media, the legacy of a true American hero regrettably became a Letterman-Leno punch-line.

Leave it to the new Red Sox owners to refocus the public's

attention back to that of Williams the hero with their production of a splendid memorial tribute at Fenway Park a little over three weeks after Williams' death. Not only did they open Fenway to fans on the morning of July 22nd for an all-day memorial tribute to Williams but they hosted a special ticketed tribute that took place that night in the park.

Among the dignitaries to pay homage to Williams that night were his Marine wingman, Senator John Glenn; broadcasters Curt Gowdy,

Ken Coleman, and Ned Martin; teammates Dom DiMaggio, Johnny Pesky, Dave Ferris, Charlie Wagner, Walt Dropo, and Frank Malzone; and an array of past and current Red Sox players that included Carl Yastrzemski, Luis Tiant, Earl Wilson, Jim Rice, Jerry Remy, Rico Petrocelli, Jim Lonborg, Johnny Damon, Nomar Garciaparra, Lou Merloni, and Tim Wakefield.

Dom DiMaggio received polite applause when he remarked, "I am saddened by the turmoil of the current controversy. I hope and pray this controversy ends as abruptly as it began and the family will do the right thing by honoring his final resting place, and may he rest in peace."

The park was beautifully decorated in mural-size photos of Williams batting, in the cockpit of his Marine jet, and with children supporting The Jimmy Fund. Groundskeeper David Mellor created a 77' by 36' number nine out of white carnations, roses, and baby's breath. Williams' Hall of Fame plaque was brought from Cooperstown for a special display near the left-field warning track.

Speakers included Red Sox principal owner John Henry who welcomed the near-capacity crowd to a program that also included Dom DiMaggio, John Glenn, TV personality Dick Flavin reciting "Teddy at the Bat," Peter Gammons, Jimmy Fund chief Mike Andrews, and Jimmy Fund patient Kate Shaughnessy who recalled Williams calling her hospital room when she was 8 years old and telling her, "everything will be ok."

The night ended with a video and musical tribute that included footage of Williams hitting his last home run in his final at bat at Fenway and the Marine band playing, "God

Bruce Springsteen became the first major musical act at Fenway since the ill-fated 1973 Newport Jazz Festival. *(Courtesy of the Red Sox)*

Bless America" The crowd exited to the strains of "Auld Lang Syne," as photos of Williams flickered on the Jumbotron.

SEPTEMBER 5, 2002

Fenway Concourse II Opens

PRESERVING A TREASURE

By Janet Marie Smith

My first trip to Fenway Park was in 1989 when I was working for Larry Lucchino, then President of the Baltimore Orioles, to spearhead the team's input into the design of Oriole Park at Camden Yards. Larry was emphatic that we take advantage of the downtown location and baseball-only facility the State of Maryland had agreed to fund, and design a ballpark (not a stadium, he constantly reminded us) that would be the spiritual kin of the classic ballparks of the early 1900s. Part of my mission was to identify the specific characteristics of these parks that could be transferred to our new home. Fenway Park, Wrigley Field, Tiger Stadium, and Comiskey Park (ironically in the state of being replaced itself) were the only living examples of this era. So off to Boston, camera and pen in hand, I went.

The Red Sox place on Yawkey Way is magical, as any baseball aficionado knows. And all the notes in the world about the irregularities of the playing field, the way the outfield geometry is dictated by the adjoining streets, the proximity of the seats to the field, the low elevation of the portals to the seats, the steel trusses, the brick façade, the granite sign band – cannot result in a composition as eclectic and yet balanced a cacophony of shapes as those that make up Fenway Park.

When Oriole Park at Camden Yards opened in 1992, we were enormously pleased with the reaction of fans to the new park – but there were times when I worried its success may have been the death toll for Fenway Park. The Boston Red Sox and countless City of Boston officials made trips to Baltimore to see the Orioles' new park and use this as an example of how Bean

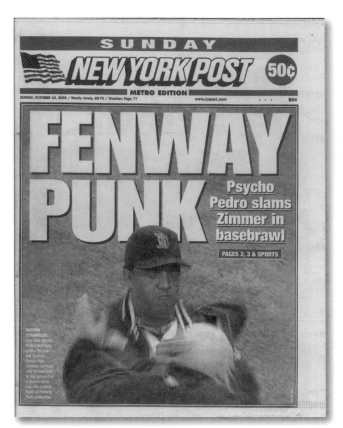

On a day in which the main drama should have focused on the pitching duel between Cy Young Award winners Roger Clemens and Pedro Martinez, headlines instead were made after a brawl erupted in the bottom of the fourth inning. *(Courtesy of the Red Sox)*

Town could create a new park and still have the Fenway charm. When Larry Lucchino phoned me in 2001, almost a full decade later to ask if I would be willing to take a look at ideas to preserve and add to Fenway Park, I could not have been more delighted – not so much for the opportunity for myself– but to know that this vulnerable ballpark was about to fall into the hands of an ownership group who not only appreciated its irreplaceable charm, but knew enough about design and construction to be willing to take on the challenge. To be sure, they also understood politics and economics and saw that a renovation would be far less costly than building new and politically much more likely to succeed.

It would not be fair to suggest that the answer to Fenway Park's future came solely from the new advocates, who now had their hands firmly on the reins of the problem, if not yet the solution. Time and ballpark trends were clearly on the side of Fenway Park. When Camden Yards opened with over 48,000 seats, followed shortly by Coors Field in Denver, Jacobs Field in Cleveland, and Turner Field in Atlanta, all with about 50,000 seats, Fenway Park's 33,000+ seats, seemed impossibly small. But by the time Tom Werner, John Henry and Larry Lucchino and their partners took over the Boston Red Sox in 2002, the average MLB Park (PNC, San Diego, and Twins) was being planned for closer to 40,000 seats. So Fenway Park's stretch goal was altered by almost 10,000 seats, making renovation a much more obtainable objective.

But these new venues also boasted things that Fenway did not have: wide concourses and convenient concessions, retail and restrooms, luxury suites and club sections, separate areas for upgraded seating sections, parking, and plenty of behind-the-scenes function spaces including weight rooms, batting tunnels, interview rooms, media truck locations, loading docks and other functions of a 21st century park. The challenge was how to develop these fundamental "amenities" into the site without altering the character and scale of Fenway Park. It is noteworthy that the square footage of Fenway Park was about 750,000 and the new parks, even the smallest such as San Francisco, was almost 2,000,000. And the site in Boston was only 7.5 acres where as the new parks sat on 20 acres or more.

Beginning with a cautious but enthusiastic dedication to Fenway

The Mother's day Walk was just one of the many special ballpark events started by the new owners. *(Courtesy of the Red Sox)*

Manny Ramirez was nothing less than a modern day Jimmie Foxx for the Red Sox as the new century brought two world championships to Fenway Park. *(Courtesy of the Red Sox)*

Apart from the new Red Sox management, Jimmy Buffett also brought "Changes in Latitudes and Changes in Attitudes" to Fenway Park in 2004. *(Courtesy of the Red Sox)*

In October 2004 David "Big Papi" Ortiz joined the Red Sox pantheon of sluggers as he contributed mightily to the miracle comeback victory over the Yankees in the ALCS and the World Series that followed. *(Courtesy of the Red Sox)*

Park itself, the team set out to invest in a series of annual improvements that would set the stage for a complete renovation of the ballpark. Initially, the criteria was to invest in projects that would have a 3-5 year payback with the notion that even if "renovation" was proved impossible, these initial improvements would have a financial return that would justify the investment before a new ballpark could possibly be constructed.

Buoyed by an enthusiastic reception from Red Sox Nation, a welcome sigh of relief from the neighbors, a series of studies undertaken by preservationists, and the team's own intuitive sensibilities of what constituted a "beloved ballpark" –the focus firmly shifted to an examination of a complete renovation and additions that would bring Fenway Park programmatically in line with other new MLB parks. There were numerous studies done during the 1990s that helped to support these efforts–from Meredith & Grew's real estate analysis to the "Save Fenway Park" and Fenway CDC sponsored design charettes to the City of Boston studies of the Fenway neighborhood historic character reports. But at the end of the day, nothing supported the renovation goals more than ownership interest to make it happen. The fact that the Red Sox were able to generate such solid financial returns on their Fenway Park investment made this goal more than just the sentimental favorite alternative to a new park.

The initial improvements were modest in scale, though dramatic in results: the neighborhood and city supported the Red Sox request to put turnstiles at either end of Yawkey Way, the street flanking the

Fenway Park on the Opening Night of the 2004 World Series. *(Courtesy of the Red Sox)*

home-plate entry to Fenway Park, adding much-needed square footage to a crowded corridor, as well as welcome in-the-park open-air grills and kiosks to augment the limited food service.

Popular new seats were added above the Green Monster left-field wall and scoreboard. Though this only added 500 new tickets, the iconic quality of the location added much excitement. Similarly, the right-field roof was structurally upgraded, and tables and stools were created to add to the menu of Fenway Park offerings.

Entrances were expanded and areas closed to fans for decades were reclaimed by moving many operations to the adjacent Fenway Garage. Storage rooms such as those under the bleachers were transformed into the "Bleacher Bar" with views of the outfield

through the original garage doors on the playing field.

With the approval of the City and State Preservation offices, the walls separating the Smith (Jeano) building at the corner of Yawkey Way and Brookline were demolished, allowing wider concourses inside the ballpark, and all-new, ADA-accessible restrooms and concessions were constructed. In the outfield, the same approach allowed the Big Concourse to double the width of the circulation area under the crowded bleacher and right field grandstand. New concessions and restrooms followed. The clubhouse was expanded to include construction of a batting tunnel under the first-base grandstand and a new weight room and interview room were built adjacent the original clubhouse so that the roof of the new areas would double as added

standing room and circulation area for the rear of the grandstand. The playing field was completely replaced to give Fenway a state-of-the art drainage system. Sidewalks were widened on all sides. Street trees and historic acorn light fixtures and bike racks were installed in the new sidewalks.

In sum, the answer to the question of how to renovate Fenway Park without losing the architectural character and charm of the scale and history of the park was in how the real estate adjacent the park was redeployed to create greater value. Many of the answers to how to add square footage were found by simply using existing spaces more creatively and in that respect, the changes at Fenway Park were good urban design solutions, opening up the ballpark to more lively street front uses. Thank goodness, the stewards of the Boston Red Sox during the Yawkey Foundation era had the good sense and foresight to acquire the Jeano Building and Fenway Garage, or there would not have been the ability for the Werner-Henry-Lucchino team to take advantage of this additional square footage in such an imaginative way.

Highly important in the equation was the decision to employ D'Agostino Izzo & Quirk (DAIQ), a Somerville architectural office with a convincing resume of historical renovations in their portfolio as well as a keen understanding of how to create "people places" as demonstrated in their years of working for the legendary developer, James W. Rouse, who had been a moving force in the redevelopment of Boston's Fanfieul Hall. I had first met DAIQ when we interviewed them for the work in Atlanta to transform the 1996 Olympic Stadium outfield area into the Braves entry plaza. They were introduced by Bowie Arnot as the only architects that Jim Rouse ever admired–a compelling testament as he felt that most architects were more concerned with their authorship of a building than of the space that people inhabited. Being a private entity, we had the luxury of being able to choose professionals we felt had the right skills and approach to solving Fenway Park's problems even though DAIQ's "sports" architecture was more limited than a public-selection process might have found acceptable.

Another Jim Rouse introduction from Baltimore which paid huge dividends—literally—for Fenway Park, was the role that Struever Bros. Eccles & Rouse (SBER) played to help the Boston Red Sox obtain historic tax credits

Manny Ramirez acknowledges the crowd on Opening Day 2005 as he prepares to receive his World Series ring. *(Courtesy of the Red Sox)*

for the ballpark. Fenway Park is the first MLB facility to obtain the historic status necessary to qualify for this financial opportunity. The Orioles had looked into this possibility for the B&O Warehouse alternations at Camden Yards, but as a publicly owned facility, the opportunity for historic tax credits did not exist. Fenway Park, owned solely by the privately owned Boston Red Sox was different. After three seasons of "improvements," from 2002–05, the Boston Red Sox, with the help of SBER, submitted a full renovation plan to the City Landmarks Commission, the Massachusetts Historic Commission, and the National Park Service and embarked on the largest project to date: the reconstruction of the seating and addition of approximately 1,300 seats to increase the capacity to 38,805 in April of 2006. The 1989 glass of the .406 Club was removed from behind homeplate so that the premium seats in that area could be free from the clutter of ramps, temporary concessions, restrooms, and scattered

HVAC units, was transformed into a more useable space to support the added seats. The good work of Leslie Donovan and Erika Tarlin of Tremont Preservation ensured adherence to both the National Park Service standards and the faithfulness to Fenway Park's historic character. The added graphic touches of Ashton Design was like putting jewelry back on the building as much of the original signage was replicated for the new areas.

Though the Boston Red Sox take appropriate pride in the fact that the hundreds of millions of funds for all 10 years of "improvements" came solely from the team, the government agencies that oversee the project deserve major credit for the renovations. Whether it was the advocacy and blessing from the neighbors and ultimately Boston City Hall and Mayor Tom Menino, who approved the concept of a ticketed "Yawkey Way" and an area over the Lansdowne sidewalk for the Green Monster seats, or the dollars from the historic tax credit from the federal and state government as a result of the conformance to the National Park Service standards—the willingness of all levels of government to support the Red Sox renovation, additions, and improvements, have ensured the teams successful investment into Fenway Park to ensure the ability of the next generations of baseball fans to enjoy this classic baseball shrine.

(Author's note: Janet Marie Smith is the award winning architect who directed the creation of both Camden Yards and Petco Park as well as the extensive renovation of Fenway Park)

APRIL 12, 2003

GREEN MONSTER SEATS UNVEILED

MAY 15, 2003

RED SOX RECORD-SETTING SELLOUT STREAK BEGINS AS 33,801 SEE MARTINEZ BEST RANGERS 12-3

AUGUST 9, 2003

KEVIN MILLAR SOCKS FENWAY'S 10,000TH HOME RUN OVER THE GREEN MONSTER

SEPTEMBER 6, 2003

Glory Days: The Boss Plays Fenway

The "Boss" captured the spirit of his memorable and historic performance as the first major rock 'n roll act to play Fenway Park when he led off with a rousing rendition of "Take Me Out to The Ballgame."

He later paid homage to Boston's music heritage with a version of the Barry and the Remains hit, "Diddy Wah Diddy," and The Standells garage classic, "Dirty Water" with supporting vocals from J. Geils frontman Peter Wolf. Fans packed the park and adjoining rooftops and several thousand even enjoyed a free concert while standing behind the Green Monster on Lansdowne Street as Springsteen roared through a set that included many songs from *The Rising* as well as hits such as "Because The Night," "Badlands," "No Surrender," "Out in The Street," "Hungry Heart," and "Born in the USA" among other standards.

The non-stop three-hour show was described by Springsteen as Fenway's "rock and roll baptism." He later observed, "There's not many places where you can walk into an empty place and feel the soul of the city, but this is one."

Ronnie Wood (left) and Mick Jagger started their "Bigger Bang" tour at Fenway in August 2005. *(Courtesy of the Red Sox)*

Fenway Park has rapidly become Boston's top tourist attraction through its ballpark tour program. *(Courtesy of the Red Sox)*

OCTOBER 4, 2003

A'S DROP SLAPSTICK AFFAIR, 3-1

OCTOBER 5, 2003

SOX EDGE A'S, 5-4, AS COMEBACK CONTINUES

OCTOBER 11, 2003

Martinez vs Clemens Redux

YANKS WIN THE OLD BRAWL GAME, 4-3

The buzz surrounding the playoff match-up between Pedro Martinez and pinstriped prodigal son Roger Clemens was like that leading up to a prize fight. Like many of the similarly hyped Fenway pitching duels of yore it promised drama, trauma, heroics, and history and delivered all four in disproportionate measure.

In a game that seemingly lasted 12 rounds instead of nine innings, Boston lost both its temper and the game as Pedro Martinez came unglued in a bizarre fourth inning.

With Boston holding a 2-0 lead, Martinez gave up 2 runs in the second on an RBI single to Yankee reserve Karim Garcia and a solo homer by Derek Jeter. In the fourth he walked Posada, surrendered a single to Nick Johnson, and an RBI single to Hideki Matsui. With first open he then plunked Garcia on his shoulder as Veritek moved to separate Garcia from Martinez. Umpire Alfonzo Maqquez then issued a warning to both benches.

Tempers flared one batter later as Garcia up-ended Sox second baseman Todd Walker and both players tussled as Garcia and Martinez shouted and Martinez, looking toward the Yankee dugout, gestured toward his head as if to threaten the Yankee catcher for his next at-bat.

In the bottom of the fourth the game entered an almost farcical dimension as the ever-unpredictable Manny Ramirez ducked away from a Clemens high fastball with the count at one and two. As soon as the Sox left fielder strode toward the mound, both benches emptied with Yankee coach Don Zimmer making a beeline for Martinez. Martinez then grabbed the (70-year-old coach and tossed him to the ground in one of the most regrettable and bizarre scenes in Fenway's long history.

Tempers flared throughout the park for the remainder of the game as rival fans scuffled as well as Yankee relief pitcher Jeff Nelson who beat up Red Sox part-time employee Paul Williams, a teacher of mentally disabled kids who assisted the grounds crew in the bullpens.

Nelson's attack came in the middle of the ninth and served as a brutal climax to an ugly afternoon.

OCTOBER 13, 2003

NIXON'S THE ONE! SOX BEAT YANKEES, 3-2

OCTOBER 14, 2003

LOWE DOWN, YANKS EDGE SOX 4-2

APRIL 16, 2004

TED WILLIAMS SCULPTURE UNVEILED

MAY 2004

MOTHER'S DAY WALK STARTED AT FENWAY

MAY 25, 2004

Sox Discuss Plans to Remain at Fenway Park

The Big Guy could not have been more direct or succinct when discussing the future of Fenway Park. "I love Fenway. I don't think you can replicate the magic you have here. It would never feel like Fenway." Red Sox principal owner John Henry after the team announced they'd add an additional 5,000 seats.

With the utterance of those words all speculation regarding a possible future waterfront or Back Bay home for the Red Sox was scuttled as the club devoted all its energies to rebounding from their heartbreaking defeat in the previous year's playoffs to the hated Yankees.

Sheryl Crow wasn't the only one having some fun at Fenway during her concert with Dave Matthews in 2006. *(Courtesy of the Red Sox)*

Dave Matthews. *(Courtesy of the Red Sox)*

JULY 24, 2004

Mueller Rocks Rivera/Yanks with Walk-off Winner

The spark for the 2004 World Championship was surely struck in one of the most memorable regular-season games in Fenway's storied history as the Red Sox won a raucous 11-10 victory over the Yankees on an afternoon marked by well-documented confrontation between Boston captain Jason Veritek and Yankee third baseman Alex Rodriguez.

Entering the game the Red Sox stood nine games behind their rivals after an 8-7 defeat the night before. By now they'd been all but written off by the Boston press and a sizable number of fans. Their revival began in the third inning with the Red Sox trailing 3-0 when Boston starter Bronson Arroyo hit A-Rod with an errant pitch. As the $25 million man strode toward first, he shouted at Arroyo and soon Veritek rushed to defend his pitcher and ended up pushing his catcher's mitt square in the Yankee's face as both benches raced onto the diamond.

The stills of the fight made every sports page and many front pages across the country the next morning, and if readers bothered to read the accompanying stories they'd have read of a team immediately unified in battle as Trot Nixon battled Yankee pitcher Tanyon Sturtze

just as Veritek and Rodriguez were being ejected.

The ending was a preview of games to come as Bill Mueller jacked a two-run game-winning home run off uber-closer Mariano Rivera with one out in the ninth inning. Not only did this break Rivera's streak of converting 23 straight save opportunities but it also was only the second home run he'd allowed all season.

Eight games out the Red Sox were born again.

AUGUST 27, 2004

Jimmy Fund Day

Safe to say there is no team in American sports and no ballpark more associated with a charity than the Red Sox and Fenway Park

Rookie Clay Buchholz surprised fans by pitching a no-hitter on September 1, 2007, in only his second big-league start. *(Courtesy of the Red Sox)*

Relief ace Jonathan Papelbon performed an Irish step dance to the strains of The Dropkick Murphys following the Red Sox come-from-behind win in the 2007 ALCS. *(Courtesy of the Red Sox)*

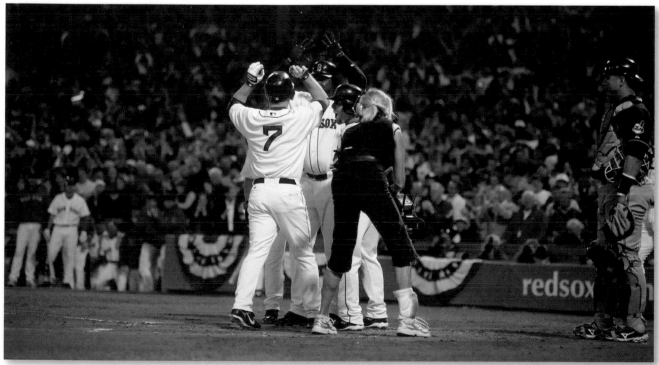

J.D. Drew is greeted at home plate by teammates and a TV camerawoman as he scores on a home run that helped Boston to a 12-2 win in Game 6 of the 2007 ALCS. *(Courtesy of the Red Sox)*

The Red Sox dugout is jubilant as the team celebrates its second pennant in four seasons in October 2007. *(Courtesy of the Red Sox)*

are with The Jimmy Fund of the Dana Farber Cancer Institute. Not only did Tom Yawkey gladly take over the stewardship of the charity from the Boston Braves when they moved to Milwaukee in 1953 but he and wife Jean were among the fund's most generous donors. Likewise, Ted Williams raised millions with his only request being that his efforts *not* be publicized lest the public think he was doing so to burnish his oft tempestuous persona.

Williams along with countless other Red Sox players have made many hours visiting the clinics and hospital rooms at the clinic as well as attending fund-rasing dinners and golf tournaments across New England to support what has become one of the greatest

cancer research and treatment facilities in the world.

Fenway is the venue for an annual Jimmy Fund Day in which both the team's radio and TV outlets join in boosting a radiothon that has raised many millions of dollars. Among the events' most ardent and generous supporters was the late George Steinbrenner.

SEPTEMBER 10 & 12, 2004

Fenway Franks & Cheeseburgers in Paradise

JIMMY BUFFETT AT FENWAY

In a season marked by contentment the Lord of Good Times, Jimmy Buffett, filled the Fens for two dates His anthem, "Changes in Latitudes,

Changes in Attitudes," could well have been sung in honor of the new Red Sox owners as not only were they making Fenway Park a bit like the multi-purpose venue of yore but their team was tearing up the league like the boys of '46, '67, and '75.

Included in Buffett's act was a skit that purported to lift the team's alleged curse and a three-song medley that ended with Neil Diamond's crowd pleasing "Sweet Caroline."

OCTOBER 8, 2004

Ortiz Blast Leads Sox Sweep Over Angels, 8-6

The overture of the Red Sox postseason opera was a mighty blow by David Ortiz that sent the Angels packing as fans relished a possible re-match with the Yankees. With two outs in the bottom of the 10th inning he smashed the first pitch from lefthander Jarrod Washburn high into the Monster seats in left.

The game was a patented Fenway Special as the Red Sox raced out to a 6-1 lead through seven innings only to march into extra innings after Anaheim scored five times in the top of the seventh.

After more than four hours the darkening skies mirrored the mood in the park until Ortiz made history.

OCTOBER 16, 2004

SOX CRUSHED 19-8, FACE YANKEE SWEEP

OCTOBER 17, 2004

ROBERTS AND ORTIZ LEAD 12 INNING COMEBACK RED SOX 6, NEW YORK 4

Not only did cancer survivor Jon Lester capture a win in the Red Sox World Series–clinching game in 2007, but he followed it up in style by pitching a no-hitter against Kansas City in May 2008. *(Courtesy of the Red Sox)*

OCTOBER 18, 2004

Ortiz, Sox Need 14 Innings to Beat Yankees, 5-4

Clutch

By Steve Buckley

For a quarter of a century, and by acclimation, Carl Yastrzemski was considered the greatest clutch hitter in Red Sox history. His Triple Crown heroics in 1967 transformed this tattered franchise from perennial cellar dwellers into American League champions; indeed, in the final two games of the season, with the Sox needing to sweep the Minnesota Twins to win their first pennant in 21 years, Yastrzemski went a combined 7-for-8 with six runs batted in.

The baseball poets called that season "The Impossible Dream," but it was Yastrzemski, more than anyone, who made the dream come true. Even Dick Williams, the fiery, rookie manager who had stripped Yastrzemski of his captaincy during spring training that year and who was a man held captive by neither sentiment nor revisionist history, would later say, "I never saw a player have a better season."

But late on the evening of October 18, 2004, as jubilant Red Sox fans spilled out into Kenmore Square following Boston's 14-inning, 5-4 victory over the New York Yankees in Game 5 of the American League Championship Series, yahoos and poets alike were daring to place the name of a modern-day,

Fenway fans had long adopted Neil Diamond's anthem "Sweet Caroline" before the man himself came to sing it and other hits on August 22, 2008. *(Courtesy of the Red Sox)*

left-handed-hitting Red Sox slugger up there on the pedestal with Yaz.

David Ortiz had begun the season with one nickname: Big Papi. Now he had another: Senor Octubre. Stepping up to the plate in the bottom of the 14th, the game tied 4-4, runners on first and second, the Red Sox facing elimination if they lost (and yet another winter of hand-wringing and finger-pointing for embittered Sox fans), Ortiz got locked into an epic battle with Yankees reliever Esteban Loaiza, a journeyman righthander whose best years were behind him. Ortiz swung and missed at the first pitch,

and then took ball one. He fouled off the next three pitches before taking ball two, and then fouled off three more. On the tenth pitch of the at-bat Ortiz lined a single into center field, bringing in Johnny Damon with the winning run and saving the season.

The Red Sox had lost the first three games of the series, and Game 3 was an embarrassment: The Yankees pounded six Boston pitchers en route to a 19-8 victory. Whereas the 2003 ALCS between the two teams had ended in newly minted heartbreak for the Red Sox—Aaron Boone winning Game 7 with a home run off

Fenway was host to a Naturalization Ceremony for hundreds of new citizens on September 17, 2008. A similar ceremony was also held in 2010.
(Courtesy of the Red Sox)

knuckleballer Tim Wakefield on a night best remembered for Sox manager Grady Little's refusal to use his bullpen to rescue a spent Pedro Martinez – the understanding going into Game 4, 2004, was that the Yankees would simply put the Red Sox out of their misery and advance to the World Series.

With the Sox clinging to life in the ninth inning of Game 4, trailing by a run, Kevin Millar worked a walk off Mariano Rivera, the great Yankee closer. Into the game now came Dave Roberts, a late-season pick-up from the Los Angeles Dodgers by Red Sox GM Theo Epstein, who, explaining the acquisitions that day of Roberts, shortstop Orlando Cabrera and first baseman Doug Mientkiewicz, said, "We need to be able to win low-scoring games in October."

How prescient that comment would prove to be. For here it was, October, Game 4 of the American League Championship Series, and the Sox were trailing 4-3 in the ninth.

When Dave Roberts retired following the 2008 season, he had stolen 243 bases. He had 40 more stolen bases in a season three times. But he had only been to the post-season once prior to joining the Red Sox, and he had never stolen a base in a playoff game. Now he broke for second on Rivera's first pitch to Bill Mueller; either hc was going to be safe, which would give Mueller a chance to tie the game, or he was going to be out, emptying the bases.

Red Sox manager Terry Francona winked. Roberts ran on the first pitch. The throw from Yankees catcher Jorge Posada was strong and accurate, but Roberts, who had taken a strong lead, beat the tag slapped down by shortstop Derek Jeter. Mueller followed with a ground ball single, and Roberts raced home with the tying run.

The Red Sox and Yankees went to extra innings. In the bottom of the 12th, the game now just over five hours old, Manny Ramirez led off with a single to left off Paul Quantrill, a rubber-armed right-hander who had made a league-leading 86 relief appearances during the regular season.

Up stepped Ortiz, who earlier in the game had driven in two runs with a single off Yankees starter Orlando Hernandez. This time, jumping on a 2-1 pitch from Quantrill, Ortiz hit a two-run homer into the Yankee bullpen to give the Red Sox an improbable 6-4

Vermont residents Phish jammed the night away on May 31, 2009. *(Courtesy of the Red Sox)*

the most shocking comeback in sports history with a pennant-clinching 10-3 victory over the Yankees.

Later, after the Red Sox swept the St. Louis Cardinals for their first World Series championship in 86 years, the entire season-long package would be captured in books, documentaries, and even a hastily re-written ending to the film *Fever Pitch*. But the snapshot that will remain forever frozen in the minds of Red Sox fans will be from October 18, 2004.

Two snapshots, actually—taken at 1:22 a.m. and on 10:59 p.m. In both of them, David Ortiz can be seen carving his name into Fenway lore.

(Author's note: Steve Buckley is a columnist for The Boston Herald *and is also a familiar presence on Boston's radio and TV airwaves. His most recent book is* Wicked Good Year *which chronicles Boston's recent sports renaissance.)*

OCTOBER 23, 2004

Sox Take Series Opener Over Cards, 11-9

What a difference a week makes. For exactly a week prior to the start of the 2004 World Series, the Red Sox lost the 19-8 stinker that left them at death's doorstep. And, unlike 2003, the 2004 World Series logo painted on Fenway's grass saw nary a brushstroke prior to the final glorious out recorded in the Bronx.

By the time the Cardinals got to Boston for the city's first World Series game in 18 years, the pennant celebration had just barely ended. Albeit subdued due to the tragic

victory. It was 1:22 a.m., October 18, 2004. Less than 16 hours later, the two teams were back on the field for Game 5, with Sox starter Pedro Martinez delivering a first-pitch strike to Jeter at 5:11 p.m.

Five hours and 49 minutes later, when Ortiz ended it with his game-winning single off Loaiza, it was stamped into the books as the biggest two-game clutch performance by a Sox player since Yastrzemski's heroics against the Twins during that frantic season-ending weekend in 1967. And Ortiz had done it in one calendar day – at 1:22 a.m. and at 10:59 p.m.

Reserve outfielder Gabe Kapler referred to what he'd just seen in those two games as "Jordanesque," referring of course to NBA great Michael Jordan. Hearing this, a surprisingly reserved Ortiz said, "That's basketball, man. One guy can do it in basketball. This is baseball. You need more than one guy."

Ortiz continued.

"Somebody else is going to have to step up," he said. "It's always me lately. That's fine, but if we're going to beat the Yankees, somebody else has to do it. Not me, not all the time. We can't win that way, not against the Yankees.

"If we keep playing that way against the Yankees, they're going to beat our asses. We've been playing the game stupid, you know? We got so many opportunities to win that game, and we just didn't execute. Stupid, man. You can't play like that against the Yankees."

His teammates listened. In Game 6 at Yankee Stadium, it was pitcher Curt Schilling, blood oozing from his sock as he limited the Yankees to one run in seven innings, and Mark Bellhorn, clocking a three-run, fourth-inning home run, who stepped up. Sox 4, Yankees 2.

The next night, every Boston starter had a hit – including Ortiz, who hit his fourth home run of the series – as the Red Sox completed

June 17, 2009 marked the historic 500th consecutive sell-out for the Red Sox. *(Courtesy of the Red Sox)*

death of Victoria Snelgrove, a student hit by a pepper canister fired by Boston police in the midst of a melee following the clincher.

Most newspaper columns and stories dwelt on the Sox's epic seven games World Series in '46 and '67 and a few even made mention of the fact that principal owner John Henry grew up in Arkansas as a rapid Cards fan.

Henry told columnist Dan Shaughnessy, "What could be better than to have these two regions-which appreciate baseball more than anywhere else in the country-that they could be in a World Series together. And I think the game means more now than before, it certainly does here."

The opener was another high scoring Fenway Park pinball machine special as the Cardinals twice came back to tie the score from respective deficits of 7-2 and 9-7. The game finally broke open in the 8th inning when Boston native Mark Belhorn belted a two-run homer off Pesky's pole to give Boston a narrow 11-9 victory.

Keith Foule earned the save by working out of an eighth-inning bases-loaded jam

Like most teams of destiny they prevailed despite not playing their best. In fact their score sheet reflected a joyous ineptitude as their four errors and 12 stranded runners were rendered irrelevant by 11 precious runs.

OCTOBER 24, 2004

Schilling, Sox Win On Bellhorn Double, 6-2

Curt Schilling awoke the morning of his first Red Sox World Series start and was nearly certain he'd have to beg off the assignment as the pain in his recently sutured and greatly celebrated ankle just could not hold up to the task. However as the day progressed, Schilling relented and informed manager Terry Francona he was good to go just hours before gametime.

Defending the honor of the city of his birth once more, Mark

Belhorn once again provided the key hit, a fourth-inning double that drove in two runs to bolster Schilling's heroic six innings of four-hit ball. Once again the Sox made four errors, three by Bill Mueller alone, but overcame them by with timely hitting by Veritek, Cabrera, and Bellhorn. Little did most fans anticipate it would be the last time they'd see their team play at Fenway in 2004.

Red Sox Commit to Fenway's Future

Red Sox ownership acknowledged today what many fans knew in their hearts for years, that being the fact that Fenway Park, more than any single player or team, is the true star of the franchise. President Larry Lucchino made the team's intention to remain at the park for the foreseeable future when he remarked, "We're establishing ourselves as longterm residents, and we share with other residents a desire for improvements to this area. You will not find a government dollar in Fenway Park or for the exclusive benefit of the Red Sox. There has been no such ask."

Sox fans continued to do their part by paying the highest prices in the majors for tickets to the perpetually sold-out park.

(Author's note: As of 2011 the team has sunk over a quarter of a billion dollars into ballpark renovations, upgrades, and preservation.)

Paul McCartney delighted fans with a show that included many Beatles songs as well as old favorites from Wings. *(Courtesy of the Red Sox)*

The Ghosts of Opening Day

Opening Day was a secular holy day long before any talk of Red Sox Nation, the Curse, or the Evil Empire.

Now that Boston is once again baseball's capital, Opening Day is not only the official end of winter but also a day to give thanks for a hardball heritage dating back to town ball on the village greens of the commonwealth. And so it was again on April 11, 2005, as Boston's baseball pre-eminence was restored in a colorful ceremony that touchingly evoked the past while taking fans to a place last visited by their great-grandparents. That the New York Yankees had to witness it was the proverbial maraschino cherry on top.

During the past 102 seasons, the Yankees and Red Sox have met 52 times in Opening Day festivities equally divided between games at Hilltop Park, Polo Grounds, and Yankee Stadium in New York and Huntington Avenue Grounds and Fenway Park in Boston. For the record, the Sox have held their rivals at a 13-game draw at home while suffering a deficit of 16-9-1 on the road. Included in those games are eight occasions on which the Sox trekked to Yankee Stadium to watch the raising of a world championship banner.

Before yesterday, the last time the Sox raised a world championship banner, their guests were the pennant-less, pre-rivalry, Ruth-less Yankees.

Prior to the home opener on May 1, 1919, (the season was

shortened due to a flu epidemic), Boston's big baseball news was the Sox's suspension of Babe Ruth for "flagrant violation of training rules." By the time the crowd of 11,500, led by Governor Calvin Coolidge, arrived at Fenway Park, Ruth was given a reprieve and was penciled in the lineup as manager Ed Barrow's left fielder.

In the *Boston Herald*, Burt Whitman reported the contest between the teams reached "a white hot stage." Sox starter Carl Mays, who'd defeated the Yankees, 10-0, in his previous start in the New Yorkers' season opener at the Polo Grounds, was thrown at twice by Yankees pitchers and had a heated shouting match with Yankees second baseman Del Pratt as the result of a hard tag applied to the pitcher.

New York settled the score with a four-run, ninth-inning rally to defeat the defending world champions, 7-3.

Unlike yesterday's festivities, May 1, 1919, didn't include the awarding of any rings or trinkets to the champs, and the crowd was less than half-capacity. In fact, the players were the victims of a petty power play by major league baseball, controlled at that point by the National Commission in the era before the introduction of an all-powerful commissioner. Because the Sox players had taken offense at the drastic reduction of their World Series share and had threatened to strike during the 1918 World Series, the powers-that-be never forgave them for eight decades. It was 74 years before the heirs of the 1918 champs were given the championship medallions so long denied their hardball ancestors.

In typical Boston fashion, the best moments yesterday arrived

un-rehearsed, with the Yankees standing as a team to applaud Sox legend Johnny Pesky, and the Fenway diehards gave Yankees reliever Mariano Rivera their loudest and most ironic ovation in years. Even Rivera, the greatest reliever of his era and perhaps the greatest ever, had to smile on this most memorable of Opening Days.

APRIL 21, 2005

HARVARD 7, NORTHEASTERN 3 (BEANPOT CHAMPIONSHIP) BOSTON COLLEGE 8, UNIVERSITY OF MASSACHUSETTS 6 (BEANPOT

JULY 15, 2005

RED SOX 17, YANKEES 1

JULY 22, 2005

RED SOX FILE FIRST PORTION OF APPLICATION FOR FENWAY PARK'S LANDMARK STATUS AND PLACEMENT ON REGISTER OF NATIONAL HISTORIC PLACES

AUGUST 21, 2005

Green Monster, Brown Sugar: The Stones Rock Fenway

The Black Eyed Peas had only just finished an opening set highlighted by their mega-hit, "Lets Get It Started," when the headlining Rolling Stones answered with their signature opener, "Start Me Up."

2010 Winter Classic Ticket. *(Courtesy of Charlie Bakst)*

The 2010 Winter Classic transformed Fenway Park into an ice palace that was used by both the NHL and NCAA as well as many schools and community groups that rented it out for games and practices. *(Courtesy of the Boston Bruins)*

In the latest of the annual Fenway Park summer concert blockbusters the venerable ballyard was the first venue for the Rolling Stones' 37-city "Bigger Bang" tour.

Celebrities such as Steven Tyler, Doug Flutie, Denis Leary, Carly Simon, and Whoopi Goldberg joined a packed house in cheering for Mick, Keith, and the lads as they played a blend of greatest hits such as "Satisfaction," "Sympathy for The Devil," "Tumbling Dice," and "Shattered," along with new songs like "Back of My Hand" and "Rough Justice."

Jagger also played homage to Ray Charles with a cover of "(Night Time is) The Right Time" on the motorized stage that took the rock icon from the edge of the infield grass out to center field. Even the great Tris Speaker never had it so good on that acre of real estate.

AUGUST 28, 2005

CURT GOWDY HONORED IN PRE-GAME CEREMONIES

OCTOBER 7, 2005

WHITE SOX COMPLETE PLAYOFF SWEEP AT FENWAY, 5-3

April 25, 2006 Boston College 10, Harvard 2 (Beanpot Championship)

April 25, 2006 Northeastern 7, University of Massachusetts 6 (Beanpot Consolation)

JULY 7 & 8, 2006

DAVE MATTHEWS AND CHERYL CROW SERENADE FENWAY

August 26, 2006 Lowell Spinners 3, Oneonta Tigers 1 (Futures at Fenway)

August 26, 2006 Pawtucket Red Sox 5, Rochester Red Wings 4 (Futures at Fenway)

SEPTEMBER 21, 2006

David Ortiz Breaks Foxx's 68-Year-Old HR Mark

At the end of a season in which the Red Sox were rebuilding after a string of postseason appearances, the show was provided by Big Papi once again as David Ortiz broke one of the longest-standing offensive records in team history, and one of the few not set by Ted Williams. In the first inning of a late season game against his old team, Ortiz socked his record-setting 51st home off fellow All-Star Joahan Santana and later added his 52nd in his last at

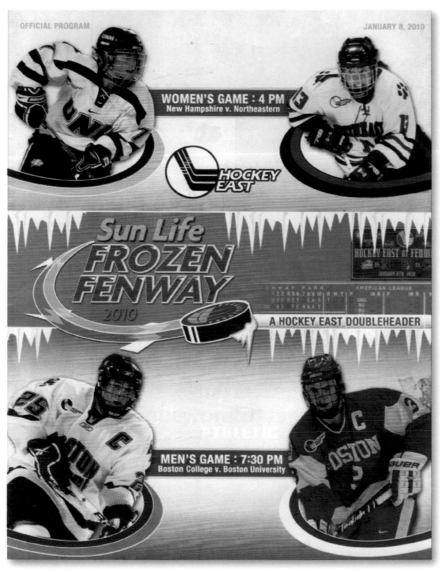
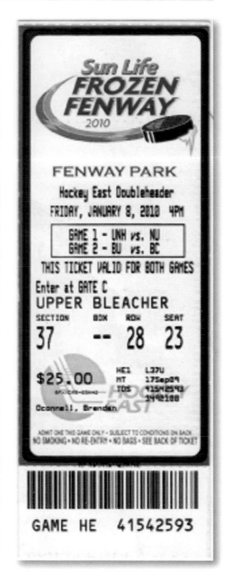

2010 College Hockey double-header program and ticket. *(Collection of the author)*

bat as the Red Sox beat the Twins by a score of 6-0.

As Ortiz circled the bases following the record-setting blast, the Fenway speakers blared the theme from *The Natural* as fans roared their approval and remained standing for several minutes. Ortiz later commented to reporters, "A great feeling, especially doing it here in front of my fans. I think the whole of Red Sox Nation enjoys when you do something like that at home. It's pretty fun. I mean, people were just going crazy out there."

SEPTEMBER 27, 2006

Pesky Honored on 87th Birthday With Dedication of 'Pesky's Pole'

The most-beloved figure in Red Sox Nation began his Boston career 64 years before the club paid him a truly unique honor by officially naming the foul pole that had been unofficially his all these many years. The right-field foul

pole was dedicated in a brief formal ceremony prior to the Red Sox/Rays game on Pesky's 87th birthday. Right fielder Trot Nixon made the formal presentation of a commemorative plaque to Pesky as former teammates Bobby Doerr and Frank Malzone also joined in the celebration.

April 25, 2007 Northeastern 2, Boston College 0 (Beanpot Championship)

April 25, 2007 Holy Cross 8, University of Massachusetts 3 (Beanpot Consolation)

"Teammates" sculpture un-veiling program. *(Collection of the author)*

SEPTEMBER 1, 2007

Buchholz No-Hits Orioles, 10-0 in Second Big League Start

In only his second major-league start rookie righthander Clay Buchholz subbed for an injured Tim Wakefield in the heat of a pennant race and thrilled fans with a dazzling no-hitter. Not only did Buchholz become the first rookie in team history to notch a no-hitter but he also ended the team's four-game losing streak and lifted Boston to a five-game lead over the Yankees with 26 games to play.

As with all no-hitters Buchholz established a pitching rhythm that quieted the crowd by the mid-innings as fans held their breath for the rookie. Teammates also observed the time-honored tradition of avoiding making contact with Buchholz on the bench. And finally, the hallmark of all no-hit games occurred in the seventh inning when second baseman Dustin Pedoia dove deep in the hole to backhand Miguel Tejada's grounder and rob the Oriole shortstop of a sure hit while preserving Buchholz's masterpiece.

Fans soon erupted when home plate umpire Joe West made an emphatic call of the game's final out on a called strike of a sweeping curveball.

After the game Buchholz told the media it was his second no-hitter, after one he'd pitched in high school, and that he'd slept badly after gathering his stuff from Pawtucket and making the trip to Boston. More than one writer

The Landmark Symphony orchestra filled the bleachers in July 2010. *(Courtesy of the Red Sox)*

remarked in the next day's sports page that manager Terry Francona, only days before, had cast himself as a bit of a seer while commenting on Buchholz's first career start, "Doesn't matter if he throws a no-hitter. He's going back down (to Pawtucket)."

Apparently that declaration didn't count for his second start as he stayed in Boston for a relief appearance and additional start before a sore shoulder shelved him for what turned out to be another world championship post-season.

OCTOBER 3, 2007

BECKETT SMOKES ANGELS, 4-0, IN ALDS OPENER

OCTOBER 5, 2007

MAN OH MANNY, RAMIREZ WALK OFF BLAST LEADS SOX TO 6-3 WIN

OCTOBER 12, 2007

SOX CLOBBER CLEVELAND, 10-3, ALCS OPENER

OCTOBER 13, 2007

CLEVELAND EVENS SERIES, BEAT SOX, 13-6

OCTOBER 20, 2007

RED SOX EXTEND SERIES, BEAT INDIANS, 12-2

OCTOBER 21, 2007

CHAMPIONS, Sox Beat Cleveland, 11-2,

MATSUZAKA GETS WIN

The tone for the evening was set before the first pitch was thrown as Boston's own "Dropkick Murphy's" sang a stirring rendition of their adaptation of Woody Guthrie's "Shipping Up to Boston" from a platform erected adjacent to the center-field bleachers. The Celtic rhythm surely stirred the ghosts of the Royal Rooters as the Red Sox pounded the Indians by a score of 11-2 to complete yet another historic comeback.

Daisuke Matsuzaka got the win while pitching five innings and allowing both Cleveland runs. Countryman Hideki Okajima then pitched two scoreless innings as Dustin Pedroia enjoyed his best game yet while knocking in five runs on three hits. Kevin Yukalis also had three hits, among them a Coke bottle shot of the left field light tower to help him win Series MVP honors.

In fact, six of Boston's first eight batters reached base as Cleveland starter Jake Westbrook pitched effectively after that only to see his bullpen surrender two runs in the seventh and another six in the eighth as Cleveland collapsed before a Fenway crowd that stood and clapped for the entire ninth inning.

The celebration that followed was Fenway's first pennant party in 21 seasons as closer Jonathan Papelbon danced an Irish jig on the infield grass, cigar in mouth, to the strains of "Shipping Up to Boston." The Sunday night crowd enjoyed the prospect of yet another night of sleep deprivation as Boston won its second league title in four seasons, a phenomena not seen since the days of Speaker, Hooper, and Ruth.

OCTOBER 24, 2007

Sox Capture Series Opener Over Rockies, 13-1

PEDROIA FIRST ROOKIE TO SOCK LEADOFF SERIES HOMER

The opening game of the 2007 World Series started with a touch ceremony in which the 20 surviving

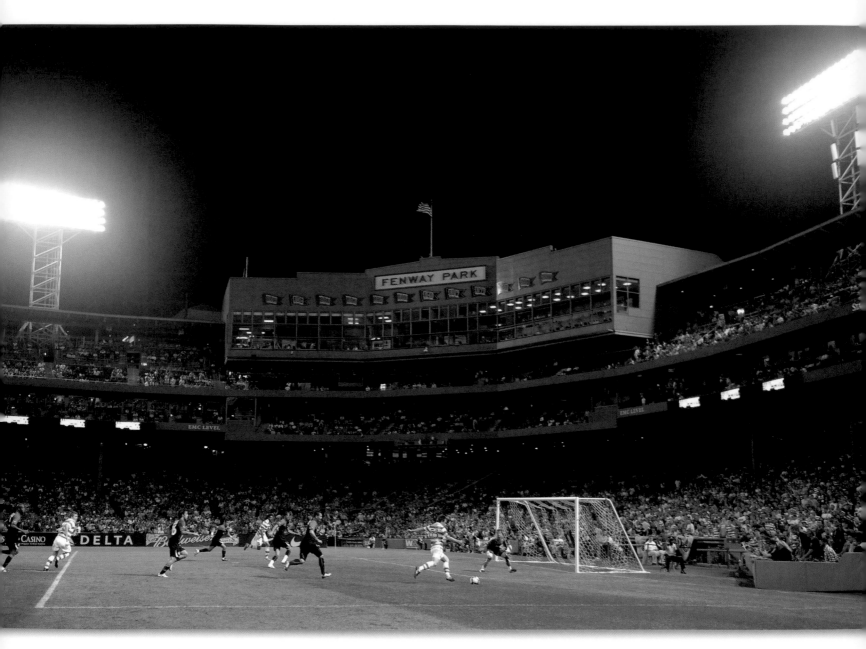

Celtic FC made their first visit to Fenway Park since 1931 in July 2010. *(Collection of the author)*

The Father's Day catch joined the Mother's Day Walk as a new ballpark tradition. *(Courtesy of the Red Sox)*

members of the 1967 Impossible Dream team strolled in from left field to join teammate Carl Yastrzemski as he tossed a ceremonial first pitch to Doug Mirabelli.

Where else but Fenway Park would the home team establish a World Series record by scoring 13 runs in the opening game? Where else would the home team's lead-off batter (Dustin Pedroia) become only the second player in Series history to lead off Game 1 with a home run? Even at sea level the Red Sox power was evident as the team had only recently overpowered the Cleveland Indians, outscoring them by a combined total of 30-5 in the final three games of their league championship series. One could only wonder what they'd do in the mile-high environs of Denver's Coors Field later in the week.

The Rockies eleven-game winning streak was but a distant memory as Josh Beckett struck out the first four Rockies batters while pitching seven innings to improve his postseason record to a perfect record-tying 4-0.

The Red Sox attack featured 17 hits, including a record-tying eight doubles and included a seven-run fifth inning that boosted their lead to 13-1. Even the light-hitting Julio Lugo got three hits to match teammates David Ortiz and Manny Ramirez.

OCTOBER 25, 2007

Schilling, Sox Edge Jimenez, Rockies, 2-1

Taking a break from their double-digit run production, the Red Sox emulated the last dynasty in franchise history and won a squeaker that Bill Carrigan and Harry Hooper would've appreciated. Not only did Curt Schilling become only the second pitcher over the age of 40 to start and win a World Series game but reliever Hideki Okajima became the first Japanese pitcher to pitch in a World Series game.

And pitch he did, as he was perfect during his 2-1/3 inning stint

while recording four strikeouts. Schilling could only marvel while exclaiming, "Okajima was perfect, just absolutely perfect—every single pitch. And that's a hell of a lineup to go through."

Jonathan Papelbon then came on in the eighth and preserved Boston's one-run lead while picking off Rockies MVP and potential tying run Matt Holliday with Todd Helton at the plate. Oops.

Boston's runs came on a fourth inning Veritek sacrifice to center to score Lowell and a fifth-inning double by Lowell off Rockies starter Ubaldo Jimenez with two outs to score David Ortiz with the go-ahead run.

Once again the Red Sox found themselves up two games to none to start a World Series, and it was beginning to look a lot like 2004 or even 1915.

April 15, 2008 University of Massachusetts 4, Boston College 3 (Beanpot Championship)

April 16, 2008 Northeastern 7, Harvard 6 (10 innings) (Beanpot Consolation)

MAY 19, 2008

Lester No-Hits Royals at Fenway, Sox Win, 7-0

Jon Lester was already a hero in Boston, having beaten lymphoma and contributed four regular-season wins and a World Series clinching victory for the 2007 world champions. His no-hitter against the Kansas City Royals was simply

Former All-Star player, coach, manager, and broadcaster Johnny Pesky is nothing less than Fenway Park's "Man of the Century." *(Courtesy of the Red Sox)*

OCTOBER 6, 2008

Red Sox Capture ALDS Series Over Angels, Win 3-2

The Red Sox avoided a late-night flight to Anaheim as rookie short-stop Jed Lowrie singled home the game-winning RBI in the bottom of the ninth to send the Angels packing yet again. For the second time in a week lefty Jon Lester bested the Angels while allowing zero runs in fourteen innings. Lester had a shut-out going until he was relieved after seven innings and 109 pitches.

The beleaguered Boston bull-pen then gave up two runs on a Tori Hunter single to right field in the eighth before Boston native and West Roxbury High graduate Manny Delcarmen held the Angels scoreless and gained the victory when Lowrie came though in the ninth.

As players popped champagne corks and toasted one another, fans departed into the night to the strains of "The Impossible Dream" being played by the organist.

a joyous exclamation point to an in-spiring run of success.

Not only was Lester's gem the first no-hitter pitched by a Boston left-hander since Mel Parnell in 1956, but he also accomplished it while tossing his first major-league complete game. Lester mastered the Royals, striking out nine batters and walking two on a career high 130 pitches.

And, as with all no-hitters, Lester was bailed out big time by a spectacular catch by center fielder Jacoby Ellsbury who dove to snare a shallow Texas leaguer by Royals outfielder Jose Guillen. And in perfect form the 24-year-old can-cer survivor struck out infielder Alberto Callaspo to end the game in dramatic fashion on a chilly night.

Catcher Jason Veritek tied a major-league record by catching his fourth no-hitter, the 18th in Red Sox history.

August 9, 2008 Lowell Spinners 4, Hudson Valley Renegades 3 (12 Innings) (Futures at Fenway)

August 9, 2008 Pawtucket Red Sox 5, Charlotte Knights 2 (Futures at Fenway)

August 23, 2008 Neil Diamond Concert

September 17, 2008 Naturalization Ceremony

OCTOBER 5, 2008

ANGELS AVOID ALDS SWEEP, WIN, 5-4

OCTOBER 13, 2008

TAMPA BAY ROCKS BOSTON, 9-1

OCTOBER 14, 2008

TAMPA SCORCHES SOX, 13-4

OCTOBER 16, 2008

BOSTON EDGES TAMPA, 8-7

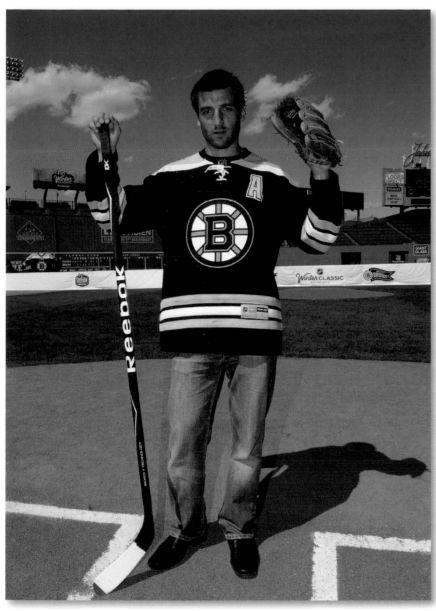

Bruins assistant captain Patrice Bergeron poses at home plate at the press cenference announcing the 2010 Winter Classic in July 2009. *(Courtesy of the Boston Bruins)*

April 13, 2009 Northeastern 5, University of Massachusetts 3 (Beanpot Championship)

April 13, 2009 Boston College 9, Harvard 5 (Beanpot Consolation)

May 29 & 30, 2009 Dave Matthews Band Concert

May 31, 2009 Phish Concert

JUNE 17, 2009

500TH STRAIGHT SELL OUT FOR FENWAY

JULY 3, 2009

WAKEFIELD RECORDS RE-CORD 383RD START FOR RED SOX

JULY 28, 2009

SOX RETIRE RICE'S NUMBER 14

August 5 & 6, 2009 Paul McCartney Concert

August 8, 2009 Portland Sea Dogs 3, Bowie Baysox 2 (Futures at Fenway)

August 8, 2009 Norfolk Tides 7, Pawtucket Red Sox 3 (Futures at Fenway)

August 26, 2009 Ellsbury Tops Harper for Sox Single-Season Theft Record

OCTOBER 11, 2009

PAPELBON FALTERS AS ANGELS SCORE COMEBACK FOR SERIES CLINCHER, 7-6

JANUARY 1, 2010 AND JANUARY 8, 2010

Frozen Fenway Hosts Winter Classic(s) Bruins Beat Philly in OT Wildcats and Terriers Headline Doubleheader

The day the ice trucks arrived in Boston the buzz began and spread through New England like a Canadian cold front. Outdoor ice, hot chocolate, pond hockey, Fenway Park. Yahoo. Yes, the Winter Classic was the marquee event, but the Fenway ice saw more skaters than any previous NHL installation because the sport had arrived in the perfect place at the perfect time with the perfect weather.

The magical rink was the site for many memorable events including a Bruins alumni gathering for

New Hampshire native Steven Tyler led Aerosmith into Fenway Park in August 2010. *(Courtesy of the Red Sox)*

the first official skate on the infield ice. Included in that exclusive gathering were such legends as 91-year-old Milt Schmidt, Cam Neeley, Terry O'Reilly, Gary Doak, Ken Hodge, Pie McKenzie, Brad Park, Ray Bourque, and the incomparable Bobby Orr, among many others.

Several teams paid dearly for ice time, including prep school teams from Connecticut and suburban Boston, and Mayor Tom Menino hosted a free public skate for city residents chosen by lottery for their special spin.

Each of the three scheduled games played over a span of eight days had a distinctive appeal. The Bruins/Flyers game was marked by clear frigid sunny weather and was overseen by NHL ref Chris Rooney of South Boston, a Red Sox season

ticket holder. The Bruins sent fans away with memories of an overtime finish that had camera flashes popping as Marco Sturm scored one of the most memorable goals in the post-Orr era.

Likewise a week later the women from UNH dominated Northeastern for a 5-3 win in a setting that was two parts Peter Brueghal and three parts Currier and Ives. For shortly after the opening faceoff, a light snow descending through the glow of the floodlights casti a frigid and spectacular rim of stardust on the proceedings.

Later the men's teams from Boston University and Boston College renewed the best collegiate hockey rivalry in America as competing head coaches and fellow Red Sox season-ticket holders Jerry

York and Jack Parker faced off for the umpteenth time since they'd first butted heads at BC High and Catholic Memorial, respectively.

As with their many battles Boston University recognized the unique distinction afforded the victors of the first ever men's collegiate hockey game at Fenway and shot out to a 3-0 lead early in the second period. As the temperature dropped to a wind chill factor of seven degrees, Boston College charged ahead and pulled to within a goal with a little over 12 minutes to go but couldn't sustain their attack as the swirling snow slowed the game by a barely noticeable measure.

Many of the snowbound spectators had toughed it out for the entire six-hour marathon on one of the most memorable and captivating nights in Fenway's long history.

JUNE 9, 2010

'TEAMMATES" WILLIAMS, DIMAGGIO, PESKY AND DOERR HONORED WITH SCULPTURE

JUNE 12, 2010

Rookie Nava Socks Grand Slam on First Major League Pitch

Fenway Park is often transformed into a true theater of dreams and such was the case for career minor leaguer Daniel Nava who introduced himself to Boston by way of his crushing a second-inning first pitch from Joe Blanton into the right-field stands for a grand slam home run that gave the Red Sox a 5-2 lead over the Phillies. Nava's remarkable feat marked the second time a rookie had crushed the first pitch he'd faced for a grand slam as Kevin Kouzmanoff did it for the Indians in 1996.

Following the game Nava's father Donald made his way to the interview room where he shared the podium with his son. The younger Nava, who also doubled to lead off the fifth inning, grinned at his dad as he said, "I was looking for something to drive. As I was rounding the bases, I think that's when I said, "Oh man, I just hit a grand slam."

According to the next day's *Boston Globe* Nava had received over 140 text messages and 200 Facebook messages before the sun had set on his day of days.

July 7, 2010 Landmark Symphony Orchestra Concert

July 10, 2010 Jamestown Jammers 7, Lowell Spinners 2 (six innings Due to Rain) (Futures at Fenway)

JULY 21, 2010

Celtic Captures "Football at Fenway," 79 Years after Prior Visit

It had been three generations since "The Boys of the Old Brigade" had last been sung at Fenway Park as an army of futbol fans clad in green and white striped shirts gathered on the infield side of the ancient ballyard to root for their Bhoys of the Celtic Football Club representing the east side of Glasgow, Scotland.

Gathered in the bleachers and right-field stands were an equal number of fans clad in the same colors in support of Sporting FC of Lisbon, Portugal.

Both squads enjoy a sizable following in the United States with a large concentration of support in New England. In fact, Celtic had last played at Fenway in 1931, and Sporting had made more numerous but infrequent trips to entertain the large Portugese-American population in the southeast corner of the Commonwealth near Fall River.

On this night both clubs transformed Fenway Park into a chamber of boisterous song, and rambunctious cheers as "Hail, Hail, The Celts are here! What the hell do we care? What the hell do we care?," and "Viva Sporting, Viva Sporting" resounded through the two-hour exhibition match.

A crowd of 32,162 were treated to a match that ended in regulation time as a 1-1 tie but was decided by penalties with Celtic by a score of 6-5. Afterwards Celtic manager Neil Lennon remarked, "It was an interesting setup. The history and the tradition of the stadium as well, it is not as corporate as a lot of stadiums would be."

July 28, 2010 Cape Cod League All-Star Game: Western Division 5, Eastern Division 0

August 14, 2010 Aerosmith and J. Geils Band Concert

September 14, 2010 Naturalization Ceremony

Requiem for the Bleachers

By Glenn Stout

In the winter, when it is cold and dark and the snow is blowing and blotting out the far shore of Lake Champlain in northern Vermont, where I now live, and I think of summer and Fenway Park, I do not think of 1967 or 1986 or 2004 or any other season best known for either victory or loss.

I think of 1982.

I had graduated from college only a year earlier and had been in Boston only a few months. Unemployment was pressing 10 percent and there was no work worth doing. For only a few pennies more than minimum wage I spent most days doing crossword puzzles and reading the *Herald* as a security guard at the Harvard Medical School.

But I lived in Kenmore Square, and that meant I was neighbors with Fenway Park. That winter and spring my walk back and forth to work each day brought me past Fenway. I would tip my cap, nod a 'hello," and with each step summer was a little bit closer.

I had first seen Fenway Park 16 years before, when I was all of eight years old. My mother was a native of Newfoundland and we were, somewhat improbably, driving there from Ohio on vacation. My father had piled us all into the old Pontiac station wagon one summer afternoon and then drove nonstop through the night. As the sun peaked over the horizon at dawn, we entered the outskirts of Boston. I remember nothing of the city as

The Dorchester-bred New Kids on The Block announce their Fenway Park concert for the summer of 2011. They were just the latest band of local lads to play on Boston's "Field of Dreams." *(Courtesy of the Red Sox)*

we drove through but the light towers of Fenway Park looming over a distant horizon.

I had never been to a major-league ballpark before and held out little hope of doing so anytime soon. My traffic-adverse father frowned on trips to either Cleveland or Cincinnati, much less Detroit or Pittsburgh or Chicago, the other cities within a reasonable driving distance from central Ohio, meaning I missed opportunities to see most of the classic ballparks of the age—Crosley Field, Tiger Stadium, Forbes Field, Wrigley Field, Comiskey Park. Even Cleveland's rusting Stalinesque Municipal Stadium, not really a ballpark at all, eluded me.

So when I moved to Boston nearly two decades later, Fenway Park was both a reason for my pilgrimage and a destination. This time I promised myself I would do more than drive by with my face pressed against the car window. I planned to spend the whole summer in my neighbor's backyard, Fenway Park.

And the miracle was that I could. I made all of $6,000 that year, bought mac and cheese by the case, and lost my old Dodge Dart to parking tickets. Yet after I cashed my check each week, I could usually still afford to slip a $20 bill in the top drawer of my desk. That was my season ticket, because depending on how many beers I decided to drink—or even if I decided to drink any at all—a $20 bill was enough to get me into Fenway Park, not just for a game

or two, but for an entire week, and still with change to spare.

General admission bleacher seats were $2. Twenty bucks was enough for an entire home stand. And the best part was back then, except for holidays and some Saturday afternoons, a ticket in the bleachers got you far more than 17" on a bench. Most of the time there was enough room to put your feet up on the bench in front of you and lean back onto the bench behind. It was like watching baseball from a Barcalounger. Despite the zillions of dollars that have since been spent on upgrades at Fenway Park, there is still no seat, including those in the luxury boxes, as spacious or as comfortable as those in the bleachers in the summer of 1982.

Okay, so the baseball, when measured by today's heady standards, was not that memorable. The Sox spent most of May and June in first place, which made the bleachers begin to get a bit crowded, but they had no starting pitching and no one ever thought they had a real chance of winning. Sure enough, like a casual fan on a hot day with one beer too many, they swooned in July and then down the aisle in August. They finished third to Milwaukee, 89-73, a record identical to that of the 2010 Sox and one which, as fall approached, left plenty of lounging room.

But these Red Sox were still entertaining. Most of us in the bleachers looked forward to seeing a beach ball or blow-up doll bounce into the bullpen. Then Bob Stanley would slowly emerge, wielding a garden rake. Conscious of the fact that all eyes were on him, he would deliberately raise it over his head, then violently burst the air-filled vinyl object like Boston's pennant dream, and the bleacher would rattle with raucous applause.

Sure, it wasn't always that wonderful out there. The bathrooms were atrocious, the ushers polite as Neanderthals, the beer warm and flat, and a bleacher ticket meant just that, and nothing more. The gate that allowed access to the rest of the park was always kept locked, segregating bleacherites from everyone else, with no chance to sneak into better seats.

None of that really mattered. It was still Fenway Park and damn near perfect. The ballpark was much quieter then, the Green Monster was unadorned by crass advertising, and everything about the park was thoroughly unpretentious. It was just a building, a simple ballpark, nothing more, full of regular people. Even when the park was full, or nearly so, hardly anyone bought tickets in advance. And if you were poor, as I undeniably was, Fenway Park was still affordable - not just on a special occasion, but virtually every day.

That's the way it had always been. When the park first opened in 1912 a bleacher ticket cost 25 cents. In an era when many workers made little more than $10 a week, that was still within range of the charwoman, the laborer, or the kid skipping school. It took nearly seven decades for the price to rise to $2. Given the rate of inflation, that actually meant that by 1982 it was even *more affordable* to go to a game than it had been in 1912.

Today of course, although there are a handful of bleachers seats available at $12, the vast majority cost $28. By 1982 standards inflation should have turned that two dollar ticket into one costing about $4.50. Instead, as our expectations of what baseball should be have changed and Fenway Park has become more tourist attraction than ballpark, all bells and whistles and hard sells and noise, over the last two decades the price of most bleacher seats has risen by about 600%. Today, instead of slipping one $20 bill into the drawer to see a week or more of baseball, I would have to skim a couple of hundred out of my paycheck and probably skip the mac and cheese altogether so I could squeeze into a seat. The Barcalounger days are long gone.

And if I wanted to sit elsewhere... well, forget it. Even when one includes the bleachers, the average price of a ticket at Fenway Park, as of 2010, was nearly the highest in baseball, more than $52, just a few pennies less than the average cost of a ticket at Wrigley Field, but still more than those at the new Yankee Stadium.

But Fenway Park is still here, and in the last decade two World Championship banners have undeniably been raised upon the flagpole. That is, I guess, the price of history, one that many fans do not mind paying.

Yet it is just as undeniable that those banners have come with a cost. For those of us who still play the lottery the ability to spend a season at Fenway Park is about as likely as hitting Megabucks. The only affordable way to spend a season at Fenway Park these days is to watch it on television.

(Author note: Glenn Stout is author and editor of nearly eighty books. Series editor of The Best American Sports Writing *since its inception, he is author of the* "Good Sports" *juvenile series, and co-author, with Richard Johnson, of* Red Sox Century. *His most recent book is* Fenway 1912: The Birth of a Ballpark, a Championship Season, and Fenway's Remarkable First Year.)

My Fenway

By Bob Ryan

Sorry, but I can recall no details from my first visit to Fenway Park in September 1963.

It was a night game, and I'm pretty sure it was against the Tigers, but it might have been the Indians. I was on a college visit trip to Boston with my aunt and I dragged

The Landmark Symphony orchestra filled the bleachers in July 2010. *(Courtesy of the Red Sox)*

her to Fenway. (She would become a major Yankee hater in later life, watching every game from her house in New Jersey, enjoying Phil Rizzuto as he rhapsodized about birthdays and cannolis while hoping the Yankees would lose every game, 10-0.)

But I well remember visit number two, 10 months or so later. Having been accepted by Boston College, I was in town to secure housing. My mother and I went to Fenway on a Sunday afternoon. The Sox were playing the Angels. It was Father and Son Day. We sat fairly far up on the first-base side, not all that far from my first season ticket location 27 years in the future.

The Red Sox won by a 9-6 score in what I would come to know as

a Fenway Special. Rookie sensation and certified Home Town Hero Tony Conigliaro won the game with an eighth-inning three-run bomb onto Landsdowne Street off Angels' reliever Bob (Ack) Duliba. Dick Radatz, in his third season of short-lived Monster glory, saved the game, throwing up both arms in his customary style after the final out. The next day Bob Coyne had a great cartoon in the morning *Record*. Don't you miss those great daily sports cartoons? I do.

I can't say I frequented Fenway during my first two springs in Boston. I was a pretty staunch Giants' and National League fan, and there was no real reason to develop an allegiance toward the Sox in the springs and summers of 1965 and 1966. I do remember

coming up for a weekend to visit my girlfriend, Elaine Murray (She has answered to the name "Mrs. Ryan" since 1969) in the summer of '66, and we went to a Saturday night game against the Twins. Somebody won big, 9-2 or 10-2. I think it was the Twins. I say that because I know Ted Uhlaender did something or other.

Understand that Fenway did not have the cachet it has now in the mid-sixties. Rather than being viewed a civic treasure (Clark Booth's celebrated anointing of Fenway as a "Baseball Basilica" would be a few years away), Fenway was more like that old sofa at Grandma's house. It had a sort of rustic charm, but the post-Thumper teams had proven to be so dreary that the structure itself lacked general appeal. The Wall? It was about this time that The Wall was starting to be regarded as as something evil, perhaps even very reason the Red Sox had not been in a World Series since 1946 or had won the whole thing, since —when was it? Oh, yeah, 1918, two months before Armistice Day. Even Tom Yawkey himself was of the opinion that Fenway was outmoded. No Fenway Romantic, he.

So there can be no doubt it was the dividing line in Red Sox history.

The year was 1967. That's when both Fenway and baseball itself were re-discovered in this town and this region. And it's when I, Bob Ryan, someone who had always regarded himself as a top-drawer baseball fan (baseball and basketball were always jockeying back and forth in the 1/1A spots in my heart), was re-bitten with a baseball bug, the effects of which have lasted to this day.

The personal epiphany took place on Memorial Day. I took Elaine Murray to Fenway for a doubleheader against the Indians. Still have a ticket stub. Game B013. Ticket number 00146. One buck. Sox won the first game, 4-3, on a George Scott homer I can still see floating toward us.

Boomer's best power always was to right-center. Sox won the second game 6-2.

I was hooked.

Before the glorious summer and early fall of 1967 had reached its deflating conclusion in Game 7 of the World Series, I would attend 25 more games. Week nights, weekends, even weekdays, such as the two mid-week games against those same Indians in the final week of the regular season. Didn't matter. Baseball was back in my life, front

and center. Fortunately, I had a girl-friend who didn't question the passion, and still doesn't.

I had a summer job working at the old City Hall. On a payday Friday late in July, I went to Fenway on my lunch hour in order to purchase some tickets. Then, as now, that big board detailing ticket availability for each game stretched over the ticket windows. I bought a pair of tickets for this game and that game, and then I saw that the Twins were in town for the final weekend. I knew I wouldn't be able to go on Saturday due to BC football (I worked for the student paper), but I thought, "Wow! Sunday. Last game of the season. That might be cool." And that's how Elaine Murray and I wound up sitting in Section 22, Box 133E, seats 9 and 10; in other words, behind the screen, for what would go down as the most electrifying and flat-out important Red Sox game played at Fenway since the Babe was young and trim. Still got both of those stubs.

I was also there the night Tony C was hit. Elaine was away for the weekend, and my decision to attend the game was impulsive. I had intended to sit in the bleachers, but a guy on the street sold me a box seat just to the left of the screen. In the first inning Jimmie Hall hit a foul ball, which bounced into my area and rolled under my seat. No one ever got an easier foul ball. Of course, I still have it.

What a strange game. Gary Bell had a perfect game into the fifth and a no-hitter into the seventh. Tony had been hit in the face by Jack Fisher in the fifth, and naturally we were all sick. But there was weird-ness all around that night. Someone threw a smoke bomb onto the field, delaying the game. Rico Petrocelli

drove in the first run when Jose Cardenal simply overran his liner to right-center. Hall broke up the no-no with a homer in the seventh, and then he hit another one in the ninth. But the Sox won. The next day was the famous 9-8 win when Norm Siebern cleared the bases with a pinch-triple off Jim Coates and Rico made a sensational play by coming in on a Bob Rodgers chopper over the mound with two outs and bases loaded in the ninth to prevent two runs from scoring. Saw that one from the bleachers.

Everyone has a specific memory of October 1, 1967. Here are a few of mine:

—- Yaz coming to the plate in the fifth with the bases loaded and I'm thinking I've never been so sure in my life that someone would get a hit.

—- Tony Oliva,standing on third, staring at Bob Allison, who had just ended the eighth being thrown out by Yaz while trying to stretch a single into a double.

—- Sandy Koufax, broadcasting the game for NBC, waving wildly at oncoming fans climbing up the screen to get off before it collapses. The photo hangs in the current press box.

—- Listening to radios carrying the WHDH pick-up of the Tigers-Angels game that would determine whether or not there would be a Monday playoff game with Detroit as we rode the Green Line back to Elaine's Brighton home.

I had no clout and therefore no World Series ticket access.

You simply cannot exaggerate the historical impact of the 1967 Red Sox on the course of franchise history. First of all, it reversed a negative course of performance. From 1951 through 1966 the Red Sox had not been a serious American League factor. But it is safe to say they have been fairly regular contenders for the past four-and-a-half decades.

As a by-product, Fenway Park itself has evolved into the ongoing star of the franchise. When people think of Boston, they think of the great schools, the great hospitals, the Museum of Fine Arts, Symphony Hall, the Freedom Trail, the Boston Common/Public Garden, and, yes, Fenway Park, which has become a certified tourist attraction, second to none. Daily tours of Fenway? Tom Yawkey would have laughed. As late as June of 1967 he went on record declaring Fenway Park all but uninhabitable.

It was only after so many good things happened in that memorable summer of 1967 that people decided that it was all good inside that old ballpark. So all hail The Wall, The Door, The Triangle and The Ladder (which is still there as an historical artifact, even though it no longer serves a function) and all those assorted nooks, crannies, and undulations that make it a unique place to play major league baseball.

And all hail the many great players and many great games that have provided me with so many additional memories since that breakthrough season of 1967.

I did not anticipate becoming a part of the process, a writer who would cover the Red Sox as both a full-time beat man (1977), multipurpose game story and feature writer (1970-76, 1978-89) and since 1989, full-time columnist.

Obviously, certain things stand out: Luis Tiant's great run from 1972 through 1978. (Was there ever a more fun trip around the bases than the one he had in Game 1

of the '75 Series?) The advent of Fred Lynn and Jim Rice in 1975. That 1977 hitting 233 homers, 16 of which came during an amazing June weekend sweep of the Yankees. It began with four first-inning homers off Catfish Hunter on Friday night and culminating with Carl Yastrzemski coming amazingly close to becoming the only person never to hit one out of the park in right by knocking a Dick Tidrow pitch off the facade. Rice smashing the ball hither and yon (15 triples) to rack up an astonishing 407 total bases in 1978.

Who could forget Yaz's weekend farewell in 1983? Who will ever forget Roger Clemens' spectacular 14-0 start in 1986? The magic wand of Wade Boggs?

First Looie, next Rog, and finally, Pedro. Looie had the bullfighter's flair and Roger had the macho swagger, but the 1998-2001 Pedro Martinez had an unmatched artist's touch. That was the finest pitching Fenway has ever seen, although if anyone can say he saw Smokey Joe Wood mowing 'em down in 1912, I might have to listen.

You know who else was special? The early Nomar Garciaparra. All he seemed to do in those first few years was either get a hit or make a hard out. Injury did him in, pure and simple. But let no one forget how enjoyable he was.

Favorite Fenway game? I was at Game 6 in 1975, and that would be an easy call. But my favorite day, or day-plus, at Fenway was that emotionally exhausting combination of Games 4 and 5 in the 2004 ALCS against the Yankees. They went 5:02 in what we recall as The Dave Roberts Game (poor Bill Mueller, let along Kevin Millar), which ended after midnight. Game 5 began

later that afternoon, and it went 5:49, the highlight of which, for me anyway, being Tim Wakefield, with that dancing knuckleball, striking out Ruben Sierra with the go-ahead run at third base (the bases loaded, in fact) in the 13th. The catcher at the time was Jason Varitek, who was not used to catching Wake. The poignancy of Wake winning that game with three stellar innings of relief a year after the infamous Aaron Boone home run was enormous.

I walked out of that game 99.9 percent sure the Red Sox would make it all the way back. No one in the Yankee camp wanted to go back to New York to play that suddenly revived Red Sox team.

Things come full cycle so often in sports, and so it was that on April 20, 2010, the Red Sox provided another great Fenway thrill. We had our then-10-year-old grandson, Conor at the game, and this was the evening when Darnell McDonald, a person unknown to us all when the day began, made his Fenway debut in the eighth with a game-tying two-run pinch-hit homer and then completed his evening in his next at-bat with a game-winning Wall job. Conor Ryan had a new Red Sox hero all his own. Isn't that the way it's supposed to be?

Bob Ryan has worked for the Boston Globe *for six decades and is one of the nation's greatest sports columnists and commentators. He is also a regular contributor to ESPN's* Sports Reporters *and* Pardon the Interruption.